British Cinema and the
Second World War

D1562905

Also available from Continuum

Pam Cook, *Gainsborough Pictures*

Michael Gray, *Song and Dance Man III*

Sue Harper, *Women in British Cinema*

Chris Jones and Genevieve Jolliffe,
The Guerilla Film Makers Handbook, 2nd edition

Geoffrey Macnab, *Searching for Stars*

Jonathan Rayner, *The Films of Peter Weir*

Nicholas Reeves, *The Power of Film Propaganda*

Ginette Vincendeau, *Stars and Stardom in French Cinema*

British Cinema and the Second World War

ROBERT MURPHY

CONTINUUM
London and New York

Continuum

The Tower Building
11 York Road
London, SE1 7NX

370 Lexington Avenue
New York
NY 10017-6503

First published in 2000

British Library Cataloguing-in-Publication Data
A catalogue record for this book is available from the British Library.

ISBN 0-8264-5138-1 (hardback)
      0-8264-5139-X (paperback)

Typeset by CentraServe Ltd, Saffron Walden, Essex
Printed and bound in Great Britain by Biddles Ltd, Guildford and King's Lynn

Contents

Illustrations

Acknowledgements

I would like to thank Sue Harper, Tim O'Sullivan, Chris Goldie, Ken Philips, Paul Marris, Pamela Church Gibson, Alan Burton, Dave Campbell, Suzanne Hartley, Kerri Marples, Jo Mills, Edward Noel and Pius Hume for their help and support; Anne Eardley for assiduously sending me useful newspaper cuttings, Sophie Noel with the compilation of the filmography, Steve Chibnall for letting me see tapes of J. Lee Thompson's war films and his perceptive analyses prior to publication of his monograph, Noel Williams for commenting on early drafts, Esther O'Neill for last-minute deliveries of *Sea Wife* and *Seven Thunders*, and Ian Aitken for letting me consult his chapter on Alberto Cavalcanti at Ealing before publication. Tom Ryall opened new perspectives on wartime cinema for me and Pam Cook and Jane Greenwood encouraged me in shaping vague ideas into book form. Ian MacKillop at the University of Sheffield, Natacha Thiéry at the Maison Française d'Oxford, Claire Tylee at Brunel University and Mark Glancy at Queen Mary College, London, allowed me the opportunity to present elements of my research to critical scrutiny at events they organized.

Inspiration for writing about British films about the Second World War dates back to Vincent Porter and Richard Collins, at what was then the Polytechnic of Central London, who introduced me to the war period; Colin Sørenson at the Museum of London, who organized brilliant programmes of old British films; to Elaine Burrows, who allowed me to preview them in the National Film Archive; and to Rod McShane, Paul Taylor and Chris Peachment, who gave me the opportunity to review them in *Time Out*. Further back, what my parents told me about their wartime experiences, my mother as a nurse at Bushey Heath, my father servicing Hurricanes on the airfields of Gloucestershire, has left an indelible impression that has made wartime cinema particularly resonant for me.

Thanks are also due to David Barker and Sandra Margolies for their editorial support and Rebecca Russell for vigilant copy editing; to the staff of Sheffield City Library and the Psalter Lane library of Sheffield Hallam University; to the Film and Video Archive of the Imperial War Museum; to Kathleen Dickson, Briony Dixon and Steve Tollervey of the National Film Archive; and to De Montfort University and the Arts and Humanities Research Board, London, whose Research Leave Scheme allowed me time to complete this book. I should also like to thank John Mackintosh and Steve Gamble of De Montfort University Computer Services Department and Spot Computer Maintenance for keeping my laptop going; the Sheffield Courts of Justice for patiently deferring my jury service; and Judy Simons and my colleagues at De Montfort University for their unstinting encouragement.

The lines from Alun Lewis, 'All Day It Has Rained', quoted on p. 239, published in Brian Gardner (ed.), *The Terrible Rain: The War Poets 1939–1945* (London: Methuen, 1983), are reproduced by kind permission of Methuen.

Finally, I am particularly grateful to Andrew Spicer, who supplied me with invaluable tapes of films I would otherwise not have been able to see, and read through the manuscript, tactfully pointing out factual errors and encouraging me to clarify obscurities.

For Edward, Sam, Alex, David and Tom

Introduction

'The people of Britain know that night after night through autumn and winter they must meet the German attack in their own streets. Marshall Goering announces that he's striking at us because we are the heart. Very well, the heart will go on beating. There are loved ones to be avenged. There are all our hopes for the future to fight for. There is the most damnable tyranny that has ever threatened mankind to destroy. Knowing this, knowing what we're about, we say, "bombs will never break us, panic will never stampede us, Britain will stick it out."' (Brefni O'Rorke in *Unpublished Story*)

The Second World War ended over fifty years ago but it continues to generate intense interest. This is partly to do with the sheer scale of events – campaigns involving millions of men, systematic genocide, the destruction of cities, conflict over all areas of the globe. But our remembrance of the war is aided and encouraged by cinematic representation. Steven Spielberg was able to draw upon the miles of footage shot by American, British and Canadian cameramen in order to recreate the D-Day landings for *Saving Private Ryan* (1998) and in so doing he revived interest in the war for generations for whom it might otherwise have receded into the mists of time.[1]

In Britain this was hardly necessary. Via television – whether it be searing documentary, like *The Nazis: A Warning from History* (1997), or situation comedy, like the perpetual re-runs of *Dad's Army* and *'Allo, 'Allo* – the war seems always to be with us. In Britain, maybe more than anywhere else, the Second World War is profoundly important to the national psyche. If, from a global perspective, the big wars were fought between Russia and Germany, America and Japan, with Britain's main achievements the defensive ones of surviving the Blitz and keeping open the shipping lanes in the Battle of the

1

Atlantic, the idea of the war – and particularly of that year between June 1940 and June 1941 when the British Empire stood alone against the all-conquering Nazis – as Britain's 'finest hour' is still a potent one. For, after the war, with an exhausted economy and a disintegrating empire, Britain's role in the world inevitably diminished.

It is not surprising, then, that the events of the Second World War should be so important to the history of British cinema. The use of film as propaganda had been eagerly taken up by governments in the First World War, but over the next twenty years cinema developed enormously. Commentary might guide the audience more effectively than written captions but audiences had grown more sophisticated in their reading of images and there could be no going back to the crudely staged 'babies on bayonets' propaganda of the silent period. In Britain in particular, the demand for authenticity, of fidelity to the ethos if not the reality of the war, meant that such Hollywood films as *Mrs Miniver* (William Wyler, 1942) and *Objective Burma!* (Raoul Walsh, 1945) were frowned upon as insufficiently respectful of the sacrifices the British people were required to make in pursuit of victory. Much was made of the influence of documentary methods on British commercial film-making. According to Dilys Powell, the war encouraged the growth of

> a new movement towards concentration on the native subject, the movement towards documentary truth in the entertainment film. The war both encouraged a new seriousness of approach by British producers and directors, and drove them to look nearer home than before in their themes. (Powell, 1947, p. 22)

It was this fusion of documentary and feature film-making practices, the quality of 'documentary truth in the entertainment film', which persuaded critics that British wartime cinema was the finest hour of the British film industry. It now looks less completely so than was thought at the time, but it helped to establish a distinctive national identity for a cinema which in the 1930s had been dominated by European and Hollywood expatriates and adventurers.

There were other reasons besides the influence of the documentary ethos for the creative development of British cinema. First, far fewer films were produced in the war years (an average of 42) than in the peak years of the 1930s (around 150 a year between 1933 and 1937). That the industry had contracted to one-third of its former size might seem an unlikely cause for celebration, but with fewer bad films around, critical and popular attention could focus on the handful of

2

good ones. The boom in cinema attendance meant that the owner of two of the three major cinema circuits, J. Arthur Rank, made big enough profits to be able to offer film-makers unprecedentedly generous financial and creative terms on which to make their films. From 1943 onwards most of the major films – from Powell and Pressburger's *A Canterbury Tale* to Laurence Olivier's *Henry V* (1945) to Leslie Arliss's *The Wicked Lady* (1945) – came from Rank-controlled companies.

Second, the war aroused patriotic feelings, which meant that British films dealing with aspects of British life and culture were more warmly received. In a class-ridden society the war provided a subject where harmony and co-operation in a common aim could be depicted without implausible distortion. From 1941 onwards, British films won critical approval and rivalled Hollywood films as box-office attractions.

Third, a generation of film-makers – Carol Reed, David Lean, Powell and Pressburger, Launder and Gilliat, Roy and John Boulting, Thorold Dickinson, Charles Frend, Robert Hamer, Charles Crichton, John Baxter, and others – who had served an apprenticeship in the 1930s as editors, writers or directors of low-budget films came of age in the war years. One might expect Reed's *The Way Ahead* to be more ambitious and proficient than his *Laburnum Grove* (1935); Powell and Pressburger's *The Life and Death of Colonel Blimp* to hold more interest than Powell's *The Red Ensign* (1935); and Asquith's *The Way to the Stars* to be more effective than his First World War film *Tell England* (1930).[2]

In the First World War Britain suffered more military casualties than in the Second, but the civilian population came under direct enemy attack only from a few bombing raids on London. In the Second World War the 300,000 servicemen killed were matched by a similar number of civilians, most of them casualties of aerial bombardment, and 40,000 merchant seamen killed when their ships were sunk by German U-boats and surface raiders. Shortages, which led to the introduction of a rationing system, and air raids, with their accompanying evacuations and blackout, transformed everyday life. During the First World War, the huge demands made on the economy had led to startling changes, particularly in the government control of industry and the use of women in jobs hitherto done by men, but between 1939 and 1945 the changes were even more radical. Women not only took over men's jobs but were conscripted into military service.

If national feeling about the First World War might be characterized as optimistic illusion followed by horror and trauma, that around the Second World War was imbued with a sober realism. What Angus Calder characterizes as 'the myth of the Blitz' – the exaggeration of Britain's contribution to defeating the Nazis, the celebration of Dunkirk as something other than an ignominious retreat, the over-estimation of resistance to the Nazis in occupied Europe – were spontaneously generated ways of coping with a situation where victory, or even survival, appeared unlikely, rather than a propaganda line imposed from above on a gullible populace. Government propaganda at its best and most effective dovetailed into pre-existing structures of feeling.[3] Film, whether fiction, newsreel or documentary, became such an essential part of wartime culture because of the way in which it reflected and shared commonly held hopes, beliefs and fears.

The shock induced by the collapse of Europe and the threat of invasion in 1940 produced a radical shift in political and social values. The deficiencies of the old ruling class had been exposed and the demand for a new and better society if and when the war was won was overwhelming. Traditional jingoism ('We don't want to fight but by jingo if we do . . .!') was superseded by a determination to fight for a new and better world order. Britain's war culture was characterized by a mixture of idealism and stoical humour rather than patriotic chauvinism, as can be seen in newspapers and journals like *Picture Post* and the *Daily Mirror*, radio shows such as *ITMA* and *Happidrome*, and documentary films like *Listen to Britain* and *Diary for Timothy*. Realist films such as *Love on the Dole* (John Baxter, 1941), *Millions Like Us* and *The Rake's Progress* openly advocated a new order which would abolish poverty and unemployment, but allegories such as *They Came to a City* (Basil Deardon, 1944), comedies such as *Dreaming*, and even costume films like *Fanny by Gaslight* (Anthony Asquith, 1944) were also important in expressing wishes for a fairer and better society.

Early wartime films such as *The Lion Has Wings* tried to present Britain as a modern industrial country with new industries, model housing projects and growing prosperity, but rural Britain provided more resonant images. Evacuation, the mobilization of the women's Land Army and the stationing of troops and RAF personnel in remote rural areas brought a new familiarity with the countryside. People in towns, benighted by the blackout, digging for victory, and envious of the open spaces where bombs rarely fell, were also lured by the attractions of the pastoral myth. Films like *Tawny Pipit*, *The Demi-Paradise*, *A Canterbury Tale* and *Great Day* effectively deploy this interest to present their celebrations of Britain's determination to win the war.

British films achieved box-office success and won critical approval during the Second World War.[4] But attitudes towards what sort of films should be made changed as the tide turned and the sweep to victory began. The critics, and film producers like Michael Balcon, wanted to continue the realist developments in film-making, especially as there were now victories to celebrate. Documentary dramas like *Target for Tonight*, *Fires Were Started* and *Western Approaches* enjoyed considerable success, as did the actuality compilation films *Desert Victory*, *Tunisian Victory* and *Burma Victory* and *The True Glory*. But from 1943 the trend in feature film production was away from the war and into costume films such as *The Man in Grey* (Leslie Arliss, 1943) and *Fanny by Gaslight*, comic fantasies such as *Fiddlers Three* and *Bees in Paradise*, and contemporary melodramas that, like *Love Story*, romanticized the war or – like *Madonna of the Seven Moons* (Arthur Crabtree, 1944) and *They Were Sisters* (Arthur Crabtree, 1945) – pretended it never happened.

During the six years of the war, British film production transformed itself from a slump-ridden industry which inspired little loyalty from audiences or critics into a popular and vital element of national culture. The war seemed to provide a theme, a subject, a common cause which could meld the conflicting influences of Continental and Hollywood cinema and the British theatrical tradition into a national style. If this manifested itself most obviously in a documentary-influenced realism in films about active service or about war on the Home Front, the war seeped into everything. In comedies, George Formby, Tommy Trinder, Will Hay, Arthur Askey and many others unmasked spies and fifth columnists; historical films such as *Lady Hamilton* (Alexander Korda, 1941) and *The Young Mr Pitt* (Carol Reed, 1942) reminded audiences of Britain's earlier struggles against Continental dictators. Even an ostensibly escapist melodrama such as *The Man in Grey* bookended its salacious period romance with a contemporary wartime setting and a message that class bigotry and sexual oppression had no place in the new society emerging from the war. Films like *Madonna of the Seven Moons* and *Brief Encounter* (David Lean, 1945) steadfastly ignore the war, but in their mood of troubled intensity they conjure up its atmosphere and act as a counterbalance to more obvious wartime subjects such as *The Gentle Sex* and *The Way Ahead*, where the need to bolster morale holds back any tendency towards darkness and despondency. Nevertheless, the drift towards fantasy and melodrama, attacked in Michael Balcon's pamphlet *Realism or Tinsel* (1944), worried the critics.

By the late 1940s, British cinema's adherence to realism appeared to have disintegrated, and with it the interest of film critics and intellectuals. Consequently, when films about the war began to regain box-office popularity from 1950 onwards, they attracted lukewarm critical support. *The Cruel Sea* and *The Dam Busters* were praised for their low-key authenticity but most war films were seen as formulaic and unnecessarily militaristic at a time when pacifism was gaining ground among intellectuals. Younger critics such as Lindsay Anderson saw 1950s war films as epitomizing the middle-class conformity which appeared to smother all creativity from British film production until the eruption of the 'kitchen sink' films at the end of the decade. These faults seem less heinous now than they did to Anderson and his contemporaries. The formulaic qualities of films about prisoner-of-war camps, the desert war, the war at sea and the exploits of the RAF, which formed such an important part of 1950s British cinema, tie them together into a short-lived but remarkably coherent genre where shared conventions allow a deepening of thematic exploration.

Clive Coultass argues that

> *The Cruel Sea* was perhaps the last British film to be sufficiently close to the events of the second world war to retain a high measure of authenticity . . . British cinema's attempt to capture the reality of the war almost began and ended with the period of hostilities itself, and flourished particularly between 1942 and 1943. (Coultass, 1988, p. 98)

This is not what contemporaries thought. Films like *The Wooden Horse* and *The Colditz Story*, based on autobiographical accounts by escaped prisoners, and films like *Reach for the Sky*, *The Dam Busters* and *Odette* which centred upon the exploits of real people, were seen at the time as improvements on the openly propagandistic films made during the war. A contemporary reviewer of *The Dam Busters* compares the film favourably with its wartime equivalents:

> The story itself is good enough and they have let it be. No sobbing WAAFs calling B for Baker, no merciless interjections of Other Rank badinage, no misty-eyed bar-maids at the Station pub, no brave upward glances at throbbing skies.[5]

Post-war films expressed the concerns of the society they grew out of but they were also able to incorporate new knowledge and offer a more complex and sophisticated view of the events of the war

In films made during the Second World War, there is a stress on everyone pulling together, on friendship between women and men, on cheerfulness and casual courage in adversity. In 1950s war films it is very much an officers' war and other ranks barely get a look in. None the less, the concentration on heroic masculinity, coupled with the use of popular stars like Richard Todd, Kenneth More and Jack Hawkins, meant that they appealed to working-class as well as middle-class audiences. The celebration of British achievement in these films now looks surprisingly fair and unindulgent. Restraint and low-key heroics can easily slide into self-congratulatory smugness and repression, and clichéd responses mar some of the films. But with hindsight their stiff-upper-lip ethos – a last manifestation of the public school morality which had dominated so much of British culture – can be seen as an appropriate and satisfactory way of dealing with the legacy of the war.

Films of the late 1950s, like *Ice Cold in Alex, Yesterday's Enemy* and *The Camp on Blood Island*, have a more cynical, less gentlemanly ethos, and the action adventure epics of the 1960s – *The Guns of Navarone, Operation Crossbow, The Heroes of Telemark, Where Eagles Dare* – are less rooted in British culture. Apart from lower-budget variants on similar themes such as the Mirisch brothers' *633 Squadron* and *Attack on the Iron Coast*, 1960s attitudes to the war were epitomized by violent, hardbitten films like André de Toth's *Play Dirty* and Peter Collinson's *The Long Day's Dying*, and Richard Lester's anti-war satire *How I Won the War*.

Big-budget epics and adventure films enjoyed a revival at the end of the 1970s but their disappointing box-office returns seemed to indicate that a decent enough interval had passed and a sufficient number of films had been made for the Second World War to have exhausted its potential as a film subject. However, such films as *Yanks* and *Hope and Glory*, written and directed by men too young to have served in the war but who grew up immersed in its mythologies, opened up new seams of interest. More radical reassessments were made in low-budget television films such as David Hare's *Licking Hitler*, Ian McEwan's *The Imitation Game* and David Pirie's *Rainy Day Women* which, by adopting contemporary concerns with feminism and the oppressive power of government agencies, viewed the war in dark, conspiratorial terms.

The shape of the book reflects my own interests in the relationship between film and society. Low-budget comedies, stoical Home Front sagas, unrealistic resistance adventures and evocations of English nationalism made during the war may have few aesthetic pretensions but collectively they are a valuable historical resource. Views expressed in these films – about the war and the new society which might emerge after it was over – cannot be taken as straightforward historical evidence but they give some indication of the issues which concerned people. The pictures they present – of relations between men and women, between Britons and foreigners, between members of different classes – conjure up a society which is beginning to slip from living memory. The first six chapters of the book examine the war period. The following two chapters attempt to remedy the neglect into which war films made between 1945 and 1960 have fallen and the final chapter offers a guide to those diverse representations of the war which have appeared in the forty years between 1960 and 2000. As the filmography shows, a huge number of British films have been made which relate in one way or another to the Second World War. I have tried to fashion arguments about them rather than dealing with them as individual entities. This means that, although I have tried to be as comprehensive as possible, some not insignificant films which do not fit into the patterns I have laid out have inevitably been neglected.

NOTES

1 Date and director are given on the first mention of films not included in the filmography.
2 Andrew Sarris describes the development of Carol Reed's style thus: 'A scene here, an image there, small advances in milieu and montage, minor elisions of obligatory dialogue, a more precise logic of camera movements and a greater variety of set-ups all signify his steady progress towards control of his medium' ('First of the realists', *Films and Filming*, September 1957, p. 9).
3 For a more theoretical approach to 'structures of feeling', see Martin Hunt, 'They don't make them like that anymore! Authenticity, integrity and the structure of feeling in British war films', paper presented at the Screen Studies Conference, University of Glasgow, July 1999, which draws upon Raymond Williams and Michael Orrom's *Preface to Film* (London: Film Drama Ltd, 1954).
4 Films about the war made between 1939 and 1945 are investigated eruditely in Aldgate and Richards (1994), Coultass (1989) and Chapman (1998b). Manvell (1974) deals with Second World War films as a world-wide phenomenon, though he devotes little space to the period after 1950. Butler (1974) is too out of sympathy with his subject to be useful. Pronay (1988), Ramsden (1998) and Chapman (1998a) continue the reassessment of post-war films begun by Geraghty (1984) and Medhurst (1984).
5 Helen Fletcher, *Time and Tide*, 28 May 1955 (BFI microfiche, *The Dam Busters*).

1

Whistling in the Dark: British Cinema in the Early Years of the War

London, when you see its sky-line at all, seems peculiarly beautiful under the black-out. And you may read a bitter, sad defiance in its silent stone. But for most nights of the month it is just a black nothingness, in which you move gingerly for fear you will meet something. (Negley Farson, *Bomber's Moon*, 1941, p. 15)

Growing up under the shadow of Hollywood, British cinema had problems establishing a viable identity. British film-makers had been innovative and inventive in the early days but they failed to keep up with their more ambitious rivals. By 1913 only around 15 per cent of the films shown in British cinemas were British; the rest came from France, Italy, Denmark and America.[1] During the First World War, Germany and Russia took advantage of the fracturing of the international market to build up popular and innovative film production industries and establish strong national cinemas. In Britain, film production, starved of finance, resources and imagination, fell into decrepitude.

As British cinema remained stuck in its technical and cultural backwater, Hollywood films flooded the British market. By the mid-1920s, British film production was on the verge of extinction. It was saved by the Cinematograph Films Act of 1927 which required cinemas to show a specified quota of British films. Though the great majority of films shown in Britain were still American, British producers now had a guaranteed share in their own market. New studios were built at Denham, Pinewood, Elstree, Ealing and Shepperton and, despite recurring financial crises, by the end of the 1930s Britain had a sizeable production industry. The outbreak of war in September 1939 seemed to threaten its survival.

The Film Industry at War

The eagerness of French and British politicians to appease Hitler stemmed from a feeling that another European war was something almost too horrific to contemplate. The indiscriminate slaughter of the 1914–18 war had tarnished for ever the idea of war as a noble and glorious enterprise. Admittedly, tanks seemed to open up the possibility of a more mobile form of warfare and the military campaigns in Abyssinia, China and Spain in the 1930s had been fought in very different ways from those of the First World War, but the massive fortifications of the Siegfried and Maginot Lines seemed to indicate that any conflict between France and Germany would result in a similar bloody stasis to that which had occurred in the last war.

What made the idea of war particularly unappealing to the leaders of the democracies was the probability of massive civilian casualties. In the First World War Britain had suffered a handful of alarming but not very damaging bomb attacks by Zeppelin airships. But in June 1917 a formation of German Gothas had bombed London and killed over two hundred people (Short, 1997b, p. 11). The belief that this was a harbinger of things to come was reinforced by Italy's use of aerial bombardment in Abyssinia, Japan's in Manchuria and Shanghai, and the Fascist raids which destroyed Guernica and devastated Madrid. War could no longer be confined to competing armies. Civilians, including women and children, would now suffer too.

Central to this view was the belief that 'the bomber will always get through', a belief confirmed by the bombing of Warsaw in September 1939.[2] In fact both Britain and Germany developed air defence systems which ensured that most bombers did not get through in daylight, and night-time bombing proved too inexact to be militarily very effective, but large cities were still vulnerable and there were good grounds for assuming cinemas would be potential death-traps. If cinemas were to be shut down, there seemed little point keeping alive a film production industry.

On Sunday 3 September 1939, after Neville Chamberlain had sadly informed listeners that 'this country is now at war with Germany', a radio announcement confirmed that cinemas, along with other places of public entertainment, would be closed until further notice. But the political consequences of alienating such a powerful trade organization as the Cinematograph Exhibitors Association and throwing large numbers of cinema employees out of work were soon made clear to the government by vigorous lobbying by employers and trade unions. The *Kinematograph Weekly* threw its weight behind the exhibitors, warning of the dire effect the closure of cinemas was having on moral standards:

> If intoxication is becoming a public scandal, if public houses have sold out of beer by 8 p.m. just because the people will insist upon being with a crowd of their fellows and there is nowhere else to go, then the time for re-opening the kinema – and the theatres and the music halls – has become an urgent public necessity.[3]

Within a week, cinemas outside the evacuation areas were given permission to reopen and in the absence of heavy bombing the reprieve was extended to all cinemas. But for the first few months there was some doubt as to whether there would be any British films to show in them.[4]

The initial response of the government to the film industry on the outbreak of war was to kill off feature film production in the expectation that Hollywood would satisfy any demand that remained for entertainment, and advertising and newsreel companies would provide propaganda and information films. Alexander Korda, the most prestigious producer working in Britain, had concluded negotiations with the Air Ministry about a film which would highlight the significance of the RAF shortly before war broke out and he suspended production on his big-budget epic *The Thief of Bagdad* (1940) to begin work on *The Lion Has Wings*. The film was later derided, but at the time of its release in November 1939 it was well received by both critics and audiences and made substantial profits. However, rather than continuing to produce similar films, Korda was encouraged by his friends in the government, particularly Winston Churchill, to go to Hollywood and promote Britain's cause there. Korda and others were to face criticism for having 'gone with the wind up', but as far as the Foreign Office was concerned, the most vital role British film-makers could play was to present Britain's cause sympathetically to American audiences – which they were more likely to be able to do by working in Hollywood than by making films in Britain.[5] The success of Alfred Hitchcock's *Foreign Correspondent* (1940), Korda's *Lady Hamilton* (1941) and Herbert Wilcox's *Nurse Edith Cavell* (1939) and *Forever and a Day* (1943) – which brought out most of the English colony in Hollywood to plead Britain's cause – seemed to vindicate this policy; but the absence of support for British film production turned the assessment of its limited appeal to the American market into a self-fulfilling prophecy. In September 1940 the American correspondent of the *Documentary News Letter* reported that: 'The films sent over have been scattered, odd, unequal, and

11

have built up no single or solid impression. The millions spent in creating a British film industry have produced no dividend of influence in England's hour of need.'[6] The Crown Film Unit's *London Can Take It* (1940), *Christmas under Fire* (1941) and *Target for Tonight* – all directed by Harry Watt – were well received, and Carol Reed's *Night Train to Munich* was an unexpected success. However, it was not until early 1942 – by which time America had been brought into the war by the Japanese attack on Pearl Harbor – that a British feature film with a strong propaganda message, Michael Powell and Emeric Pressburger's *49th Parallel* (US title *The Invaders*), was released successfully in America.

Faced with uncertain financial prospects, requisitioning of studios and vacillating and contradictory government policies, many British producers called it a day. The two big vertically integrated companies which dominated the industry – the Gaumont-British Picture Corporation (GBPC) and the Associated British Picture Corporation (ABPC) – were already suffering financial difficulties. John Maxwell, the Chairman of Associated British, was a sick man and he died in October 1940, leaving his company rudderless. ABPC's main studio at Elstree was taken over by the government and production was reduced to the making of low-budget B-films at a small studio in Welwyn Garden City. Isidore Ostrer, the founder of Gaumont-British, was a financier with little interest in the day-to-day running of companies.[7] In the late 1930s he remarried and, because his second wife suffered from tuberculosis, moved to South Africa. In October 1941 he sold his shares in Gaumont-British to J. Arthur Rank, though his brother Maurice remained in control of the corporation's Gainsborough studio until 1945. Shepperton and Pinewood had been dark for most of 1939, victims of a slump that had hit the industry in 1937, and the big modern studios at Borehamwood, which MGM would later acquire, had been mothballed to prevent further over-capacity.[8] All these studios were requisitioned and used for a variety of purposes, from storing sugar and cardboard coffins to the printing of money for the Bank of England (though Pinewood was later derequisitioned to house the Crown Film Unit and the film units of the Army and the RAF). The task of keeping alive the British film industry fell upon three modest companies: Associated Talking Pictures at Ealing, British National at the Joe Rock studios, Elstree and Gainsborough at Shepherd's Bush.

Throughout the war, Ealing, Gainsborough and British National remained the backbone of British film production, providing around two-fifths of the annual output. In the early years the numbers were made up by low-budget efforts from Butchers, a production and distribution company dating back to before the First World War, Warner Bros., the most active of the American companies, with its own British studios at Teddington (until they were destroyed by a flying bomb in 1944), and ABPC at Welwyn. After 1942 a more important rival emerged, Filippo Del Giudice's Two Cities, which like the film-makers grouped together under the Rank-financed Independent Producers, made bigger-budget pictures aimed at boosting Britain's prestige abroad as well as at home.

When Ealing was founded by theatrical impresario Basil Dean in 1931, he claimed that it would be 'the studio with the team spirit'. Michael Balcon, who took over as head of production in 1938, continued the tradition, recruiting a team of directors – Basil Dearden, Charles Crichton, Robert Hamer, Charles Frend, Sergei Nolbandov, and the documentary film-makers Alberto Cavalcanti and Harry Watt – who made films exclusively for Ealing. Balcon had flirted with big-budget international films earlier in his career, but he was now a firm advocate of medium-budget, indigenously British films, and convinced of the importance of maintaining a supply of such films in wartime.

Gainsborough had been set up by Balcon in 1924 but had been taken over by the Gaumont-British Picture Corporation four years later. When war broke out, Gainsborough moved into the Gaumont-British studios at Shepherd's Bush, which were larger and less likely to be bombed than its own studios in Islington, a converted power station with a tall chimney, uncomfortably close to railway lines running into King's Cross and St Pancras. Production was controlled by Maurice Ostrer and Edward Black, one of a family of music hall and cinema entrepreneurs whose cinema chain had been absorbed by Gaumont-British.[9] Black's aim was to produce a varied programme which included comedies, musicals, thrillers, war films and costume melodramas. Ostrer was more aggressively anti-realist, although it was only after the success of a flamboyant melodrama, *The Man in Grey* in 1943, that he imposed his ideas on studio production policy.

British National had been set up by J. Arthur Rank and Lady Yule in 1933. Their first film, *The Turn of the Tide* (Norman Walker, 1935), had been a critical success but had lost money and Rank moved on to weightier ventures such as the building of Pinewood studios. The company had struggled on, making low-budget B-films, but the outbreak of war spurred Lady Yule to action, occupying studio space at Denham after Korda's departure for America and taking over the Joe Rock studios at Elstree. British National was more prolific and less tightly controlled than Gainsborough and Ealing. Its most regularly employed director, John Baxter, provided a radical populist ethos for the studio and a major critical success with *Love on the Dole* in 1941. Baxter directed a succession of similar films – *The Common Touch* (1941), *Let the People Sing* (1942) and *The Shipbuilders* (1943) – but with less critical or commercial success and he interspersed them with mundane but probably more profitable vehicles for Old Mother Riley and Flanagan and Allen. British National's most successful films came from directors who worked only irregularly for the studio: Powell and Pressburger with *Contraband* and *One of Our Aircraft Is Missing*, Leslie Howard with *Pimpernel Smith* and Thorold Dickinson with *Gaslight* (1941). Through the efforts of the National Film and Television Archive and the spread of video distribution, interesting British National films – such as Maurice Elvey's Home Front drama *Salute John Citizen* (1942), Vernon Sewell's *The World Owes Me a Living* and most of the Baxter films – are seeping back into circulation, but the studio remains an under-explored area of British cinema.

It should be borne in mind that throughout the war years at least three-quarters of the films shown in British cinemas came from Hollywood and the majority of them ignored the war. British war films like *49th Parallel*, *In Which We Serve* and *The Way to the Stars* were competing with *Rebecca*, *Gone with the Wind* and *The Philadelphia Story*. But in the early years of the war, insufficient resources were available for British films to compete very effectively. The achievement of British film production, like Britain itself, was to survive.

Early War Films

Ealing, British National and Gainsborough all expressed their desire to make patriotic films supporting the war effort, but they had problems finding suitable subjects in the first year of the war. The 'phoney war' period, during which little seemed to happen as far as the West was concerned, ended abruptly in April 1940 with the German invasion of Denmark and Norway. Holland, Belgium and France fell soon after and the British Expeditionary Force had to beat a rapid retreat from Dunkirk. A number of impressive films were made about the army later in the war including *Next of Kin*, *Nine Men*, *The Way Ahead* and the feature-length documentaries *Desert Victory*, *Tunisian Victory*, *Burma Victory*, *The True Glory* and *Theirs Is the Glory*. But in the early years of the war, it was difficult to conceive of a way of showing the army in a favourable light.

Old Bill and Son, directed by Ian Dalrymple, who had produced *The Lion Has Wings*, is a curious *mélange* of the pseudo-sophisticated Korda comedy and the sort of working-class characters who generally only appear in low-budget comedies made by Butchers and Mancunian.

Morland Graham plays Bruce Bairnsfather's First World War stoic, Old Bill, who is initially turned down by the recruiting officer ('The officer means we haven't got enough bath chairs. Move along old cock, there's others waiting.') but soon finds himself back in France meeting up with old pals and young officers who have risen to high positions since the last war. He has to compete with his spiv-like son (John Mills), who has exchanged his loud suit and layabout ways for a life in the Army, and an adopted daughter (Rene Ray) who is also determined to do her bit in uniform, but the sort of trench-raiding warfare shown is misleadingly reminiscent of the First World War.

Heroic acts were performed by small units during the retreat from Europe in 1940 (such as that glimpsed in the opening sequences of Harold French's *Unpublished Story*) and a number of films – *Mrs Miniver*, *The Day Will Dawn*, *Unpublished Story* – devote some attention to Dunkirk, but there was little in the way of victory to celebrate. The Eighth Army had easily defeated the Italians in North Africa but had then been pushed back by Rommel's Afrika Corps, and it was not until the end of 1942 that the Battle of El Alamein swung things decisively in Britain's favour.

The RAF had played a major role in attempting to slow the German advance into Western Europe but the most modern and effective RAF fighters – Hurricanes and Spitfires – had been held back for the defence of Britain and the planes that were used – Gloster Gladiator biplane fighters, Bristol Blenheim and Fairey Battle bombers – were slow and vulnerable. When Spitfires and Hurricanes were committed to the battle (to provide cover for the evacuation of the British Expeditionary Force from Dunkirk) they intercepted German planes before they reached the beaches and were rarely seen by the troops. Bombing raids, which would later constitute Britain's main attack on Germany, were begun cautiously. Aerial attacks on German warships brought heavy British casualties and, reluctant to provoke the Luftwaffe into carrying out raids on Britain and wary of the danger posed by German fighter planes, the RAF had not attempted large-scale bombing of Germany.

The Royal Navy was still regarded as the most powerful fleet in the world but it suffered some nasty shocks in the early part of the war. On 14 October 1939 a German U-boat penetrated the Royal Navy anchorage at Scapa Flow and sunk the battleship HMS *Royal Oak*; and in the first year of the war the Germans sank an aircraft carrier (HMS *Glorious*, in April 1940, attacked while withdrawing from the Norwegian campaign with her decks so cluttered with evacuated Hurricanes and Gladiators that they could not be used in her defence), a battleship, three destroyers, five auxiliary cruisers and 440 merchant ships (Deighton, 1993, p. 64). Fortunately there were victories as well. In December 1939 three battlecruisers – HMS *Exeter*, HMS *Ajax* and the New Zealand ship *Achilles* – tracked down the German pocket battleship *Admiral Graf Spee* and forced her to take refuge in Montevideo harbour. Denied sufficient time or facilities to repair the damage inflicted on his ship and convinced that a British squadron was waiting for him, the captain decided to save his crew from unnecessary slaughter and the dishonour of defeat by blowing up the ship himself. In fact the British forces were much weaker than he thought and the *Graf Spee* might easily have escaped.

A more decisive victory was won in May 1941 when the *Bismarck*, the most modern and powerful battleship in the German Navy, was sunk on her way back to the French deep-water port at St Nazaire, though only after the British battlecruiser HMS *Hood* had been lost with all but three of her 1419 crew. The battle of the Atlantic was to be a hard and vicious one and until the end of 1941 it looked as though the Germans might win, but the convoy system instituted at the beginning of the war proved increasingly effective and the war at sea a source for bold deeds that could be celebrated on film. For example, Gainsborough's *For Freedom* incorporates the victory over the *Graf Spee* into its story of the travails of a newsreel editor; Ealing's *Convoy* treats the hazards of the convoy system with a degree of fidelity; and its successor, *Ships with Wings*, deals with the under-resourced but increasingly important Fleet Air Arm.

The Lion Has Wings used the talents of three directors – Michael Powell, Adrian Brunel and Brian Desmond Hurst – and was completed in six weeks. It falls into three parts, the first of which, put together by Korda's American editor William Hornbeck in *March of Time* style, is a clever montage contrasting British with German values and achievements. It presents a Britain of modern flats and health centres, leafy parks and new industries, a prosperous and contented country now threatened by Nazi military aggrandizement. Englishmen play games for their own sake (and Scotsmen throw 'heavy things about for reasons only Scotsmen understand') while Germans strive only to win; Hitler addresses massed ranks of automata-like Nazis while King George VI, in a kilt and open-necked shirt, sings 'Under the Spreading Chestnut Tree' with a troupe of boy scouts. For the international audience there was a danger that the image of Britain as a country run by bumbling amateurs would be reinforced; and for less well-off members of the domestic audience questions might surface about whether the British way of life they were being asked to fight for related in any way to their own lives. None the less, its public schoolboy attitude to history is expressed with enthusiasm and conviction. The Germans are once again barbarians, threatening the humane, tolerant civilization of the British Empire just as they had threatened Rome 1500 years earlier.

The next section of the film deals with an air attack on the Kiel Canal – the vital passageway for German ships from the Baltic to the Atlantic avoiding the long and dangerous trip round Denmark. The RAF had sent fifteen Bristol Blenheims to bomb Wilhelmshaven and fourteen Vickers Wellingtons to bomb Bransbüttel, the German naval bases at the North Sea entrance to the Kiel Canal, the day after war was declared. Michael Powell was at RAF Mildenhall when the order came through despatching eight of the squadron's Wellingtons on the raid and he pleaded to be allowed to go with them to shoot aerial footage. This was a step further than the RAF was prepared to go, but he was allowed to film bombs being loaded on to the planes and obtain footage of the crews after they returned.

The actual raid was reconstructed with the use of a damaged Wellington fuselage (which 'stood until Christmas week a spectre in the studio car park').[10] Idiosyncratic but not overly well-known actors like Anthony Bushell and Derrick de Marney stand in convincingly for the real RAF crews.[11] The commentary stresses that German warships represent a legitimate and difficult target and that pains were taken to avoid civilian casualties. Misrepresentation occurs only in the degree of success which the raid is shown to have achieved. The film shows bombs raining down on German ships and though the commentary admits that not all the planes returned safely, it insists that 'they had achieved what they set out to do and they drew first blood in a war that was none of their making'. In fact, only four of the Wellingtons managed to find their target and their bombs – many of which failed to explode – inflicted little damage. Two of the aircraft failed to return. The Blenheims inflicted some damage on the pocket battleship *Admiral von Scheer* and the battlecruiser *Emden* but at a terrible cost: five planes were lost and their crews killed. Later attacks – by the Fleet Air Arm against Italian ships anchored at Taranto and by Japanese planes against the American fleet at Pearl Harbor – showed that aerial raids on warships could be devastatingly effective, but at Kiel on this and later raids most of the cards seem to have been held by the defenders.

The final section of *The Lion Has Wings*, which deals with Britain's air defences and a fictional German attack on London, is the least convincing. According to Powell, 'my sequences in the film were to show how an all-out attack by Nazi bombers, supported by fighters, was completely wrecked by the use of radar by the fighter squadrons of the RAF' (Powell, 1986, p. 334). During the Battle of Britain in the summer of 1940, the defence system which British developments in radar technology had made possible did give the RAF an advantage which made up for the Luftwaffe's superiority in numbers of aircraft and nullified the element of surprise that the attacker might expect to enjoy. As Angus Calder explains: 'Had the radar chain not existed, Fighter Command would have wasted its strength ineffectively in standing patrols; as it was the British planes could rise relatively late to anticipate the intruders' (Calder, 1971, p. 166). Radar stations, control rooms, the Royal Observer Corps, the Post Office War Group, the engineers and mechanics who kept the planes flying, not to mention the aircraft workers who built the planes at such prolific rates that the RAF finished the Battle of Britain with more aircraft than it had at the start, all played a vital role. The Spitfire and Hurricane pilots were the cutting edge of a highly effective fighting machine.

Official secrecy ensured that little evidence of radar remained in the film. There is more emphasis on barrage balloons and the German raiders are repelled with ludicrous ease. Possibly some antidote to Korda's earlier production *Things to Come* (1935), which had shown civilization collapsing under the impact of aerial bombardment, was thought necessary, but such over-optimism sits uneasily with the realist ethos of the rest of the film. The artificiality of the final section is heightened by a skimpy story about an overworked RAF commander played by Ralph Richardson. After orchestrating London's defences and repelling the German raiders, the commander returns home early in the morning just ahead of his wife (played by Korda's wife, Merle Oberon), who is working as a Red Cross nurse, and rather than go to bed they drive out into the countryside and sit together under a tree in the early morning sunshine. Graham Greene, in a perceptive review that recognized the film's strengths as well as its weaknesses, was particularly disappointed by this ending:

> Miss Oberon in nurse's uniform is speaking for all the women of England, telling the world, through United Artists, that we are fighting for 'Truth and beauty, and fair play, and . . .' with whimsical hesitation and a professional quaver, 'kindness.' As a statement of war aims, one feels, this leaves the world beyond Roedean still expectant.[12]

Ian Dalrymple, soon to become head of the Crown Film Unit, was prepared to admit to a degree of sentimentality in this last scene, but he pleaded in its defence that 'in present uncertainty our emotional reactions change from day to day' and 'had there been a *blitzkrieg* [he was writing in February 1940] what is now sentimental might have seemed real'.[13] The patriotic peroration was to become a staple of films made during the war but here it is poorly written and unconvincingly delivered.

Gainsborough's *For Freedom*, directed by Maurice Elvey and the newsreel editor Castleton Knight, offers a much sharper critique of pre-war Britain. Elvey, whose career stretches back to the silent period, had been responsible for *Sons of the Sea* (1939), a stiffly patriotic spy film with unsympathetic characters but enriched by Dufaycolor photography and location shooting at Dartmouth Naval College. *For Freedom*, starring the Scottish comedian Will Fyffe, is much more boisterous. Gainsborough and its parent company, Gaumont-British, had evaded British Board of Film Censorship (BBFC) restrictions to make covert criticism of Nazi Germany in such films as *Jew Süss* (Lothar Mendes, 1934), an adaptation of Leon Feuchtwangler's novel about the oppression of the Jews in seventeenth-century Rhineland, and *The Lady Vanishes* (Alfred Hitchcock, 1938), in which the villains are to all intents and purposes Nazis.[14] *For Freedom* has a sketchy storyline about the pacifist son of a newsreel editor, who redeems himself by scooping the scuppering of the *Graf Spee* from his exile in South America, but it is lively and topical. The first half of the film concerns the old newsreel man (Will Fyffe) making a film about the iniquities of Hitler's Germany, allowing Gainsborough to make the sort of open attack on the Nazi regime which censorship had prohibited until war was declared – blaming the Nazis for the burning of the Reichstag and the assassination of the Austrian Chancellor, Dollfuss, condemning the persecution of Jews, the concentration camps, and the lack of political liberty.[15] He brushes aside objections that Britain is not yet at war with Germany by pointing out that 'peace is running a temperature of a hundred and five with double pneumonia and pleurisy thrown in'. But news of the Munich agreement seems to prove otherwise and his son, Stephen, persuades him to put together an international film showing how the social, artistic, scientific and cultural achievements of Britain, France, Germany, Russia and the United States can each contribute something to making the world a better and safer place.

We see preliminary footage for Stephen's section, which shows a Britain not dissimilar from that depicted in *The Lion Has Wings*, and the German contribution, which is angrily dismissed by Fyffe as militarist bombast. But before we can see what the Russians and the Americans have to show, news comes in of the German invasion of Czechoslovakia and the project is pushed aside to make way for a film about the gathering clouds of war.

With the disintegration of the international community represented by the newsreel contributors, the story is virtually abandoned.
Stephen returns with his vital footage from Montevideo and it is
rushed to the processing laboratory, but what we are shown is a
reconstruction which makes no pretence to being the newsreel footage he might have shot. It begins with the sinking of one of the *Graf
Spee*'s victims, the merchant ship *Africa Shell*, and follows her captain
onto the German ship where he joins other British captives and
witnesses the ensuing battle. Powell and Pressburger adopt the same
structure in *The Battle of the River Plate* with Bernard Lee playing
Captain Dove of the *Africa Shell*. In *For Freedom*, Dove plays himself
and proves to be a natural actor, busily disposing of his ships' papers
through the porthole and cheekily misunderstanding German
requests for his secret papers by offering them his cigarette papers.
The Germans are played by actors (Captain Langsdorff had shot
himself and most of his crew escaped back to Germany), but in
contrast to the foreigner's English spoken by Nazis in most British
war films, they speak German among themselves. Model shots of the
battle are rudimentary, but apart from playing down the precariousness of the victory there was little need for exaggeration or distortion
and the enthusiasm and conviction of everyone concerned is
infectious.

A postscript to the *Graf Spee* sinking occurred two months later
when on 16 February 1940 the Royal Navy invaded neutral Norwegian waters and rescued British seamen from the *Altmark*, the
German supply ship onto which many of the *Graf Spee*'s victims had
been transferred. The film shows the liberated sailors marching
through London in what looks like a victory parade and ends with a
speech by Winston Churchill, then First Lord of the Admiralty,
celebrating that

> under the nose of the enemy and amidst the tangles of one-sided
> neutrality, the rescue of British captives . . . proves that the long
> arm of British sea power can be stretched out not only for foes but
> also for faithful friends.

With Fyffe's bulldog-ish belligerence and the appearance of
Churchill himself, *For Freedom* might be regarded as 'Churchillian'
rather than 'Chamberlainite'. But like Chamberlain's comment on 4
April that 'Hitler has missed the bus', the film's optimism proved ill-
founded. By the time it went on general release in May 1940, Hitler's
armies were marching through Holland, Belgium and France.

Gainsborough attempted to emulate the success of *For Freedom* with *Neutral Port*, casting Fyffe as the cantankerous skipper of an old steamer which he has saved from the breaker's yard. His sense of outrage and injustice at being sunk by a U-boat leads him to hijack a German merchant ship – which is sunk as soon as he runs up his flag – and the German battleship the *Scharnhorst*, which is then sunk by the Royal Navy. Marcel Varnel, who directed many of the best Will Hay and George Formby films, is here defeated by a weak script with badly worked out sub-plots. The same elements – an awkward, roguish individualist who wages his own personal war, a neutral port filled with refugees desperate to get out, a bar where the various nationalities compete with each other in singing their national anthems – would be combined more successfully in *Casablanca* (Michael Curtiz, 1942).

Conrad Veidt plays an equally cussed merchant ship captain in Powell and Pressburger's *Contraband*, though here he is a Dane and it is the British not the Germans he has problems with. Eager to avoid delay, he tries to outrun British Contraband Control and is only stopped by a shot across his bows. Once he has been boarded he soon establishes a rapport with the efficient, fair and gentlemanly British officers, but this is merely the prologue to the main plot, which begins when Captain Andersen follows two of his passengers, the spivvish Mr Pidgeon (Esmond Knight) and the glamorous Mrs Sørenson (Valerie Hobson), to London. They are both British agents – reporting on German attempts to disguise their merchant ships as neutrals – and they fall victim to a nest of spies and fifth columnists in London from whom Andersen and the staff of a Danish restaurant, the Three Vikings, rescue them.

Veidt and Hobson had played against each other successfully in *The Spy in Black*, Powell and Pressburger's first collaboration, a First World War thriller which found a receptive audience in the early months of the war, and *Contraband* was made as a follow-up. The relationship between the characters played by Veidt and Hobson is more straightforward than in *The Spy in Black*, where he is a ruthless but likeable German spy and she metamorphoses from collaborator to secret agent. In *Contraband*, Mrs Sørenson is a wilful passenger who refuses to wear her life-jacket, but the antagonism between her and the captain only thinly veils their mutual attraction. Hobson is the first of Powell's strong, resourceful, intelligent women, brave in the face of danger and never frilly or helpless. Veidt, who had played the somnambulist in *The Cabinet of Dr Caligari* (Robert Wiene, 1919) and would go on to Hollywood to become Humphrey Bogart's adversary in *Casablanca*, had left-wing views and a Jewish wife and represented everything the Nazis detested. *Contraband* provided him with a rare opportunity to play a good German (albeit in the guise of a Dane) – correct, formal, gentlemanly, courteous, brave, a precursor of Anton Walbrook's Theo Kretschmar-Schuldorff in *The Life and Death of Colonel Blimp* – rather than a Nazi villain.

Powell recalled the film as 'basically a chase in the blackout', and much of the film's interest derives from its re-creation of blacked-out London. It was not until 7 September 1940 that hundreds of German bombers attacked London and started the Blitz, but in expectation of such raids a blackout had been imposed since the beginning of the war. Even without bombs it had a dramatic effect on social life in Britain. The task of blacking out homes was time-consuming and difficult. A chink of light would provoke a visit from the ARP (Air Raid Precaution) warden and possibly a fine.[16] Factories that kept working though the night often had to be permanently blacked out, making them even more dingy and badly ventilated.

Once cocooned within the home, people were tempted to stay there. The outside world could appear alien and hostile. As Calder notes:

> For to make one's way from back street or suburb to the city centre was a prospect fraught with depression and even danger. In September 1939 the total of people killed in road accidents increased by nearly one hundred per cent. This excludes others who walked into canals, fell down steps, plunged through glass roofs and toppled from railway platforms. (Calder, 1971, pp. 72–3)

In *Contraband*, the blackout is exciting and dangerous; it causes Andersen to lose his bearings after escaping from the spies but this necessitates a tour round the nightclubs of the West End in a search for the singer and banjo player he could hear while imprisoned.

The final shoot-out is set in the storerooms of 'Patriotic Plaster Products', stocked with unsold busts of Neville Chamberlain, many of which are shattered by the villain's bullets. The film was made at the end of 1939 when the war had hardly begun as far as Britain was concerned and Chamberlain's position as Prime Minister was secure, but by the time it went on general release in May 1940 the situation had changed dramatically and Chamberlain had been swept away.

War and Melodrama

Britain was heavily dependent for food, munitions and raw materials on imports brought in by sea, and despite the strength of the Royal

Navy, the merchant ships were very vulnerable to German U-boats and *panzerschiffe*, specially designed surface raiders like the *Graf Spee* and the *Deutschland*, classed by the British as 'pocket battleships' because of their formidable armaments. Ealing's *Convoy*, directed by Pen Tennyson, takes on these problems in a much more sober and serious way than *Neutral Port*, though it too features an awkward, individualistic merchant navy skipper (Edward Chapman). Tennyson's previous two films – *There Ain't No Justice* (1939) and *The Proud Valley* (1940) – were both unusual in that they penetrated below the middle-class surface upon which most British films dwelt. In *There Ain't No Justice*, based on a radical low-life novel by James Curtis, he explores dead-end working-class life (albeit less bleakly than in the novel) and the iniquities of the fight game; in *The Proud Valley*, the black American communist Paul Robeson sings his way to acceptance among the coal-mining communities of south Wales. Tennyson joined the Navy after completing *Convoy* and was asked to take over a unit making training films. His promising career was cut short when he was killed in a flying accident in July 1941.[17]

Convoy seems to mark a return to the conventions of middle-class cinema, with naval commander Tom Armitage (Clive Brook) annoyed to find that the man for whom his wife left him, David Cranford (John Clements), has been posted to his ship. Geoff Brown comments that

> the extensive location material shot in the North Sea had to fight it out with Clive Brook festooned with gold braid viewing the war through binoculars, a dull romantic triangle, and a U-boat crew who talk about firing 'torpedo number Zwei'. (Brown, 1997, p. 192)

The *Documentary News Letter* took a similar view at the time, joking that 'we must not be surprised to find His Majesty's Navy tacking round the eternal triangle in the intervals of duty' and complaining about the representation of Germans 'as conventional automata punctuating their sadism with heel clicks'. But Tennyson's 'picture of naval life and ritual aboard ship . . . the rigid code of the wardroom, the etiquette of the bridge' was noted with approval.[18]

A year later *Convoy* was followed by a similar naval drama, *Ships with Wings*, directed by Sergei Nolbandov, the associate producer of Tennyson's three films. It is much more melodramatic than *Convoy*, with John Clements playing a larger and more flamboyant role as a disgraced officer who redeems himself through outstanding heroism (a role he had perfected in Alexander and Zoltan Korda's Technicolor epic *The Four Feathers* (1939)). As Charles Barr puts it:

> All the embarrassing elements in *Convoy* are doubled: the heroics are more unlikely, the men more deferential, the enemy more caricatured. . . . The whole effort is a theatrical one, belonging to the West End theatre and to a national cinema which had never decisively broken with it: this tradition encompasses its acting style, its dramatic conventions, its class assumptions and its implicit audience. (Barr, 1977, p. 26)

In *Convoy*, Cranford's reckless act – contradicting the captain's orders and detaching a destroyer and a plane from the convoy to rescue a merchant ship under threat from a German submarine – links into the message of the film that the survival of the convoy must override the safety of particular individuals. It also links up the romantic triangle (the commander's wife is on board the merchant ship) and the subplot of the rogue merchant ship which endangers, but in the end ensures the survival of, the convoy. Cranford's death at the end is shown as part of a general willingness of the crew to sacrifice their lives to ensure the safety of the ship.

The main plot remains securely anchored around Armitage's task of escorting a convoy of merchant ships across the North Sea. Judy Campbell's Lucy Armitage is refreshingly independent – it turns out she left Cranford, not the other way round, and she is affectionate to both men without indicating any sign that she wants either of them back – but Tennyson shows little interest in the romance and devotes more time and energy to the unruly life below decks. It is possible to see this bunch of grumbling, argumentative and undeferential Jack Tars as working-class stereotypes but they have a raw vitality which contrasts favourably with the stiff formalities of the upper deck. The battle with which the film ends suffers from modestly budgeted studio model work, but the danger involved in a light cruiser taking on a more heavily armed German raider (here supposedly the *Deutschland*) with a much greater range for its guns is not minimized and the battered cruiser sailing into port sends a very different message to the easy optimism of *The Lion Has Wings*, *For Freedom* and *Neutral Port*.

Ships with Wings, despite its extensive documentary footage of HMS *Ark Royal*, is essentially a romantic melodrama. Dick Stacey (John Clements) undertakes the aerobatic display which causes his downfall purely to impress the admiral's daughter and his flamboyant death at the end of the film is more about redeeming his character than winning the war. In *Convoy*, contradictions about Lucy's character are

Convoy. Strange shipmates: Edward Chapman, Edward Rigby and Judy Campbell. Supplied by BFI Stills, © courtesy of Canal + Image.

left unresolved and the fact that Cranford has sent two airmen to their death is easily forgotten because they are of relatively little importance to the film's main plot. In *Ships with Wings*, the action of the war is subordinated to the demands of romance. A carrier-based air raid on an Italian port (echoing the attack by Fleet Air Arm Swordfish on the Italian navy at Taranto in November 1940) seems to have been a success but it has to be transformed into a potential disaster in order for Stacey to fully redeem himself by a suicidal attack which saves the day.[19]

Convoy had met with government approval and considerable naval co-operation had been offered on *Ships with Wings*. Consequently, Balcon was shocked and dismayed when he was told that Churchill had seen the film and was attempting to block its release on the grounds that it would cause 'alarm and despondency' (Balcon, 1969, p. 133). In the event, Churchill agreed to let the final decision rest with the First Sea Lord, Admiral Sir Dudley Pound, who raised no objection to its being shown, and when *Ships with Wings* was released at the end of 1941 it proved almost as popular as *Convoy*. However, it

Convoy. 'The unruly life below decks'. Supplied by BFI Stills, © courtesy of Canal + Image.

attracted considerable hostility from the press for its unrealistic and melodramatic tone. The *Documentary News Letter* considered that 'The propaganda line of the film would be more appropriate to a Ruritanian campaign than to the Second World War' and fulminated against the *Ark Royal* having been used in what it dismissed as 'a pretty cheap business'.[20] This confirmed Balcon in his view that the way forward was towards greater realism in the cinema and he claimed that '*Ships with Wings* was our last film that could attract this particular type of criticism, because from then on we learned to snatch our stories from the headlines and they had a ring of truth' (Balcon, 1969, p. 133). In fact, he allowed Nolbandov to make another full-blooded melodrama starring John Clements, *Undercover*, and by 1944 Ealing had succumbed to the prevailing demand for fantasy, but his attitude towards *Ships with Wings* fitted the critical orthodoxy about wartime cinema.

In 1987 Jeffrey Richards set out to challenge that orthodoxy, using evidence from Mass Observation surveys to demonstrate how little critical irritation with lack of realism and plausibility impinged on audience approval. He argued that films 'which celebrate the class

26

Celia (Jane Baxter), the Admiral's daughter, with her suitors (left to right: Michael Wilding, Michael Rennie, John Clements) in *Ships with Wings*. Supplied by Flashbacks, © courtesy of Canal + Image.

system, perpetuate the division between officers and other ranks and are by the standards of progressives backward-looking' were none the less successful at the box-office (Richards, 1987, p. 138). It is a seminal article, challenging received ideas about what is important with regard to wartime cinema – marking its continuity with the cinema of the 1930s, the overwhelming dominance of Hollywood films, the importance of non-realist traditions of melodrama and the slenderness of the realist strand upon which such high critical hopes were centred. Richards is right to stress the popularity of critically despised fantasy films but he steps into more dubious territory by denying the box-office appeal of the realist films. While critics and audiences may have disagreed on the relative merits of a dramatized documentary like *Western Approaches* and a sensational melodrama like *Madonna of the Seven Moons*, those films applauded by the critics and incorporated into a canon of approved British war films – *Target for Tonight, The Foreman Went to France, One of Our Aircraft Is Missing, In Which We Serve, The Gentle Sex, Millions Like Us, San Demetrio London, The Way Ahead, The Way to the Stars* and *Western Approaches* – were popular with audiences as well as critics. On the other hand, films which retained the old melodramatic style, such as Nolbandov's

Undercover and George King's *Tomorrow We Live*, interesting though they might be, failed to attract much enthusiasm at the box-office.[21]

Critics were uneasy about a return to the jingoistic film propaganda of the First World War, not only because it negated all the advances made in the use of films for educational and informational purposes by the British documentary movement but because it would not be acceptable abroad – particularly in the United States. Films like *49th Parallel* and *Convoy* were welcomed as harbingers of a new style of cinema; *Ships with Wings* was despised as a reversion to crude melodrama. Comic book dialogue such as 'Get up you filthy Hun, I want to hit you again!' and 'Well, you can't argue with Germans, you've just got to kick 'em in the pants' which *Ships with Wings* indulges in would find no place in the scripts of Emeric Pressburger, Terence Rattigan and Noël Coward.

Richards challenges Balcon's view that it was *Ships with Wings'* lack of authenticity which Churchill objected to. Some of Roy Kellino's special effects now look ridiculous – which is hardly surprising given the implausibility of what he was asked to provide – but the sequence where the British carrier's planes attempt to land and take off from a bomb-damaged flight deck is alarmingly convincing. Most of them are engulfed in flames, and Churchill's worries about the effects such scenes might have on morale seem entirely understandable, particularly in view of the fact that the *Ark Royal*, the aircraft carrier which plays such a large part in the film (as HMS *Invincible*), had been sunk by a German U-boat in the Mediterranean in November 1941.

Richards' Mass Observation figures show that over 80 per cent of cinemagoers liked the film (99 per cent of women in naval ports) and 'men and particularly young men, after seeing the film felt that they would like to join the Navy' (Richards and Sheridan, 1987, p. 375).[22] But these were immediate reactions from audiences as they left the cinema. Nolbandov is a good storyteller and the film builds up to a dramatic conclusion which, at a time when the war was going badly but looked set to improve (with the entry of the Americans), might allow a final gasp of unreasonable optimism.[23] Audience tastes, along with much else, were soon to change. Roger Manvell claims that

almost everyone knew something of the war through the common experience of sons and daughters, husbands and lovers. Almost everyone knew the sound of bombing and the vivid state of tension before the crash of explosion. The film producers were dealing with a psychologically aware audience. They could not afford, even if they had wished to do so, to turn into melodrama stories so close to the heart of Britain. Care was taken therefore to make the reconstruction of warfare on land, sea or in the air accurate to the conditions involved rather than spectacular for its own sake. (Manvell, 1974, p. 85)

This is not entirely wishful thinking. Audiences might have responded positively to the class-bound melodramatic heroics of *Ships with Wings* at the beginning of 1942 but later in the year they were welcoming the very different style and ethos of films like *The Foreman Went to France*, *One of Our Aircraft Is Missing* and *In Which We Serve*. That much of what was seen as a new national cinema now seems cautiously conservative should not obscure the fact that it was a more nuanced and sophisticated style of cinema than that embalmed in a historical curio like *Ships with Wings*.

The style of film-making where characterization and plausibility are sacrificed to pace and excitement remained central to commercial cinema and was used vigorously in such British war films as Nolbandov's *Undercover*, George King's *Tomorrow We Live* and *Candlelight in Algeria*, Lawrence Huntington's *The Tower of Terror* and Karel Lamac's *They Met in the Dark*, which make up exciting stories about the war. But the films that emerged as big box-office successes from 1943 onwards were either nostalgia-tinged realist films such as Noël Coward and David Lean's *This Happy Breed* and Terence Rattigan and Anthony Asquith's *The Way to the Stars*, romantic melodramas like Herbert Wilcox's *I Live in Grosvenor Square* and *Piccadilly Incident* and Leslie Arliss's *Love Story*, which use the war as a background against which intense dramas of sacrifice and loss are played out, or melodramas such as *The Man in Grey*, *Madonna of the Seven Moons*, *The Seventh Veil* and *The Wicked Lady*, which turn their back on the war to spin their complex webs of intrigue and passion.

A film like *In Which We Serve*, with its vision of Britain as a happy and efficient ship where everybody knows their place and does their duty, might appear condescending to modern audiences but it is light years away from *Ships with Wings* in its treatment of romance, heroism, and the relationships between officers and men. Its realism and restraint were to set the tone for most subsequent British war films. The concentration on heroic officers and the marginalization of those from the lower ranks would re-emerge in 1950s war films when there was no longer any need to promote the idea of a 'people's war' with everyone pulling together. However, in stylistic terms, films like *The Cruel Sea*, *The Dam Busters* and *Reach for the Sky* adhered to the sober realism established in the middle years of the war.

NOTES

1 See Rachel Low, *The History of the British Film, 1906–1914* (London: Allen and Unwin, 1949), p. 134.

2 The phrase was first used in a speech made by Stanley Baldwin to the House of Commons on 10 November 1932, though the idea had been heavily promoted by Lord Trenchard, who led the RAF in the years after 1918 and successfully prevented it from being absorbed by the Army and Navy.

3 *Kinematograph Weekly*, 7 September 1939, p. 4.

4 Morgan (1948) is a fascinating history of the Granada cinema circuit in the war years and an invaluable source for cinemagoing during the war.

5 It was Sir Seymour Hicks (who appears as the anti-Nazi General von Grotjahn in *Pastor Hall*) who wrote the 'Gone with the Wind Up' article. See Morley (1984), p. 172.

6 'The other side of the Atlantic', *Documentary News Letter*, September 1940, pp. 2–3.

7 Isidore Ostrer's books *A New International Currency* (1921) and *The Conquest of Gold* (1932) expressed the same sort of anti-monetarist arguments as John Maynard Keynes and Roosevelt's New Deal adviser Waddill Catchings. In the political arena, Ostrer solidly supported the National Government. According to Hollins, the Gaumont-British Newsreel was 'particularly sympathetic to conservative aims during the 1930s' and in 1935 'a clear but highly secret link' was established between Ostrer and the National Publicity Bureau which co-ordinated government publicity (Hollins, 1981, pp. 367–8).

8 In the early months of the year, Two Cities' First World War comedy *Spy for a Day* (directed by Mario Zampi), which improbably unites Lancashire comic Duggie Wakefield and the deep-voiced nightclub singer from *Contraband*, Paddy Browne, was made at Shepperton.

9 The cinema circuit owned by the Blacks was actually taken over by Sir Edward Gibbons's General Theatre Corporation, which in turn was taken over by Gaumont-British. The eldest brother, George, ran the flagship of GTC's and subsequently Gaumont-British's music hall circuit, the London Palladium.

10 John Ware, *The Lion Has Wings: The Epic of the Famous Korda Film* (London: Collins, 1940), p. 176, quoted in Short (1997b), p. 24. Most of the factual information here is derived from Short's meticulously researched monograph.

11 Bushell acted in a huge number of films, most notably in *The Ghoul* (T. Hayes Hunter, 1933), *The Small Back Room*, and as Colonel Breen in the 1963 television series *Quatermass and the Pit*. De Marney was equally prolific and enterprising. In the early 1940s he formed a production company, Concannen, with Leslie Howard. His most notable acting role was as a sinister Victorian villain trying to cheat his niece out of her inheritance in *Uncle Silas* (Charles Frank, 1947).

12 *Spectator*, 3 November 1939.

13 Ian Dalrymple, 'On the lion having wings', *Cine-Technician*, Feb–March 1940, p. 11.

14 *Jew Süss* was remade – with a viciously anti-Semitic slant – in Germany by Veit Harlan in 1940.

15 The American newsreel *March of Time* did carry out hard-hitting examinations of the world situation in its editions on the Italian war in Abyssinia, the settlement of Jews in Palestine, the Japanese seizure of Manchuria, the Spanish Civil War, and life inside Nazi Germany, though they were subject to British censorship. See Manvell (1974), pp. 15–21.

16 In *Mrs Miniver*, the Minivers are threatened with a forty-shilling fine, but the ARP warden is the local grocer and is using his powers – jokily – to increase orders in the shop.

17 For Tennyson see *Penrose Tennyson* by C.T. (Charles Tennyson), privately published, 1943; and 'Pen Tennyson writes a letter', *Cine Technician*, July–August 1941, pp. 82–4.

18 'Film of the month: *Convoy*', *Documentary News Letter*, August 1940, p. 9.

19 Acts of suicidal courage certainly occurred. During the raid on Wilhelmshaven on 4 September 1939, the pilot of a stricken Blenheim deliberately crashed his plane into the German cruiser *Emden* (Short, 1997b, p. 39). Narracott (1947) includes the following extract from Leonard R. Gribble's *Heroes of the Fighting RAF*:

> An unnamed sergeant pilot was just taking off in his yellow-painted Anson training aircraft from an aerodrome in the West Country when bombs began falling all round the landing field. As he climbed he saw a Heinkel 111 swooping. The Heinkel began sending a stream of machine-gun bullets at the unarmed pilot. He could not hit back. . . . Deliberately the unarmed sergeant flew at the enemy that was trying to shoot him out of the sky. His Anson turned suddenly and crashed into the bomber. The Heinkel crashed, and its crew of five perished. The Anson crashed after it.

20 *Documentary News Letter*, 2 December 1941, p. 221.

21 Josh Billings, who compiled the 'Box Office Winners of the Year' for the *Kinematograph Weekly*, stresses himself that his surveys are based on his general knowledge of the film trade rather than on hard statistical evidence, but in the absence of more concrete evidence his conclusions are generally accepted. He mentions *Love on the Dole* as one of the more successful British films of 1941 (*Kinematograph Weekly*, 8 January 1942, p. 8), puts *One of Our Aircraft Is Missing* ahead of *Ships with Wings* in 1942 (*Kinematograph Weekly*, 14 January 1943, pp. 46–7), and includes *San Demetrio London* among the top films of February 1944. Richards' evidence to the contrary comes from the detailed box-office returns compiled by Julian Poole for a cinema in Macclesfield (Poole, 1987) and a speech made by W. J. Speakman of the solidly conservative CEA to what one might suppose would be an audience of left-wing intellectuals at a BFI summer school in 1944 (in *Film Appreciation and Visual Education*, BFI: London, 1944, p. 42).

22 Richards and Sheridan (1987), pp. 364–80, reproduces the Mass Observation files on *Ships with Wings*.

23 Nolbandov reverted to his role as producer after *Undercover*. He produced *This Modern Age*, Rank's answer to *March of Time*, and worked with Stewart McAllister and Alfred Hitchcock on Sidney Bernstein's (never released) documentary about the Nazi concentration camps. His later credits include Philip Leacock's *The Kidnappers* (1953) and *Mix Me a Person* (1961), directed by Leslie Norman for Ian Dalrymple's company, Wessex, and starring Adam Faith, Anne Baxter and Donald Sinden.

2

The World Turned Upside Down: War Comedy

'Don't hit the sergeant with a hammer.
Into deeds of violence do not be led.
Don't hit the sergeant with a hammer.
Use the butt end of your rifle instead.'
(Nat Jackley, Norman Evans, Dan
Young, Tony Dalton, *Demobbed*)

Clive Coultass points out that during the early years of the war, 'none of the films made within the period shows any understanding of the likely course of the conflict or the immense effort and resolution that would be needed to defeat Nazi Germany' (Coultass, 1989, p. 37). This is hardly surprising when few of Britain's military and political leaders themselves came anywhere near a true assessment of German military might. In retrospect, though, it does seem extraordinary that jaunty, madcap comedies like *Let George Do It* and *Gasbags* (originally titled *We're Going to Hang Out the Washing on the Siegfried Line* after Bud Flanagan and Chesney Allen's popular song) which were conceived and made during the 'phoney war' period before the German armies marched into Western Europe, should have proved so popular when they were released in the autumn and winter of 1940 when Britain was under siege.

Criticism of *Ships with Wings* centred upon the banality of its romantic entanglements and the implausibility of its special effects. Negative comment gathered by Mass Observation came from those who had gone to see the film in the expectation that they would be shown what the Navy was doing and found they were presented with 'another fairy-tale' (Richards and Sheridan, 1987, p. 373). Stacey's feat of piggybacking his stricken plane onto a German bomber and steering it into the dam could be seen as a trivialization of the real dangers faced by the men of the Fleet Air Arm, but in comedies similar exploits were entirely acceptable. In *Let George Do It*, George Formby outwits the crew of a U-boat and survives being fired from a torpedo tube to land in the arms of the glamorous British agent who loves him. In *Spare a Copper*, he escapes from the fifth columnists he has exposed in a miniature car which enables him to evade his pursuers by going under a fence, a lorry and, finally, a horse. In *Gasbags*, the Crazy Gang drift into Germany on a barrage balloon and make their escape in a machine designed like a mechanical mole which burrows back to Britain – disrupting the Siegfried Line and intersecting with a London tube train before emerging in the office of their irate sergeant major.

The shortage of good news in the early years of the war meant that film-makers had to fall back on spy thrillers or stories of resistance to the Nazis, such as *Night Train to Munich* and the Boulting Brothers' much grimmer *Pastor Hall*. Above all, the uncertainty and confusion of this period led film-makers to take the safe path of making comedies. Of the 98 British films released in 1940 and 1941, 44 were comedies or comedy-thrillers.[1] Some of these films, like ABPC's *Spring Meeting* (Walter Mycroft, 1940) and *Banana Ridge* (Walter Mycroft, 1941), ignored the war, as did adaptations of upper-middle-class stage comedies like Esther MacCracken's *Quiet Wedding* (Anthony Asquith, 1941). But most of them eagerly adapted to the new situation either by depicting the mishaps of their comic characters when they joined up or by exploring the possibilities opened up by such phenomena as the blackout, the need to shelter from air raids, the creation of large numbers of evacuees and the seeming prevalence of spies and fifth columnists.

Early War Comedies

War disrupted the normal pattern of everyday life and quickly imposed its own rhythms and culture. Evacuation of urban women and children had long been planned and was begun on 1 September, before war was declared. Despite reportage like George Orwell's *The Road to Wigan Pier*, there was considerable ignorance of how life was lived either side of the class divide. Middle-class families were shocked to receive lice-ridden children unused to knives and forks and green vegetables. Slum children were puzzled by hot running water and flushing toilets, not to mention the dangers and excitements of the countryside. Inevitably, hasty, patchy organization led to an odd mismatching of evacuees and their hosts:

Elderly gentlemen found their retirement invaded by half a dozen urchins from the slums of London or Liverpool. Neat spinsters who had agreed to take a schoolchild might be gifted instead with a sluttish mother who arrived smoking a cigarette over her baby's head and disappeared with her offspring as soon as the pubs opened. (Calder, 1971, p. 47)

When Goering failed to send over his bombers, the scheme crumbled. By the beginning of 1940, around four out of ten children and nine-tenths of the mothers evacuated in England and Wales had returned home. In Scotland the drift back was even more marked. But a substantial number of children remained and they feature regularly in wartime films set in rural Britain.

The tough street gang from *Front Line Kids* soon trek back to London, bored with the countryside where 'there ain't nothing to look at, no shop windows or nothing'; and Old Bill's wife (Mary Clare) fiercely rejects the suggestion that, with the rest of the family at war, she should evacuate herself to the countryside:

'Now look here you, just get this clear. I hate my sister and I hate my sister's husband and I hate my sister's husband's mother worse than the lot. I hate the nasty little farmers. I hate the countryside and everything concerned with it – pigs, cows, chickens, all the smelly lot.'

But George Cole in *Cottage to Let* and Harry Fowler in *Went the Day Well?* find plenty to do in a countryside swarming with Germans and fifth columnists, and streetwise Vera Francis helps Arthur Askey outwit the German spies in *Back Room Boy* and George Formby his Home Guard rivals in *Get Cracking*. In *Tawny Pipit*, two evacuees attempt to steal the pipits' eggs but they are quickly converted into guardians of the nest. In *Gert and Daisy's Weekend*, the party of unruly evacuees shepherded by the two women to the safety of a stately home make life hell for the butler but catch a country house con-man who has stolen the family jewels. Similarly, British National's *Those Kids from Town* has both Harry Fowler and George Cole billeted on an earl. Evacuees were thus absorbed into the fabric of popular mythology, though a serious approach to the phenomenon had to wait for Alan Parker and Jack Gold's television films *Evacuees* (1975) and *Goodnight Mr Tom* (1999).

Mobilization inspired a group of joining-up films – *All at Sea, Laugh It Off, Old Bill and Son, Old Mother Riley Joins Up, Pack Up Your Troubles* and the series of films starring Frank Randle, *Somewhere in England*,

The Cockney evacuee: Ronald Mittsby (George Cole) regarded with bemused affection by Miss Fernsby (Muriel Aked) and Mrs Barrington (Jeanne de Casalis) in *Cottage to Let*. Supplied by BFI Stills, © courtesy of Carlton International.

Somewhere in Camp, *Somewhere on Leave* and *Somewhere in Civvies* – generally involving a comedian's encounter with service life. As Sandy Powell, Tommy Trinder, Morland Graham, Arthur Lucan and the rest invariably played working-class characters, this often produced guarded references to the problems of a class-divided society. Upper-class women are caricatured in *Old Mother Riley Joins Up* (as is the languorous telephone chatterer in *Do It Now*) and ritually humiliated by Frank Randle in the *Somewhere* films. The friendly but deferential relationship that Old Bill has with his commanding officers contrasts sharply with his son's attitude, making fun of the accent of his well-educated sidekick (Manning Whiley) and assuring his sweetheart that 'you don't have to be a toff to be an officer nowadays'. The traditional working class is represented as cheerily irreverent, like naughty children, by the older characters played by Arthur Lucan, Sandy Powell, Leslie Fuller and Edward Rigby, but the new generation is eager for social mobility. Old Bill's son looks set to overcome his spivvish habits and become an officer, Old Mother

Riley's daughter (Kitty McShane) qualifies as a doctor and wins the heart of the general's son, and Tommy Towers' (Tommy Trinder) ability to put on a show in *Laugh It Off* qualifies him for a commission as Entertainments Officer. In the *Somewhere* films, an upper-middle-class young man often finds himself serving as a private alongside Frank Randle and his cohorts, but like the principal boy in a panto-mime his story seems to exist alongside rather than form a part of the chaotic goings-on of the comic characters.

The *Somewhere* films continued long after Trinder, Old Mother Riley and the rest had been demobbed. In these films the prospect of action seems far off and life centres around shambolic parades by a squad which no amount of drill will mould into an effective fighting force. Medical inspections reveal the misshapen, semi-decrepit state of Randle and his pals. Simple cleaning and tidying tasks around the camp lead to an orgy of wreckage and destruction, and attempts to put on a show provide an excuse for monologues and sketches.

Randle was a Lancashire variety performer noted for his anarchic stage act and the problems of incorporating him into a conventional film narrative were beyond the talents of John E. Blakeley. According to Jeff Nuttall, Blakeley and his cameraman Ernie Palmer

> took no identity on themselves other than the identity normally taken by audience and theatre producer. The picture frame was static as a proscenium arch. The camera angle was eye-level frontal throughout. There was no zooming, little panning, no dollying and no change of angle. The camera was in fact a man in a music hall. (Nuttall, 1978, p. 52)[2]

Zoom lenses were not available until after the war and Palmer, Geoffrey Faithfull and Stephen Dade, the cinematographers who worked on the Mancunian films, showed considerable visual flair on other films they worked on. But Nuttall grasps the essential point about the films: that they are valuable less for what they reveal about life in the Army or for any aesthetic qualities and more for the glimpse they allow into unsanitized, undeferential working-class culture.

The *Somewhere* films and several other of the service comedies did very well at the box-office but most of them were low-budget affairs destined for the bottom part of the double bill. Vehicles provided for the likes of George Formby, Arthur Askey, Will Hay and the Crazy Gang were a little more costly and their directors – Marcel Varnel, John Paddy Carstairs, Herbert Mason and Walter Forde – higher in the pecking order than Oswald Mitchell, Maclean Rogers and John

E. Blakeley. This end of the market was very much dominated by Gainsborough and Ealing, with British National pushing up from below but tending to lose out between the grass roots working-class audience tapped by Butchers – which seemed to be able to call up an inexhaustible supply of popular variety acts around which to construct their low-budget films – and the mainstream audience reached by its better-established rivals.[3]

Ealing's strongest card was George Formby, whom Balcon inherited from his predecessor, Basil Dean. Balcon had little time for Formby, and despite the huge success of his first two wartime films, *Let George Do It* and *Spare a Copper*, he seems to have made little effort to persuade him not to transfer his allegiance to the American company Columbia.[4] Balcon had managed to poach Will Hay, with whom he had worked in the 1930s, from Gainsborough, and a promising start was made with *The Ghost of St Michael's*, with Claude Hulbert and Charles Hawtrey giving the sort of comic support Hay had had from Moore Marriott and Graham Moffat at Gainsborough. The story runs on similar lines to Hay's most successful 1930s film, *Oh, Mr Porter!* (Marcel Varnel, 1936), with successive headmasters of a boys' public school, which has been evacuated to the Isle of Skye, falling victim to what is supposed to be the castle ghost but who is actually a fifth columnist signalling to German submarines from the ramparts. By 1941 the rules of this type of film were so firmly set that our suspicions are successfully displaced onto usual suspects Raymond Huntley and Manning Whiley – already typecast as spies, fifth columnists or Nazis – to distract us from the real villain.[5] Hay's next two films, *The Black Sheep of Whitehall* – where Hay and John Mills unmask a gang of fifth columnists who have kidnapped an economics expert – and *The Goose Steps Out* – where Hay is helped by a group of Austrian youths led by Charles Hawtrey to steal a German secret weapon – seem cruder and less funny. Hay's final film, *My Learned Friend* (Basil Deardon, 1943), ignores the war; reuniting him with Claude Hulbert, it is a black comedy which looks forward to Ealing's later successes *Kind Hearts and Coronets* (Robert Hamer, 1949) and *The Ladykillers* (Alexander Mackendrick, 1955).

Ealing's third string was Tommy Trinder, a Cockney comedian lured from British National where he had made *Laugh It Off*. His first film for Ealing, *Sailors Three*, teamed him with Claude Hulbert and Michael Wilding in a comic parallel to *Convoy* and *For Freedom*. The three sailors are part of the crew of HMS *Ferocious*, which is despatched to the South Atlantic to find and sink the German pocket battleship *Ludendorff*. After putting ashore at a South American port, the three sailors get very drunk and board the *Ludendorff* in mistake for their own ship. Their plan to get the Germans to abandon their ship is sabotaged by two monstrous children but all turns out well in the end. Walter Forde, who had been responsible for Ealing's two best non-war comedies – *Cheer Boys Cheer* (1939) and *Saloon Bar* (1940) – directs the film with his usual professionalism as a British equivalent to *Follow the Fleet* (1936). However, Tommy Trinder and Carla Lehman, a young Canadian actress who became a staple of British wartime cinema, are less charismatic than Fred Astaire and Ginger Rogers, and Claude Hulbert and Michael Wilding are under-used in their supporting roles. Though the film was successful enough to inspire a sequel – Harry Watt's *Fiddlers Three* – Trinder was more effective when he exchanged the role of romantic lead to play comic characters in two serious war films, *The Foreman Went to France* and *The Bells Go Down*, and the *lion comique* George Leybourne in Caval-canti's *Champagne Charlie* (1944).

Before the war, Gainsborough and Gaumont-British had assembled an impressive team of comedy performers but during the financial crisis of 1937 they lost Jack Hulbert and Cicely Courtneidge and the Aldwych farceurs (Ralph Lynn, Tom Walls and Robertson Hare), and in 1939 Will Hay defected to Ealing. This left only Will Fyffe and the Crazy Gang and by 1941 they too had drifted away. In contrast to Butchers' reliance on old-style variety acts, Gainsborough turned to the radio to recruit new talent. *Band Waggon*, starring 'Big-hearted' Arthur Askey and Richard 'Stinker' Murdoch, takes on much of the baggage of the radio show from which it takes its name but stiffens it up with a good script from the studio's regular comedy writing team – J. O. C. Orton, Val Guest and Marriott Edgar. Askey comedies continued to pour out from the studio until 1944, though the format and the supporting cast changed radically in an attempt to maintain his popularity.

Gainsborough had less success with its other radio stars. American husband and wife team Ben Lyon and Bebe Daniels failed to secure much of an audience for *Hi Gang!*, which, apart from a few moments of redeeming vulgarity from Will Hay's old sidekicks Moore Marriott and Graham Moffat, is Gainsborough's least funny comedy. Tommy Handley's *ITMA* (*It's That Man Again*) also failed to make a successful transition from radio to film. The ITMA radio show appealed to all classes and ages and provided many of the catchphrases of wartime society. According to Angus Calder,

> In any one week, more than sixteen million people would listen to ITMA. RAF pilots shouted 'I'm going down now' as they dived to attack; a small boy trapped under a pile of rubble in Bath piped out

to the rescue squad, 'Can you do me now, sir?' When ITMA was off the air for a few weeks, the public could work its magic for themselves by repeating the catchphrases. Capable, by some alchemy, of making fun of Dame Austerity herself ... ITMA sparkled through the life of the nation like bubbles through soda water. (Calder, 1971, p. 418)

Unfortunately, Gainsborough's team of expert scriptwriters – Launder and Gilliat, Guest, Orton and Edgar – seem to have been too busy on other projects, and Ted Kavanagh, Handley's gag writer, and Howard Irving Young came up with nothing better than the tired old warhorse of putting on a show in a ruined theatre. Walter Forde does his best but he was given little opportunity to capture the strangely surreal world that Handley and his pals transmitted across the radio waves. He was given more scope with *Time Flies* (1944), for which Orton helped construct a more original script. The ITMA cast was dispensed with and Handley was supported by an odd collection of talents including Gainsborough stalwarts Moore Marriott and Graham Moffatt, the distinguished character actor Felix Aylmer (as a Doctor Who-like time traveller), Stephane Grappelly (as an Elizabethan troubadour) and Evelyn Dall, a dynamic American blonde who seemed to combine the comic zest of Barbara Windsor with the musical dynamism of Debbie Harry. Sue Harper praises the way in which the film 'renders complex philosophical ideas about time in a palatable form' and admires the art direction of John Bryan, particularly his time machine. 'It is spherical, and thus immeasurably suggestive: perfect, symmetrical, with a massive interior, able to hover at will, and its doors are invisible. It is the egg of time' (Harper, 1997, pp. 91–2). Along with Val Guest's *Give Us the Moon*, it is the most interesting of Gainsborough's attempts to stretch the boundaries of British film comedy, but it failed to appeal to audiences and Handley returned to the radio microphone where he reigned supreme until his death in 1949.[6]

The early war comedies that are now the most watchable are the most extravagant: *Let George Do It* and *Gasbags* – both of which take advantage of their foreign settings to lurch into outrageous fantasies. *Let George Do It*, scripted by Ealing regulars John Dighton, Austin Melford and Angus MacPhail, along with Basil Dearden, who also acted as associate producer, is the best of Formby's wartime films. A strong supporting cast and a clever script combine to give Formby the lift-off he never quite gets from his subsequent films. Phyllis Calvert, as a British agent, has more to do than the sympathetic simpering that most of George's heroines are reduced to; Garry Marsh's jovial bullying makes him a more formidable adversary than the cardboard villains of *Spare a Copper*; and Coral Browne's slinky femme fatale is more dangerous than the usual 'cheeky fast cat' who threatens to invade George's virginal shyness. The plot, which revolves around Marsh's band transmitting musical Morse code messages to German U-boats, was good enough to be recycled for Karel Lamac's *They Met in the Dark* in 1943, but here it is particularly appropriate, serving as a means of integrating George and his ukulele into the story and avoiding the usual problem of the narrative having to come to an abrupt halt while George sings his songs.

Anti-Nazi propaganda is also effectively integrated. After being slipped a truth drug in his coffee and spilling the beans to the villains, George goes into a deep sleep and dreams he is at the gates of heaven but is refused entrance until he can return with 'the ace of knaves – Adolf Hitler'. He drifts down to Germany on a barrage balloon and spots Hitler addressing a rally. Shouting 'Hey Adolf I want you', he proceeds to knock him out. The stormtroopers on the platform, rather than arresting him, applaud wildly and George wakes up fighting with the sheets. It all seems rather silly now, but according to a Mass Observation survey, audiences at the time loved it.[7]

A similar irreverence is displayed in *Gasbags*. The Crazy Gang, a combustible combination of three double acts – Jimmy Nervo and Teddy Knox, Bud Flanagan and Chesney Allen, Charlie Naughton and Jimmy Gold – were protégés of George Black, the manager of the London Palladium whose brother Edward produced all of Gainsborough's films between 1937 and 1944. They had made *Okay for Sound* (Marcel Varnel, 1937) and *The Frozen Limits* (Marcel Varnel, 1939) before the war but stayed together for only one more film – *Gasbags* – although Flanagan and Allen made four films with John Baxter: *We'll Smile Again* (1942), *Theatre Royal* (1943), *Dreaming* (1944) and *Here Comes the Sun* (1945). The narrative form of a feature film was not really flexible enough to provide equal opportunities for each of the jealously competitive performers, and Charlie Naughton's clowning, Jimmy Nervo's wisecracking and Bud Flanagan's wordplay tended to give them a prominence over their partners not allowed in their stage acts. *Gasbags* is a ramshackle affair, but the way in which it casually incorporates barrage balloons, concentration camps, secret weapons, the SS and Hitler into its zany, irreverent, knockabout comic world robs them of terror. They become new toys, new targets to make fun of. Put into the most fantastic situation, the Crazy Gang seek out practical solutions. When Charlie Naughton inhales so much of the balloon gas that he swells up and floats off, the others hold him down and pump him out into a gas ring on which Flanagan cooks them fish for breakfast. Confronted by myriad Hitler lookalikes, Jimmy Nervo changes his hairstyle and becomes one of them, bravely volunteering to fill in for the Führer.

The Askey films are more conventional and less chaotic. In *Band Waggon*, 'Stinker' and 'Big', sick of waiting for an audition at the BBC, take up residence in the attic of Broadcasting House, hanging out their washing between the aerials and keeping their goat, cock and pigeons on the roof. When they are ejected by the irate Director General they drive out into rural England and find shelter in a haunted castle which is being used as a base by a nest of German spies. The fact that the spies are transmitting television pictures back to Germany might seem unnecessarily extravagant, but it allows Askey the opportunity to interrupt a broadcast of Hitler addressing a rally, and for Askey, Murdoch and other artists shut out by the BBC to challenge its monopoly by setting up a pirate television channel broadcasting popular entertainment.

In *Band Waggon*, 'Stinker' and 'Big' are to all intents and purposes a gay couple. Askey puts a bolster between them when they have to share a bed in the castle, but the clanking of the ghost (Moore Marriott) soon has them clutching each other in terror. This was all very well on the radio but it was deemed too risqué to flourish in British cinema and the string of films that follow try different solutions to the problem of what sort of man the gnome-like Askey should play. In *Charley's Big-Hearted Aunt* (Walter Forde, 1940) and *I Thank You*, he spends much of the film disguised as a woman. In *The Ghost Train*, he is a manic little sprite responsible for a group of travellers missing their connection and having to spend the night in a lonely, haunted station waiting room. There he torments them with jokes, macabre stories, gramophone records (until an enraged passenger throws the gramophone out through the door) and an inextinguishable effervescent cheerfulness. In these three films Murdoch sheds his effeminacy and becomes a straight romantic lead, but by the time *Back Room Boy* went into production he had joined the RAF and in his absence Askey is allowed a rudimentary romance (with Joyce Howard, an English Rose type who had been the victim of Nazi sexual beastliness in *Freedom Radio*). Ten minutes into the film, however, she rejects Askey in favour of a radio announcer and he exiles himself to a remote lighthouse where he is helped by a Cockney evacuee (Vera Francis) and harassed by Moore Marriott and Graham Moffat, a gang of German spies and a troupe of querulous shipwrecked showgirls led by Googie Withers.

Collar the Lot

MI5 had been remarkably successful in rounding up German agents in the early months of the war, though this had as much to do with the unpreparedness of the Nazis as the efficiency of British counter-espionage. Both Britain and Germany had invested far more in attempting to infiltrate left-wing groups than in preparing for war against each other. Ironically, several MI5 agents belonged to the Right Club, the virulent right-wing, anti-Semitic group set up by Conservative MP Captain Ramsay. It was no secret that several members of the establishment – from the Duke of Windsor down – were admirers of Hitler and had no objection to German expansionism as long as it was directed eastwards. The collapse of Western Europe in the spring and summer of 1940 led to a dramatic shift of attitudes and newspapers like the *Daily Mail* switched from a pro-Fascist stance to a concern to seek out enemies within who might threaten Britain's security.

The rapid capitulation of Norway, Holland, Belgium and France was blamed on the treachery of quislings and fifth columnists, and similar elements were thought to be at work in Britain.[8] Suspicion fell upon the enemy aliens, despite the fact that the great majority of them were refugees from Nazi persecution. The Home Office had divided them into categories and, at the outbreak of war, interned the small number thought to be actively sympathetic to the Nazi cause. By the end of May a combination of pressures – from newspapers (particularly those with a guilty conscience about their own less than firm stance against Nazi aggression), MI5 and the Foreign Office – led to the round-up of over 30,000 of those hitherto not thought to be a security risk. Italians who had spent most of their lives in Britain, Polish Jews who had come to Britain before the First World War, Jewish scientists working on government projects were interned.

Fifth columnists, spies and traitors figure prominently in a range of British films from the knockabout farce of *Front Line Kids* to the grim realism of *The Next of Kin*. The Germans and their agents tend to be depicted as sinister, bullying and ruthless but there is little attempt to show them as exceptionally grotesque or sadistic. Nor are they charismatic, unlike some of the spivs and black marketeers of late 1940s films. In most cases they are interchangeable with the villains of pre-war comedy thrillers and tend to be played by a fixed group of actors – Garry Marsh, Raymond Lovell, Julien Mitchell, Eliot Makeham, Frank Pettingell, Manning Whiley, Raymond Huntley, Mary

Clare, Bernard Miles – many of whom had already established a villainous persona. There is an emphasis on fifth column activity but there is no targeting of either foreign nationals or particular trades and professions.[9] Waiters, barmen/maids, theatrical agents, shopkeepers and businessmen of various sorts, stuntmen, shipping clerks, taxidermists, piano-tuners, post-office sorters, doctors and dentists, headmasters, cooks, matrons, nurses, fishermen, bandleaders, estate agents and fairground owners all prove untrustworthy. But the spirit of the films is one of cheery resilience and there is no hint of xenophobia or paranoia.

Looking back, Michael Balcon commented that

> there was little to laugh about in life and our Will Hay comedy, *The Ghost of St Michael's*, *Sailors Three* with Tommy Trinder, and our two Formby comedies, *Spare a Copper* and *Turned Out Nice Again*, provided some respite for a public that had known nothing but bad news for a long time. (Balcon, 1969, p. 132)

Films taught that the war did not have to be taken seriously all the time, that the deadly threat facing Britain could be laughed at. In response to the danger within, they show that appearances can be deceptive and that spies and fifth columnists are everywhere but it is not something to worry about. On the contrary, rooting them out is great fun and dangers are more than compensated for by the prospect of romantic success. British comedies of the early war years were popular because they wear their propaganda burden so lightly. Later in the war, influences by the Ministry of information on the industry shifted production in favour of realism and social responsibility, and films display that enlightened paternalism which was to give birth to the Welfare State. But in the early years these comedies present a less mediated response to the war.

In the atmosphere of gloom and anxiety preceding the war a rash of spy films had emerged: *Q Planes* (Tim Whelan), *The Spy in Black*, *Spies of the Air* (David Macdonald), *Among Human Wolves* (John Baxter), *The Four Just Men* (Walter Forde), *An Englishman's Home* (Albert de Courville) and *Traitor Spy* (Walter Summers) were all released in 1939. Fewer spy thrillers were made after war was declared and their tone, paradoxically, was lighter.

The Gainsborough team made three films featuring the radio detective Inspector Hornleigh for 20th Century-Fox. *Inspector Hornleigh* (Eugene Forde, 1939) is a clever whodunnit involving some impressively seedy settings and characters, three murders and the theft of the Chancellor of the Exchequer's Budget Bag. *Inspector*

Hornleigh on Holiday (Walter Forde, 1940) was completed just before war broke out but with a few minor modifications it could qualify as a fifth columnist thriller. Hornleigh (Gordon Harker) and Sergeant Bingham (Alastair Sim) are relieved to have their rainy seaside holiday enlivened by a suicide which they skilfully discern to be murder. Their investigations lead them to the Upside Down Bridge Club, which is a front for a gang carrying out life insurance frauds. In a pre-echo of how the resistance would work, the criminal master-mind organizing the racket transmits his instructions in the form of gardening tips on amateur radio and is caught by Hornleigh and Bingham with the help of a radio detector van.

Inspector Hornleigh Goes to It begins with Hornleigh dictating his memoirs, leaving blank the last chapter but heading it 'The Fifth Column'. To his indignation and annoyance, the fifth column case is assigned to his rival, Inspector Blow (Percy Walsh), and Hornleigh and Bingham are ordered to enlist as privates to investigate pilfering from Army stores. However, Bingham's infatuation with a barmaid who makes suspiciously frequent visits to the dentist ('Either she's what I think she is or the way you kiss her knocks her teeth in') puts them on the trail of the fifth columnists. Phyllis Calvert, who had inspired George Formby to do his patriotic duty in *Let George Do It*, is recast as a slinky femme fatale who outwits the gullible Bingham. But they eventually solve the mystery of how the spies appear to be constantly on the move by tracking them down to the London to Scotland night mail train, where the GPO sorting supervisor transmits the gang's coded messages from the train.

Though the Hornleigh films were well received, Sim had outgrown his subordinate role and the team split up. Harker reverted to his pre-war persona as a colourful bookie in *Saloon Bar* and a publican with a shady past in *Once a Crook* (Herbert Mason, 1941) but returned to fight spies and fifth columnists determined to kidnap Winston Churchill in *Warn That Man*. Sim stayed on as a detective in Anthony Asquith's *Cottage to Let*, though he muddies the waters by posing first as a loquacious birdwatcher and then as the leader of the fifth columnists. Asquith withholds from us for as long as possible who is and who is not a fifth columnist. John Mills as an injured Spitfire pilot seems to flaunt his conquest over his devoted nurse (Carla Lehman) in a caddish way but, along with the Cockney evacuee played by George Cole, we cannot bring ourselves to believe that a fighter pilot – particularly one played by John Mills – could really be a traitor. On the other hand, Sim draws too much attention to himself to be a convincing villain, and Michael Wilding as a shy backroom boy playing postal chess with a correspondent in Switzerland and making odd assignations with the dubious-looking cook seems to be getting such a raw deal in the romance stakes that it is difficult not to sympathize with him. The evacuee turned amateur sleuth, the inventor who cannot be bothered with security, the butler who is obviously (to the streetwise evacuee at least) a policeman in disguise, the fluttering upper-class hostess, and the birdwatcher who turns out to be not what he seems, provide a typical Asquithian gallery of eccentrics, but they are more than a match for the coldly ruthless fifth columnists.

Night Train to Munich, scripted by Frank Launder and Sidney Gilliat from a story by Gordon Wellesley, deliberately retained the comedy-thriller ethos of *The Lady Vanishes* and played down the horrors of Nazi brutality. Its original title was *Gestapo* and it was, according to Carol Reed, 'rather serious. But when the war came on, we felt it was wrong to make something so heavy at such a time, so we made it more amusing' (Samuels, 1978, p. 14). A scene in the concentration camp where a young man (Paul Henreid before going to Hollywood for *Casablanca* and *Now Voyager*) defies the camp guards and is beaten up seems brutal but it later proves to have been a sham, a set-up to establish the credentials of a Nazi spy out to gain the confidence of the heroine. The interplay between Rex Harrison and Margaret Lockwood seems to deliberately echo that of Lockwood and Michael Redgrave in *The Lady Vanishes*, and the cricket-loving Englishmen, Charters and Caldicott, are on hand to help out when they are needed. But this is something more than a pale copy. Deliberately light-hearted though it might be, there is an edge of urgency and anxiety not present in *The Lady Vanishes*, an acknowledgement that the enemy being fought is ruthless and well organized.

Pimpernel Smith moves further towards gentlemanly escapism, with Leslie Howard reworking his Scarlet Pimpernel persona for a contemporary wartime story. Exploiting the Nazis' contemptuous underestimation of dreamy intellectuals, he ventures into Germany to save victims of Nazi oppression. As he tells his students: 'You see, when a man holds the view that progress and civilization in every age depends upon the hands and brains of a few exceptional spirits, it's rather hard to stand by and see them destroyed.' Jeffrey Richards defends Howard and the character he plays against the charge of elitism, pointing out that the rescue of artists, scientists and intellectuals is central to his idea of a civilization under threat from the forces of barbarism and ignorance (Aldgate and Richards, 1986, p. 61). It was an idea shared by Kenneth Clark at the Ministry of Information who, in a paper called 'It's the Same Old Hun', argued that:

It would seem in our interest to stress the very great difference between the Germany of 1914–18 and today, by pointing out how in the last war all the best elements of German culture and science were still in Germany and were supporting the German cause, whereas now they are outside Germany and supporting us. (Quoted in McLaine, 1979, p. 156)

This was written in January 1941 when large numbers of these 'best elements of German culture and science' were still in the internment camps where the 'collar the lot' policy of the previous summer had deposited them. But their supporters were eventually to secure their release by stressing how such a policy damaged Britain's image as a beacon of tolerance and civilization.

Intertwined with the jokes about Nazis mystified by the English sense of humour and the schoolboy japes in *Pimpernel Smith*, there is a dark plot strand about a Polish expatriate forced to work for the Gestapo to ensure the survival of her imprisoned father. One of the reasons cited for the internment of refugees as enemy aliens was the anxiety that pressure could be brought to bear on them by the Nazis if members of their family were still in Germany, and Mary Morris's Ludmilla Koslowski is treated with appropriate seriousness. She agrees to help the Nazis unmask 'the Shadow' and quickly realizes it is Professor Smith. But he is as quick to understand her predicament and they form an alliance to rescue her father. This leads to an unexpected romance which adds depth and poignancy to the film. Ludmilla is prepared to sacrifice herself but Smith promises to rescue her too. In an earlier scene he has talked to her about his ideal woman, and shown her a photograph of the statue of Aphrodite we saw him admiring at the beginning of the film. Given his brusque treatment of women throughout the film this is not unexpected, but he then proceeds to tear it up, showing that his fusty misogyny is as much a pretence as his ineffectual other-worldliness.[10]

Harold French's *Unpublished Story* has an element of screwball comedy in its central romance between two rival newspaper reporters (Valerie Hobson and Richard Greene). However, it's at its most interesting in dealing with the events of 1940 to 1941 – the last days of the British Expeditionary Force (BEF) in France, the withdrawal from Dunkirk and the London Blitz – before nostalgia had time to settle in, and its treatment of people opposed to the war. After witnessing the collapse of France, sports reporter Bob Randall (Greene) tells his editor (Brefni O'Rourke) that 'it wasn't only the German army they had to fight. They had to fight panic and confusion behind their lines – fifth columnists giving false orders, refugees flooding the roads, traitors within the gates.' Determined that 'it mustn't happen here', he roots out the peacemongers of a pacifist organization, one of whose members tells a meeting that 'prosperity, lawful commerce, the orderly stratification of society – in fact everything that goes to make life worth living' have been 'hindered, forgotten or tied to the blood-bespattered wheels of the chariot of Mars'. Randall's fellow reporter Carol Bennett (Hobson) is sympathetic to the well-meaning clerk who heads the organization but her moderate, unsensational story is only run after Randall's story ('Peace Apostle Bolts When Siren Sounds') is spiked by Ministry of Information censorship. Suspecting that the fifth columnists have already penetrated the government, he meets the official responsible and discovers that he is an MI5 agent on the verge of rounding up the ringleaders of what they suspect to be a Nazi front organization.

Given that one of the villains in *Unpublished Story* comes to Britain disguised as a Belgian refugee ('one refugee is very like another if he has the right papers'), it might seem surprising that the film was made for Two Cities, a company founded by two expatriate Italians, Filippo Del Giudice and Mario Zampi, in 1938. They had been arrested and interned on the Isle of Man as enemy aliens while working on *Freedom Radio* in the summer of 1940 and Zampi (who specialized in directing comedy films), unable to convince the authorities that he posed no threat, was shipped out to Canada. Del Giudice, a lawyer with a gift for cultivating good contacts in high places, was released in September and, with the help of Anthony Havelock-Allan, a successful producer of 'quota quickies', set about reviving the fortunes of Two Cities.

Unpublished Story is on an altogether different scale to Two Cities' earlier films, with an elaborate crane shot showing the arrival of a train carrying exhausted soldiers from Dunkirk and impressive footage of London burning and the aftermath of ruined buildings.[11] Its focus on the dangers of fifth columnists – the spreading of rumours and the distribution of anti-war pamphlets to people enduring endless nights of bombing raids – shows that opposition to the war was not quite unthinkable, but as with so many of these films the emphasis is less on fear and betrayal (the leader of the organization realizes too late that he has been duped and his fellow directors are not just Nazi sympathizers but Germans) than on the stoicism and resilience of ordinary people.

Mansell (Edward Rigby) looks askance at the beard sported by Commander Heritage (James Mason) in *They Met in the Dark*. Supplied by BFI Stills, © courtesy of Carlton International.

Later War Comedies

After 1941, comedies abandoned the search for spies and fifth columnists except for Askey's ingenious lighthouse mystery, *Back Room Boy*, two undistinguished comedies from British National (*Lady from Lisbon* and *We'll Smile Again*) and Formby's *Bell Bottom George*, notable chiefly for the sinister taxidermist played by Eliot Makeham. Comedy thrillers with a wartime theme virtually disappeared after *Cottage to Let*, apart from Lawrence Huntington's *Warn That Man* and Karel Lamac's *They Met in the Dark*. Lamac was an extremely prolific Czech director who impressed Rank sufficiently to gain funding for this ambitious production which attempts to launch Joyce Howard as a star and presents James Mason as a Royal Navy captain with a fully fledged beard.[12] This ill-matched romantic couple are set against a threatening band of fifth columnists – Karel Stepanek's womanizing hypnotist, Ronald Chesney's mouth-organ virtuoso and Tom Wall's unctuous theatrical agent – and the film is atmospherically lit by the

Czech cinematographer Otto Heller. But it was not a success, and it put an end to the cycle unless one counts Frank Launder's *I See a Dark Stranger*, made three years later.

Comedies remained important during the war, however, and found new themes: the threat posed by black marketeers and spivs in *Gert and Daisy Clean Up* and *Old Mother Riley, Detective*; and the pleasures and pains of life in the Home Guard in Formby's *Get Cracking* and Alfred Drayton and Robertson Hare's *Women Aren't Angels*. There was a reversion to the putting on a show formula, most inventively in John Baxter's adaptation of Priestley's *Let the People Sing* and MGM's attempt at a radio spin-off, *Happidrome* (Phil Brandon, 1943). Gainsborough tried various ways of packaging Arthur Askey in *King Arthur Was a Gentleman* (1943), *Miss London Ltd* (1943) and *Bees in Paradise* (1944). Two Cities boldly revived upper-class comedy, realizing the comic potential unleashed by social upheaval which made a butler the commanding officer of his former mistress (*English without Tears*); led a traditional English community to welcome a Bolshevik engineer as its guest of honour (*The Demi-Paradise*); showed an upper-class family on their uppers and willing to give up their legacy to the local villagers (*Don't Take It to Heart*); and united all sections of a rural community – from crusty colonel to Cockney evacuees – in defence of a pair of nesting birds (*Tawny Pipit*).

The alternative response was to escape from contemporary society altogether. Ealing transported Tommy Trinder and his chums to Nero's Rome in *Fiddlers Three*; Gainsborough sent Tommy Handley, Evelyn Dall, George Moon and Felix Aylmer to Shakespeare's London in *Time Flies*; and shipwrecked Arthur Askey on a tropical island ruled by women in *Bees in Paradise*. This might be seen as a utopian vision of the future, though for the diminutive Askey, chosen as a mate by the bulky singer Anne Shelton, it is an uncomfortable one. More mundane but perceptive glimpses into the future are provided by *Give Us the Moon*, *Demobbed* and *29 Acacia Avenue*.

In Gainsborough's *Give Us the Moon*, Peter Pyke (Peter Graves) is an ex-fighter pilot uninterested in running his father's new Eisenhower Hotel. He is drawn by Nina (Margaret Lockwood), a Russian adventuress, into the world of the White Elephant Club, whose members think that the world is made up of two types of people – the suckers who work and those who think there is something better to do with your life. Led in different directions by Vic Oliver's zany mid-European Pied Piper (ironically, Oliver was Churchill's son-in-law) and Jean Simmons' wilful teenage anarchist, the Elephants offer a very different spread of eccentrics to the cosy crew Asquith introduces us to in *Quiet Wedding*, *Cottage to Let* and *The Demi-Paradise*.

These artists, bohemians and intellectuals offer a whiff of Soho/ Fitzrovia society and look forward to the Goons, existentialism and the Theatre of the Absurd.

Mancunian's *Demobbed* is a continuation of the *Somewhere* series with Norman Evans, Nat Jackley and Tony Dalton substituting for Frank Randle, Harry Korris and Robbie Vincent and with Dan Young continuing to serve as a monocled toff. The thin storyline dissolves into musical burlesque but there is more of an attempt to integrate the antics of the comic characters into the middle-class world of work and romance. Demobbed from the Army, the four privates find themselves reunited with their unloved sergeant in a factory. They proceed to play cards, disrupt production and generally make a nuisance of themselves – offering a foretaste of the bolshie, skiving workforce which, in popular mythology at least, characterized post-war British industry – but their perspicacity in exposing the manger as a crook gets them all a seat on the board of directors.

An alternative view of the future was provided by Henry Cass and Sydney Box's *29 Acacia Avenue*. The Robinsons (Gordon Harker and Betty Balfour) are a lower-middle-class couple living in suburbia, slightly less respectable than the Briggs of *The Briggs Family*, slightly more prosperous than the Buntings of *Salute John Citizen* and the Gibbons of *This Happy Breed*. They are tempted to compete with their upwardly mobile neighbours (Henry Kendall and Noele Gordon) by going on a Mediterranean cruise, leaving their almost grown-up children at home. The daughter, Joan (Jill Evans), invites her fiancé (Hubert Gregg) to stay the night while the son, Peter (Jimmy Hanley), is tempted into an adulterous relationship with an older woman (Carla Lehman). Neither of these adventures progresses very far. Joan banishes her fiancé to the living-room sofa after an argument about social habits which reveals the deep divisions between different strata of the English middle classes; before Peter can overcome his virginal inhibitions he is interrupted by the wronged husband; and Mum and Dad cancel their cruise and spend their holiday at the seaside lodging house in Bognor they have frequented for the past twenty years. Even so, Rank considered it immoral and its successors, *Holiday Camp* (Ken Annakin, 1947) and the Huggett films, are pitched slightly lower in the class structure where illicit sexual opportunities in the purlieus of the tennis club are not available. But the ambience of a pleasant, prosperous suburban life remained a modest ideal towards which post-war society strove.

After 1945, Second World War comedies were almost entirely confined to life in the services – *Worm's Eye View*, *Reluctant Heroes* (Jack Raymond, 1951), *Private's Progress*, *Desert Mice*, *Light Up the Sky*,

On the Fiddle – though there were occasional attempts to explore more bizarre subjects in *Appointment with Venus, The Night We Dropped a Clanger* and *Soft Beds, Hard Battles.* A trilogy of genial comedies directed by Norman Cohen appeared at the end of the 1960s – *Till Death Us Do Part* (1968), *Dad's Army* and *Adolf Hitler – My Part in His Downfall* – but the function of comedy to defuse anxiety and familiarize the abnormal had shifted from cinema to television where situation comedies such as *Dad's Army* (w. Jimmy Perry/David Croft, 1968–77), *It Ain't Half Hot Mum* (w. David Croft 1973–81) and *'Allo 'Allo!* (Jeremy Lloyd/David Croft, 1984–5) enjoyed a durable popularity.

NOTES

1 These are rough calculations based on Gifford (1986). I have included only films of over 60 minutes and have reclassified some films that Gifford lists as crime films and musicals.

2 Palmer, who photographed *It's a Grand Life* (John E. Blakeley, 1953), had proved inventive on Bernard Vorhaus's *The Ghost Camera* (1933) and Michael Powell's *The Edge of the World* (1937); Stephen Dade, who was responsible for *Somewhere on Leave*, went on to shoot such big-budget Technicolor films as *Christopher Columbus* (David MacDonald, 1949) and *Ivanhoe* (Richard Thorpe, 1952).

3 Butchers' talent pool contained – besides Frank Randle – Nat Jackley, Norman Evans, Jimmy James, Wilson, Kepple and Betty, Bunny Doyle and Betty Driver, Betty Jumel, Albert Modley and Robb Wilton.

4 Formby made seven films for Columbia between 1942 and 1946: *South American George* (Marcel Varnel, 1942), *Much Too Shy* (Marcel Varnel, 1942), *Bell Bottom George* (1943), *Get Cracking* (1943), *He Snoops to Conquer* (Marcel Varnel, 1944), *I Didn't Do It* (Marcel Varnel, 1945) and *George in Civvy Street* (1946). He also acted as associate producer on two of Columbia's Vera Lynn vehicles, *We'll Meet Again* and *Rhythm Serenade*.

5 The same trick is played in *Bell Bottom George* where Manning Whiley, accomplice to the treacherous taxidermist played by Eliot Makeham, is revealed at the end to be a British Secret Service agent.

6 *Time Flies* has a similar plot to that of Mark Twain's *A Connecticut Yankee in King Arthur's Court*, filmed in 1931 with Will Rogers and in 1948 with Bing Crosby, William Bendix and Rhonda Fleming.

7 Richards and Sheridan (1987), pp. 331–49, reproduce in full the Mass Observation investigation into audience response to *Let George Do It*.

8 Vidkun Quisling was the leader of a Fascist organization in Norway whose treachery was thought to have contributed substantially to the rapid German takeover of the country. In fact, he was not considered reliable enough to trust with the date of the invasion, and the German victory was achieved through speed and surprise. The term 'quisling' was used gener-

ally for traitors and those prepared to collaborate with the Nazis. The fifth column was the term used by Franco for his supporters within the Republican stronghold of Madrid and subsequently for all traitors.

9 Most of these actors were allowed at least one chance to redeem themselves by playing a good character – Eliot Makeham, for example, is a patriotic priest in *Uncensored* and the cathedral organist in *A Canterbury Tale* – but only Bernard Miles, an ambitious and original actor, made a full transition from bad to good roles.

10 Leslie Howard was killed in 1943, when the unarmed passenger plane he was travelling in from Lisbon was shot down by German fighters.

11 Cinematographer Bernard Knowles had used a similar crane shot for the discovery of the murderer at the end of Hitchcock's *Young and Innocent* in 1937.

12 James Mason shaves off his beard fifteen minutes into the film. He and Joyce Howard had appeared together in an atmospheric low-budget thriller, *The Night Has Eyes* (Leslie Arliss, 1942). Gainsborough rightly discerned that it was not the romance between Mason and Howard that made the film special but Mason's sadistic behaviour towards her, and cast him as the cold, cruel Lord Rohan in *The Man in Grey* (Leslie Arliss, 1943).

3

Myths and Fictions: Film and Propaganda

The war, to which we have brought a unity of feeling never known before in our island history, was somehow not quite our war. Nobody told us right out to mind our own business, but often something of the sort was implied. There were too many snubs and cold-shoulders about. (J. B. Priestley, *Postscript*, Sunday 23 June 1940)

B ritish propaganda was thought to have played a vital part in undermining German morale and bringing about victory for the Allies in 1918, and one of the startling innovations of the Nazi regime had been the establishment of a powerful Ministry of Propaganda under Joseph Goebbels. New worries during the next two decades such as the effect of aerial bombardment and enemy radio broadcasts on civilian morale seemed to indicate that propaganda would play a vital role in any future war.

The government had made plans for a Ministry of Information (MoI) as early as 1935 but when it finally came into operation in the autumn of 1939 all was muddle and confusion. An editorial in the *Kinematograph Weekly* described it as 'a conglomeration of individuals, built up like a lot of misplaced higgledy-piggledy sandbags'.[1] The Minister, Lord Macmillan, a retired judge and a friend of Neville Chamberlain, proved ineffectual and in January 1940 he was replaced by Sir John Reith, previously Director General of the BBC. Reith was a more formidable figure, used to running a large public service organization, but Churchill found him difficult to work with and shifted him to the Ministry of Transport in May 1940. His replacement, Duff Cooper, felt frustrated at the work of the Ministry being ignored or counteracted by more firmly established branches of government such as the Foreign Office and the Service ministries and was happy to hand over responsibility to Brendan Bracken in June

1941. *Documentary News Letter*, summing up its sorry history, argued that

> the Ministry of Information has never recovered from the wounds to its self-esteem which were inflicted during early battles with the press, parliament and public. Nowadays, in its relations with other Government departments, the Ministry too often occupies the role of a wounded dog which is set upon by the rest of the pack and viciously mauled at every opportunity.[2]

Bracken, a close friend of Churchill and the proprietor of the *Financial Times*, proved more adept at fighting his corner and gradually built up the power and prestige of the Ministry, where he remained until the end of the war.

The Films Division of the MoI, responsible for newsreels, documentary and information films and relations with the commercial film industry, also had its problems. The first Films Officer, Sir Joseph Ball, was a staunch Chamberlainite who as head of the Research Department of the Conservative Party in the 1930s had pioneered the use of film for party political propaganda. *Kinematograph Weekly* welcomed him as 'an outstanding example of the man who knows how to use the velvet glove'.[3] As an ex-MI5 agent he was certainly adept at undercover work. J. C. Davidson, who when Chairman of the Conservative Party had recruited Ball, recalled him as a man who 'is steeped in service tradition, and has as much experience as anyone I know in the seamy side of life and the handling of crooks' (James, 1969, p. 272). Ball had been involved in the Zinoviev Letter affair which helped the Conservative Party to victory in the 1924 general election; and had managed to infiltrate the Odhams Press print works, allowing him sight of Labour Party leaflets, pamphlets and reports before they reached Labour headquarters (James, 1969, p. 272). He had good links with the newsreel companies and advertising agencies, but he failed to attract the support of the surviving commercial film production companies and aroused hostility and contempt from the small but influential documentary movement. Over-rigid censorship quickly alienated the newsreel companies and Ball's inability to work out a response to the inaction of the 'phoney war' led to stagnation. By the end of the year he had been replaced by Kenneth Clark, director of the National Gallery.[4] Clark – with patrician disdain – found that

> there was nothing to be learnt from my predecessor in the job. He was a man named Sir Joseph Ball, who had secured the patronage

of Mr Neville Chamberlain because he owned a reach of the River Test, and asked Mr Chamberlain down to fish. I paid him a routine call, and found a small, fat man sitting behind an empty desk with lines of cigarette ash stretched across the folds of his waistcoat. He cannot have moved for a long time. He did not bother to be polite to me, and when I asked him about his staff said that he had never met them. (Clark, 1977, p. 10)

Ball was by no means a spent force, going on to become deputy chairman of the Home Defence (Security) Executive, the body responsible for coercing a reluctant Home Office into the indiscriminate internment of aliens in the summer of 1940, but the film industry had quickly become disillusioned with him and no tears were shed at his leaving (Gillman and Gillman, 1980, pp. 127, 144). Not that there was much enthusiasm for Clark, who had no experience of film production and was viewed with suspicion as a highbrow dilettante by the industry. However, he was a respected member of the intelligentsia and liable to be more appreciative of the documentary-makers. His lack of experience of the film industry did not prevent him from vigorous intervention – presenting a paper on the use of feature films as propaganda, coercing the Treasury into providing finance for a programme of feature films (though only *49th Parallel* was made), suggesting a programme of five-minute films sponsored by the Ministry for cinema distribution and simplifying the complicated system of control by which the GPO Film Unit, though part of the MoI, was still run by a Post Office official. He was rewarded by being promoted to Controller of Home Propaganda and his position as Films Officer was filled by Jack Beddington, who had been head of publicity at Shell.[5]

Beddington was initially regarded with as much hostility as Clark by the film industry. 'Tatler' in the *Daily Film Renter*, after dismissing Clark as a young man with 'an excellent drawing room manner', complained that 'it is an absolute scandal, to my way of thinking, that we should have foisted on us somebody whose knowledge of the film trade is practically nil'.[6] Beddington was astute enough to recruit two very able deputies – Sidney Bernstein, head of the Granada cinema chain (and later Granada Television) and Sir Arthur Elton, a key member of the documentary movement – and he gradually won the respect of at least part of the industry, but his relations with Michael Balcon at Ealing proved to be particularly stormy.[7]

In 1938 Balcon had attempted to alert the government to the importance of feature film production in wartime:

I sent a memorandum to a government department outlining my plans for the harnessing of films to the national effort: a memorandum which I need hardly add had no effect at all. Yet the important thing remains that in those years I began to believe, along with other people, that films could serve to fight against Fascism both in this country and elsewhere, and to project the democratic idea for which all right-minded people, as well as the left-minded people, are fighting today. (Balcon, 1944, p. 5)

Throughout the war he remained a vigorous advocate of the use of feature films for propaganda purposes. Ealing had made three short films for the 'Careless Talk Costs Lives' campaign and *Sea Fort*, a seven-minute film directed by Ian Dalrymple and produced by Alberto Cavalcanti, and Balcon was keen to do more.[8]

In April 1940 it was announced in the trade press that Cavalcanti, the head of the GPO Film Unit, would take up a position at Ealing. It appears that Balcon had grandiose ambitions to take the whole unit under Ealing's wing. But Beddington was already beginning to find his feet, and excusing himself on the grounds that the Film Unit still technically belonged to the GPO, he rejected Balcon's offer. Harold Boxall, studio manager at Denham, was asked to examine the structure and organization of the Unit and when Cavalcanti left for Ealing, he was replaced by Dalrymple, another Denham man (though he had also worked with Balcon as supervisory editor at Gaumont-British).[9] One of Boxall's recommendations was that the Film Unit should change its name (though his suggestion of 'Victory' was rejected in favour of 'Crown', which allowed the unit to retain its GPO symbol); another was that it should move out of its primitive studios at Blackheath and take up residence at Denham. This was accepted and the Crown Film Unit became the main production arm of the MoI, making around twelve films a year, most of them relatively prestigious assignments for cinematic distribution in contrast to the hundreds of information films turned out by the likes of Paul Rotha's Realist, Donald Taylor's Strand and Sydney Box's Verity units for the non-theatrical circuit.

Cavalcanti's move to Ealing (followed in 1942 by Harry Watt) is often cited as evidence of the influence of documentary-makers on the mainstream commercial industry. The significance of the Crown Film Unit's move to Denham, under a Denham producer, has tended to be ignored. The MoI's closest collaboration with commercial filmmakers was with Michael Powell and Emeric Pressburger – a relationship which even survived the furore over *The Life and Death of Colonel Blimp* (see pp. 65–70) – and with Filippo Del Giudice's Denham-based

Two Cities Films. This Denham connection – and behind it the spirit of Alexander Korda – was to ensure that government film propaganda was never entirely confined to the didactic documentary ethos espoused by John Grierson.[10]

Documentary and Newsreel

After the war had ended, the *Documentary News Letter* judged that:

> The failure of the Ball regime was because he did not, perhaps could not, realise that he was facing a public which did not require sobstuff appeals to make it fight (it had made up its mind already about this) but which was hungry for objective clear information, which the documentary school had always claimed could be given a dramatic and emotional appeal of its own. It was this new frame of mind which compelled the powers to bring out again what perhaps they hoped had been put away for good – the contentious, obstinate, unruly yet disciplined documentary school of film-makers who had trained under Tallents and Grierson and whose pre-occupation with a world of new social values was in key with the new public temper.[11]

But the documentary-makers were by no means the obvious choice to become the focus of the government's wartime film policy. They had little economic muscle – Ball had not been far from the truth when he claimed that apart from the GPO and Shell film units, the documentary companies 'were not production companies, just a name on the door and a typewriter', and their political outlook hardly matched that of the government (Pronay and Thorpe, 1980, p. 26). Most of the documentary film-makers were left-wing and had been ferociously critical of Chamberlain's policies, and it was hardly surprising that a staunchly Chamberlainite MoI did not rush to secure their services. The replacement of Chamberlain by Churchill in May 1940 opened up the possibility of a reconciliation. Churchill was no less right-wing, but he was considerably more pragmatic and his wholehearted commitment to winning the war commanded a wide spectrum of support. Labour MPs joined him in a coalition and effectively took charge of domestic policy, and left-wing intellectuals found that their contribution to the war effort was now valued.

One of John Grierson's ambitions had been the development of a non-theatrical circuit where non-fiction films could be shown and seriously discussed. During the war, the Films Division developed such a circuit, with mobile film units showing programmes of documentaries in town and village halls, Women's Institutes, factories, libraries and schools. Efforts were also made to reach the popular cinema audience. One of Kenneth Clark's initiatives had been to launch a series of 'five-minute films' (in practice most were longer) employing well-known actors and directors to put across messages in a witty and dramatic way. *Miss Grant Goes to the Door* (Brian Desmond Hurst, 1940), for example, shows Mary Clare and Martita Hunt intrepidly dealing with a German paratrooper; in *The Nose Has It* (Val Guest, 1942), Arthur Askey damages the war effort by coughing and sneezing and spreading diseases; and *Partners in Crime* (Frank Launder and Sidney Gilliat, 1942) sees Irene Handl reprimanded for unpatriotically dabbling in the black market. They were distributed free to cinemas and were a relatively painless way of absorbing government propaganda.[12]

A more ambitious strategy, which evolved from the film-making ambitions of the Crown Film Unit, was the production of feature-length dramatized documentaries. Harry Watt's hour-long *Target for Tonight*, which follows the crew of an RAF Wellington bomber on a raid on Germany, was an unexpected box-office success and led to other drama documentaries such as Jack Holmes' *Coastal Command*, Jack Lee's *Close Quarters*, Humphrey Jennings' *Fires Were Started* and Pat Jackson's *Western Approaches*. Equally successful in the cinemas were the feature-length films made by the Army Film and Photographic Unit and the RAF Film Production Unit: *Desert Victory, Tunisian Victory, Burma Victory, The True Glory, Theirs Is the Glory* and *Journey Together*. Documentary thus became an essential part of government propaganda. But the expert self-publicity of the documentarists has tended to mask the fact that as far as the government was concerned documentary was always of secondary importance to the newsreels.

Ball's downfall had less to do with his under-appreciation of the documentary-makers than with his failure to work effectively with the newsreel companies. Compared to the estimated fifteen million people a year who attended the Ministry's non-theatrical screenings, the newsreels could count on a weekly audience of around twenty million. Newsreels were given 'top priority in the matter of stock and personnel allocation coupled with a far greater degree of attention and control than was given to the more artistic products of the Films Division' (Pronay, 1982, p. 174). Harry Watt, for example, found that a brilliant shot obtained by his cameraman Jonah Jones for *The Front Line* was appropriated by the newsreel men:

We were shooting a convoy being shelled in the Channel – we bloody near copped it – and suddenly I heard the sound which tells you a plane is being shot down. . . . There coming right down towards us was a plane. I said, 'Look Jonah!' We had the longest-focus lens, about a seventeen-inch lens on. So he whipped up the lens, and he picked this thing up and he followed it right down. It hit the water a few hundred yards in front of us and bounced, and then hit the water again and disappeared. And you actually saw the body coming out of the cockpit, if you looked closely as it hit. It was a fantastic shot. . . . All the stuff you sent to London was censored at the War Office. When the newsreels were having their stuff censored at the same time as ours (we were sitting there with Jack Beddington), they saw this shot and they said, 'Jesus Christ, what a shot! Can we have it? Can we have it? And he gave it away. He gave it to the newsreels. (quoted in Sussex, 1975a, pp. 122–3)

Watt was still able to use the shot, but he complained that everyone had seen it by the time *The Front Line* reached the cinema screen.

If the MoI's reliance on the makers of advertising and commercial feature films for its documentary and informational films in the first months of the war was a mistake, its reliance on War Office personnel to provide newsreel footage was a disaster. On 10 September 1939 the War Office had banned photography of military subjects. It was obviously important that there was no leakage of information useful to the enemy – the whereabouts, size and strength of military units, for example – but the War Office seemed to think that revealing anything newsworthy might be dangerous.

While German news film – shown widely in neutral countries from Norway to the USA – pictured vast armies marching into Poland, the only film available of the British Army was of 'a platoon of Royal Engineers marching through a suburban street, carrying shovels and pickaxes' (Pronay, 1982, p. 183). The British Expeditionary Force had not been filmed on its departure for France and there was no film reporting of its activities there. This could only help Goebbels' campaign to demoralize the French Army with questions like 'Where ARE your British Allies?', and Pronay points out that 'British audiences, at home and in the Empire were reduced to seeing the start of the war chiefly through German footage purchased in neutral countries' (Pronay and Thorpe, 1980, p. 22). Sir Edward Villiers, the civil servant put in charge of newsreels at the Films Division, made wholly impractical plans to bypass the newsreel companies – which had international distribution networks – with a Ministry-controlled unit. By the time of the D-Day landings, Army and RAF cameramen were able to shoot millions of feet of film but in the early months of the war most of the film shot for the War Office was too amateurish to be shown.

When Reith took over in January 1940, this sort of bungling ended. Censorship remained strict but henceforth the newsreel companies were treated as equal partners rather than troublesome outsiders and harmonious relationships were built up between them and the Ministry. Paramount News, for example, suffered only 166 cuts (most of them for reasons of morale or military security) in the 1500 stories it put together between 1940 and 1944 (Pronay, 1982, p. 198).

Feature Films as Propaganda

Feature films appeared to present more intractable problems than either newsreels or documentaries. There were unresolved questions as to whether entertainment and propaganda could be combined; whether the government should invest directly or merely encourage projects which seemed favourable to its cause; how strict censorship should be and what form it should take; how the public could be persuaded to watch films that were good for them; and what sort of films were good for them. Balcon's views on the importance to morale of presenting war stories which would show what Britain was fighting for did not go unchallenged. The *Kinematograph Weekly*, for example, in arguing its case for the reopening of the cinemas, had suggested a less exalted and cosier role for cinema:

> Our immediate duty is to offer some outlet for the intelligence; to present in pleasant, harmless form a relief from the very ugly world in which we are living today. Can one think of a safer anodyne to the disturbed public mind than the screenplay?[13]

This conflict between 'escapism' and 'propaganda', between what Balcon was later to differentiate as 'realism or tinsel', was to prove a key issue of wartime cinema.

Kenneth Clark, who was quick to recognize the importance of feature films, told his Policy Committee that 'If we renounced interest in entertainment as such, we might be deprived of a valuable weapon for getting across our propaganda (quoted in Aldgate and Richards, 1994, p. 11). He had already set out how this was to be done in a paper entitled 'Programme for Film Propaganda', which stressed the importance of documentaries and newsreel, but also proposed that feature films be used as covert propaganda.[14] Three types of film were recommended: documentary-inclined stories about aspects of the war and the war effort; films celebrating British ideals and traditions; and films dealing with British life and character.

Clark determined to invest directly in feature film production. A film was planned on Anglo/French co-operation but had to be abandoned when France surrendered to the Germans. A second project, about minesweepers, was suggested to Michael Powell, but Powell persuaded Clark that a film set in Canada would be more useful. He argued that Canada's example in coming into the war might be used to persuade America to do likewise and, with Emeric Pressburger, he devised a story, *49th Parallel*, involving six survivors of a U-boat crew making their way across Canada and coming into contact with various types of Canadian (and an Englishman). In the process, Nazi ideology is exposed as brutal and stupid while the Canadians (and the Englishman) show tolerance, kindness and resourceful intelligence.

In August 1940, while the film was being made, a Parliamentary Select Committee on Government Expenditure reported on the activities of the Films Division and recommended that it 'should not in future assume direct responsibility for the production of feature films by the provision of public money' and that 'no further commitments should be entered into in connection with the proposed scheme of non-theatrical display, unless very clear evidence is obtained from experience that it is making a contribution to the war effort commensurate with its expenditure'.[15] It is a measure of the growing assurance of the Films Division that it managed to subvert both these rulings. The number of mobile film units was expanded from 76 in 1940 to 130 in 1942, and although there was no further large-scale investment in feature films (despite the fact that *49th Parallel* was the top box-office film of 1941), subtle ways of moulding feature film production without direct government investment evolved (Forman, 1982, p. 224). Such films as *Millions Like Us* and *The Way Ahead* were made as commercial feature films, but they were effectively sponsored by the Ministry of Information and carried desirable propaganda messages about the contribution women could make to the war effort by working in factories and the team spirit and comradeship men would find when they joined the British Army.

Though the day-to-day job of film censorship remained with the British Board of Film Censorship (BBFC), the MoI was able to exert considerable pressure as to what sort of films were made. Whereas the BBFC employed a proscriptive regime of censorship, prohibiting the filming of controversial or sensitive subjects – those concerned with politics, sex, race and royalty, for example, and anything which might be regarded as immoral or in bad taste – the MoI played a more positive role. According to Sidney Bernstein, the left-wing cinema owner who became a vital link between the government and the industry,

> the Ministry both advised the producers on the suitability of sub-jects which they had suggested, and proposed subjects which we thought would do good overseas. Whenever the Ministry had approved a subject, we gave every help to the producer in obtaining facilities necessary to make the film. For instance, we helped them get artists out of the services, we aided them to secure raw-stock, travel priorities and so on. (Bernstein, 1945, p. 12)

The liberal intelligentsia, who increasingly dominated the MoI Films Division, had more robust sensibilities than the BBFC censors, and were generally sympathetic to film-makers who wished to make films which were meaningful and socially relevant. Attempts to film Walter Greenwood's controversial novel *Love on the Dole*, for example, had been rejected by the BBFC in the 1930s as liable to show 'too much of the tragic and sordid side of poverty'.[16] But in 1941 it presented no threat to the propaganda aims of the MoI. Criticizing the mistakes of the past damaged only those politicians who had already been rejected as 'yesterday's men', and permitting a grim picture of industrial life in the 1930s to be made demonstrated Britain's commitment to freedom of speech. As Dilys Powell explained, *Love on the Dole*

> savagely attacked a social and economic structure which wasted human lives in idleness and poverty, and its picture of the slump in a Lancashire factory town held no flattery for the British. Yet those who most bitterly attacked the conditions it showed could not but praise the public honesty which permitted the showing. (Powell, 1947, p. 21)

In marked contrast to BBFC policy in the 1930s, the MoI required something more than harmless entertainment from the industry. Faced with a plea from the British Film Producers Association for fewer war films and co-operation over the release of actors for films which would give people 'relaxation and entertainment from the stress of events', the MoI expressed its willingness to support all sorts of films, including comedies and dramas, but insisted that they should be of 'the highest quality and neither maudlin, morbid nor nostalgic for the old ways and old days' and ought to deal realistically with everyday life 'in the factory, the mines and on the land' (quoted in Aldgate and Richards, 1994, p. 12). The MoI used its powers to push feature film production into the realist channels it thought would serve its purposes. However, it would be wrong to believe that it totally controlled the output of the British film industry during the war, as the following three examples demonstrate.

In Which We Serve

Two Cities had managed to survive the internment of its two directors, Del Giudice and Zampi, and though Zampi was exiled to Canada for the duration, Del Giudice's ambitions remained unchecked. The company's biggest success had been *French without Tears* in 1939, where a promising young playwright, Terence Rattigan, had been teamed with a talented director, Anthony Asquith, and allowed untrammelled creative freedom to make a film to which both men were enthusiastically committed. After making *Unpublished Story*, Del Giudice approached Noël Coward with the idea of shooting a film about the Royal Navy.[17] Coward's experience with screen adaptations of his plays had been less than happy, but Del Giudice's willingness to allow him complete creative control tempted him to write a screenplay based on the naval experiences of his friend Lord Louis Mountbatten, whose destroyer HMS *Kelly* had been sunk during the Battle of Crete.

In Which We Serve became the most successful British film of the war years, even doing good business in the US market. It is structured from a series of flashbacks centred around three representatives of different layers of society. Captain Kinross (Noël Coward) is an officer and a gentleman; Petty Officer Walter Hardy (Bernard Miles) is the epitome of lower-middle-class eccentricity; and Able Seaman Shorty Blake (John Mills) is a representative of salt of the earth working-class pluckiness. The film tends now to be seen as a semi-official film presenting positive propaganda about the Royal Navy and illustrating how all sections of the nation were pulling together to win the war, but the film was made in the teeth of opposition from the MoI and certain sections of the press. Coward himself was seen as representing the wrong sort of values. A leader in the *Sunday Express*, complaining about him being sent on official duties to America, insisted that: 'His flippant England – cocktails, countesses, caviar – has gone. A man of the people, more in tune with the new mood of Britain, would be a better proposition for America' (quoted in Aldgate and Richards, 1994, p. 190).

In fact, Coward had been an outspoken critic of Chamberlain and the Munich agreement and he eagerly adapted to the 'new mood of Britain'. In a radio broadcast in Australia, he claimed:

> The provinces of England have, I think, contributed more to the glory of the country than the streets of Mayfair, and perhaps one of the few benefits that emerge from this war will be the final destruction of those false snob values which have imposed themselves upon the honest heart of London. As a matter of fact, a change is already taking place in the ARP canteens, in the buses and tubes and air raid shelters. There is a new comradeship growing in London between people of all creeds and classes. All they are enduring makes it increasingly apparent that true democracy needs no veneer. (Quoted in Aldgate and Richards, 1994, p. 192)

As a result of Mountbatten's influence at the Admiralty, Coward was able to proceed with the film but his critics persisted in their attacks while the film was in production. The *Daily Express*, for example, considered 'it is wrong to have a professional actor dressed in the gold braid of a British naval officer'. More serious opposition came from the MoI, dubious about the propaganda value of a film centring on a lost battle and a sunk ship. Mountbatten had sufficient political clout to overrule Beddington, and when the film was completed it pleased everyone. But it is important to note its troubled gestation.

The Life and Death of Colonel Blimp

Within a very short period Michael Powell had risen from the ranks of obscure quota quickie directors to become (particularly in the absence of key figures like Alfred Hitchcock, Victor Saville, Herbert Wilcox and Alexander Korda, all of whom were in Hollywood) one of the top film-makers in Britain. In 1942 he was approached by J. Arthur Rank and given virtual *carte blanche* to make what he wanted. Rank now owned the Gaumont and Odeon cinema circuits, Pinewood, Denham, Shepherd's Bush and Islington studios, General Film Distributors (the major British distribution company), and Gainsborough, one of the most prolific production companies. He was soon to face criticism for the threat of monopoly he posed to the British film industry, but in 1941 he was able to buy so much because nobody else wanted it. In November 1940, the *Economist* had gloomily forecast that 'Probably nothing but the return of peace can put the cinemas on their feet'.[18] But cinema-going survived the blackout and

Colonel Clive Wynne-Candy (Roger Livesey) demonstrates that he can still use a gun when roused. *The Life and Death of Colonel Blimp*. Supplied by BFI Stills, © courtesy of Carlton International.

the Blitz and became more popular – and more profitable – than it had been in peacetime. The lack of alternative entertainment, the large numbers of displaced people denied the comforts of their family home, the solace of fantasy amidst the traumatic events of war, combined to push attendance figures to record heights. With money pouring in from over six hundred cinemas (and subject to Excess Profit Tax), Rank could afford to be ambitious. In 1942 he set up Independent Producers (IP) to provide services and finance to a group of producers who had been backed financially by GFD – Marcel Hellman, Norman Walker, Gabriel Pascal – and Rank encouraged Michael Powell and Emeric Pressburger to come in under the IP umbrella.

Powell and Pressburger's first film for Rank, *The Life and Death of Colonel Blimp*, proved controversial. It grew, innocently enough, from an incident cut out of *One of Our Aircraft Is Missing*, where the ageing rear gunner (Godfrey Tearle) tells the young pilot officer (Hugh Burden): 'You know, you are like what I was when I was young and I'm like you will be when you're old.' This became the starting point for a script showing the evolution of a dashing young officer into a conservative old military buffer. However, according to Powell,

> As it progressed and became more and more an epic, a saga of a wonderful, half lovable, half infuriating character, it occurred to one of us, I don't know which, to lug in Colonel Blimp. It was probably because the whole idea seemed to chime together and the thought of dramatising the life of Colonel Blimp appealed enormously, because at the time Blimp was a household word. (Badder, 1978, p. 10)

Blimp was a cartoon character created by David Low who represented all that was most bigoted, incompetent and old-fashioned about the British military hierarchy. Powell, who had hitherto had extremely good relations with the MoI, began to run into problems:

> Approved by the Ministry of Information, the script went up to Sir James Grigg, the Minister of War, who had to approve our borrowing of Army material: uniforms, guns, transport etc. I don't know whether he actually read the script, but he must have had a scathing report from touchy underlings. He turned our request down point blank, and sent a memo to Churchill and to Brendan Bracken, the Minister of Information, telling them what he thought of it. The fat was in the fire. . . . 'Do you forbid us to make the film?' I asked the Minister and Jack Beddington. 'Oh my dear fellow, after all we are a democracy, aren't we? You know we can't forbid you to do anything, but don't make it, because everyone will be really cross, and the Old Man will be *very* cross and you'll never get a knighthood.' (Powell, 1986, pp. 402–3)

The Old Man did get very cross, and Powell never did get a knighthood, but the film did get made – as a lavish big-budget film, using Technicolor and lots of Army props, though without Laurence Olivier, whom the MoI refused to release from his military duties to play Colonel Blimp. After the film was completed, a special screening was arranged for Grigg, Churchill and Bracken where it was decided that Churchill's claim that it was 'detrimental to the morale of the Army' could not be sustained and the film could not be banned. However, government pressure combined with commercial considerations to effect a reduction of the film's length (though most critics thought that at two and a half hours it was still far too long) and Churchill's continuing opposition delayed, though it did not finally prevent, the film from being shown abroad.

In an odd, yet interesting essay, Nicholas Pronay and Jeremy Croft argue that this was all a sham: that the MoI were secretly backing the film.[19] They start out with a useful reminder that there was no single voice controlling propaganda:

> The case of the *Life and Death of Colonel Blimp* (1943) illustrates most clearly and fully the conflicts which could arise, by the middle years of the war, between the expert and sophisticated propaganda policies of the MoI, and the policies of the amateur propagandists outside it. (Pronay and Croft, 1983, p. 155)

Conflicts certainly existed, as can be seen in the case of *In Which We Serve*; though in that case the Admiralty proved rather more sophisticated than the MoI. They argue that the intention behind *Colonel Blimp* was

> to show to the Americans, whose soldiers were to come over in large numbers, that the British Army had shed its ineffective, upper-class, 'Blimp' officer attitudes, that it had become essentially a 'democratic' citizen army and that it had also acquired the necessary mental attitudes to become an efficient, tough fighting force, capable of matching the professionalism of the Germans. (Pronay and Croft, 1983, p. 156)

However, there is no evidence that this is how Powell and Pressburger presented their script to the MoI, and it certainly bears little resemblance to the finished film. Undeterred, the authors go on to claim:

> Camouflage was, therefore, essential. If the War Office had provided the usual 'facilities' for the production; if the MoI had released Laurence Olivier, the one British superstar recognized in America, from his well-publicized job in the Fleet Air Arm, so that he could act in the film; and indeed, if it was produced by the Rank Organization (British Films), which was recognized by Americans as being as fully integrated into the wartime scheme as MGM was in their own country, the cloven hoof would obviously have protruded and negated the purpose of the exercise. (Pronay and Croft, 1983, p. 157)

In fact, Rank was unknown in America in 1943, and only crass stupidity could substitute an actor nobody in America had heard of for 'the one British superstar' if success with American audiences was the primary aim.

More seriously, Pronay and Croft insist that it would have been impossible for a producer to get either the film stock or the military facilities to make an ambitious film like *Colonel Blimp* without MoI collusion. However, the evidence they present for the MoI's (rather than the Board of Trade's) control of film stock is conjectural, and their suggestion that control over rare and expensive Technicolor film stock might be even more rigorous is misguided. In the 1940s the Technicolor process relied on black-and-white film (albeit of a specialized grade manufactured in the USA); it was the camera – which ran three strips of film simultaneously – and the processing that produced the colour (Coote, 1993, pp. 122–5).[20] There were only four of these highly complex, technically sophisticated cameras – which the cinematographer Jack Cardiff compares to a Rolls-Royce – in the country and they were jealously guarded by Technicolor. On *Western Approaches*, Cardiff had been allowed to take one of the cameras out on the open seas for the lifeboat sequences, but had been prohibited from crossing the Atlantic with it for fear of U-boats, and had to use a conventional camera using a new type of monopack colour film for the convoy sequences (Cardiff, 1996, p. 80; Jackson, 1999, p. 238). Powell seems to have had no problem obtaining Technicolor's co-operation on what was a well-funded and ambitious production with a distinguished cinematographer, Georges Perinal, but there is no evidence to suggest that the MoI had any influence on the company's decision.

Pronay also points to the extensive use of military equipment and uniforms in the film as evidence for covert official support, but Powell supplies a more convincing explanation:

> I have often been asked how we managed to obtain military vehicles, military uniforms, and all the fixings after being refused help by the War Office and the Ministry of Information. The answer is quite simple: we stole them. Any prop man worth his salt – and we had one of the best – would laugh at the question. There may have been one or two forged passes too. Who knows? It was all part of the war effort. The Archers were famous now, and we had friends in all sorts of quarters, high and low. (Powell, 1986, p. 406)

Correspondence between Churchill and Brendan Bracken shows that, despite being a close friend of Churchill, Bracken did not share his ferocious hostility towards the film.[21] Having worked successfully with Powell and Pressburger in the past, and having initially approved the script, it is unlikely that the MoI would have been over-vigorous in attempting to suppress the film, and as Bracken repeatedly points out, it had no powers to do so. *Colonel Blimp*'s success in Britain, where it was marketed as 'the film the government tried to ban', gives a veneer of plausibility to Pronay and Croft's theory that the MoI put up a smokescreen of protest to conceal the propaganda embedded in the film, but the fate of the film in America offers decisive proof to the contrary. Strenuous efforts were made by the MoI's adviser, Sidney Bernstein, to persuade American distributors to show films which did endorse government policy, such as the Crown Film Unit's *Target for Tonight*, which reached a wide audience despite the fact that it had no stars, little dramatic action and the sort of upper-class voices which were generally considered to alienate American audiences (Moorehead, 1984, pp. 132, 134). By contrast, *Blimp* was left to flounder in a distribution jungle unused to and uninterested in selling non-Hollywood product. As Geoffrey Macnab reports:

> United Artists tried to sell the film as a ribald tale of a lusty old soldier, a sort of Colonel Bluebeard. On the posters the slogans read as follows – 'The lusty lifetime of a gentleman who was sometimes Quite a Rogue! Duelling – hunting big game – and pretty girls – life's a grand adventure with Colonel Blimp!' (Macnab, 1993, p. 68)

Cut to 88 minutes and marketed as *The Loves and Adventures of Colonel Blimp*, it attracted few customers.

The Way Ahead

Unlike *In Which We Serve* and *The Life and Death of Colonel Blimp*, *The Way Ahead* was very much an MoI-backed film. After the success of *In Which We Serve*, Beddington asked Noël Coward to make a similar sort of film about the Army. Coward refused, but Del Giudice expressed an interest, and was put in touch with a group of army officers – Major David Niven (of the Rifle Brigade), and Captain Carol Reed, Lieutenant Eric Ambler and Private Peter Ustinov (all of the Army Kinematograph Service) – who worked together on a script outline. Niven told Jack Beddington that they wanted to make a film which would make everyone who saw it say: 'There, that's what our Bert is doing, isn't it wonderful?' He also warned that it should be on a proper commercial scale and have 'first class entertainment value' (Litewski and Porter, 1981, p. 111). Del Giudice agreed to make the film in close collaboration with the MoI and the War Office.

The script drew heavily on *The New Lot*, a 40-minute Army training film on which Ambler, Reed and Ustinov had worked. Here, as in *The*

Way Ahead, men from different walks of life are brought together and, after initial resistance, welded into an efficient fighting unit. Niven had pointed out to Jack Beddington that 'after three years of war the cinema-going public can smell pure propaganda a mile off' and the film eschews heroic messages and exhortations to duty and self-sacrifice (Litewski and Porter, 1981, p. 111). It also presents a much less hierarchical view of British society than *In Which We Serve*. Middle-class and working-class recruits soon submerge their differences and Lieutenant Perry (David Niven), despite his gentlemanly accoutrements, is carefully established as a garage mechanic who served as a sergeant in France before getting his commission. Here, the British Army really does shed its ineffective, upper-class, 'Blimp' officer attitudes and becomes essentially democratic. Rank agreed to back the film only on the condition that Niven (then under contract to Samuel Goldwyn) was given the leading role. Niven's Hollywood connections were seen to represent not only an entrée into the American market, but a guarantee of that sort of democratic classlessness which made Hollywood films so appealing to British audiences.

Propaganda, as Niven had specified, lies not on the surface but embedded in the structure of the film. The conflict between the new recruits and Sergeant Fletcher (William Hartnell), for example, deals cleverly with the widely held belief that the British Army was run on bull and bullying. Fletcher's obsession with drill and discipline appears to embody all the worst aspects of military life. But he is gradually revealed to be a warm and humane man who cares for the recruits. His harshness is necessary to steel the men for the ordeals that will confront them once they go to war. Our attitude towards Fletcher is influenced by the high opinion held of him by Lieutenant Perry. In a key sequence, two of the middle-class recruits, Stainer (a car salesman played by Jimmy Hanley) and Lloyd (a rent collector played by James Donald), lead a revolt against what seems to them a pointless exercise and deliberately get themselves 'killed' so they can get back to base early. Consequently, the platoon lets down the company, which lets down the battalion, which loses the 'war'. Lieutenant Perry understands what has happened but instead of putting them on a charge, soberly explains to them that in the real war, not being able to rely on your colleagues inevitably leads to defeat. Fletcher's emphasis on discipline and order suddenly has meaning, and Perry's speech is not just about unmilitaristic recruits letting down the traditions of the regiment – it is also about the selfish, short-sighted habits of pre-war society undermining the 'People's Army'.

The Way Ahead is generally regarded as one of the most successful films of the war period, but as Litewski and Porter (1981) point out, as propaganda it failed. When a film was first proposed in mid-1942, the war was going badly and there was considerable discontent about Army pay and conditions. *The Way Ahead* presents the Army in a convincingly positive light, but by the time the film went on general release in July 1944, the Normandy landings had already begun and the end of the war seemed in sight. Attitudes within and towards the Army had changed. Essentially, the film was preaching to the converted. From a longer-term view, however, *The Way Ahead*, along with another MoI-backed film, *Millions Like Us*, was successful in propagating a democratic 'everyone-pulling-together' ethos which became one of the key myths of the war.

In his reassessment of how we understand the Second World War, *The Myth of the Blitz*, Angus Calder warns that 'the word "myth" should not be taken to be equivalent to "untruth", still less to "lies"' (Calder, 1991, p. viii). More usefully, it should be seen as the elevation of one particular aspect or set of aspects about a situation into a generally accepted truth. *The Life and Death of Colonel Blimp*, with its contrast between modern and traditional methods, *In Which We Serve*, with its happy and efficient ship, *The Way Ahead*, with its moulding of clerks and stokers and second-hand car salesmen into a fighting unit, create coherent meaning out of the chaos of wartime events. Admittedly they ignore equally important aspects of reality – that anachronistic and anti-democratic practices and structures abounded in the British Army and Navy, that for most soldiers and sailors the war was a combination of extreme danger and extreme boredom – but it would be simplistic to regard these films as promoting an official ideology.

The pre-war BBFC had excluded certain topics, representations, forms of language from British films, but the MoI Films Division went beyond negative censorship. However, their aim of using feature films as positive propaganda was difficult to achieve. Against MoI expectations, *In Which We Serve* proved highly effective propaganda, in both Britain and the USA. Powell and Pressburger, who had proved the MoI's best ally with their wartime feature films – *Contraband*, *49th Parallel* and *One of Our Aircraft Is Missing* – insisted on making *The Life and Death of Colonel Blimp*, a film the Ministry did not support and which Churchill vehemently opposed. Even when things went completely smoothly, as with *The Way Ahead*, there were problems in making a film quickly enough for it to be still relevant to the propaganda needs it had been set up to fulfil.

Film and Social Change

The British documentary movement in the 1930s was part of an influential intellectual trend. As Paul Addison explains:

> Both Marxists and progressives became obsessed by the problem of communicating with the mass of the public, and equally with the effort to explain to the middle classes how the working classes lived. There was a movement, part literary and political, part commercial, to radicalize domestic communications. The growth of the documentary film movement under John Grierson, the formation of Mass-Observation by the poet Charles Madge and the anthropologist Tom Harrisson, the establishment of Penguin Books by Allen Lane and of *Picture Post* by Edward Hulton and Stefan Lorant, the transformation by Cecil King and Guy Bartholomew of the *Daily Mirror* from a right-wing paper for women into a left-wing *vox populi*, all occurred during the 1930s and were all related developments. (Addison, 1977, p. 143)

Apart from the Crown Film Unit, only two fully-fledged documentarists – Arthur Elton and Thomas Baird – were directly employed by the MoI, but a substantial number of the documentary and information films made for the Ministry were written, directed or produced by participants in the documentary film movement. Nicholas Pronay argues that there was an 'open conspiracy' of left-wing intellectuals to influence the masses, and that this was particularly effective in the routine documentaries shown on the non-theatrical circuit, which were less scrupulously supervised than prestige films like *Target for Tonight*, *Fires Were Started* and *Western Approaches*. Although these films reached a much smaller market than they would have done if shown in commercial cinemas, he insists that the radical message of the documentary-makers, hammered home repeatedly in films as ostensibly apolitical as *Power for the Highlands*, *Manpower* and *The Harvest Shall Come*, played a crucial role in changing the political climate and preparing the way for a Labour government:

> Coming to factories, working-men's institutes, church halls, adult education classes and the like at regular intervals of every five weeks or so, and thus being projected not in an entertainment context but in a context designed to lead to 'structured discussion' afterwards (for they were accompanied by MoI lecturers drawn from the Left wing of the intelligentsia), it was in fact a classic

Soviet-type Agitprop operation. In that light the figures of attendance, which amount to about one and half million for each *cycle*,
may very well have significantly raised 'political consciousness' and
helped to politicise a 'cadre' section of the working class and in
particular its self-taught functionary-intelligentsia. (Pronay, 1983,
p. 72)

There was no secret about the left-wing bias of the documentary
movement or of its determination that the war should be followed by
social change. In November 1940 the *Documentary News Letter* argued:

For the present war, if it is to be worth fighting at all, is a war
between two ideas, and not between two groups of nations. It is a
war to decide whether the ordinary decent men and women of all
countries shall have the power to live not only according to their
own lights and their own standards, but also more fully and more
freely. (p. 3)

But the documentary-makers were swimming with rather than
against the tide. At a time when the survival of Britain was at stake,
it became possible to ask fundamental questions even about the
sacred right of property. In his BBC Postscript broadcast on 21 July
1940, J. B. Priestley invited his audience to consider whether the
concept of private property was now outdated:

Property is that old-fashioned way of thinking of a country as a
thing . . . instead of thinking of a country as the home of a living
society, and considering the welfare of that society, the community
itself, as the first test. . . . Near where I live is a house with a large
garden, that's not being used at all because the owner of it has
gone to America. Now according to the property view, this is all
right, and we, who haven't gone to America, must fight to protect
this absentee owner's property. But on the community view, this is
all wrong. There are hundreds of working men not far from here
who urgently need ground for allotments so that they can produce
a bit more food. Also, we may soon need more houses for billeting.
Therefore, I say, that house and garden ought to be used whether
the owner, who's gone to America, likes it or not. (Priestley, 1940,
pp. 37–8)[22]

The desire for change was something that permeated all levels of
society. The novelist John Braine, in his biography of Priestley, recalls
that as a young soldier he and his colleagues did not need propaganda

to convince them of the need of doing 'a dirty job which had to be done', nor did they need to be told what they were fighting for:

> About our war aims, having had the benefit of our father's experience, we were quietly determined. There would be a change. We honestly didn't expect great things from the change: but any change from the middle of 1939 would be a change for the better. (Braine, 1978, p. 110)

If people responded positively to Priestley's radio Postscripts or the message of the documentarists, it was because they were being told what they wanted to hear.

The struggle between traditionalism and radicalism – often ending up as odd mixture of both – can be seen in the ways in which film-makers attempted to represent Britain on the screen. With simplistic King and Country patriotism discredited, there were problems in establishing a positive image of the Britain people were fighting to save. As Antonia Lant explains, the way in which British society, character and culture should be portrayed was not something which could be easily agreed upon:

> National identity is not a natural, timeless essence, but an intermittent, combinatory historical product, arising at moments of contestation of different political and geographical boundaries. . . . War produced the need for images of national identity, both on the screen and in the audience's mind, but British national identity was not simply on tap, waiting to be imaged, somehow rooted in British geology. 'National characteristics' could not simply be 'infused into a national cinema' however much later writers wished that version of the story to be true. Instead, the stuff of national identity had to be winnowed and forged from traditional aesthetic and narrative forms, borrowed from the diverse conventions of melodrama, realism, and fantasy, and transplanted from literature, painting, and history, into the cinema. (Lant, 1991, p. 31; her reference is to Powell, 1947, p. 8)

Film-makers were very aware of these problems. Ian Dalrymple, the producer of *The Lion Has Wings*, tried to give some durability to the film by concentrating on the virtues of the English character and the achievements of democracy: 'I opened our film with the suggestion that there was a British ideology arising from our national character; that it was valuable to the world; and that it should not be lost.'[23]

Lady Loxfield (Mabel Terry-Lewis), her daughter Philippa (Frances Rowe) and Cudsworth (Norman Shelley) the businessman, among the stylized sets of *They Came to a City*. Supplied by BFI Stills, © courtesy of Canal + Image.

It is easy to laugh now at Merle Oberon's final speech in the film – 'We must keep our land, darling. We must keep our freedom. We must fight for what we believe in: truth and beauty and fair play and [pause] kindness' – which she declaims to her snoozing husband under an oak tree. Even at the time this was seen by many as being outdated and slightly ludicrous. The image of England presented in the film's documentary footage of new flats, happy people, swimming pools and health centres is less easily dismissed. Economic growth and rising living standards for those in employment were as much a part of the 1930s as high unemployment, the Jarrow March and the Means Test, but the desire for social change meant that the pre-war period was looked back on critically rather than with nostalgia. Feature films such as John Baxter's *Love on the Dole* and *The Shipbuilders* (1944) are outspoken about the injustices of the past, and if the utopian visions he presents in *The Common Touch* (1941), *Let the People Sing* (1942) and *Dreaming* (1944) now look whimsically sentimental, they nevertheless look forward cheerily and confidently to a new society. Basil Dearden's adaptation of Priestley's play *They Came to a*

City is achingly idealistic, but, like Launder and Gilliat's *Millions Like Us* and *Waterloo Road* and Carol Reed's *The Way Ahead*, it is more cautious about the new society where 'people don't work to keep themselves out of the gutter but because they've got something big and exciting to do', which no longer seemed guaranteed by victory in the war.

In 1941 George Orwell was convinced that 'We cannot win the war without introducing Socialism, nor establish Socialism without winning the war. At such a time it is possible, as it was not in the peaceful years, to be both revolutionary and realistic.'[24] He was optimistic that victory and socialism could be achieved:

> Everywhere in England you can see a ding-dong battle raging to and fro – in Parliament and in the Government, in the factories and the armed forces, in the pubs and the air-raid shelters, in the newspapers and on the radio. Every day there are tiny defeats, tiny victories. Morrison for Home Secretary – a few yards forward. Priestley shoved off the air – a few yards back. It is a struggle between the groping and the unteachable, between the young and the old, between the living and the dead. But it is very necessary that the discontent which undoubtedly exists should take a purposeful and not merely obstructive form. It is time for *the people* to define their war aims.[25]

In December 1942 the government published the Beveridge Report outlining plans for a comprehensive welfare scheme: children would be financially supported through a family allowance; a national health service would be provided; and the unemployed would be eligible for benefits until they could return to work. It sold 635,000 copies and a Gallup Poll taken two weeks after its publication reported that nine people out of ten thought its proposals should be carried out. The most popular policy of a new political party, Common Wealth, launched in July 1942, was full and immediate implementation of Beveridge's proposals. Priestley, who had helped to create it, resigned by the autumn, but Common Wealth won its first by-election victory in April 1943 and continued to harry and embarrass the government until it was swamped by the Labour landslide in July 1945.

By December 1944 Orwell recognized that socialism would not be triumphant: the war was being won and, although movement had been made towards a planned economy, there was 'no real shift of power and no increase in genuine democracy'.[26] Orwell admitted that he had underestimated the vulnerability of the old order, 'over-emphasised the anti-Fascist character of the war, exaggerated the social changes that were actually occurring, and underrated the enormous strength of the forces of reaction'.[27] The victory of the Labour Party in 1945 indicated a continuing desire for change, but socialist revolution was no longer on the agenda. Anthony Howard, looking back with hindsight from 1963, saw that

> 1945 was not merely a political watershed: it had at least the potentiality for being a social one too. The war had not only buried the dinner jacket – it had reduced famous public schools to pale, evacuated shadows, it had destroyed the caste system in the Civil Service, it had eroded practically every traditional social barrier in Britain. (Howard, 1986, p. 18)

Unfortunately, the Labour government, saddled with a grossly distorted economy, a huge American debt, and an empire it could no longer afford to police, was reduced to patching and mending. Howard concludes that 'Far from introducing a "social revolution" the overwhelming Labour victory of 1945 brought about the greatest restoration of traditional social values since 1660' (Howard, 1986, p. 19). From the perspective of 1963, with another Labour victory in sight which seemed to promise radical change, Howard's view is understandable. Power structures remained intact and class privilege remained after 1945; none the less, the war had a genuine democratizing effect. No longer would the working class be content with their lot at the bottom of society. Wage demands, materialism and a willingness to help children grasp opportunities unavailable to their parents were the manifestations of this new society rather than anything Orwell would have recognized as socialism, but the old hierarchical, deferential society, which had lingered on through the 1920s and 1930s, was killed off by the Second World War.

NOTES

1 Samuel Harris, 'Who is the fool?', *Kinematograph Weekly*, 11 October 1939, p. 5.
2 *Documentary News Letter*, June 1941, p. 1.
3 *Kinematograph Weekly*, 14 September 1939, p. 4.
4 Clark, later famous for his *Landscape into Art* (1964) and *Civilization* (1969) series for BBC Television, can be glimpsed sitting next to the Queen in the Myra Hess lunchtime concert sequence of *Listen to Britain*.
5 At Shell, Beddington had 'abandoned the conventional chorus-girl-cum-petrol-pump style of advertising and had developed the finest output of

posters that any company in Great Britain has ever had'. '12 Months – a survey of the MoI', *Documentary News Letter*, September 1940, p. 5.

6 *Daily Film Renter*, 15 April 1940, p. 2.

7 Arthur Elton and Edward Anstey jointly directed *Housing Problems* (1935) and *Enough to Eat* (1936), which had broken new ground in exploring social conditions in working-class areas of Britain.

8 Ealing's three 'careless talk' films were *Now You're Talking, Dangerous Comment* and *All Hands*, all directed by John Paddy Carstairs; see Coultass (1989), p. 27, for a critical assessment of them. The cameraman on *Sea Fort* was Ernest Palmer, later to shoot some of the Mancunian films.

9 In June 1943 Dalrymple left the Crown Film Unit to rejoin Korda, who had returned from Hollywood to work in unhappy alliance with MGM-British. Like many of the arrangements Korda made during this period it didn't work out, and Dalrymple set up his own company, Wessex, which achieved box-office success with *The Wooden Horse* (1950). His successors at Crown were Jack Holmes and, finally, Basil Wright.

10 For Powell and Pressburger's loyalty to Denham, see Powell (1986), p. 340. Powell insisted on making *Contraband* at Denham, despite British National having available studio facilities at Elstree. He also points out that *In Which We Serve* used essentially the same crew as *One of Our Aircraft Is Missing*, with David Lean promoted from editor to director (*ibid.*, p. 397).

11 *Documentary News Letter*, September 1945, p. 85.

12 Clark (1977), p. 11, claims that it was Korda who suggested that very short propaganda films would be acceptable to cinema exhibitors.

13 *Kinematograph Weekly*, 7 September 1939, p. 4.

14 'Programme for film propaganda' is reproduced in Christie (1978). According to Aldgate and Richards (1994), p. 26, and Chapman (1998b), p. 26, Clark developed ideas outlined by Lord Macmillan in an MoI Policy Committee Paper of December 1939 entitled 'The principles underlying British wartime propaganda'.

15 Quoted in *Documentary News Letter*, October 1940, p. 3.

16 Report by film censor Miss N. Shortt in 1936. Quoted by Jeffrey Richards, *The Age of the Dream Palace* (London: Routledge, 1984), p. 119.

17 *Unpublished Story* seems to have had disappointing box-office results and not received the attention it deserved, though Lejeune reviewed it favourably and perceptively in the *Observer* (see BFI microfiche, *Unpublished Story*).

18 *Economist*, 9 November 1940, p. 587.

19 James Chapman (1995) fully and adequately refutes Pronay and Croft's argument but, given the number of student essays which uncritically reproduce it, I deduce that conspiracy theories require repeated bludgeoning before they expire.

20 This is a simplification: the Technicolor camera worked on a 'bi-pack plus one' system (Coote, 1993, p. 125).

21 The correspondence is reproduced in Christie (1978) and Powell and Pressburger (1994) and is analysed in detail in both.

22 The fact that Priestley's own large and not fully utilized house on the Isle

of Wight had been requisitioned by the Army as its General Headquarters for the island in June 1940 might have provoked this train of thought (Cook, 1997, pp. 180–1).

23 *Cine Technician*, Feb/March 1940, p. 10.
24 'The lion and the unicorn', Orwell (1968), vol. 2, p. 117.
25 *Ibid.*, p. 118.
26 'London letter to *Partisan Review*', Orwell (1968), vol. 3, p. 336.
27 *Ibid.*, p. 339.

4

The Secret War:
Films of Resistance and Subversion

... the persevering efforts put into clandestine recruiting, grouping, organization of future insurgents, were a sort of Penelope's web, continually unpicked by the Gestapo, of which the bloody threads were obstinately re-knotted night by night. (Adrien Dansette, 1946)[1]

The evacuation of the British Expeditionary Force from Dunkirk and the surrender of the French Army three weeks later might easily have brought a close to the war. Hitler's ambitions did not encompass the invasion of Britain or the destruction of the British Empire. Yet there was no serious discussion of peace between Britain and Germany.[2] This was partly to do with British pride. Britain in 1940, with its huge empire intact, still had pretensions to being the premier world power. And if Britain stood alone, it was with the backing of Australia, New Zealand, Canada, India and substantial parts of Africa, linked together by the unchallenged might of the Royal Navy with its fortified island bases in Gibraltar, Malta and Singapore. The retreat from Dunkirk had been a reverse and a humiliation, but there had been no defeat and the Navy and Air Force had acquitted themselves well in facilitating the evacuation. British chauvinism sustained a stoical pride in the task of facing up to Germany unencumbered by difficult and unreliable Continental allies. Britain could present itself as the last bastion of democracy and civilization – a stance that was reinforced by the presence in London of governments-in-exile of Czechoslovakia, Poland, Norway, Holland and Belgium.

Had the 'Men of Munich' still been in power, peace might have been a plausible option. But on 5 May 1940, as German troops poured into Belgium and Holland, Churchill displaced Chamberlain as Prime Minister and Labour and Liberal politicians were brought into the government in a national coalition. Churchill's government was unable to prevent the conquest of Western Europe but it had not been in power long enough to be held responsible for it. Instead, guilt attached to those who had appeased Hitler.

When Churchill addressed the House of Commons on 4 June, he ended his speech with the now famous declaration: 'We shall fight on the beaches, we shall fight on the landing grounds, we shall fight in the fields and in the streets, we shall fight in the hills; we shall never surrender.' It was an appropriate and not wholly unrealistic note of defiance. The problems involved in launching a German invasion of Britain were considerable and, without an internal collapse of morale, unlikely to be successful. Britain still had control over the sea and the only way in which the German Navy could get an invasion force across the Channel would be to do so under protective air power. Thus all depended on the Luftwaffe knocking out the RAF. The struggle for power in the skies in August 1940 really was a Battle of Britain.

Churchill's bulldog-like determination to fight on crystallized a national mood, but he knew that without financial and military support from the United States, Britain would not be able to continue the fight. Awareness of Britain's economic weakness did not extend beyond the highest echelons of government; rather there was widespread belief in Germany's political and economic instability. Xenophobia and a contempt for despotism combined to reinforce the belief that Hitler and the bunch of mavericks and misfits who made up the Nazi hierarchy had only a precarious and temporary grip on power and that as soon as the military and economic climate worsened they would be ousted. Similarly, Britain's adherence to monetary orthodoxy throughout the 1930s encouraged the belief that Germany's economic recovery was inherently unsound, that massive government expenditure had resulted in an economic boom which would inevitably collapse, leaving Germany militarily and economically over-extended. This collapse was to be hastened by Britain's naval blockade and by the bombing of key German industrial and communications installations.

There was a danger, of course, that Germany would profit from its military expansion – that the invasion of Poland, Czechoslovakia, Norway, Denmark and most of Western Europe would make it economically self-sufficient. It was expected, however, that the high level of resistance the Nazis would have to face in the occupied countries would make them more of a burden than a prize. Europe, it was supposed, was a seething mass of discontent, a time bomb which would one day explode. To facilitate this explosion, in July

1940 Churchill authorized the setting up of the Special Operations Executive (SOE) as part of the Ministry of Economic Warfare. 'And now,' he exhorted Hugh Dalton, the minister in charge, 'set Europe ablaze' (Dalton, 1957, p. 366).[3]

Resistance Strategies

The idea that Europe was on the verge of revolt was as important to British morale as that of the German economy being gradually extinguished by the RAF's bombs and the Royal Navy's blockade. The surrender of the French Army left a gaping hole in Britain's military strategy. Millions of British and Commonwealth soldiers had fought in the First World War but victory had only been achieved in conjunction with the French and United States armies. It was unrealistic to expect Britain to build an army strong enough to cross the Channel and drive back the Germans. To defeat Germany, it was hoped that British forces would act as a catalyst for the oppressed peoples of occupied Europe. In December 1941, Churchill told his generals that an invasion of Europe would be supported by a mass uprising:

> It need not be assumed that great numbers of men are required. If this incursion of the armoured formations is successful, the uprising of the local population for whom weapons must be brought, will supply the corpus of the liberating offensive. (quoted in Taylor, 1983, p. 626)

Churchill's involvement in the disastrous Gallipoli campaign of 1915, which saw large forces of British and Australian troops unable to break out of beachheads they had established on the Turkish coast, and his positive experience with lightly armoured car patrols – 'motorized guerrillas' as he termed them – when commanding a battalion on the Western Front, inclined him to favour unorthodox military methods. Hugh Dalton (whose own First World War experience had been with the small British contingent fighting with the Italians, rather than in the trenches of Flanders) told Lord Halifax:

> We must organise movements in every occupied territory comparable to the Sinn Fein movement in Ireland, to the Chinese guerrillas now operating against Japan, to the Spanish irregulars who played a notable part in Wellington's campaign or – one might as well admit it – the organisations which the Nazis themselves have

developed so remarkably in almost every country in the world. We must use many different methods, including industrial and military sabotage, labour agitation and strikes, continuous propaganda, terrorist acts against traitors and German leaders, boycotts and riots. (Dalton, 1957, p. 367)

Since the Second World War subversion and guerrilla warfare have become commonplace, but in 1940 the most important precedents – T. E. Lawrence's exploits in Arabia, the activities of the Bolsheviks in the Russian Civil War and the struggles over Irish independence – had not seriously affected military thinking, and their adoption as part of government strategy marked a very radical shift from the early days of the war when the Air Minister, Kingsley Wood, objected to an RAF plan to set fire to German forests on the grounds that they were private property (Taylor, 1983, p. 560).[4]

Dalton stressed the importance of establishing links with trade unions and left-wing organizations in Europe, though a good public school education and the right family background tended to be more useful qualifications than left-wing activism or experience in the Spanish Civil War for recruitment as an SOE agent.[5] SOE's sponsoring of subversion, under the Labour firebrand Dalton – the only Labour minister directly involved in military affairs – did not go unchallenged. The Secret Intelligence Service (SIS/MI6) resented the intrusion of another subversive organization in the field and the Foreign Office was alarmed at the political ramifications SOE aid to left-wing guerrillas might have on the post-war world (after all, Britain was an imperial power and hoped to retain its empire). In February 1942 the Foreign Secretary, Anthony Eden, and the Minister of Information, Brendan Bracken (who was eager to wrest control of black propaganda from the Ministry of Economic Warfare), contrived to have Dalton replaced by the impeccably conservative Lord Selbourne.

Even so, when the war ended, SOE was seen as an embarrassment and military historians like Basil Liddell Hart condemned its willingness 'to defy authority and break the rules of civic morality' and 'its wider amoral effect on the younger generation as a whole'.[6] The first volume of its official history, M. R. D. Foot's splendid *SOE in France*, was not published until 1966, and subsequent volumes dealing with SOE's activities in the Far East and Scandinavia did not surface until the 1980s.[7]

Though SOE's achievements were eventually considerable, the Nazi hold over Europe was more tenacious than had been hoped and setting the Continent ablaze proved a slow and uncertain process.

David Stafford quotes the SOE war diary on the situation at the end of 1940:

> in the belligerent, occupied and so-called neutral countries of Central and Western Europe, no field staff existed; SO2's problem is to get the horse in after the stable door has been shut; and first of all the horse must be found. (Stafford, 1983, p. 49)[8]

By the end of 1940, belief in a viable opposition to Hitler in Germany had faded.[9] The Czech and Polish governments-in-exile both claimed to control large secret armies, but supply lines were hazardous. The long flight to Central Europe could only be managed by ponderous and unwieldy Whitley bombers and accurate dropping of men and material was impossible.[10] Resistance certainly existed, despite Nazi ruthlessness, but the strategy of the Czech and Polish governments-in-exile was to build up secret armies capable of taking over their countries with the support of an Allied invasion rather than to attract German reprisals by acts of sabotage. In May 1942 the Czechs were goaded into action and assassinated Reinhard Heydrich, deputy leader of the SS and 'Protector of Bohemia and Moravia'. It was a spectacular success, but it led to execution of nearly 2000 people and the erasing of the village of Lidice from the map. Similar atrocities were carried out in Yugoslavia and Russia, but in these countries all-out partisan war raged. In Czechoslovakia the savage clampdown severely damaged clandestine organizations and, for a time at least, 'the spirit of open resistance' was broken (Stafford, 1983, p. 108).

In Eastern Europe the Czechs and Poles and other Slavs were treated with contemptuous brutality; in the West the Germans were more circumspect. Initially at least, there was an attempt to win over the Norwegians, Danes, Dutch, Belgians and French and to encourage collaboration. According to Kenneth Macksey:

> Usually the various nationalities 'policed' themselves and so the Germans needed but a few thousand men of their own to deal with exceptional outbreaks. . . . The Occupation in no way over-stretched Germany and, indeed from the economic point of view, redoubled her strength. . . . Nobody in Western Europe was ready for sacrifices in 1940, when it was better to wait and see if unification under Germany might produce long-term benefits – as a unified Europe might well do of itself. (Macksey, 1975, pp. 55–6)

After its great victories, the German Army could afford to be generous, and though Dutch, Belgian and Norwegian governments-in-exile were established in London, they could not claim the sort of mass support enjoyed by their Czech and Polish counterparts.

The situation in France was complicated by the existence of the neutral French government based in the spa town of Vichy. By the terms of the armistice agreed on 22 June 1940, the eastern provinces of Alsace and Lorraine were incorporated into Germany, and northern France, including Paris, was occupied by German troops. But Marshal Pétain was allowed to maintain control over the southern two-fifths of France and to maintain an army and navy. The French Army, defeated and demoralized, was no longer a significant force, but the French fleet was of considerable strength and if it was combined with that of the Germans, the ascendancy of the Royal Navy would be seriously threatened. By the terms of the armistice, the French fleet was to be disarmed and neutral, but Britain, mistrustful of the security of Nazi promises, demanded that it be surrendered to the Royal Navy. The French commander refused and on 3 July 1940 his fleet was attacked in the North African harbour of Mers-el-Kébir: two battleships and a battlecruiser were sunk, resulting in the death of more than a thousand French sailors (Deighton, 1993, pp. 238–40). It was a national humiliation for France and caused considerable bitterness. Anglo-French relations were at a low ebb for the rest of 1940; though as General de Gaulle had proved an ineffective ally in attempts to turn French North Africa towards Britain's cause and as yet had only a small following in France, attempts were made to build bridges with the Vichy regime rather than to sever them irretrievably.

SOE's strategy was to send into occupied Europe – by boat, by plane, by parachute – trained agents to organize and co-ordinate resistance. Apart from the time-consuming and dangerous tasks of organizing the reception of agents, arms and munitions, SOE networks were charged with two main tasks: first, to organize secret armies ready for the day when an all-out attempt would be made to eject the Nazis; second, to carry out sabotage on military and industrial targets. SOE networks were also a useful source of information about the strength of local resistance, the location of German arms and ammunition depots, and the nature and direction of troop movements. But SOE agents were not specifically trained in intelligence work, which remained the jealously guarded preserve of the SIS.

Dalton hoped that SOE would be forged into a 'fourth service' which would play as vital a role in the war as the Army, Navy and

Air Force. But hostility from the three other services made its growth and development difficult. The Navy resented risking its ships landing agents in heavily guarded coastal waters. Attempts to send agents into France via the Atlantic shoreline were abandoned after 1941, though a regular service by felucca (shallow-keeled, 20-ton fishing vessels crewed by expatriate Poles) was run into southern France via Gibraltar until the end of 1942, after which Germany's occupation of Vichy France made it too dangerous.

The Army remained sceptical of the value of poorly armed, irregular secret armies and disapproved of the sort of sabotage, ambush and assassination SOE agents were required to carry out. Its own clandestine units – commandos trained to strike behind enemy lines and the more radically unorthodox Long Range Desert Attack Group, Special Air Service (SAS) and Special Boat Service (SBS) – were rigorously trained, highly disciplined and always wore uniform.

The RAF disapproved as much as the Army of ungentlemanly methods of war. An attempt by five French SOE agents to ambush a bus carrying German pathfinder pilots to their airfield near Vannes in March 1941 aroused the ire of the RAF chiefs:

> When Portal and Air-Marshal Harris heard that the ambush was to be laid by plainclothesmen they objected on the ground that this was the sort of operation with which the RAF would not wish to be associated. It was a matter of ethics, the difference between dropping a spy and encouraging assassins. It threatened, too, the survival of ordinary airmen shot down in combat. In law it was wrong, giving the Germans justification for taking reprisals against civilians. (Stafford, 1983, p. 49)

Whereas the Russian Air Force was almost entirely concerned with supporting its armies – and the partisans operating behind German lines – the RAF was allowed to pursue its own agenda of extensive night-time bombing designed to shatter German morale and the German economy. SOE's increasing demands for parachute drops and secret landings by plane (the tiny, fragile Lysanders, occasionally supplemented by larger Hudsons) were persistently resisted by the Air Minister, Lord Portal, and the head of Bomber Command, Sir Arthur Harris, who resented any diversion away from the bombing campaign they believed could win the war. SOE was to complain continually that 'owing to the inadequacy of air transport, resistance in the occupied territories cannot be further increased' (Stafford, 1983, p. 107).

SOE faced less overt but more deadly rivalry from the SIS, which resented the attention SOE acts of derring-do attracted from German Military Intelligence (the Abwehr) and the Sicherheitsdienst (SD), the intelligence arm of the SS, in areas where SIS agents had been quietly building networks.[11] The SIS was slow to pass on vital information derived from the Ultra code-breaking operation at Bletchley Park, persistently denigrated SOE's achievements and had no scruples about sacrificing SOE agents in its own counter-espionage games.[12]

The Resistance Cycle

SOE was a secret organization and its activities could obviously not be celebrated in film while the war was going on, but an interesting cycle of films depicting resistance activity in Europe was made between 1940 and 1943. According to Dilys Powell, the film critic of the *Sunday Times*,

> From the Continent across the Channel, travellers came back with stories beyond the invention of men; a dark curtain of secrecy had been lowered but the British knew that beyond it a great war of sacrifice and desperation was being fought. It is easy enough to dismiss as fairy tales the series of adventure films about Occupied Europe which were made in British studios and, later, in Hollywood. Many of them, certainly, were made without knowledge or imaginative understanding of the ordeal of the European peoples. But at least some of them were an attempt at understanding. And, when all is said and done, the British contribution to the series is not negligible. (Powell, 1947, p. 23)

Apart from Michael Powell and Emeric Pressburger's *One of Our Aircraft Is Missing*, none of these films are particularly outstanding aesthetically. However, from a historical point of view they are fascinating and valuable. The cycle began with Roy and John Boulting's *Pastor Hall*, Carol Reed's *Night Train to Munich*, Leslie Howard's *Pimpernel Smith* and Anthony Asquith's *Freedom Radio*, conceived when subjects which could be at all positive about the war were being sought. *Pastor Hall*, based on an anti-Nazi play which the BBFC had discouraged the Boultings from filming before war broke out, told the story of a German priest, Pastor Martin Niemöller, who is made to suffer for his outspoken condemnation of the Nazis from his pulpit (in the play he is imprisoned, in the film he escapes but after

delivering a passionate sermon goes out to face his SS executioners).
It was respectfully received in Britain, but the American correspondent of the *Documentary News Letter* reported that

> the film has been admired for certain intrinsic production qualities,
> but it is observed that concentration camps and other European
> cruelties create only a sense of distance in the native mind and a
> feeling of 'Thank God we emigrated from Europe to a decent
> country.' . . . Jewish maltreatment, concentration camps, sadistic
> lashings are, one is afraid, old stuff, slightly discredited and do not
> command people's deepest attention.[13]

Fourteen-year-old girls coming home pregnant from labour camps
and old men being given 25 lashes now seem almost insignificant
compared to what the Nazis proved themselves capable of, but First
World War atrocity stories which later proved to be fabrications had
left a miasma of scepticism that was not finally dispelled until the
liberation of Belsen and Auschwitz.

Both *Night Train to Munich* and *Pimpernel Smith* were box-office
successes but *Freedom Radio*, a dourer and less inspiring film, was
more typical of the subsequent resistance cycle. Clive Brook's Dr
Roder is a society doctor who takes time off from his illustrious Nazi
patients to run a pirate radio station which vows to reveal to the
German and Austrian people the truth behind Nazi propaganda. He
dies in a hail of bullets, but his Nazi-sympathizing wife (Diana
Wynyard playing an interesting Leni Riefenstahl/Thea von Harbou-
like character who becomes Hitler's 'director of pageantry') is dis-
abused of her illusions and dies with him, and his compatriots ensure
that Freedom Radio remains on-air. The fact that Dr Roder is an
Austrian seems less important than the fact he is a gentleman,
offended and moved to action by the brutal methods of the Nazis.
Louis MacNeice, writing in the *Spectator*, warned that the film's
attitude to the Nazi menace was dangerously simplistic:

> Propaganda either against the Nazis or to the German people must
> treat the Nazi revolution as something more than Machiavellian
> mumbo-jumbo if it is to make it comprehensible – and we must
> comprehend our enemy in order to combat him . . . we need more
> psychological subtlety and depth, a more imaginative grasp of that
> Nazi world which we ourselves – however indirectly – helped to
> create; it is a fantastic and horrible world, but it is not outside
> nature.[14]

In fact, interest in understanding the Nazi world view waned almost to extinction. In the early months of the war MoI policy had been to distinguish between good Germans and Nazis, and in October 1939 an MoI pamphlet had gone so far as to suggest that 'National Socialism began as an honourable experiment' whose 'leaders started with many fine ideals and the German people had every right to expect that they would be realised'.[15] But the conquest of Western Europe, the threat of invasion, and the Blitz led to such distinctions being jettisoned in favour of blaming the whole German nation for the war (in order to justify the growing bombing campaign against German towns and cities). Except in the officially disapproved-of *Colonel Blimp*, there would be no more good Germans in wartime films and it was the gallant Czechs, Serbs, Belgians, Dutch, French and Scandinavians who would be depicted resisting the Nazis.

Melodrama and Realism

A dozen resistance films followed over the next two years: *One of Our Aircraft Is Missing*, *The Day Will Dawn*, *Uncensored*, *Secret Mission* and *Tomorrow We Live* in 1942; *The Silver Fleet*, *The Night Invader*, *Undercover*, *Escape to Danger*, *The Flemish Farm*, *Schweik's New Adventures* and *The Adventures of Tartu* in 1943, after which the cycle came to an abrupt halt.[16]

Norway and Denmark had one film each. In *Escape to Danger*, the American actress Ann Dvorak plays an English schoolmistress who poses as a traitor to root out German agents in Denmark. In *The Day Will Dawn*, Hugh Williams plays a newspaper racing correspondent, Colin Metcalfe ('a typical product of a good-for-nothing minor aristocracy run to seed'), who is recruited by Naval Intelligence to organize a commando raid on a submarine base in a Norwegian fjord. But it was not until twenty years after the war ended that Anthony Mann's *The Heroes of Telemark* told the story of Knut Haukelid's successful attack on the hydro plant at Vemork which destroyed its capacity for producing heavy water and Germany's hopes of producing an atomic bomb.[17]

The most favoured locations for resistance films made during the war were Belgium (*Uncensored* and *The Flemish Farm*) and Holland (*One of Our Aircraft Is Missing*, *The Night Invader* and *The Silver Fleet*).[18] *The Flemish Farm*, despite being made by youngish, left-wing filmmakers (Jeffrey Dell, Jill Craigie and Sydney Box), is virtually a throwback to the 'honour of the regiment' heroics of *Ships with Wings*. Jane Baxter, who had played the admiral's daughter, is again a

Judas unforgiven: Father de Gruyte (Griffith Jones) refuses to exonerate Neels (Peter Glenville) for his betrayal of Belgian patriots in *Uncensored*. Supplied by BFI Stills, © courtesy of Carlton International.

determined young woman who plumps for a handsome, upright officer (Philip Friend in place of Michael Wilding), and the fact that she is supposed to be a Belgian peasant hardly impinges on her upper-class vowels. Clive Brook is the commander of the last remnants of the Belgian Air Force and though he later becomes a leading member of the resistance, he surrenders nothing in the way of courtly decorum and finds it as incongruous as we do that he is labelled a 'Jew Communist' before being shot by the Nazis.

Uncensored is much more central to the cycle – a sophisticated reworking of the themes Asquith had explored earlier in *Freedom Radio*, with the less gentlemanly Eric Portman replacing Clive Brook as the patriot determined to tell the truth (in a news sheet, *La Libre Belgique*) and undermine Nazi lies. Objectively, it would be difficult to argue that the characters are more realistic than those in *Freedom Radio*, but the darker mood of the film makes it more intense and compelling. Returning to Brussels after the shattering of the Belgian army, André Delange (Portman) is shown a burnt-out house where advancing German troops have incinerated women and children.

Later, confronted by a sentry from the battalion responsible, he disarms him and cold-bloodedly bayonets him to death. There are lighter moments – the Germans played by Raymond Lovell, Felix Aylmer and Irene Handl are essentially comic caricatures – but the sardonic gloom which seems to float around so many of the characters Portman plays permeates the whole film.

Delange is allowed a conventional romance with a fiery patriot played by Phyllis Calvert, but the film is structured around his relationship with his stage partner, Charles Neels (Peter Glenville). From the start it is established that Neels' ambitions exceed his talent and that Delange is carrying him. In a typical Asquith set-piece, Neels attempts a solo act and is rewarded with applause and laughter. What he doesn't see is that the plaudits are for a backstage cat which, woken by his playing, climbs out of the grand piano and sleepily washes itself during his act. When Delange agrees to go on a tour of German bases – without his partner – in order to facilitate his resistance activities, the hysterical Neels ('He was leaving me to starve after all these years') betrays him to the Gestapo. Although one might assume that if Neels knows about his partner's (carefully concealed) resistance work, he might also understand why he has to take up the German offer, the film is unusual in capturing the emotional truth that personal jealousies and rivalries in the hothouse world of resistance and subversion could result in bizarre behaviour and unexpected betrayal.

In March 1943 SOE proudly claimed that in Holland 'an organisation of some 1,500 men has been very carefully built up on a definite plan of action for the day of invasion' (Stafford, 1983, p. 108). Unfortunately, such optimism was ill-founded. In Holland both SIS and SOE were comprehensively outwitted by German intelligence. In October 1939 the two top SIS agents in Holland – Sigismund Payne Best and Major Richard Stevens – had been lured to the border town of Venlo by the promise of an intrigue with dissident German army officers. Snatched by a Sicherheitsdienst squad, they were rushed to Berlin, where they were made to reveal information which led to the break-up of the SIS's Continental networks (Marshall, 1988, p. 37). In March 1942 Major Giskes, head of Abwehr counter-espionage in Holland, was even more successful against SOE. Having arrested an SOE radio operator, he persuaded him to transmit to London under Abwehr instruction. The agent hoped that someone would realize something was wrong when he failed to use his secret security check. Unfortunately, they did not. As Macksey put it:

> With an ineptitude that is hard to credit, SOE allowed the Germans
> to substitute their own operators for the original SOE men and

authorized newly arrived groups to contact each other, thus breaching the bulwarks of secrecy which were meant to immunize one group from another. The Order Service [the non-communist Dutch resistance group] was penetrated via SOE: far worse, from the allied point of view, certain courier links from Holland into Belgium and France and right through to neutral Switzerland and Spain came into German hands. In due course various SOE circuits in the other occupied countries were infected and in Belgium the Armeé Blanche was infiltrated. (Macksey, 1975, p. 110)[19]

Out of the 56 SOE agents sent into Holland over the next eighteen months, 43 were arrested, along with many of the people who helped them, and 200 drops were intercepted.

Of course, none of this was known when Michael Powell and Emeric Pressburger began making *One of Our Aircraft Is Missing*, their most straightforwardly patriotic film. After the success of *49th Parallel*, J. Arthur Rank expressed an interest in backing Powell and Pressburger's next film. But Pressburger's script outline, about a British bomber crew bailing out over occupied Holland and attempting to escape back to England, was considered too downbeat by Rank's distributor, C. M. Woolf. Insisting that as film-makers they were the best judge of what was an appropriate subject, Powell turned back to British National, who agreed to back the film and allow Powell and Pressburger to make it under the banner of their own production company, the Archers.

In *49th Parallel*, a rigidly hierarchical group of German submariners make their way across Canada hoping to find sanctuary in the then neutral United States and are hindered at every turn. Only their leader (Eric Portman) survives, and he is captured just at the point when he thinks he has escaped. In *One of Our Aircraft Is Missing*, the egalitarian crew of an RAF Wellington bomber bail out of their stricken aircraft and make their way across Holland. They are helped by sympathetic Netherlanders and are picked up by the Royal Navy and brought safely home to England.

The ostensible hero is the 51-year-old Sir George Corbett, but as played by Godfrey Tearle he is no more than a first among equals (it might have been different if Ralph Richardson, Pressburger's first choice, had been able to take the role); and as in subsequent films such as *The Gentle Sex*, *The Way Ahead* and *Two Thousand Women*, the real hero is a group of characters who represent the nation. Tensions within the group supposedly exist between the aged Sir George and his young colleagues.[20] As Pressburger explained to Powell:

'Just imagine, Michael, what a bore such an old gentleman must seem to the young men who make up the bomber's crew. They would want to get rid of him. They would think he should be grounded and yet such a man, when they are trying to find their way home through enemy-occupied territory, would be invaluable. Airborne, *they* are the professionals. On the ground *he* is. For them it is a new and frightening experience. But he is an old soldier. He has been lost before, sometimes alone, sometimes with a scouting party, perhaps with a whole regiment.' (Powell, 1986, p. 392)

There is some friendly rivalry between Sir George and the navigator, Frank Shelley (Hugh Williams), an actor unused to military discipline; but there is remarkably little conflict within the group.

Pressburger shows no interest in the English class system and a cavalier disregard for American sensibilities – the American rear gunner is ditched in favour of Sir George for the crucial mission and never seen again. His characters – a footballer, Bob Ashley (Emrys Jones), a mechanic, Geoff Hickman (Bernard Miles), a sheep farmer, Tom Earnshaw (Eric Portman), a baronet, Sir George (Godfrey Tearle), a diplomat, John Glyn Haggard (Hugh Burden), and an actor, Frank Shelley (Hugh Williams) – are obstinately individual. They lack the resonance of the deeply etched portrayals of John Mills, Bernard Miles and Noël Coward in *In Which We Serve* but they are also less open to caricature.[21] There is no attempt to conceal the fact that a deferential class system is still very much in place. In the officers' mess Sir George admits to pilot Haggard, co-pilot Earnshaw and navigator Shelley that he has used his influence to fly with them that night, while in the sergeants' mess wireless operator Ashley and the front gunner Hickman commiserate with the displaced American rear gunner. Haggard drives up to the bomber in his sports car and casually orders the mechanics to sort out its non-functioning indicator, as if they were his personal servants. But this is naturally and casually transcended in the intercom conversation between Hickman and Haggard about the relationships they have both had with Stuttgart nurses as they approach the city which they are going to bomb.

Pressburger's grandson complains that the film 'has limited appeal to modern audiences. It seems dated and somewhat formulaic' (Macdonald, 1994, p. 194). But his disappointment might be to do with confused expectations. Powell and Pressburger are noted for their defiance of realist orthodoxy, yet here they devote themselves whole-heartedly to an austere realist ethos. According to Powell,

I had decided on complete naturalism. There would only be the natural sounds of a country at war. It was not a documentary; it was a detached narrative, told from the inside, of what it is like to be a pawn in the game of total war. . . . One of Emeric's very best ideas was to hear Germans everywhere, but only to see them in the distance, if at all. We picked all the dozens of voices carefully, whether they were making jokes as they signed civilian passes, or barking orders. The audience saw military vehicles packed with soldiers careering along with their klaxons blaring, but we never got close to a German in the whole film, except in the sequence in the church. (Powell, 1986, p. 389)

The film's mixture of blatant propaganda and verisimilitude is remarkable, and Powell's attention to detail pays rich dividends in terms of authenticity. The crawling around the fuselage necessary for the gunners to get into their positions, the edgy delay as the crew jump from the stricken aircraft, capture something of the mystery, danger and excitement of wartime flying. Romance is only touched upon: a mutual attraction between Haggard (who, despite the casting of the chinless Burden, might be seen as Powell's alter ego) and Pamela Brown's Else Meertens; Geoff Hickman's admiring glances at small and fiery Jo Van Dieren (Joyce Redman); the odd, delicate flirtation between Frank Shelley, an actor devoted to his radio star wife, and Jo de Vries (Googie Withers), keeping the home fires burning for her exiled patriot husband. But there is a strong female presence (the absence of which Powell was to lament in *Ill Met by Moonlight*). Pamela Brown, making her first screen appearance, is strikingly effective; but it is Googie Withers, who hitherto had played only light comic roles – in films like Powell's quota quickie *The Love Test* (1935) and opposite George Formby in *Trouble Brewing* (Anthony Kimmins, 1939) – who dominates the film. Withers delivers the film's strongest propaganda message, telling the airmen that the help she and her compatriots have given them is reciprocated by the bombs RAF crews are showering over their occupied country:

'You see, that's what you're doing for us? Can you hear them running for shelter? Can you understand what that means to all the occupied countries, to enslaved people having it drummed into their ears that the Germans are masters of the earth, seeing those masters running for shelter, seeing them crouching under tables and hearing that steady hum, night after night, that noise which is oil for the burning fire in our hearts?'

With financial backing from J. Arthur Rank, Powell and Pressburger were able not only to proceed with their expensive Technicolor epic *The Life and Death of Colonel Blimp* but also to act as producers of another resistance film, *The Silver Fleet*, directed by Vernon Sewell and Gordon Wellesley. *One of Our Aircraft Is Missing* begins with the low-flying Wellington bomber crashing into an electricity pylon and exploding before we are taken back in time to be shown that the crew have already bailed out. The beginning of *The Silver Fleet* is equally effective: we see into a submarine lying on the seabed and discover that all its crew are dead before the tale which led to this watery grave is unravelled through the diary of Jaap Van Leyden (Ralph Richardson). Like *Pimpernel Smith*, this is yet another story of a man who is not what he seems, carrying out effective subversion against the Nazis. Van Leyden is a Dutch shipyard owner forced to build U-boats for the German Navy or else see his workforce starve. Overhearing a patriotic schoolmistress (Kathleen Byron) telling her pupils the legend of Piet Hein, who sank the Spanish silver fleet when Holland was fighting for its independence in the seventeenth century, he is inspired to organize a secret resistance network which will sabotage the boats built in his yard. According to Kevin Macdonald, Pressburger was not pleased with the finished film. 'It was exactly the type of polite, anodyne war film which Emeric had been reacting against and he withdrew his name from the writing credits' (Macdonald, 1994, p. 201). Certainly, the film is less original and more conventional than any of Powell and Pressburger's own films, but the mysterious beginning and the flashback device of the shipbuilder's wife (Googie Withers) reading the story from her now dead husband's secret diary give it a poignancy that is far from anodyne.

However, the propaganda in the film has the same sort of grandiose patriotism that one sees in *Freedom Radio*, *Pimpernel Smith*, *The Day Will Dawn* and *Undercover*. *The Silver Fleet* ends on Van Leyden's words:

'As long as Dutchmen live in Holland I shall be here. Because I was one of the seeds from which Freedom grew again. I shall not die! Does a seed die when it is buried in the earth? Has the wind died when it ceases to blow? Are the waves dead when the sea is calm? The truth is that a Nation will only live as long as it has people ready to die.'

This is precisely what Pressburger avoids doing in *One of Our Aircraft Is Missing*. The propaganda message is equally strong – in fact, it could be considered even less realistic in that Jo de Vries's call for friendly bombs to rain down was unlikely to have been shared by many people in occupied Europe. But it is clearly motivated and integrated into the story that the film wishes to tell. Jo's husband has supposedly been killed during a British bombing raid, giving her good reason to hate the British and help the Germans, but this is a cover story, and her husband is in fact continuing the struggle from England. The bombing raid is a significant moment in the film's narrative – the airmen can only escape when the corridor leading them out of hiding is left unguarded during a raid. This event has been carefully prepared for. After all the disguises, the airmen are back in uniform (another realistic detail Powell insists upon – if they are caught in uniform they will be treated as prisoners of war, if they are in disguise they can be shot as spies) and Jo is out of her workaday overalls and wearing a dress. Sir George offers a toast to 'a brave woman and a fearless country', promising 'a growing help, an attack which will sweep these Germans . . .', and the sound of the approaching planes finishes his sentence. The seeming truth of Jo's speech about the joys of seeing the swaggering Nazis running for shelter seems to be endorsed in the high-angle shot from the window of them scurrying around below. This level of sophistication was not present in *The Silver Fleet* or any of the other resistance films, but to some extent their crudity makes more transparent their ideological significance.

The invasion of Italy, which began in July 1943, enhanced the importance of resistance activity in Yugoslavia, Greece and Albania. Sabotage, ambushes, the disruption of roads and railways would weaken the resolve of the Italians and ease pressure against the invaders. Once bases had been established in Italy, supplies could more easily be carried to the partisans. By April 1944 five squadrons of British Halifax bombers and US Army Dakotas, plus a Polish Halifax flight and two squadrons of Italian aircraft, were flying 900 sorties a month to Yugoslavia and Albania (Macksey, 1975, p. 168). A directive from the Chiefs of Staff to SOE on 20 March 1943 put the Italian-held islands Corsica and Crete at the head of a list of priorities for resistance activity, with the Balkans second, France third, Poland and Czechoslovakia fourth, Norway and the Low Countries fifth and the Far East last (Stafford, 1983, p. 256).

Yugoslavia, where Tito organized a partisan force which controlled large areas of the countryside and withstood a series of major German offensives, attracted only one film, *Undercover*, and to producer Michael Balcon's embarrassment it celebrated the supposed achievements of General Mihailović's Chetniks (the original title of the film

Difficult decisions: Milosh Petrovitch (John Clements) defies his father (Tom Walls) and his wife (Mary Morris) in opting for prudence rather than hot-headed revenge in *Undercover*. Supplied by BFI Stills, © courtesy of Canal + Image.

was 'Chetnic'), a singularly ineffectual force which spent more time harrying Tito's partisans than it did fighting the forces of occupation. According to Balcon:

> Alas, halfway through the production Churchill withdrew British support for Mihailović . . . changes were made in the script . . . and the film's title became *Undercover*. Tito was now the boss and he would have no part of King Peter, Prince Paul or General Mihai-lović. (Balcon, 1969, p. 141)

Balcon could hardly be blamed for his mistake. SOE's first major success had been to help plot the overthrow of Prince Paul of Yugoslavia after he signed a treaty with Germany in March 1941. It was a pyrrhic victory, for a few days later the Germans invaded, with the excuse that they were restoring the rightful government. SOE remained tied to Mihailović and the remnants of the Yugoslav Army that provided the backbone of his Chetnik resistance group. Great things were hoped from them and repeated warnings of Chetnik reluctance to fight, except against the rival communist partisans, were ignored. It was only after Churchill was presented with irrefutable evidence of Chetnik collaboration in the form of decoded Enigma messages, and reports from two men he trusted completely – William Deakin, a Cambridge historian who had befriended him in his wilderness years, and Fitzroy Maclean, an SAS captain he sent as his personal agent to make contact with Tito – that the tide turned. As late as May 1943 (a month before *Undercover* was released), Dalton's successor, Lord Selbourne, was still stoutly defending Mihailović.[22]

Like Nolbandov's earlier *Ships with Wings*, *Undercover* has been neglected because it is alien to what has come to seem the realist ethos of Ealing. It makes good use of Welsh locations (and Welsh actors Rachel Thomas and a young Stanley Baker), but Nolbandov was the one director at Ealing totally impervious to the realist proclivities of Balcon and Cavalcanti and there are none of the underplayed heroics of other Ealing films, such as Watt's *Nine Men*, Cavalcanti's *Went the Day Well?*, Dearden's *The Bells Go Down* or Frend's *San Demetrio London*. In terms of the issues raised and the conviction of the action, however, this is by no means an insignificant or trivial film.

The German governor (Godfrey Tearle) wants to pursue a path of collaboration with 'the real leaders of the people' and tries to use an eminent doctor, Stephan Petrovitch (Stephen Murray), as a link to patriotic but pragmatic Yugoslavs who are willing to find a *modus vivendi* with the conquerors – more or less reflecting the attitude of the Chetniks (though most of their dealings were with the Italian rather than the German occupying forces). This is not what happens here, though, and when opposition proves intractable, the iron fist beneath the velvet glove is revealed. Stephan's brother Milosh (John Clements) is a leader of the guerrilla forces and his wife (Mary Morris), the village schoolmistress, is brutally interrogated, but her pupils help her escape to the mountain to join her husband. When the schoolchildren refuse to divulge the whereabouts of the guerrillas, six boys are shot. Old Petrovitch (Tom Walls) brings his son the news and assumes that retribution will be swift and terrible, but he is confounded by Milosh's decision that 'we can't afford to throw away lives just for revenge'. In *Convoy* and *Ships with Wings* the characters played by John Clements are notable for their passionate but reckless courage. Here he seems to have learnt his lesson and insists to his wife and his father that 'you can't fight a war if you let your feelings run away with you'. The irony is nicely marked by the fact that it is the cautious and respectable Stephan who is called upon for the heroic act of self-sacrifice we might have expected from Milosh.

Old Petrovitch, vowing to prove that the old ways are best, attempts to sabotage a railway tunnel and is captured and used as a hostage to draw Milosh from the mountains. Stephan, acting as go-between for the Germans, carries a suitcase full of explosives timed to go off as they pass through the now heavily guarded tunnel. Old Petrovitch, put on the train to guarantee Stephan's safety from guerrilla attack, dies with him, happy that the job he fumbled has been pulled off by his son. Milosh continues the struggle from the mountains.

Apart from the presence of ex-Yugoslav Army soldiers in the resistance force, there is little to indicate that Milosh and his men are led by Mihailović rather than Tito, and the film's apolitical stance echoes the pragmatism of Churchill's policy of aiding whoever seemed most determined to resist the Nazis.

The problem that resistance to the Nazis did not necessarily over-ride domestic divisions proved a continual thorn in SOE's side. As Kenneth Macksey points out:

> SOE teams, composed mostly of young men of action rather than elders with diplomatic wisdom, were plunged into negotiations to disentangle complex political intrigues which could mould Europe's future, instead of pursuing military operations designed to harm the Axis. (Macksey, 1975, p. 146)

In Yugoslavia things eventually worked out well. British backing for Tito helped him to maintain a distance from Moscow and ensured warm relations between Britain and Yugoslavia until its break-up in the 1990s, proving that short-term military pragmatism and long-term political strategy were not inevitably incompatible. Unfortunately, this was not the case in Greece, where Churchill, firmly committed to a royalist government-in-exile which enjoyed little popular support, fulminated against SOE aid to the communist ELAS groups whom he considered 'a mere scourge on the population' and his Foreign Secretary, Anthony Eden, described as 'a thoroughly unscrupulous gang of communist fanatics' (Stafford, 1983, pp. 126, 163). Despite pro-Hellenic feeling dating back to Lord Byron and the Greek War of Independence in the early nineteenth century, and the fact that by 1943 there were seven resistance groups – five of them with SOE advisers – with a collective strength of around 10,000 men (even if their efforts were often diverted into internecine strife), there were no British films celebrating the struggles of the Greek resistance until Michael Powell and Emeric Pressburger's *Ill Met by Moonlight* in 1957. Here, valiant Cretans led by 'a party of public-school educated,

Homer-quoting soldiers' kidnap a German general, war is played by the most gentlemanly rules, and there is no hint of internal conflict (Macdonald, 1994, p. 359).[23]

In the case of the Czechs and Poles, political complications did not arise until 1944 when it became obvious that the British-backed governments-in-exile, with their associated resistance movements, would not be able to accommodate themselves to the Russian forces driving out the Nazis and intent on fostering communist-dominated regimes in their place. Britain continued to send in agents and arms and to encourage sabotage, but the sort of support needed to sustain the Slovak and Warsaw uprisings in the autumn of 1944 would have involved a major redirection of the war effort and risked a serious breach with the Russians.[24]

Heroic Poles play bit parts in a handful of British films, and in *Dangerous Moonlight* (1941) Anton Walbrook stars as a Polish airman who gives up a brilliant career as a concert pianist in America to fight in the Battle of Britain. But the situation within Poland, partitioned and brutally repressed, was too grim to inspire any resistance films.[25] After the rescue of the Czech scientist in *Night Train to Munich*, Czechoslovakia disappeared from British screens until two films emerged late in 1943. Karel Lamac's *Schweik's New Adventures* is a very low-budget affair, notable for Lloyd Pearson's likeable performance as the Czech folk hero Schweik, who materializes as the valet of the Chief of the Gestapo and, with little regard for the realities of life in Czechoslovakia, rescues resistance activists, blows up an ammunition train (with the help of Richard Attenborough as a railway worker) and brings about the death of his employer. Harold S. Bucquet's *The Adventures of Tartu*, by contrast, was a prestige production made for MGM-British and is closer in style and ethos to Alexander Korda and Ernst Lubitsch's Hollywood film *To Be or Not to Be* (1942).[26]

Robert Donat plays a bomb disposal expert sent to Czechoslovakia in the role of a Fascist Romanian engineer to penetrate and destroy a factory producing poison gas 'somewhere near Pilsen'. His cover is that of a (deceased) Romanian Iron Guard, Tartu, and his troubles stem from the fact that as a double agent he is distrusted by both sides. Just as he begins to convince the Germans that he is a loyal Fascist, the Czech resistance decide that he is a Nazi spy attempting to infiltrate their ranks. To avoid reprisals, Maruschka (Valerie Hobson), Tartu's resistance contact, who has been passing herself off as a collaborator to mask her patriotic activities, convinces a jealous German officer that Tartu is a British agent (which of course he is, though his seeming betrayal of her friend has convinced her that he isn't) and that it would enhance his reputation – and win her sexual favours – if he shot him. There are more games of bluff and double bluff before the film rushes to its dramatic conclusion and, with Donat switching cleverly between his two identities and falling in love with a woman who is equally dangerous as a Nazi collaborator and a vengeful patriot, the film is very much in the tradition of the Hitchcockian thriller. But it is also one of the few British wartime films that, despite its studio sets, gives a real sense of life under a ruthlessly repressive regime. The high price paid for sabotage, the poverty and injustice, the humiliation of having to defer to swaggering bullies, leave a dark stain of meanness and misery on what is otherwise an exciting adventure story.

Resistance in France

The proximity of France and the importance of French opinion as a barometer of Continental attitudes to the Nazis meant that SOE afforded it a special importance. There were four separate sections dealing with resistance in France: D/F, running escape lines through Brittany, Spain and the Mediterranean coastline; EU/P, fostering sabotage and subversion among the immigrant Polish industrial workers of Lille and St Etienne; and two entirely separate resistance networks – R/F section, affiliated to General de Gaulle and his Free French movement; and F section, with a brief to work with anyone, from nationalists to the right of de Gaulle (who had been condemned to death as a rebel by the Vichy regime) to communists far to his left.

After the war, France became the *locus classicus* of resistance stories. The RAF Film Unit chose France as the setting for its account of SOE's activities in *Now It Can Be Told* (1946).[27] *Odette* (1950) and *Carve Her Name with Pride* (1958), *Orders to Kill* (1958) and *Circle of Deception* (1960) are all set in France. The BBC's television series *Moonstrike* (wr. Robert Barr, 1963) told weekly tales about the French Resistance and the British air forces supporting them; LWT's *Manhunt* (wr. Vincent Tilsley, 1970) pitched an English squadron leader among squabbling resistance groups in France and featured Robert Hardy as an Abwehr officer modelled on Sergeant Bleicher; and *Wish Me Luck* (LWT; wr. Lavinia Warner/Jill Hyem, 1988) followed the fortunes of two women agents from training through to the execution of their mission in France in 1942.[28] Thus it is surprising that only two films made during the war – *Secret Mission* and *Tomorrow We Live* – dealt with resistance in France.[29]

Secret Mission confines resistance activity to the margins. Peter Garnett (Hugh Williams), like the character Williams plays in Harold

French's other resistance film, *The Day Will Dawn*, is given the task of locating a major German installation which must be destroyed. This time he is an army officer and he is landed on the French coast with three companions, two of whom have family contacts with French women: Nobby Clark (Michael Wilding) is a Cockney married to a French café-owner; Raoul de Carnet (James Mason) – an officer in the Free French army – is a local landowner whose sister still lives in the family home and runs the estate. The Germans had set up a security zone 25 kilometres deep along the north and west coasts of France which people were not allowed to enter without permission. Thus the sort of secret mission depicted here became virtually impossible. But realism is not really the film's forte.[30] The main dramatic action involves Peter and his fellow officer Red Gowan (Roland Culver) penetrating the German HQ by pretending to be French champagne salesmen (Raoul is disqualified by his inability to speak German), which is funny but totally implausible; and a commando raid on an underground control room.

The most interesting aspect of the film is Michèle, Raoul's sister. In contrast to Jo de Vries in *One of Our Aircraft Is Missing*, she thinks resistance is futile and is bitterly resentful of the RAF. Hearing the sound of British bombers overhead, she complains that they provide cover for the local resistants to carry out their own activities and she rebuts the patriotic stoicism of Violette (Nancy Price), the family's faithful old retainer:

'No! The people are fools. We have signed an armistice with Germany. They make things more difficult for themselves by these stupid acts of sabotage. It isn't worth it. . . . Not even for freedom. I have tried banging my head against a brick wall.'

British bombing of occupied Europe was a controversial issue, particularly in France, where Marshall Pétain's government enjoyed substantial support and attitudes towards Britain were extremely ambivalent. The legacy of bitterness left by the British attack on the French fleet was only gradually overcome, and Anthony Eden temporarily aligned himself with SOE to oppose Eisenhower's plans for the saturation bombing of France and Belgium in preparation for D-Day because of the political damage heavy civilian casualties would cause Anglo-French and Anglo-Belgian relations (Stafford, 1983, p. 159).

Consequently, *Secret Mission* is circumspect in the way that it deals with resistance and collaboration. Michèle, the film's heroine, is played by Carla Lehman, a popular Canadian actress who appears

Secret Mission: Carla Lehman, James Mason and Hugh Williams listen to British bombers overhead. Supplied by BFI Stills, © courtesy of Carlton International.

in several British wartime films. It is difficult to imagine a less French-looking woman (her lack of family resemblance to James Mason's Raoul prompts Peter – who will eventually fall in love with her – to assume she is his wife rather than his sister), and one might assume that the casting of the blonde, Aryan-featured Lehman as the spokesperson of French anti-British views is deliberate. Nevertheless, by the end of the film her contempt for the Boche (Nazis are almost always called 'the Boche' in French and Belgian resistance films) and her growing affection for the cool, civilized English officer win her over and it is she who saves the mission from failure.

Secret Mission might be regarded as representative of the mainstream of resistance films along with *The Day Will Dawn* and Asquith's *Freedom Radio* and *Uncensored*, where there are similar stormy romantic relationships, gentlemanly heroes and thuggish Nazis, and a stress on the need to preserve freedom and democracy.[31] *Freedom Radio, The Day Will Dawn* and *Secret Mission*, along with *Pimpernel Smith* and Harold French's fifth column film *Unpublished Story*, are also linked by the fact that they were co-scripted by the writer Anatole de

Grunwald, who also produced most of Asquith's films from 1943 onwards. De Grunwald also co-scripted *Tomorrow We Live*, but its director, George King, best known for his film versions of Victorian melodramas like *Sweeney Todd, the Demon Barber of Fleet Street* (1935), *Maria Marten, or the Murder in the Red Barn* (1936) and *Crimes at the Dark House* (1940), starring the famous stage villain Tod Slaughter, ensured that it would be a much more extravagant affair.

Tomorrow We Live was made with the co-operation of the Free French and focuses on a resistance group whose symbol, like de Gaulle's, is the cross of Lorraine. Jean-Baptiste (John Clements), a roguish Frenchman whose papers are not in order and who needs to avoid the Germans, is helped by a dress-shop owner, Maria Duchesne (Greta Gynt), and the denizens of a friendly café. He joins the local resistance and they are successful in blowing up an ammunition train. The Germans round up hostages and threaten to shoot them unless the saboteurs give themselves up. Maria and some of the hostages refuse to believe that the Germans will shoot innocent people. Jean-Baptise does believe it: 'They've shot hostages before, people just as innocent, in Paris and Bordeaux, shot like dogs, buried like paupers in a common grave.' Indeed they had. In October 1941, 48 hostages had been shot in reprisal for the killing of two German officers in Nantes and Bordeaux, and an attack on German soldiers in the Rex cinema in Paris in September 1942 led to 116 hostages being shot (Macksey, 1975, p. 88).

The question of reprisals was an important one. Most of the governments-in-exile were reluctant to alienate their compatriots by what Michèle in *Secret Mission* calls 'stupid acts of sabotage'. At least until the tide began to turn at the end of 1942, resistants were by no means universally popular. According to Kenneth Macksey, 'Agents had to survive in an atmosphere of hatred whipped up by the Germans as an anti-partisan measure. Propaganda infiltrated every layer of society, turning friends into enemies and breaking down trust' (Macksey, 1975, p. 115). And Liane Jones, tracing the history of SOE women agents in France, reports that 'Many, many people in France at this time were ill-disposed towards the Resistance – maybe because they were Pétainistes, maybe because they believed the Resistance to be composed of thugs and gangsters' (Jones, 1990, pp. 72–3) – a belief, she adds, assiduously promoted by Vichy and German propaganda.

The desire by the governments-in-exile to cautiously gather intelligence and recruit secret armies ready to strike in support of an invasion often conflicted with the pressure from SOE for industrial and military sabotage and the stirring up of unrest which would tie down German troops. After Germany's attack on Russia, communists throughout Europe began resistance activities and their willingness to involve themselves in sabotage and assassination regardless of reprisals – acting on the Leninist principle that 'the worse it is the better it is for us' – meant that they often proved more effective allies than their non-communist rivals. In France the communist FTP (Francs-Tireurs et Partisans) was the most active resistance group between 1941 and 1944 and received substantial supplies of arms and ammunition from SOE.

Reprisals were a thorny problem to handle in films as well as in real life. In *The Day Will Dawn*, the Germans round up hostages after the RAF attack on the submarine base and threaten to shoot them unless the Englishman they hold responsible for guiding the bombers to their target is surrendered to them. The moral problem is solved when, to save his Norwegian hosts, the Englishman (Hugh Williams) gives himself up and the Germans reveal the depth of their duplicity by deciding to shoot the hostages anyway. *Tomorrow We Live* is bolder in that there are many more hostages and they represent a cross-section of French society. By no means all of them are ready to die, but they are reconciled to their fate by a patriotic speech from their mayor (Godfrey Tearle):

'Listen, my children. There have been hostages before us. Have they saved themselves? If they pleaded for mercy, denounced their compatriots, they could have obtained their freedom. None have done so. And why? Because they knew that at the first murmur, at the first sign of weakness, all the Boche would have to do would be to make a few arrests. They would know that someone would be denounced, they would know that someone would plead for mercy, and they would know that our spirit was broken. The torch of freedom has been passed into out keeping. It is a sacred torch. Let us be sure we pass it on, not quench it now. For in us the spirit of France lives or dies.'

Then, as the indomitable patriot played by Yvonne Arnaud gets everyone to join her in a heartfelt rendering of the 'Marseillaise', they march out proudly to die.

Rules of Resistance

The resistance cycle very quickly developed generic conventions. Some of them – like the escape of the protagonist despite overwhelming obstacles – recur in standard adventure films, but others are more specific to the resistance cycle. Primarily, they concern people not being what they seem. We might guess that the old, shaggy-bearded, accordion-playing beggar in *Tomorrow We Live* will turn out to be a sprightly member of the resistance, and it is only because the Germans are exceptionally stupid that they fail to realize that the comic protagonist of *Schweik's New Adventures* is working against them rather than for them, but other disguises are less obvious. Time after time men and women who appear to be collaborators are in fact exploiting their friendly contacts with the Nazis to further their work with the resistance. This is the central focus of *The Silver Fleet* but it also figures in *Uncensored*, *Undercover* and *The Adventures of Tartu*. In the reality of occupied Europe there were many instances of, for example, French gendarmes turning a blind eye to and even working with resistance groups, but more often collaborators were exactly what they seemed and organizations like the French fascist Milice, with their grass-roots local knowledge, proved extremely dangerous to resistants.[32] In both *Secret Mission* and *Tomorrow We Live*, a once respected member of the community and his daughter (Percy Walsh and Anita Gombault in *Secret Mission*; Godfrey Tearle and Greta Gynt in *Tomorrow We Live*) brave contempt by appearing to collaborate with the Nazis. In *Secret Mission*, Fayolle and his daughter are peripheral characters, though it is their example which encourages Michèle to become actively engaged against the Boche; but in *Tomorrow We Live*, the collaboration disguise is crucial to the development of the plot.

We know from the start that Maria and her father are on the side of the angels and that her relationship with the German commandant is undertaken as a distasteful but patriotic duty. However, Jean-Baptiste is less privy to her real intentions, and when he seems to have been passed over in favour of the German, he retaliates by romancing the waitress from the café (Judy Kelly), who then sells information to the Germans which allows her to buy dresses (from Maria's shop) to make herself more desirable and increase her chances of winning Jean-Baptiste.

This device of the woman who may or may not be a collaborator appears frequently in several films. Maruschka (Valerie Hobson, reprising her role in Powell and Pressburger's *The Spy in Black*), in *The Adventures of Tartu*, flaunts her pro-Nazi credentials before dramatically disclosing her key role in the Czech resistance. Mary Morris in *Pimpernel Smith* and Deborah Kerr in *The Day Will Dawn* reluctantly collaborate with the Nazis to protect their fathers and for a time have to deceive the British agent – Leslie Howard in the former, Hugh Williams in the latter – they secretly love. In *Yellow Canary*,

Anna Neagle plays a Nazi-sympathizing socialite (as Ingrid Bergman would pretend to be in Hitchcock's *Notorious*) before revealing, more than halfway into the film, that she is working for British intelligence.

The generic quality of this group of films is enhanced by the use of particular actors. In several of them the protagonist is an English gentleman: Rex Harrison, Clive Brook, Leslie Howard, Ralph Richardson, Hugh Williams and Robert Donat all bring their own individual inflections but they share the same virtues. Richardson is quirkily eccentric, Brook suave, Williams urbane, Howard, Harrison and Donat boyishly enthusiastic, but they are all unostentatiously courageous, cultured, made angry by injustice and prepared to risk their lives for their beliefs. Aside from the clubbish and more middle-aged Richardson, they all exercise great charm over women. It is only when Donat assumes the identity of a base character – the oily and boastful Tartu – that there is an attempt to give him 'foreign' characteristics. Brook's Dr Roder in *Freedom Radio* and Richardson's Jaap Van Leyden in *The Silver Fleet* could not be more English.

The same might be said for the resistance leaders played by John Clements in *Tomorrow We Live* and *Undercover*. Clements' characters are less bookish and more action orientated; but they are Englishmen first and Frenchmen and Serbian guerrillas a poor second. Indeed, it is easy to make the mistake that Jean-Baptiste's exaggerated Frenchness is the unsubtle disguise of a British agent and that at some stage he will take off his beret, stop singing French ditties and reveal himself as a proper Englishman.[33]

If the underground war against the Nazis was led by reassuringly familiar Englishmen, the villains were rarely terribly threatening either. Eric Portman – a disturbing presence even in such films as *Uncensored, Millions Like Us, One of Our Aircraft Is Missing* and *A Canterbury Tale* where he plays good characters – is a formidable adversary in *49th Parallel*, as is Godfrey Tearle in *Undercover*, where he reverts to the smiling villainous role he played in Hitchcock's *The 39 Steps* (1935). But Nazis usually consisted of hateful young thugs played by Griffith Jones (*The Day Will Dawn*) and Marius Goring (*Pastor Hall* and *The Night Invader*); gleeful sadists such as Hugh Sinclair (*Tomorrow We Live*); sneering cynics played by Raymond Huntley (*Night Train to Munich, Freedom Radio* and *Pimpernel Smith*); and blustering bullies played by Francis L. Sullivan (*Pimpernel Smith* and *The Day Will Dawn*) or Raymond Lovell (*Uncensored*).

Women in resistance films tend to be heroic. Some are innocent victims of Nazi viciousness – Lina Barrie in *Pastor Hall*, Joyce Howard in *Freedom Radio*, Glynis Johns in *The Adventures of Tartu* – but larger roles are granted women who are passionate and brave and stead-fastly oppose the Nazis. This type of heroine is epitomized by Mary Morris in *Pimpernel Smith* and *Undercover* and Deborah Kerr in *The Day Will Dawn*, while Pamela Brown and Googie Withers in *One of Our Aircraft Is Missing* offer a more austere counterpart. Older women, such as Nancy Price in *Secret Mission* and Yvonne Arnaud in *Tomorrow We Live* and the impressively gaunt Phyllis Morris in *The Adventures of Tartu*, are generally trustworthy and ready to die for their country. Judy Kelly in *Tomorrow We Live* offers a rare example of a traitorous woman, but even here there are mitigating circumstances and she is allowed to redeem herself through death. More usually, the heroine – Maria in *Tomorrow We Live*, Maruschka in *The Adventures of Tartu* – appears to be susceptible to the Nazis but is using this as a front to pursue anti-Nazi activities (Jo de Vries does so too, in *One of Our Aircraft Is Missing*, but we and the good characters are complicit with her deception throughout).

In *One of Our Aircraft Is Missing*, *Tomorrow We Live* and *The Adventures of Tartu*, women are more than helpful sidekicks or noble victims; they use a combination of intelligence, steadfastness and duplicity to lead a double life carrying out difficult and dangerous work. Though this might be thought to have as much to do with the requirements of melodramatic action as it has to reality, it was prescient of the real contribution women played in the European resistance movements. Of the 400 F-section agents SOE sent into France, 39 were women (another eleven went as R/F agents). They were sent as couriers and wireless operators rather than as organizers, but the risks, the hard-ships and the endurance required of them were equal to those of the men.

Else Meertens and Jo de Vries in *One of Our Aircraft Is Missing* are entirely plausible as representatives of the sort of women running escape lines throughout Europe. The double game played by Maruschka in *The Adventures of Tartu* faintly reflects the turbulent career of Mathilde Carré, an R/F agent turned by the Abwehr's Sergeant Bleicher (who became her lover) but persuaded to return to her original loyalties by her fellow SOE agent Pierre de Vomécourt. The Pimpernel-like Maria Duchesne in *Tomorrow We Live* is more obviously a fantasy figure, but her secret leadership of a resistance group might be seen as a melodramatic variation on the role played by the English SOE agent Pearl Witherington. When her organizer, Maurice Southgate, was caught by the Gestapo in May 1944, she took over a large section of the circuit around the Massif Central and overcame the problem of Frenchmen not wanting to take orders from a woman (women did not even have the vote in France until after the war) by finding a 'complaisant local colonel to mouth the orders she composed' (Foot, 1966, p. 381).

The sort of dangerous activity undertaken by women recruited to SOE was considered remarkable even in Britain, where women were mobilized for action more radically than anywhere else, and in the two films made about such women in the 1950s – *Odette* and *Carve Her Name with Pride* – there is an emphasis on the burden such work places on their heroines by tearing them away from a peaceful and happy domestic life and their role as mothers. Such a stress, however, doesn't prevent them from showing the grim fate that awaited women once they were captured, and both films are at their most impressive in showing their heroines' resilience under the burden of torture and deprivation.

In retrospect, what is so remarkable about the resistance films made during the war is how upbeat and ungloomy they are. In *Secret Mission*, Raoul is shot and Michèle blames the Englishmen, but she soon comes to her senses and helps them to escape. In *Tomorrow We Live*, a hundred hostages are rounded up and shot, the resistance base is discovered and its key members killed in the resulting shoot-out, and it is only in the confusion caused by a British bombing raid that Jean-Baptiste and Maria make good their escape to England. But the fact that everyone – and it is almost literally everyone – goes to their death willingly, even gladly, makes it all seem noble and worthwhile. The treachery, pain, danger, anguish, torn loyalty, isolation and brutality involved in resistance to the Nazis – which would be explored in later films – was glimpsed only fleetingly in the wartime resistance cycle. Ironically, the legacy of these films was a set of myths and stereotypes which would be exploited for comic effect in such films as Roy Boulting's *Soft Beds, Hard Battles* and in the television series *'Allo, 'Allo!*[34]

The entry of the Americans into the war at the end of 1941 had a fundamental effect on military strategy. Even before the attack on Pearl Harbor the Americans had pointed out that 'it should be recognised as an almost invariable rule that wars cannot finally be won without the use of land armies. Such land armies would have to be as large as the enemy's' (quoted in Stafford, 1983, p. 80). By June 1944 an Allied army had assembled in Britain which was strong enough to engage the Germans in conventional warfare. Partisan activity did contribute significantly to the success of the invasion, but the build-up of American troops in Britain from mid-1942 onwards led to a diversion of the popular imagination away from resistance activities to the forthcoming invasion and the interesting complexities of Anglo-American relations, explored in such films as *A Canterbury*

Tale, I Live in Grosvenor Square, The Way to the Stars, Great Day and *Journey Together*.[35]

Post-War Resistance Films

After the war, resistance was re-examined along with most other aspects of the war. Some large-scale adventure films – *The Guns of Navarone, Operation Crossbow, The Heroes of Telemark, Force Ten from Navarone* – focus upon daring commando raids that rely in varying measures on assistance from the local resistance. However, the real appendage to the resistance cycle is a group of films that deal directly with the activities of SOE agents – *Against the Wind, Odette, Carve Her Name with Pride* – and two films – *Orders to Kill* and *Circle of Deception* (discussed in Chapter 7) – which examine the difficult ethical decisions posed by resistance activity. All of these films benefit from being able to draw upon Teddy Baird's dramatized documentary *Now It Can Be Told*, which shows with meticulous realism the recruitment and training of a Frenchwoman and an English officer (Jacqueline Nearne and Harry Rée – both of whom were real F-section agents). They are dropped into the Vendée region of France where they establish a resistance network, arrange arms drops, carry out acts of sabotage, survive the depredations of the Gestapo and arrange the escape of the crew of a Lancaster bomber. James Chapman complains that 'the film as a whole lacks the human and dramatic interest of the Crown features and for once the performances of the non-professional actors are unconvincing' (Chapman, 1998b, p. 158). He has a point. Rée and Nearne are no Mulder and Scully. Quirky bits of realism – Nearne's reluctance to wear the 'awful cloche hat' allotted to her as part of her new persona and her inability to employ Mata Hari techniques ('I tried sex appeal – it was a complete flop'); Rée's 'ridiculous thought' that he could run his Austin 7 for three years on the petrol the plane flying him into France is using – fail to cohere into a dramatic pattern, and despite the exciting subject matter the film lacks dramatic tension. On the other hand, the film is an invaluable mine of factual information and Baird's reluctance to rely on fictional devices gives it a clumsy authenticity, which makes it a useful yardstick against which more commercial accounts of SOE activity might be judged.

Against the Wind, directed by Charles Crichton and scripted by T. E. B. Clarke and Michael Pertwee, is Ealing's only war film between *The Captive Heart* in 1946 and *The Cruel Sea* in 1953, and little attention has been shown it. Like Powell and Pressburger's *The Small*

Wartime reversals: Michèle (Simone Signoret) amused by Johnny (Gordon Jackson), who makes the old-fashioned assumption that men are stronger than and superior to women in *Against the Wind*. Supplied by BFI Stills, © courtesy of Chanel + Image.

Back Room, it suffered from bad timing. Audiences in 1948 were not quite ready to revisit the war and the downbeat tone of these two films did not encourage commercial success. In retrospect, however, freed from the burden of not doing anything which might undermine morale and untouched by the nostalgia and myth-making of later films, those few war films made during the 1945 to 1950 period now seem to achieve a level of truth other war films only rarely reach.

In the film, Father Phillip Eliot (Robert Beatty), a Canadian Catholic priest brought up in Belgium, is recruited to what is to all intents and purposes the Belgian section of SOE – based in back rooms of the Natural History Museum in South Kensington, London. He is trained and dropped into Belgium where, with the connivance of the bishop, he sets up as a parish priest and uses his church as a base from which to organize the rescue of a leading resistant who has been caught blowing up the local records office. The other members of his team consist of three Belgians (played by Simone Signoret, Paul Dupuis and John Slater), a Scotsman (Gordon Jackson) and an older man, Max Cronk, with a Belgian mother and a German-American father. Cronk is played by Jack Warner, the epitome of Cockney good humour, and here again he is jolly and kindly – a sort of father figure to the group. But in an odd little scene with an Irish girl who contemptuously brushes aside his sexual advances ('kissing and treason are bad mixing'), it is casually revealed that he is a traitor. His meeting has been observed but initially it is taken for a sexual pick-up, and by the time the girl's IRA links have been discovered, Cronk is in France.

Treachery is a key theme running through the film. Simone Signoret's character, Michèle, is embittered because her former lover has turned traitor. Andrew (Peter Illing), the resistance leader, tells Father Phillip the war has produced strange bedfellows: 'It's often the way: a good friend becomes a collaborator, the man you despised dies for you.' Later, he lectures the group on the need to disown one's colleagues if they are arrested rather than endanger one's own safety. 'There is no sentiment in our job, so beware of it. Duty always first and friendship a bad second. Once you start mixing duty and affection you start digging graves, your own and others'.' Michèle has obviously learnt her lessons well. Setting up her transmitter/receiver in a farmhouse while Cronk shaves at a sink in the corner, they chat together (in an earlier scene he has comforted her when she is drunk and distressed). She establishes contact with London, registers the knowledge that Cronk is a traitor, cautiously takes out a gun, calls to him so that he faces her and shoots him dead. There is no catharsis. Our balance of sympathies have turned against Cronk but not to the extent that we enjoy seeing him shot in cold blood.

This bleak moment is matched later in the film by a glimpse of optimism. Gordon Jackson's Johnny, a young explosives expert, is in love with Michèle. He has conservative views about the place of women being in the home, not in uniform, and is continually wrong-footed by Michèle's assurance and competence. When he threatens to object to the Section Officer about her going on the mission, she points out that, as he is in love with her and she is not in love with him, it is more likely he will be the one ordered not to go. In Belgium he develops toothache and has to go to the dentist. He comes out dazed from the anaesthetic and steps in front of a German staff car. When he is questioned his inability to speak French is revealed and he is arrested. Michèle, waiting a few yards away, heeds Andrew's advice and doesn't attempt to rescue him. At police headquarters, Jacques (Paul Dupuis) who – at the cost of alienating his sweetheart who now regards him as a traitor – has passed himself off as a collaborator, engineers Johnny's escape, but sacrifices his own life to do so. Johnny is understandably depressed and demoralized but is revitalized by Michèle's expression of love for him. It is a delicate moment, for she could be merely showing pity. But Signoret's performance is such that both Johnny and the audience recognize that her relief at seeing him alive – even at the cost of her compatriot's death – indicates she really has come to love him. The subsequent successful mission and the uniting of Johnny and Michèle create an optimistic strand, but this is a far more harrowing film than the resistance films made during the war.

Odette and *Carve Her Name with Pride* were both based on the experiences of SOE F-section agents. Liane Jones explains: 'In the 1940s, with the British government using the preservation of family life, wifely and motherly duties as tools of propaganda, it simply wasn't imaginable that the same government was sending women on armed missions behind enemy lines' (Jones, 1990, p. 30). When it was revealed that this was what had happened, it aroused considerable curiosity and Herbert Wilcox, a pedestrian director but an outstanding showman, was quick to realize its commercial potential. Wilcox's wife, Anna Neagle, was Britain's top box-office star by the late 1940s. She and Wilcox had returned from Hollywood in 1941 and made a topical biography of Amy Johnson, *They Flew Alone*, an effective spy thriller, *Yellow Canary*, two wartime melodramas, *Piccadilly Incident* and *I Live in Grosvenor Square*, and a string of similarly titled but much lighter films, *The Courtneys of Curzon Street* (1947), *Spring in Park Lane* (1948) and *Maytime in Mayfair* (1949). With *Odette*, however, they reverted to the sober and respectful tone of their 1930s films, *Victoria the Great* (1935) and *Sixty Glorious Years* (1936). The film is an open celebration of the achievements of SOE – with a valedictory introduction from the head of F section, Maurice Buckmaster – but the story is too chilling to be considered in any way triumphalist.

Odette Sansom, a 30-year-old Frenchwoman married to an Englishman and with three young daughters, was recruited by SOE in 1941. She was trained and sent to France in a felucca, landing at Cassis, to the east of Marseilles, on Halloween night 1942. Her mission was to travel north and establish her own circuit in the Auxerre region, but her contact in Cannes, Peter Churchill, was in desperate need of a courier for his own circuit, and given the increased danger in the area after the German occupation of Vichy France (which happened ten days after she landed) she agreed to stay with him. When their circuit was penetrated by the Abwehr, Churchill, Sansom and their radio operator Adolphe (diplomatically changed to Adam or Alex in some accounts) Rabinovitch escaped to St Joriot on the shore of Lake Annecy in the Haute Savoie, where they established links with a vigorous local resistance group. Unfortunately, they were traced by the double agent Roger Bardet who introduced his controller Sergeant Bleicher of the Abwehr as 'Colonel Henri', a dissident officer who wanted to be put in touch with SOE to discuss possible means of undermining Hitler. This was by no means implausible, but Odette distrusted both Bardet and 'Henri'. She (and Rabinovitch) managed to steer a new organizer, Francis Caemmerts, away from Bardet, but she and Churchill (who had just returned from England) were arrested.[36]

With extraordinary tenacity she managed to convince the Abwehr, and even the Sicherheitsdienst (SD) when they got their clutches on her, that she and Churchill were married (they did marry after the war) and that he was the nephew of Winston Churchill and a feckless playboy whom she had coerced into espionage. This succeeded in keeping them both from being shot, though she was imprisoned at Ravensbrück, kept in solitary confinement and subjected to extremes of heat and cold, light and dark, and had to listen to her fellow agents being shot outside her cell. When the Allies were a few miles from the camp, its commandant, Fritz Suhren, drove her to an American base and presented her as the niece of Winston Churchill, 'in the vain hope', as Foot puts it, 'that it would save his neck' (Foot, 1966, p. 430).

In the film (three times) and in real life Odette Sansom protests that 'she is just an ordinary woman' but this is misleading modesty. Her SOE training report described her as 'excitable and temperamental', and reached the conclusion that she 'has not quite the clarity of mind which is desirable in subversive activity' (quoted in Jones,

1990, p. 82). Nevertheless, she impressed Buckmaster sufficiently for him to send her out as an organizer and Peter Churchill thought enough of her abilities to persuade her and Buckmaster that she should stay and work with him. Anna Neagle – as histrionic an actor as Laurence Olivier – plays her with great zest and conviction, impressively displaying Odette's transition from middle-class house-wife to excited and inexperienced agent to confident resistance organizer to haggard concentration camp survivor. The melodramatic impact of Odette's story is such that Wilcox and his scriptwriter Warren Chetham-Strode are content to follow its lines with only minor fictionalizations.[37] Her mission to Marseilles was to deliver a suitcase full of money, not the plans of Marseilles harbour; the deserted aerodrome from which Churchill is picked up for his report back to London turned out not to be deserted at all and nearly led to disaster; the Paris headquarters of the SD in the Avenue Foch becomes the headquarters of the Gestapo; and 'Colonel Henri', as depicted by Marius Goring, becomes a sinisterly romantic figure who utters such lines as 'I hate war, it interrupts my music' and 'what a pity Herr Hitler doesn't like Mendelssohn', as he plays the music of the forbidden Jewish composer on a grand piano.

Kenneth Macksey complains that in *Odette* 'Emphasis was placed on the courage, the horror and the pity, but so mingled as to obscure the socially destructive significance of the partisan war, with its fundamental undermining of civilisation.' He concludes that 'Partisan warfare had been etched indelibly into an image of respectability which transcended the environment of degradation in which the guerrilla frequently existed' (Macksey, 1975, pp. 253–4). This sort of sanitization is a criticism that can be levelled at most war films.[38] Wilcox does an excellent job in shaping the events of Odette's experiences as an agent into a moving and exciting story, but there is no place for the sort of incident Odette Sansom recounts to Liane Jones (1990) of a long, boring, cold, uncomfortable and dangerous journey ending with her contact not turning up and a fruitless return. The demands of dramatic entertainment inevitably change Odette's role from that of a small and relatively unimportant cog into a heroine of the war and use the war as a backcloth for a melodrama about a woman suffering and surviving.

Carve Her Name with Pride is a more anaemic and sentimental film, though the fact that its heroine was shot by the Nazis meant there could be no happy ending. Violette Szabo was an atypical SOE agent in that she was a lower-middle-class girl from Brixton whose previous job had been in the Bon Marché department store in Brixton High Street. Her mother was French, her father English, and she had married an officer in the French Foreign Legion who was killed at El Alamein in October 1942. Despite having a young daughter, she was fiercely determined to work undercover in France. After training, she was dropped with an experienced SOE organizer, Philip Liéwer, to work with the Salesman *réseau* around Rouen. Unfortunately, the resistance in Rouen had been smashed by the Gestapo and there were posters up offering a reward for Liéwer's capture. A few days later the pair returned to England. Her next mission – again with Liéwer – was to be dropped into the Limoges area two days after D-Day. Attempting to warn local resistance groups of advancing German reinforcements, she and a *maquis* leader ran into an advance party of SS troops. They made a run for it but she twisted her ankle and fell, and though Violette's covering fire allowed the *maquis* leader to escape, she was wounded and captured. After interrogation by the SD at the Avenue Foch she was sent to Ravensbrück and, as the Allies advanced in the spring of 1945, taken out and shot along with two other SOE agents, Denise Bloch and Lilian Rolfe.

This rather thin narrative has much less dramatic potential than Odette's story and the tone of the film might have been set by a remark made by Liéwer (renamed Fraser in the film and played by Paul Scofield):

> 'All those months of training, blood and sweat and tears, building up, you think, to a tremendously exciting climax. And suddenly here you are in the middle of the night with your little suitcase, trotting off in a tiny, unarmed aircraft to fight the German Army all by yourself. Crazy, isn't it?'

Instead, Lewis Gilbert, a director not noted for his subtleness, takes the easy path of padding out the story with sentiment, devoting the first half-hour of the film to the courtship of Violette and her future husband, Etienne Szabo; showing Violette and her fellow female agents getting up to jolly japes on the SOE training course; and stressing the importance of Violette's relationship with her father and baby daughter. Whereas Wilcox's embellishments are unobtrusively plausible, Gilbert's strain credibility. Arriving in Rouen, a smoking ruin after British bombing raids, Violette nevertheless manages to rally the surviving members of the resistance to destroy a viaduct as an ammunition train is crossing it. On her second mission, pursued by a platoon of elite SS troops, she manages to shoot down at least half a dozen of them before she is overpowered.[39] These flaws, however, have to be balanced against the fine performances Gilbert draws from his actors, particularly from Virginia McKenna as Violette.

In his biography of Hugh Dalton, Ben Pimlott characterizes SOE women as 'plucky, outdoor types who enhanced the male camaraderie' (Pimlott, 1985, p. 301). This is a misleading simplification. Virginia Hall, a tall, red-haired American woman with a wooden leg; Noor Imayat Khan, described by a fellow agent as 'a splendid vague dreamy creature, far too conspicuous – twice seen never forgotten'; the Amazonian Nancy Wake who, according to Liane Jones, 'was strapping, voluptuous' and 'radiated sexuality'; Violette Szabo, 'really beautiful, dark-haired and olive-skinned, with that kind of porcelain clarity of face and purity of bone that one finds occasionally in the women of the South West of France', all contradict Pimlott's stereotype (Foot, 1966, p. 337; Jones, 1990, pp. 250, 246). And the training reports that Foot and Jones quote from show that, for the SOE instructors at least, dismayingly few of the other SOE women conform to it either.[40] It does, however, fit Virginia McKenna's version of Violette Szabo perfectly. Hers is a much more naturalistic performance than that of Anna Neagle – she really does seem a fairly ordinary woman, a suburban south London girl, shy but decisive, tomboyishly boisterous with her brother and devoted to her father (Jack Warner, reverting to type as a solidly good-hearted lower-middle-class dad). The first 40 minutes of the film, set in England and largely shot outside the studio, gives little impression of London at war and the ethos of the film seems indelibly of the 1950s. It is the juxtaposition of this primly English girl – she still appears virginal even after marriage and a baby – with the horrors of the war that gives the film its power and effectiveness. Her death at the end seems unfair and unsatisfactory and it is only partially compensated for by the sugary coda in which her daughter – now finally old enough to wear the dress her mother bought her in Paris – goes to Buckingham Palace to receive her mother's posthumous George Cross. The contradiction between the need for a satisfactory resolution of the narrative and the need to be faithful to the facts creates a tension that makes the film genuinely disturbing.

Part of the commercial appeal of *Odette* and *Carve Her Name with Pride* comes from their showing true stories of women doing things which contradict the roles to which wartime society – and even more so 1950s society – confined them. David Hare's play *Plenty*, filmed by Fred Schepisi in 1985, is structured around the inability of its heroine, Susan Traherne (Kate Nelligan in the play; Meryl Streep in the film), to adjust to peacetime society after the excitement of life as an SOE agent in France during the war. In fact, women seem to have had less trouble adjusting than men. The pressure to go back and live normal lives with husbands and children after their exceptional experiences might have been more beneficial than the pressure on men to live up to the high points of wartime excitement. Some women were able to capitalize on the organizing abilities they had displayed during the war – Pearl Witherington pursued a successful career as a banker in France; Odette Churchill, Nancy Wake and Yvonne Cormeau used their experiences to good effect as advisers on films and television series about SOE activities; many simply re-adjusted to civilian life – but they had broken the mould of women as either helpless victims or Mata Hari-like spies.

NOTES

1 Adrien Dansette, *Histoire de la Libération de Paris*, quoted by Foot (1966), p. 198.
2 The dramatic crash-landing of Rudolf Hess in Scotland in May 1941 with proposals for peace were not afforded serious consideration. When Hitler invaded Russia the following month there was relief that the fight against Germany would no longer have to be borne by the British Empire alone, but it was not seen as an opportunity for withdrawing from the war. A conspiracy to restore the Duke of Windsor to the throne and negotiate a deal with Hitler forms the plot of John Mair's *Never Come Back*, stylishly adapted by David Pirie and directed by Ben Bolt for BBC Television in 1989.
3 See Foot (1966), pp. 7–39, for the establishment and organization of SOE.
4 Wood continued to serve in the government, as Chancellor of the Exchequer, until his death in 1943; Chamberlain stayed on as Lord President until his death in 1941.
5 Ben Pimlott points out that the accusation that SOE was made up of 'crackpots, communists and homosexuals' could more justly be levelled at the SIS; Pimlott (1985), p. 301.
6 Quoted by Stafford (1983), p. 5, from Liddell Hart's *Defence of the West* (1950).
7 Charles Cruikshank's *SOE in the Far East* was published in 1983, his *SOE in Scandinavia* followed in 1986, both for OUP. The official history of SOE remains incomplete, though Davidson (1980) and Maclean (1949) offer authentic accounts of British involvement with the partisans of Yugo-slavia. In January–February 2000, Channel 4 broadcast a three-part series on SOE, *Churchill's Secret Army*, fronted by Sebastian Faulks, author of the novel *Charlotte Gray*, which centres around a woman being recruited as an SOE agent and sent to France. In September 2000 BBC1 broadcast a similar four-part series, *Secret Agent*.
8 SOE was divided into SO1, which was concerned with black propaganda and absorbed into the Political Warfare Executive in September 1941; and SO2, which was concerned with sabotage and the setting up of secret armies of resistance.

9 The Abwehr dangled the tantalizing carrot of German Army hostility to Hitler in front of SOE noses, most successfully in the form of Sergeant Bleicher's 'Colonel Henri', who ensnared Henri Frager and – despite her suspicions – Odette Sansom. SIS had been more carelessly gullible at the beginning of the war over the Venlo Incident. See Marshall (1988), p. 34, and below p. 92.

10 See Macksey (1975), p. 57, for Polish resistants who discovered that they had parachuted into Germany.

11 The Gestapo was a branch of the Sicherheitspolizei – the security police – but they too were part of Himmler's SS and often overlapped with the Sicherheitsdienst (SD) and tended to be lumped together by resistants, just as the Germans saw SOE and SIS as parts of the same 'British Intelligence' organization. The SD became increasingly powerful, eventually eclipsing the Abwehr, whose leader, Admiral Canaris, was implicated in the plot to assassinate Hitler and executed in April 1945.

12 Early in 1944 'SIS was circulating a report that fewer than 2000 French guerrillas could be expected to work together in conjunction with an invasion' (Stafford, 1983, p. 150). In fact, SOE agents who had forged successful links with the *maquis*, like Francis Caemmerts, George Wood and Pearl Witherington, each controlled bands of over 1000 men which provided effective support for the invading armies. Robert Marshall presents a convincing case that Jacques Derricourt, SOE's most important 'traffic controller' arranging flights in and out of France, was a double agent controlled by Sir Claude Dansey, Deputy Head of MI6, who instructed him to betray information about SOE activities to maintain his cover with Karl Boemelburg, head of the Paris SD. See Marshall (1988), *passim*.

13 'The other side of the Atlantic', *Documentary News Letter*, September 1940, p. 4.

14 Louis MacNeice, *Spectator*, 31 January 1941 (BFI microfiche, *Freedom Radio*).

15 McLaine (1979), p. 141, quoting from *Hitler and the Working Man*, October 1939.

16 One might also include the two short films made by Alfred Hitchcock in French in 1944 – *Aventure Malgache* and *Bon Voyage* – and Humphrey Jennings' *The Silent Village* (1943), a moving and grimly convincing re-creation of the fate of Lidice in a Welsh mining village, Cwmgiedd. The mood and style of Jennings' film reappears in Kevin Brownlow and Andrew Mollo's *It Happened Here* (1964). Such films as *This Was Paris*, *Lisbon Story* and *Candlelight in Algeria* are closely associated with this cycle, but concentrate more on the exploits of British agents than on resistance movements.

17 For the Vemork raid in February 1943 and an earlier attempt by British glider-borne commandos, see Macksey (1975), p. 108.

18 Two further resistance films followed after the war, *Against the Wind*, set in Belgium, and *But Not in Vain*, set in Holland. They both make much of the dangers of betrayal.

19 Macksey is scrupulously fair, but as an ex-tank commander, he is dubious

120

about the merits or the effectiveness of the sort of warfare propagated by SOE. Foot's experience in counter-espionage enables him to point out that 'wireless reception from the field was often so bad, or so badly jammed, or the operators' morse so unsteady, that not even an expert decoder could always tell which of the myriad mistakes were intended and which were accidental' (Foot, 1966, p. 107). Liane Jones (1990), p. 246, prints an example (warning that the Rouen resistance group which Violette Szabo was to have joined had been smashed) of a mistake-ridden radio message. Marks (1998) offers a detailed insight into the world of codes and decoders.

20 Maurice Southgate, who organized the highly successful Stationer network in France, joined SOE after he was passed over as too old at 30 for active service in the RAF. Sir George's real-life model, Sir Arnold Wilson, however, did serve with the RAF as a rear gunner and was shot down over Holland.

21 *In Which We Serve*, like *One of Our Aircraft Is Missing*, was shot at Denham and used many of the same crew, including editor David Lean, art director David Rawnsley and cinematographer Ronald Neame.

22 Davidson (1980), pp. 102–36, provides a useful account of the internecine war within SOE between rival supporters of Mihailović's Chetniks and Tito's partisans. Maclean (1949) describes in fascinating detail his experiences of the war in Yugoslavia fighting alongside Tito's partisans.

23 The only other notable Greek to appear during the war is Edward Chapman's sweaty but good-hearted air ferry manager who is beaten to death by a Nazi while proclaiming 'Greece will always be free' in *Ships with Wings*. Beddington had suggested to the Ideas Committee that the MoI would support a film dealing with 'true stories of Greek heroism in Crete and Greece' in May 1942, but he doesn't seem to have had any takers (Chapman, 1998b, p. 266, n. 69). In the 1961 epic *The Guns of Navarone*, the Greek resistance is represented by Gia Scala (who has turned traitress because she cannot bear pain) and Irene Papas (who is very tough and shoots her when the men prove reluctant to do it themselves).

24 The Poles had established such a high reputation for bravery and resilience that it was impossible to abandon them entirely. According to Stafford, between April and July 1944 there were 174 successful sorties to Poland; 114 men were dropped and 219 tons of supplies (Stafford, 1983, p. 184).

25 Andrzej Wajda's film trilogy *Generation* (1954), *Kanal* (1956) and *Ashes and Diamonds* (1958) deals convincingly with anti-Nazi resistance in Poland.

26 Harold S. Bucquet is best known for the string of Dr Kildare films he made for MGM in the 1930s. *To Be or Not to Be*, which is set in Warsaw during the German invasion of Poland, was produced in Hollywood by Alexander Korda.

27 A shorter version of the film, retitled *School for Danger*, was released commercially.

28 F-section agent Yvonne Cormeau acted as adviser on *Wish Me Luck*. The writers Lavinia Warner and Jill Hyem were also responsible for *Tenko* (1981–4), a television series about women in a Japanese prison camp.

29 *The Man from Morocco*, although not really a resistance film, is interesting in its depiction of International Brigade veterans of the Spanish Civil War and their shabby treatment by the Vichy government.

30 According to Macksey (1975, p. 178), 'Penetration by agents of vital target areas – such as the U-boat bases, Atlantic Wall fortifications, the newly built rocket weapon sites aligned against England and, indeed, the entire coastal belt – was almost impossible due to the density of German troops and the watchfulness of their guards.'

31 French followed Asquith's *French without Tears* (1939) with *English without Tears* (1944) and Asquith's *Quiet Wedding* (1941) with *Quiet Weekend* (1946).

32 Faulks (1998), in a novel which focuses around the recruitment and mission of an SOE agent in France, devotes considerable attention to the Milice.

33 There is a nice parallel in an episode of *'Allo, 'Allo* in which René (Gorden Kaye), annoyed at having two English airmen disguised as nuns (but with their RAF moustaches intact) dumped on him, tells Michèle (Kirsten Cooke), the resistance leader, to speak to them in their own lingo and she switches from French-accented English to upper-class Oxbridge English.

34 The parallels between *Tomorrow We Live* and *'Allo, 'Allo* are so close one suspects that the film provided the sitcom's writers, Jeremy Lloyd and David Croft – consciously or unconsciously – with a model, though there are also parallels between *'Allo, 'Allo* and *Secret Army* (Gerrard Glaister/ John Brason, BBC 1979–81), where Bernard Hepton organized resistance in Belgium from a black-market café. There were plenty of real-life absurdities to draw upon too. Foot cites, for example, a scene in a Toulouse café favoured by the Gestapo: 'two men in blue battledress came in from the street and walked up to the cashier; one said with a loud and strong English accent "Nous – officers RAF – pouvez-vous aider?"' (Foot, 1966, p. 98).

35 Foot (1966) and Stafford (1983) credit resistance groups with a considerable contribution to the Allied invasion of Europe. Macksey (1975) is much more sceptical.

36 Confusingly, Cammaert's code name was 'Roger' and this is what he is called in the film; Roger Bardet is known as Jules in the film.

37 According to Liane Jones (1990), p. 342, Odette told her biographer Jerrard Tickell: 'If you are fond of me as you say, don't let the film be done by the Americans. They will make it a Hollywood story and my story is a Hollywood story enough.'

38 Compare, for example, the opening sequence of *Saving Private Ryan*, terrifying though it is, with Foot's grim tale of the British sappers who landed on the beaches before the main invading force: 'Three battalions of British sappers had to go ashore at low tide with the first light of early dawn, and make safe the mine-laden obstacles strewn on the beaches.

Three quarters of them were shot down at their work; but they did it' (Foot, 1966, p. 348).

39 In fairness, one should add that nobody survived to make an accurate tally and Foot reports that Violette Szabo was 'one of the best shots and the fieriest characters in SOE' (Foot, 1966, p. 382).

40 Women recruited to SOE were made members of the Women's Transport Service – known as the FANYs (First Aid Nursing Yeomanry) – which, ironically, was thought of as the easiest and most glamorous of the women's service units.

5

Visions of Britain: Cinema, War and Realism

If you spend thousands of hours of a man's leisure time training him to expect human action to be dressed up and made all of a climax so that he shall live in a progressive state of pleasing tension, that is what will happen. They will laugh at the real thing. They will grow tense and hushed only at the artificial. . . . The conventions of melodrama have predisposed our twenty-five million cinema addicts to anticipate well-groomed artificial faces, dramatically timed gestures and action, the finesse of the well-paid artist. (Roger Manvell, 'They laugh at realism')[1]

Realism and Film

Realism as the dominant critical theory for the study of film seemed to grow out of the war, banishing Impressionist, Expressionist and Surrealist experiments and the montage theories of Pudovkin and Eisenstein to the sidelines. Immediately after the war, the French film critic André Bazin celebrated the use of deep-focus photography and long takes in the films of Orson Welles and William Wyler as an alternative to montage, and the use of real locations, non-actors and stories of everyday life in the films of Roberto Rossellini, Vittorio De Sica and Luchino Visconti, as indications of a new cinema which would reflect the very different priorities of a democratic post-war world. Bazin overestimated the commitment of Welles and Wyler to the realist cause. But left-wing American film-makers – such as Jules Dassin, Elia Kazan, Edward Dmytryk, Joseph Losey and Abraham Polonsky – fostered a cinema of socially concerned realism in such films as *The Naked City* and *Thieves' Highway* (Dassin, 1948; 1949), *Boomerang* and *Panic in the Streets* (Kazan, 1947; 1950), *The Prowler* (Losey, 1950) and *Force of Evil* (Polonsky, 1948) – at least until it was snuffed out by the House of Representatives Un-American Activities Committee.

Britain could be seen as something of a pioneer in so far as realism was concerned. When John Grierson capitalized on the success of his film *Drifters* in 1929 by persuading the Empire Marketing Board to let him set up a film unit, he had clear ideas about the way film could be used to improve society. He was later to insist that the documentary movement 'began not so much in affection for film *per se* as in affection for national education', and that its origins 'lay in sociological rather than aesthetic aims' ('The course of realism', in Hardy, 1979, p. 78). From Grierson's point of view the aesthetic achievements of the documentary movement were an almost irrelevant by-product:

> What confuses the history is that we had always the good sense to use the aesthetes. We did so because we liked them and because we needed them. It was, paradoxically, with the first-rate aesthetic help of people like Flaherty and Cavalcanti – our 'fellow travellers' so to speak – that we mastered the techniques necessary for our quite unaesthetic purpose. . . . We were reformers open and avowed: concerned – to use the old jargon – with 'bringing alive the new materials of citizenship', 'crystallising sentiments' and creating those 'new loyalties from which a progressive civic will might derive'. ('The Documentary Ideal: 1942', in Hardy, 1979, pp. 112–13)

This might seem very different from Bazin's Catholic phenomenology with its search for a realist essence of film; but despite their different philosophical groundings, Bazin and Grierson shared a common belief in the vital role film could play in building a democratic new society, and Grierson's undogmatic attitude towards aesthetics allowed his followers a degree of flexibility.[2] Grierson himself had been very influenced by the montage theories of Eisenstein and Pudovkin, and *Drifters* shared a programme with Eisenstein's *Battleship Potemkin* (1925) at the Film Society in London in 1929. Thus, he was happy to see Cavalcanti introduce modernist experimentation into such GPO films as *Coal Face* (1935), *Pett and Pott* (1934) and *Night Mail* (1936).

The intellectuals of the documentary movement had little time for the commercial industry, and the hostility and lack of respect were mutual. The slightest hint of intellectual sophistication was sniffed at suspiciously by the film trade unless – as with Hitchcock – it was wrapped so tightly in showmanship that they did not realize it was there. All this was changed by the war. After the initial hiccups, documentary became fashionable and the documentarists eagerly seized their opportunities both as film-makers and as critics. The fusion of documentary and feature film techniques was celebrated as the foundation of a new, progressive and genuinely British school of cinema. Dilys Powell, in her influential pamphlet *Films since 1939*, writes about 'the interchange that took place between commercial and documentary fields' epitomized by the commercial director David Macdonald working with Cavalcanti on a documentary, *Men of the Lightship* (1940); of *Target for Tonight* as the first of a new genre in cinema: 'a fact, a fragment of actual life which still held the emotional tremor of fiction'; of 'the movement towards documentary truth in the entertainment film' hinted at in *The Proud Valley* and *Convoy* and fully realized in *In Which We Serve*; of the 'mingling of documentary technique and native character' which marked such films as *Nine Men*, *The First of the Few* and *The Gentle Sex* (Powell, 1947, pp. 13, 14, 22, 26, 29).

During the war, the two main elements attributed to documentary appear to have been an attachment to realist methods and a socially progressive outlook, but the way in which they were mixed up resulted in very different compounds. Such diverse films as John Baxter's *Love on the Dole*, Powell and Pressburger's *One of Our Aircraft Is Missing*, Charles Frend's *The Foreman Went to France*, Noël Coward and David Lean's *In Which We Serve* and Harry Watt's *Nine Men* were all praised for their documentary qualities. The documentary movement itself had split into two camps in the late 1930s. Grierson and his principal followers (Arthur Elton, Edgar Anstey and Basil Wright) strove to expand the educative and informational role of documentary as a non-fictional format, while the group centring on Cavalcanti and Harry Watt borrowed techniques and strategies from the commercial cinema to create a story form of documentary that could dramatize the events of everyday life. Whereas Grierson put his faith in the development of a non-theatrical circuit of mobile and temporary cinemas, Cavalcanti and Watt wished to broaden the appeal of their films sufficiently to attract the mainstream cinema audience. The split was never absolute and during the war the Griersonians of the *Documentary News Letter* guardedly welcomed the dramatized documentaries made by the Crown Film Unit. However, it is important to acknowledge the extent of different film-making practices that documentary was deemed to cover.

Arthur Elton, who became Beddington's principal adviser on non-theatrical documentaries, claimed after the war that at the MoI there had been a battle between

> the old-fashioned people, who would have liked to fight the war in terms of society ladies dressed as Britannia, and some of the rest of

us who believed the only way to fight the war was to be very realistic about it. (Sussex, 1975a, p. 119)

At the time, this battle could be seen in the *Documentary News Letter's* scathing comparison of Anthony Asquith's *Channel Incident* (1940), in which a society lady co-opts a couple of reluctant men from the lower orders to sail to France to rescue her husband from the beaches of Dunkirk, and Harry Watt's brief portrait of life in Dover, *The Front Line* (1940), in which housewives and tradesmen defiantly ignore German shells and carry on with their lives. As the writer (probably Basil Wright) concludes:

> *The Front Line* is about US, and that's all right and as it should be; *Channel Incident* is about THEM, and they're a miserable section of the citizenry whose Sunday-night castigation by Priestley partly sums up what we feel about them.[3]

The Crown Film Unit itself was by no means immune from the criticism of its colleagues. Edgar Anstey dismissed Humphrey Jennings' *Listen to Britain* (1942) as 'the rarest piece of fiddling since the days of Nero', and there was a certain amount of animosity from the independent documentary units as well as the commercial industry over the Crown Film Unit's relatively generous budgets and – after it moved into Pinewood studios – high-quality facilities.[4] Various fusions did occur, most obviously through the influence of Cavalcanti on production at Ealing and in the MoI's Ideas Committee, which brought together directors and producers from different sides of the industry to discuss future projects, but these fusions were less straightforward than they might seem.

Realism or Tinsel?

Michael Balcon had entered the film industry in 1922 as an enterprising young producer, importing an American star, Betty Compson, for his first film – *Woman to Woman* (1923) – and seeking out co-production deals with German companies like Ufa in Berlin and Emelka in Munich. When his production company Gainsborough was bought up by the Gaumont-British conglomerate, he took charge of production at the corporation's Shepherd's Bush studio as well as supervising that of Gainsborough in Islington. At Gaumont-British he rivalled Alexander Korda in making big-budget films he hoped would break into the American market, and though the policy proved unsuccessful, when MGM looked around for someone to head their production unit in Britain they chose Balcon.

After making only one film for MGM-British – *A Yank at Oxford* (1937) – Balcon left to become an independent producer. His experience of having to take orders from Louis B. Mayer seems to have destroyed for ever his desire to ally himself with Hollywood and henceforth he was to champion the production of moderately budgeted indigenous British films. He found an ideal niche for doing this when he became head of production at Ealing studios in 1938. Ealing had been built in 1931 as a home for Associated Talking Pictures, a company set up by the theatrical impresario Basil Dean to make film versions of his West End plays. Things had not quite worked out as Dean had expected: a deal with the American company RKO-Radio was soon terminated, the theatrical adaptations did not prove a great success, and Ealing survived by making popular film vehicles for Gracie Fields and George Formby. In 1938 Fields was enticed away by 20th Century-Fox and Dean was ready to abandon films entirely (during the war he organized ENSA). When Balcon took over at Ealing, he was able to bring in two directors who had worked with him at Gaumont-British, Walter Forde and Robert Stevenson, and give his protégé Pen Tennyson the opportunity to direct (though, ironically, Dean's most promising director, Carol Reed, was recruited by Gainsborough/Gaumont-British). Balcon's first twelve Ealing films (not counting the Formby films, which continued with little change from the Dean period) were all directed by these three directors, and such films as *Cheer Boys Cheer*, *There Ain't No Justice*, *Saloon Bar* and *The Proud Valley*, released in 1939 or the early months of 1940, seemed to capture perfectly Balcon's ideal of an indigenous British cinema.

The outbreak of war threatened this stability. Stevenson, a pacifist, left for Hollywood (where he became a highly successful director for Disney); Anthony Kimmins, who had directed the Formby films, joined the Navy; Tennyson joined up after completing *Convoy*; and around the same time Forde left Ealing for Gainsborough. Balcon's bid to take over the GPO Film Unit is indicative not only of his commitment to realism and propaganda but of his need for new talent.

Cavalcanti became a cornerstone of the new Ealing, but it would be a mistake to equate him too closely with the British documentary movement. Before he joined Grierson, his impressionist city symphony, *Rien que les heures* (1926), had won him international acclaim, and his next film, *En rade* (1927), pioneered the sort of gloomy poetic realism which Jean Renoir, Julien Duvivier and Marcel Carné would make the characteristic style of 1930s French cinema. He had then begun a career as a commercial director, remaking a number of Paramount's Hollywood films in French, before leaving to work with Grierson. He was a highly effective producer and teacher. At the GPO Film Unit Harry Watt and Pat Jackson both attributed their later success to what they learned from Cavalcanti, and at Ealing he guided another group of film-makers in their craft. Monja Danischewsky, who moved from managing Ealing's publicity to work as associate producer on *Whisky Galore* (1948), commented that 'if Mick was the father figure, Cavalcanti was the Nanny who brought us up' (Danischewsky, 1966, p. 134).

It took some time, however, before the new regime produced significant results. After the last of the Tennyson and Forde films were released, the studio produced two George Formby films (his last for Ealing): *Spare a Copper*, directed by John Paddy Carstairs, and *Turned Out Nice Again*, directed by Marcel Varnel; two Will Hay films: *The Ghost of St Michael's*, directed by Varnel, and *The Black Sheep of Whitehall*, directed by Hay and Basil Dearden; and Nolbandov's *Ships with Wings*. Cavalcanti was largely responsible for three documentaries produced at Ealing for the MoI in 1941 – *Yellow Caesar*, *The Young Veteran* and *Mastery of the Sea* – none of which was particularly outstanding, and acted as associate producer (in effect, as producer, but Balcon kept that credit for himself) on *The Big Blockade*, the first film directed by Charles Frend, released in January 1942.

The Big Blockade provides a fascinating glimpse of the Ministry of Economic Warfare (MEW), shown operating from the buildings of the London School of Economics. The Ministry's main activity, centred on SOE, concerned sabotage and the establishment and supply of secret armies of resistance, and, until its SO1 branch was absorbed into the Political Warfare Executive in September 1941, black propaganda. But this was a relatively well-kept secret and *The Big Blockade* justifies the existence of this large new ministry by stressing its role in enforcing a blockade of Germany. There was little evidence to suggest that the blockade was having much effect on the German economy and the film relies on bluff and bluster, offering a crude caricature of life in Germany and occupied Europe where people exist on ersatz products and spend most of their time sheltering from British bombing raids.

Action sequences pay little regard to authenticity. A destroyer hunting down a U-boat looks forward to Frend's *The Cruel Sea*, but the much more protracted treatment of a bombing raid on Hanover is as frivolous as the worst sections of *The Lion Has Wings*. Harry Watt's *Target for Tonight* had obscured the fact that night bombing was too inexact to hit specific targets and gave little indication of the heavy losses suffered by bomber crews, but it does convey a feeling that bombing raids were cold, dangerous and risky. In *The Big Blockade* Michael Rennie and John Mills, despite flying a slow and vulnerable Hampden bomber, nimbly dodge a night-fighter and make repeated runs over their target, blowing it to smithereens before making an untroubled run home.

The narrator's comment that what we see is 'a fantasy for us but a hideous reality for the conquered nations' indicates that we are not meant to take the scenes of bullying or servile Germans, buffoonish Italians and grotesque quislings too seriously, but it is an uneasy and unsatisfactory mix of styles. Ian Aitken mounts a defence of the film in terms of its 'tone of disinterested parody' and the 'tongue-in-cheek acting performances' that Cavalcanti coaxes from his cast (Aitken, 2000, p. 196). However, *The Big Blockade*, like *Yellow Caesar* before it, seems to fly in the face of the subdued realism which characterized the films of the Crown Film Unit. It was rapidly succeeded by a group of films that represent a sudden flowering of realist cinema at Ealing. Cavalcanti and Frend went straight on to make *The Foreman Went to France*, and its production schedule overlapped with Thorold Dickinson's *The Next of Kin*; they were followed by Harry Watt's *Nine Men*, Basil Dearden's *The Bells Go Down*, Cavalcanti's *Went the Day Well?* and Charles Frend's *San Demetrio London*.

The change in style from *The Big Blockade* to *The Foreman Went to France* is remarkable. The reassuringly wise officials of the MEW are replaced by complacent factory owners and officious bureaucrats; caricatured Germans give way to convincingly treacherous Frenchmen. In *The Big Blockade*, Robert Morley plays a hysterically over-the-top gauleiter; in *The Foreman Went to France*, he is a sinisterly over-friendly mayor. In *The Big Blockade*, Will Hay and Bernard Miles casually shoot down a Heinkel which is attacking their boat while they argue about 'navy certs'; in *The Foreman Went to France*, Gordon Jackson shoots down a Stuka dive bomber, but he pays for it with his life.

The combination of humour and propaganda in a story of ordinary citizens doing their bit for the war effort was carried through from *The Foreman Went to France* into *The Bells Go Down*, *Went the Day Well?* and *San Demetrio London*. Thorold Dickinson's *The Next of Kin* has a rather different ethos. Dickinson was unusual in that he was a left-wing intellectual who had established his career in the commercial film industry as opposed to the documentary movement. He worked as assistant director to the veteran silent film-maker George Pearson, and edited such films as Basil Dean's *Sing As We Go* (1934). He considered that the two films he made in 1938 with Sidney Cole about the Spanish Civil War, *Behind Spanish Lines* and *Spanish ABC*, were 'not documentary films but news reports: any eloquence depended on the immediacy of the images captured at the moment'.[5] By the end of the 1930s he had established himself as a feature film director with a witty thriller, *The Arsenal Stadium Mystery* (1939), and an atmospheric adaptation of Patrick Hamilton's play *Gaslight* (1940).[6] *The Next of Kin* was planned as a short training film for the Army, but Balcon thought the idea of a film about careless talk costing lives would be relevant to the public at large, and agreement was reached with the War Office to turn it into a full-scale feature film, with Ealing adding £50,000 to the War Office's £20,000 budget.

Dickinson makes no compromises in his insistence in the film on the importance of security. A young officer who asks what will happen to the fan dancer he has been infatuated with and who has been ensnared into working for the Germans is told she will be taken to London, tried and hanged. We share his sense of subdued shock; but any sentimental regard we have for her evaporates in the final section of the film when the commando raid on a U-boat base on the French coast suffers heavy casualties because the Germans have had prior warning. In contrast to *Nine Men* and *The Way Ahead*, which show British soldiers as virtually invulnerable to enemy bullets, *The Next of Kin* shows that when they are outnumbered and out-gunned they retreat or die. According to Clive Coultass (1988, p. 85), cuts were imposed before the film was considered safe to show the public. Nevertheless, it is a harder-hitting film than any other made during the war. The fact that it misrepresents the reality of Germany's very poor intelligence network in Britain does not invalidate the psychological realism of how romance, loneliness, carelessness or simply a trusting friendliness could allow vital information to leak out. There is none of the clumping caricature of *The Big Blockade*. The traitors – the coke-addicted dancer and her evil dresser; the bookshop owner who takes in a Dutch refugee in order to blackmail her; and the two German agents sent to work with them – are mundane enough to be plausible. Most of them are efficiently rounded up, but the most cautious and effective agent – all the more sinister for being played by the kindly Welshman of so many other films of the period, Mervyn Johns – slips through the net.

In 1943 Balcon lectured the Film Workers' Association in Brighton on the choice the film industry faced between 'realism' and 'tinsel', extolling the virtues of realism and promising that Ealing's forthcoming naval drama, *San Demetrio London*, would be 'the best example of the final departure from tinsel which the film industry can make without any misgivings on the part of the shareholders'. However, he warned his audience that there might be 'a violent reaction towards tinsel when hostilities have ceased' (Balcon, 1944, pp. 11, 12). The new form of realist, documentary-influenced film he advocated was to flourish only briefly at Ealing, and the turn away from realism did not wait for the end of the war. In 1944 Ealing released two allegories based on stage plays, *The Halfway House* and *They Came to a City*, both directed by Basil Dearden; *Champagne Charlie*, a celebration of the Victorian music hall starring Tommy Trinder and Stanley Holloway, directed by Cavalcanti; and *Fiddlers Three*, a time-slip musical fantasy, incongruously, and not altogether successfully, directed by Harry Watt. Only Charles Crichton's directorial debut, the 67-minute *For Those in Peril*, appeared as a guilty reminder of Balcon's pledge to realism. The following year, Cavalcanti, Dearden, Crichton and Robert Hamer would work together on a rich, dark, macabre set of tales of the supernatural, *Dead of Night*. Cavalcanti was certainly a formative influence on the new generation of Ealing directors but it was not simply the documentary-realist tradition he bequeathed them.

Ealing has become such a central part of British film culture that it is tempting to go along with Charles Barr's contention that the studio 'quickly acquired a semi-official status' (Barr, 1977, p. 22). But Balcon's dispute with the MoI over his wish to take over the GPO Film Unit left a legacy of bad feeling. In December 1940 Balcon announced that Ealing would accept no more commissions for MoI shorts, and the making of *The Big Blockade* in co-operation with Hugh Dalton's Ministry of Economic Warfare can be seen as a deliberate act of defiance (Chapman, 1998b, p. 76). *The Next of Kin* was also made without MoI involvement, though it was one of Beddington's honorary advisers, Sidney Bernstein, who negotiated the release of the film in America. Much to Dickinson's annoyance, he accepted the advice of David Selznick that the film needed to be drastically cut if it was to avoid 'giving the impression that England is overrun by traitors' (Moorehead, 1984, p. 148).[7] The regularity with which Ealing films paralleled those made by the Crown Film Unit – *The Bells Go Down* and *Fires Were Started* were both released in May 1943, and but for the problems Pat Jackson had in shooting a Technicolor film in an open boat in the North Sea, *Western Approaches* would have been released around December 1943 when *San Demetrio London* appeared – suggests a continuing rivalry between Ealing and the MoI.[8]

Realism in the Mainstream

Undeniably there was a greater mixing of what had been before the war two mutually exclusive groups. According to Paul Rotha, the MoI enlisted the support of the most talented and inventive makers of both fiction films and documentaries and brought them together to discuss ideas:

> Jack Beddington, that admirable man, when he was the director of the films division at the Ministry of Information, had the idea of bringing together what he called the ideas committee. This consisted of a number of writers and directors from feature films and a number of directors and others from documentary, who met round a table over beer and rather lousy sandwiches, once every fortnight. He started this about 1942, and it went on throughout the war. We would talk backwards and forwards across the table for about a couple of hours, and then we'd go down to the theatre and see some films, and this was a very healthy and excellent thing. It broke down the barrier which had existed between feature and documentary. (quoted in Sussex, 1975a, pp. 140–1)

At the opposite end of the political and film-making spectrum, Michael Powell comments equally favourably on Beddington's attempt to bring the different factions together:

> He had a very good mind himself, and as well as understanding publicity he understood artists and creative people and he took great pains, he and the Ministry, to put us in touch with the people who were doing documentaries and training films. He took great trouble that feature film-makers should be well-informed, much better informed than the average person about what was going on in the war. (quoted in Badder, 1978, p. 11)

Powell no doubt welcomed the opportunity to view documentaries which informed him of aspects of the war he might wish to investigate further, just as Noël Coward asked Basil Wright to screen him a selection of documentaries while he was writing *In Which We Serve* (Sussex, 1975a, p. 139). Powell and other experienced directors like Carol Reed and Anthony Asquith were happy to work in collaboration with the MoI and to infuse a measure of propaganda into their films, but Reed and Powell did not need the documentary-makers to incite their concern for realism.

Reed's pre-war films – *Bank Holiday* (1937) and *The Stars Look Down* (1939), in particular – had been acknowledged as landmarks in the creation of a realist British cinema concerned with social justice and the lives of ordinary people. But Reed's realism was founded on his interest in emotionally complex characters troubled by conflicting loyalties, a subject he was to return to with less concern for surface realism in films like *Odd Man Out* (1946) and *The Third Man* (1949). Reed's politics were of the right rather than the left – indeed he seemed embarrassed by the reception of *The Stars Look Down* as a serious social critique and retreated to the safety of the past in *Kipps* (1941) and *The Young Mr Pitt* (1942). Thus his two war-realist films, *The Way Ahead* and *The True Glory* (co-directed with Garson Kanin from the millions of feet of film shot by British and American army cameramen to record the Allied victory in Europe), with their broadly populist view, might be seen as an anomaly.[9] But if the vision of a democratic Britain with class barriers brushed aside presented in *The Way Ahead* is very different from that of *Ship with Wings*, and even from *In Which We Serve*, it is perfectly compatible with the 'middle way' conservatism of rising politicians like Harold Macmillan and R. A. B. Butler. Similarly, the combination of a blank verse commentary and the voices of ordinary soldiers and citizens in *The True Glory* can be seen as representative of the democratic ideals promoted by Roosevelt and Truman in pre-McCarthyite America. Reed's films are important reminders that there was a broad consensus about the need for a fairer and more equal society.

Michael Powell had spent most of the 1930s directing quota quickies like *The Love Test* (1935), a light-hearted look at intrigue in a chemical laboratory, and *Something Always Happens* (1934), in which a penniless gentleman restores his fortunes by setting up a network of petrol stations throughout the country. But in 1937 he had made a more personal film, *The Edge of the World*, shot entirely on location on the island of Foula in the Hebrides. It can be seen as a companion piece to *Man of Aran* (1934), made by the American documentary pioneer Robert Flaherty for Balcon at Gaumont-British, on which Harry Watt had worked as Flaherty's assistant. Powell's film is at least as successful in capturing a sense of life on these windswept Celtic islands, but Powell was interested in realism less as a progressive creed and more as an element of a visually impressive, artistically ambitious cinema. If *One of Our Aircraft Is Missing*, with its discursive dialogue, total absence of scored music and idiosyncratic characters, now looks closer to *Fires Were Started* and *Western Approaches* than to the carefully constructed re-creations of Two Cities and Ealing, its realism was as much an aesthetic choice as the ones made to recreate the Himalayas at Pinewood studios for *Black Narcissus* (1947) or to insert an expressionist sequence into the otherwise grimly realistic *The Small Back Room* (1949).

For Powell, realism was an essential part of doing his job as professionally as possible. The unrealistic setting and effects of *The Lion Has Wings* could be excused by the speed and limited resources with which the film had to be made, but given substantial financial backing, he made strenuous efforts to ensure things looked right. For example, in *49th Parallel* Powell had his construction chief, Syd Streeter, build a life-size replica of a German U-boat out of canvas, wood and steel; he then reassembled it off the coast of Newfoundland and proceeded to blow it up with three 1000-pound bombs donated by the Canadian Air Force (Powell, 1986, pp. 371–4). This dedication to authenticity, combined with extensive location shooting, gives *49th Parallel* a different aesthetic to ideologically very similar films such as *Pimpernel Smith*, but it has little to do with the realism espoused by the documentarists.

Without doubt those film-makers ambitious enough to believe that they could incorporate war propaganda into their films found the Ideas Committee a useful forum. According to Paul Rotha, *Millions Like Us* 'was completely based on the documentary *Night Shift*' (which Rotha directed) and *The Way Ahead* was 'entirely based on a film called *The Common Lot*, a two reeler which Carol [Reed] saw and which gave him the idea of making *The Way Ahead*' (quoted in Sussex, 1975a, p. 141). In fact, Launder and Gilliat claim never to have seen *Night Shift*, and the two-reeler which served as a prototype for *The Way Ahead* was called *The New Lot* and directed by Reed himself. Nevertheless, *Millions Like Us* and *The Way Ahead* seem to share with the documentarists the concept of a people's war, and both films have been viewed as typical examples of the fusion between documentary and fiction film-making.

Millions Like Us has a fully developed fictional story which begins, like earlier Home Front films such as *The Briggs Family* and *Salute John Citizen*, as the chronicle of a family responding to the changes wrought by the war. Here the focus is less on the father (Moore Marriott) than on the younger daughter (Patricia Roc). As a 'mobile woman', she is called up and her dreams of joining the FANYs and chauffeuring officers around are replaced by the reality of work in the huge aircraft factory at Castle Bromwich. She falls in love with a young airman (Gordon Jackson) and they marry. But he is killed in action and she is supported in her grief by the women who work with her and have become her friends. Andrew Higson argues that documentary and fiction films employ different methods to draw the spectator into the text and the combination of these two systems creates a new form of cinema: documentary realism. He contends that in *Millions Like Us*:

> Certain sequences depend entirely upon a montage construction, such as the sequence showing the production process of assembling a complete aeroplane (or the arrival of the 'mobile women' at the factory where they are to engage in the production of just one small part of the aeroplane engine). On the other hand, there are scenes which depend on the classical narrative editing strategies of moving from establishing shot to point of view shot, particularly through shot/reverse shot structures and eyeline matching. (Higson, 1986, pp. 87–8)

Persuasive though his analysis is, it is posited on there being a coherent documentary style characterized by montage that could combine with an equally firmly established 'classical narrative' style which

> tends to draw the spectator into the organisation of looks within the diegesis, within the world of the fiction played out for us 'up there' on the screen, by means of the devices of point of view, shot/reverse shot, and eyeline matching. . . . The developing form of British documentary realism as an articulation of the public and the private is, then, dependent on the different ways in which these two systems of looking are combined in the films. (Higson, 1986, p. 86)

However, style in both documentary and fiction was more fluid and unsettled than Higson contends.

Once the documentary-makers began to incorporate fictional elements into their films, they had to pay as much attention as did studio directors to the grammatical rules of eyeline matching and point of view. Pat Jackson recalls Harry Watt's annoyance and frustration at 'crossing the line' while shooting a party of railway workers which made the sequence of them chatting together impossible to edit: instead of looking in opposite directions across the screen (an eyeline match), and thus appearing to look at each other, they were all looking in the same direction, and thus away from each other (Jackson, 1999, p. 26). The achievement of Cavalcanti, as far as directors like Jackson and Watt were concerned, was in teaching them that filmic construction required something more than fidelity to the real world. Watt recounts how when he was filming the first proper story documentary, *The Saving of Bill Blewett* (1936),

> Cavalcanti found me battling to get close-ups against the cottage, and he said, 'Don't you realise, Harry, that a wall's a wall. . . . You don't need to shoot Bill here. Take him into the sun over there, and put him against any cottage, and then you can cut back to the long shot outside this cottage.' Of course this is such a simple thing for features, but it was a revelation to me. The documentary thing was so ingrained that you would insist on shooting somebody outside the real cottage. (quoted in Sussex, 1975a, pp. 86–7)

To the extent that documentary-makers like Watt and Jackson talk about their work, their prime concern seems to be with what is and what is not acceptable to fictionalize. Brian Winston contends that

> Filming re-enactments was central to the 'creative treatment of actuality', as Grierson's famous definition of the documentary has it. It was not only permitted; it was in fact the cardinal mark of what made documentary different from other forms of non-fictional film-making such as newsreels. (Winston, 1999, p. 58)

I would argue that this is unacceptably simplistic. Much of documentary – including such films as Basil Wright's *Song of Ceylon* (1935) and Humphrey Jennings and Stewart McAllister's *Listen to Britain* (1942) – assembled actuality footage in a creative way that did not involve re-enactment, and these films were clearly different from fictional propaganda shorts like Brian Desmond Hurst's *Miss Grant Goes to the Door* (1940) and Launder and Gilliat's *Partners in Crime* (1942) in which trained actors follow a written script. What emerged in films like *Target for Tonight*, *Fires Were Started* and *Western Approaches* was a new form of film-making that diverged radically from the path mapped out by Grierson for documentary.

In *Target for Tonight*, Harry Watt sticks to a straightforward storyline about a squadron of Wellington bombers on a bombing raid over Germany. He introduces dramatic tension by showing the crew of F for Freddie, on whom he concentrates, being attacked and having to limp back to base on one engine, but he relies on devices which retain the documentary ethos. The nervousness of the airman playing the wireless operator is used to express his discomfort at being wounded; a last lingering look at the empty locker room before the raid begins is justified by the return of an airman who has forgotten his goggles. When he does stray into fictional narrative devices, they

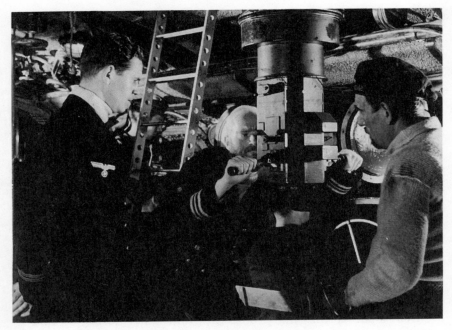

The German U-boat captain spies his prey in *Western Approaches*. Supplied by
BFI Stills, © courtesy of the Central Office of Information.

are not always successful: the sudden switch from the interior of F
for Freddie to a German anti-aircraft battery firing at the British
bombers, for example, seems an unnecessary disruption of our point
of view.

In *Western Approaches*, Pat Jackson went much further in creating a
fictional story that would fulfil the Admiralty's request for a film
which would show how effectively they were defending the essential
trade routes between Britain and America. Jackson's solution to the
problem of showing the operation of the convoy system in a way
which eschewed romance or unlikely heroism but was nevertheless
dramatically interesting, led him to a plot which had three main sites
of activity: a lifeboat, a German U-boat which picks up the SOS signal
and lies in wait to torpedo any ship that comes to the rescue, and a
merchant ship, the *Leander*, which is drawn into the U-boat's trap.
This was a more complex narrative than that of many mainstream
fictional films, and the idea of using the lifeboat as a decoy posed a
dilemma for Jackson:

I realised that if I used it, not only would it provide me with the
suspense elements for which I had been seeking so agonisingly and

which would make the story viable, but that I would also be betraying the sacred tenets of 'documentary' as currently accepted. To show an enemy periscope as seen above the waves was within the law. But to show a shot as seen through an enemy periscope, let alone find the camera in an enemy U-boat with the crew speaking German with English sub-titles, this was betrayal, if not treason. (Jackson, 1999, p. 117)

Within the framework of what has become a fictional film rather than a documentary, there is no sense of this 'betrayal'. Jackson cast a German-speaking Dutch minesweeper captain as the commander and Sudetenland Czechs as his crew, and the U-boat sequences are as convincing as those in the lifeboat. They compare interestingly with the depiction of life on a submarine in Anthony Asquith's *We Dive at Dawn*.

In an article discussing the fusion of documentary and fiction techniques, Asquith claimed that feature film directors 'realise that they have an immense amount to learn from the documentary approach, not only in accuracy but in a true picture of the lives and work of the men they want to portray'.[10] He compares *Western Approaches* with *We Dive at Dawn*, and though effusive in his praise of Jackson's film, he nevertheless manages to find a sequence in his own film which he considers more effective both as realism and as drama. The commander of a submarine (John Mills) finally sights a German battleship he has been pursuing and moves in to attack. The action consists of little more than the upping and downing of the periscope accompanied by Mills' orders and periscope silhouettes of the German ships above. According to Asquith:

What made it exciting was the imaginative way in which Mills drew the picture of a man whose brain has, so to speak, to be in two places at once. That is to say he has to issue orders which apply to the moment while his mind is already concentrated on the next move. The weight of his thought is never behind the spoken word which is really only the mechanical physical expression of what he had been thinking a moment before. In my opinion he conveyed this in a way which no real submarine captain could hope to do unless he was a superb actor.[11]

It is indeed a remarkably authentic-seeming sequence and one which looks forward to the convincing post-war naval drama *The Cruel Sea*, where actuality footage and actorly performances do at last seem to meld together. But Asquith's stress on performance marks his

Up periscope! John Mills with crew (Eric Portman wearing headphones) in *We Dive at Dawn*. Supplied by BFI Stills, © courtesy of Carlton International.

fundamental difference of approach as compared with documentary directors like Watt, Jennings and Jackson. *We Dive at Dawn* does incorporate a considerable amount of location shooting – in contrast to the contemporary Crown Film Unit submarine film, *Close Quarters*, directed by Jack Lee, most of which was shot at Pinewood. However, suspicions that Asquith might not quite be in tune with the realist project are aroused by the fact that the downplayed attack on the German battleship – we do not even know whether or not it has been successful – is followed by a conventional and melodramatic action sequence in which the submarine surfaces in a small Danish port and, with the support of the locals, holds off the German garrison long enough to refuel. Asquith is right to stress the importance of performance to his films – Wendy Hiller and Leslie Howard in *Pygmalion* (1938), Olivier in *The Demi-Paradise* and the ensemble cast of *The Way to the Stars* give a depth and resonance to his best films which make them very memorable – but it is difficult to find any link here with documentary.

Jackson, who pursued an unhappy career in Hollywood after *Western Approaches*, expressed his admiration for actors like Clark Gable and John Hodiak but he remained wedded to the idea that non-actors – if they were able to articulate their emotions and perform before a camera – were more fascinating to watch than actors assuming the guise of characters who experience emotions the actor can only imagine. *Western Approaches* seems to bear him out. John Mills makes an excellent British submarine captain and his character is all the more interesting for seeming to update the caddish, womanizing officer-type John Clements had played in *Convoy* and *Ships with Wings*. Mills has a Mayfair flat and a string of girlfriends but the gritty reality of war does not give him the chance to get near them. In the close confines of the submarine the naval hierarchy remains intact but there is much less formality and deference. Mills' performance is at the core of *We Dive at Dawn*; Jackson's U-boat commander has much less to do but it is miraculously good casting. On a visual level, the tall, red-bearded Dutchman is strangely fox-like and his actions with the periscope – the men in the lifeboat realize they are being used as decoys and wave in the opposite direction to the *Leander* to mislead the U-boat as to its whereabouts – is as impressively tense as that of Mills in the attack on the German battleship. These German submariners are dangerous adversaries but they are not stereotyped villains.

Indeed, Jackson succeeds too well in arousing our sympathies for the Germans. When the *Leander* turns the tables and fires at the surfaced U-boat, those of the crew who manage to get out jump into the sea. But we must deduce for ourselves whether they are picked up by the crew of the damaged *Leander* or whether they are left to drown. This is less a problem of a mismatch of documentary and fictional techniques than that of a narrative strand being opened out which resists easy closure.

The other problem for Jackson was that the main action of *Western Approaches* is set on an open boat. For a studio film this would present problems of shooting in a confined space (something which exercised Hitchcock in his 1944 Hollywood film *Lifeboat*). Jackson had additional problems, among them seasickness, which particularly afflicted his cameraman, Jack Cardiff; a mutiny among his cast of tough merchant seamen unused to the slow, repetitive business of filming; and innumerable difficulties with lighting, electricity and seagulls. *In Which We Serve* had avoided these problems by shooting in a studio tank and dissolving from the raft – to which the survivors cling – to protracted flashbacks. *San Demetrio London* (based on a true wartime story of a band of sailors who abandon a sinking oil tanker but then rediscover her still afloat and decide to sail her back to England) stayed with her crew in the lifeboat and tried to distract from the obvious back-projection by rocking the boat vigorously and showering the cast with cascades of water. The men row strenuously but without any sense of where they are going (as it turns out, it is round in a circle) and turn their noses up at soggy ship's biscuits. In *Western Approaches*, the reality of filming on location imposes its own order. The captain carefully plots a route (and is warned of the dangers of landing on the rocky west coast of Ireland), the men row in shifts, and rations are shared out carefully. The condition of the men in the lifeboat looks uncomfortable and dangerous, but there is also something awesome about the attempt to keep their spirits up and survive.

Harry Watt thought that films like *Desert Victory*, compiled from actuality footage of fighting shot by army cameramen, superseded the story documentaries he had pioneered. In fact, much of what seemed to be newsreel footage was recreated, though generally with the sort of commitment to truth and integrity which Watt himself had tried to abide by. The sorts of problems films like *Desert Victory* and its successors confronted – balancing truth and propaganda, linking disparate footage into a coherent narrative – were separate and distinct from the problems of combining a documentary ethos with fictional forms, which Watt, Jackson and the other Crown Film Unit directors wrestled with and which were to be inherited by later film-makers such as Ken Loach.

Charles Barr points out that 'There was no special political or aesthetic rigour in the documentary tradition which created a barrier to its easy assimilation by a commercial studio. . . . Perhaps the main influence was in the areas of: location shooting, editing techniques, sober narratives' (Barr, 1974, p. 97). Several directors did become more concerned with realism during the war. David Macdonald, whose career in the 1930s had revolved around low-budget thrillers like *Dead Men Tell No Tales* (1938), made *Men of the Lightship* (1941) for the GPO Film Unit and went on to produce *Desert Victory* and *Burma Victory*. The latter two films were directed by Roy Boulting, who had joined the Army after making *Pastor Hall* and *Thunder Rock* with his brother John – who joined the RAF and made *Journey Together*. Brian Desmond Hurst co-ordinated *Theirs Is the Glory* to commemorate the Battle of Arnhem after making the romantic wartime melodrama *Dangerous Moonlight*, and Asquith made *A Welcome to Britain* to introduce American GIs to English customs. Several of these directors, along with Powell and Pressburger, Launder and Gilliat and the Ealing directors, also made fiction films which dealt directly or indirectly with the war. But as in America, where Hollywood directors such as John Ford, William Wyler, Frank Capra and John Houston enlisted for similar sorts of propaganda work, there was no permanent shift towards realism.

The coming together of documentary and fiction is a coming together of intentions. The feature film sacrificed some of its concern to entertain and embraced – to some extent – the documentary's concern to inform, to act as a channel of communication between the state and the people. The documentary extended into fictional realms to reach as wide an audience as possible. Given the increase in the number of documentaries made during the war, it is hardly surprising that several of the new generation of film-makers who emerged once it was over had served their apprenticeship there rather than on quota quickies. But if Ken Annakin and Compton Bennett, Jack Lee and Philip Leacock emerged as competent, even interesting directors, they were hardly a match for Carol Reed, David Lean, Michael Powell and the Boulting brothers, and – in the 1940s at least – Anthony Asquith, Thorold Dickinson, and Launder and Gilliat who had learnt their craft in the hurly-burly of the commercial studios.

Harry Watt expressed the view that in the early years of the war, 'we were better film-makers than the features people, and of course the trade had suddenly woken up to it, after ten or twelve years of contempt' (quoted in Sussex, 1975a, p. 138). It is an exaggerated claim; Watt's *Target for Tonight*, Jennings' *Fires Were Started* and Jackson's *Western Approaches* remain isolated triumphs and the influence of the group of committed documentary realists was limited. Watt managed to carve out a successful career making films for Ealing in Australia and Africa, but he remained nostalgic for his work in documentary and after a final film for Ealing in 1959, *The Siege of Pinchgut*, he left the industry. Few of his documentary colleagues prospered as commercial film-makers. Jackson was signed by Alexander Korda for MGM and summoned to Culver City where he offended the studio bosses by refusing to direct a remake of *Owd Bob* – a sheepdog film which Robert Stevenson had made for Gainsborough with Will Fyffe and Margaret Lockwood – as a vehicle for Lassie. On returning to Britain he was able to make two realist melodramas – *White Corridors* (1951) and *The Birthday Present* (1957) – and a witty comedy, *What a Carve Up!* (1961), of which he could be proud, but he found it difficult to negotiate the political minefield of the British film industry in the 1950s, and he directed his last feature film in 1962. Two other documentary adherents – Jack Lee and Philip Leacock – fared well enough in the 1950s, and with *The Wooden Horse*, *Appointment in London*, *A Town Like Alice*, *Circle of Deception* and *The War Lover* were responsible for some of the best Second World War films of the period. However, Lee emigrated to Australia in 1960, and Leacock made only occasional films after 1963. Considering that today's mainstream British cinema is still characterized by realism, it is remarkable that directors who struggled to maintain the tradition should have had such a hard time making the sort of films they wished to make and enjoyed so little recognition for their efforts.

The one documentary director who has won enduring recognition, Humphrey Jennings, was killed in an accident while scouting locations in Greece in 1952. This has perhaps made it easier to acknowledge his one feature-length film, *Fires Were Started*, as a masterpiece, but it is a film which has stood up to the passage of time. Like *The Bells Go Down*, it was made as a tribute to the Auxiliary Fire Service (AFS) and released shortly before Dearden's film in June 1943. Its narrative is much simpler than that of *Western Approaches*: a new man, Barrett (the writer William Sansom), joins an AFS squad in the East End of London and after a day's training goes out at night to fight a warehouse fire started by a heavy bombing raid. One of his colleagues is killed but the fire is brought under control and a munitions ship moored nearby escapes damage. Within this modest framework, Jennings (and his editor, Stewart McAllister) evolves something which is radically different from a conventional feature film and is without equal in its combination of propaganda with human drama.

Ian Dalrymple, who was to rejoin Korda at the end of 1943, points to the limitations on the story documentaries made by the Crown Film Unit:

it must be remembered that, although our major films were in dramatic form, they were denied the depth of a playwright's scenes of interplay of characters. They contained no dialogue not precisely to do with the functional duties of the 'actors', who were all servicemen or servicewomen or ordinary civilians, allotted as available, which gave directors little chance of careful casting. Arising from all this, there was an ingredient which became of vital importance to us – music. (Dalrymple, 1982, p. 219)

This is particularly evident in *Fires Were Started*. Jennings uses music as a means of holding the disparate parts of the film together. Barrett's rhythmic piano playing takes us out from the fire station into the streets and we see the sky darkening as the time for the night bombers to return approaches. His rendition of 'One Man Went to Mow' is a way of reintroducing us to each of the men as they come into the canteen, and acts as a bridge from the preparation and training of the first part of the film to the action of the warehouse fire. At the end, William Alwyn's quiet, solemn music links together the men carrying Jacko's coffin and the munitions ship moving gracefully away down the river.

Comparing *Fires Were Started* with *The Bells Go Down*, Brian Winston points out that Jennings' film devotes much more time to the procedures and organization of the fire service and argues that

> Jennings' painstaking efforts to explain the abandoned pre-N.F.S. structure of command, mainly through the crude use of explicit establishing shots of signs and maps, are the least successful part of the film. This was not entirely his fault, since the various controls – local, district, O.P. and brigade – employ W.A.F.S. with telephones who answer every call at whatever level, confusingly, 'Control'. (Winston, 1999, pp. 62–3)

This rather misses the point. Jennings is not interested in exposition and no one is likely to come away from *Fires Were Started* with much of an understanding of 'the abandoned pre-N.F.S. structure of command'. He uses the voices of the telephone operators passing on weather reports, the progress of the fires and the availability of pumps and units as a reassuring chorus, as atmospheric and evocative as the sounds of *Listen to Britain*. In a film where there is no deeply personal interaction, and conflict never rises above the level of friendly banter, the informational component of the film, like the music, helps to give a rhapsodic structure to the film.

In *Listen to Britain*, Jennings had cut from Flanagan and Allen singing in a huge factory canteen to Dame Myra Hess playing Mozart at a lunchtime concert at the National Gallery, illustrating the harmony between classes, the common ground shared by high and low culture during the war. In *Fires Were Started*, Jennings has one of the firemen, Rumbold, recite Sir Walter Raleigh's 'Oh eloquent, just and mighty death, whom none could advise, thou hast persuaded' and Shakespeare's 'Ay, in the catalogue, ye go for men', provoking the *Documentary News Letter* reviewer to complain that he 'goes all arty for a moment'.[12] But Jennings inserts these high art intrusions in as casually a surreal way as his images of a horse being led to safety through the flaming streets and a one-legged man hopping determinedly through the rubble. The ode to death prepares us for the events of the night, the speech from *Macbeth* is an elegy for Jacko: they are part of a complex framework. In contrast to the speeches on freedom and liberty and the need to fight Nazi tyranny which sprout from fiction films about resistance and national identity, the propaganda in *Fires Were Started* works on a deeper level, setting very solidly the foundations for a view of London during the Blitz which has proved remarkably durable.

Although it uses an unconventional narrative structure and relies on information and atmosphere rather than romance and suspense, *Fires Were Started*, like *The Bells Go Down*, climaxes with the death of a fireman. In *The Bells Go Down* the firemen fight a fire at a hospital and the chief officer, McFarlane (Finlay Currie), is trapped under a fallen roof beam. He is freed by the cheery, irreverent auxiliary played by Tommy Trinder, just before the floor falls in. They are trapped on a ledge and Tommy – who has been continually reprimanded for smoking on the job – offers his chief a cigarette. He grins and takes one but as they light up a huge wall collapses on to them. Dearden's willingness to sacrifice realism for pathos and visual effect is evident earlier in the film. From his ladder, the young married fireman (Philip Friend) sees a telephone through an open window of a burning building and reaches through to ring the call-box outside his home and speak to his wife. She rushes down to answer the phone and narrowly escapes being blown up when a bomb explodes nearby. It is a visually and dramatically satisfying sequence but seems implausibly reckless behaviour. Similarly, the death of Tommy and McFarlane is spectacular enough – until now the film has been a light-hearted affair – to draw the film to a close, but it is essentially arbitrary. In *Fires Were Started*, Barrett and Jacko help their injured chief off the roof of a burning warehouse and Jacko stays to hang on to a guide rope which will prevent his body being dashed against the building. Before the ladder can return, he has been engulfed by the flames. Jacko's death is as shocking as Tommy's, but in retrospect we can see that Jennings has made meticulous preparations for it. Jacko is the one fireman we see with a life outside the fire station (running a small newsagent's), and his wife tells him not to do anything silly as he goes out; he is introduced as 'our little ray of sunshine' and is almost a mascot for the squad, embodying their doggedness, loyalty and unostentatious bravery. Arriving at the station, he tells of dozing by his fire, when 'a big lump of coal fell out'; though it is treated as a joke ('You're doing it all wrong, having a fire in your own home'), it is clearly an omen.

Tommy's death adds a slightly darker tinge to *The Bells Go Down*, but the film would not have been radically different if he had survived. Jacko's death is crucial to *Fires Were Started*. Without it the film would still be an interesting and worthy tribute to the AFS – as, for example, *Coastal Command* is to the long-distance flying boats which gave air cover to the Atlantic convoys – but it would lose its intensity and resonance.[13]

Andrew Higson points out that the division between 'realism' and 'escapism' is not reducible to a distinction between 'fact' and 'fiction':

> The aesthetic implications of Grierson's maxim, 'the creative inter-pretation of actuality', refuses such a reductionism, which is further complicated by the development of the story documentary form, which employs some of the devices and strategies of the narrative film – that is, the fiction film. (Higson, 1986, p. 81)

However, the category of documentary-realist film Higson outlines is undermined by the occasional incompatibility of documentary and realism. If it is a perfectly appropriate term for films like *Western Approaches* or *Fires Were Started*, it fits ill with such films as *The Lion Has Wings* and *For Freedom*, which combine unrealistic fiction with documentary. And even the most fervid advocate of the fiction/documentary fusion would probably wish to disown Gordon Welles-ley's *Rhythm Serenade*, despite its use of documentary-like footage of a commando raid and images of women working in factories. The fact that it was produced by George Formby for Columbia-British and stars Vera Lynn would probably be enough to put it beyond the pale, but a more legitimate reason for excluding it from the canon of approved films would be the shallowness of its characters and the implausibility of its plot. As the enthusiasm for films like *This Happy Breed* and *The Way to the Stars* indicates, emotional depth as embodied by characters that audiences – and critics – could identify with was at least as important as location shooting or the use of non-actors in the creation of a realist national cinema.

Emotional Realism

Roger Manvell, discussing 'Britain's self-portraiture in feature films' in 1953, points out that

> The dramatist and the film-maker, who both depend in their story-telling on self-revelation through speech and action, are faced with the dilemma of stripping the mask of shyness from our brows and revealing the warmth and the tenderness, the strengths and the weaknesses beneath. A particular style has had to be evolved to do this effectively while actually maintaining the principle of the national reserve. The film-makers and the film critics call it 'under-statement'. In our best films like *The Way Ahead, The Way to the Stars* and *Brief Encounter*, the understatement of emotion – resolved by

eloquent silences or by giving a certain pathos to the *clichés* of accepted behaviour, or by side-tracking emotion by using laughter in its place – is as indigenous as our green, sweet and rain-quenched landscapes.[14]

Finding an appropriate tone for the expression of emotional truth was particularly important for films that touched on the war because of the likelihood of their having to deal with death.

Death finds its way into most films – subsidiary characters die to progress the main plot, to reveal hidden depths in the main characters, to act as a cause of revenge or as a reminder of the precariousness of life, though the death of a main character tends to happen only after a careful build-up. Early war films conform to this pattern. The death of David Cranford in *Convoy* tidies things up, cementing the respect which Commander Armitage now feels towards him, and allowing Lucy to express her lingering affection. In *Ships with Wings*, there is a scale of emotional resonance attached to the various deaths, but it is set by the trajectory of the narrative rather than by any attempt to deal with the reality of the war. Young Wetherby, killed in a plane he had no right to be in, is significant only because his death brings about Stacey's disgrace and ends his romance with Celia, the admiral's daughter. Kay, the self-sacrificing other woman shot by the German agent while trying to warn Stacey, is more important. Her death is allowed a certain poignancy, but its function is to steel Stacey for the deed of reckless courage which will bring about his self-destruction.

Later films attempt to make arbitrary wartime death seem worthwhile and meaningful. In *The Day Will Dawn*, Old Alstad (Finlay Currie) is shot while helping Colin Metcalfe (Hugh Williams) guide the British planes to their target. He is an old man and this is a much better end for him than incarceration in a Nazi prison. But he is loved intensely by his daughter. Metcalfe breaks the news to her with warmth and sympathy and without much sense of English restraint – hugging her to him and promising to take care of her. Peter Garnett (Hugh Williams) is less successful in consoling Michele in *Secret Mission* when her brother is killed. The romance between them is at a tentative stage and she screams and shouts at him and blames him for Raoul's death, but his quiet patience eventually wins her over and she comes to see it as part of a greater struggle.

Films with Continental characters license a degree of emotionalism, whereas the keynote for British characters is restraint. *In Which We Serve*, as with so many things, set the tone. Walter Hardy (Bernard Miles) and his wife have an affectionate rather than a passionate

148

relationship. He is writing to her when Shorty Blake (John Mills) brings him the news that she has been killed during a bombing raid, but his niece (Shorty's wife), who has been living with her, is safe and has given birth to a son. Walter politely congratulates Shorty on becoming a father and then goes out on to the deck. Noticing that he is still holding the letter, he crumples it up and throws it in the sea. Nothing is said to express the seismic emotional disaster he has suffered; Miles conveys raging emotion by remaining calm. David Lean's direction cleverly builds up emotional intensity by making the space in which Walter sits seem increasingly claustrophobic, but the sequence is moving rather than clichéd because it draws on the depth of emotion between this odd, inhibited couple.

Celia (Patricia Roc) in *Millions Like Us* is more openly emotional about the death of her young husband, but we witness her distress obliquely. At work, she is called to the manager's office; a clergyman's presence alerts us to the probability of bad news; someone opens the door to ask for a glass of water; the foreman tells her friend to take her home; Celia stands beside the window of the dismal room that she and her young husband were going to make into a home. The next time we see her she is in the factory canteen, sad and subdued but gradually warmed to life as variety artiste Bertha Willmott sings 'Waiting at the Church' – a song sung at her wedding reception. While British bombers fly overhead, she is encouraged by her friends to join in the singing.

The Way to the Stars, more than any other British war film, dwells upon death and its impact on the bereaved. The strength of the film comes from its sensitivity in tracing the emotional lives of its characters and intertwining them into its theme about the need to go on forming deep emotional relationships despite the possibility of their being shattered by sudden death. The first part of the film is dominated by David Archdale (Michael Redgrave), and his death acts as a hinge between the two parts of the film. He leaves his wife and baby to go out on another bombing raid but cannot find his lucky charm, a cigarette lighter. When the planes return, aircrew troop into the mess and Peter Penrose (John Mills), Archdale's closest friend, discovers the lighter behind a pin-up picture. We hardly need to be told that he has been shot down and the following scenes, in the room the two men shared and at the hotel run by Archdale's wife, are concerned with exploring the reactions to his death. Penrose tries to isolate himself emotionally – initially refusing to break the news to Toddy (Archdale's wife) and breaking off his relationship with Iris (Renee Asherson), the woman he was about to propose to. Toddy (Rosamund John), despite her grief, remains emotionally open, mak-

The Way to the Stars: Michael Redgrave, Basil Radford and David Tomlinson –
the anxious wait to see who hasn't returned. Supplied by BFI Stills,
© courtesy of Carlton International.

ing Penrose read Archdale's poem (John Pudney's 'For Johnny'), and
eventually passing on the lighter to the American airman with whom
she forms a deep friendship. He is also killed, but she remains resilient
and helps Penrose break out of his emotional numbness to resume
his relationship with Iris.

The restrained emotionalism of this and other films about the war
is sometimes difficult for modern audiences to take seriously. Their
metaphors for powerful emotion are more sophisticated than the
howling winds and fast-flowing rivers of silent cinema, but they rely
heavily on performance and devices borrowed from the theatre. This
does not mean that they are artificial or insignificant, but it is difficult
to discern much trace of documentary influence now of films such as
In Which We Serve and *The Way to the Stars*. Higson's contention that
'under the unique circumstances of World War II, the documentary
idea came to inform both much commercial film-making practice and
the dominant discourses of film criticism' is more true of 'the dominant discourses of film criticism' than of commercial film-making
practice (Higson, 1986, p. 72). What was 'realist' was assumed mis-
takenly to be 'documentary'. But realism was not a gift bestowed by

the documentary movement on the commercial industry; it was something which came from greater involvement with the real world by film-makers from both sectors. The movement towards realism was part of a more general feeling that it was right and necessary to show people from all walks of life pulling together for the common good.

NOTES

1 *Documentary News Letter*, March 1943, p. 188.
2 Grierson's philosophical background is explored fully in Aitken (1990).
3 'Films and a people's war', *Documentary News Letter*, November 1940, p. 3.
4 *Documentary News Letter*, 1942, reproduced in Sussex (1975a), p. 144. See Sussex, pp. 137, 156, for Rotha's and Wright's comments on 'the luxury unit' at Pinewood.
5 Thorold Dickinson, 'Experiences of the Spanish Civil War', *Historical Journal of Film Radio and Television*, vol. 4, no. 2, p. 189.
6 *Gaslight* was later remade in Hollywood and released in Britain as *The Murder in Thornton Square* (George Cukor, 1944).
7 Selznick's view, though backed by that of Nunnally Johnson, was not necessarily typical of American opinion. Darryl F. Zanuck, the head of 20th Century-Fox, who was in Britain serving as a colonel in the US Army, thought *The Next of Kin* 'a fine film', and General Eisenhower made it required viewing for US personnel stationed in Britain. See Jeffrey Richards, 'Careless talk costs lives,' in Aldgate and Richards (1986), p. 112.
8 Ian Dalrymple attributes *We Dive at Dawn*, which came out at about the same time as Crown's submarine film, *Close Quarters*, in 1943, to Balcon at Ealing. In fact, it was made for Gainsborough. See Sussex (1975a), p. 139.
9 Of *The Stars Look Down*, Reed told Charles Samuels: 'I simply took the novel by Cronin, I didn't feel particularly about his subject (nationalisation of mines). One could just as easily make a picture on the opposite side' (Samuels, 1978, p. 16).
10 'Realler than the real thing', *Cine-Technician*, March–April 1945, p. 26.
11 *Ibid.*, p. 27.
12 *Documentary News Letter*, vol. 4, no. 4, 1943, p. 200.
13 See also the perceptive analyses of *Fires Were Started* by Daniel Millar in *Sight and Sound*, Spring 1969, pp. 100–4, and Jeffrey Richards in Aldgate and Richards (1994), pp. 218–45.
14 Roger Manvell, 'Britain's self-portraiture in feature films', *Geographical Magazine*, August 1953, p. 222.

6

Passion and Loss:
The Role of Women in
Wartime Cinema

'Oh Dizzy, he's such a dear little man. If I weren't there to wind him up and start him off for the office every morning, he'd run down like a clockwork mouse.' (Deborah Kerr in *Perfect Strangers*)

Women had played an active role in the First World War, taking over men's jobs on the trams, buses and railways, recruited in large numbers for the munitions factories, and serving with the armies in France, as well as in Britain, as nurses and canteen workers. Most of them returned to their homes when the war was over, though around five million women were employed in industry, commerce and the armed services by 1939 (Smith, 1986, p. 211). Most of these women were young and single. Marriage was still seen – by women as well as men – as a woman's true vocation. A marriage bar existed for those employed as civil servants, nurses, local government officers, schoolteachers and doctors, and in many industries women were dismissed upon getting married.

As homekeepers, women suffered along with men in areas of high unemployment and the decline of the cotton textiles industry threw large numbers of them out of work, but changes in the economy broadly favoured women. Contraction in the coal, steel and ship-building industries, which relied almost exclusively on men, was matched by a growth in light engineering and service industries which relied much more on women. J. B. Priestley's discovery of 'factory girls looking like actresses' on his English journey of 1933 was an indication of the new economic role played by women (Priestley, 1979, p. 375).

Britain had lost three-quarters of a million men in the First World War, which meant that many women who would otherwise have married were unable to.[1] This was not wholly disadvantageous, particularly for women in the higher income brackets. Casualty rates among young officers had been particularly high and the death of fathers and brothers meant that women were more liable to inherit wealth. The shortage of suitable marriage partners made it more likely that it would be retained – or spent on leisure activities, conspicuous consumption and travel – rather than passed on to another man. Upper- and middle-class single women in Britain were a large enough group to create their own networks and lifestyles and to enjoy a remarkable degree of freedom.

Through the agency of the Women's Voluntary Service (WVS), women were largely responsible for organizing the Home Front – canteens, evacuation and the provision of services for those made homeless by German bombing. Half a million women joined the ATS, WRNS, WAAF, FANY and Air Transport Auxiliary (ferry pilots) and another two million were drafted into industrial jobs. For some, this opened up new opportunities and provided exciting, formative opportunities; for others it meant drudgery, disruption and boredom. Such films as *The Gentle Sex*, *Millions Like Us* and *Perfect Strangers* stressed the positive side of wartime changes and showed women coping enthusiastically with their new responsibilities. Other films – for example, *A Canterbury Tale* and *Piccadilly Incident* – are more ambivalent, but are equally interesting in their exploration of the changes in male–female relations and the benefits and sacrifices brought about by the war.

Transformations

The Gentle Sex and *Millions Like Us* were both made with the encouragement of the MoI and show women from a variety of backgrounds coming together to become proficient servicewomen and effective workers in war factories. They also express a desire for a fairer and better society to which these newly confident and competent women can contribute. *The Gentle Sex*, directed by Leslie Howard for Two Cities, brings together seven women as recruits to the ATS (Auxiliary Territorial Service).[2] All the women's services, but particularly the ATS, attracted rumours of sexual promiscuity, and a parliamentary committee was set up in November 1941 to investigate. It found 'no justification for the vague but sweeping charges of immorality which have disturbed public opinion' and offered this explanation for their prevalence:

The British, though they fight when called upon to do so with unfaltering courage and determination, are not a military race. They cherish a deep-rooted prejudice against uniforms; consequently ... The woman in uniform becomes an easy target for gossip and careless talk. To be seen drinking a glass of beer in a public house is to provide a text for fluent remarks about the low standards of the Services. (Quoted in Costello, 1986, p. 82)

By 1943 the ATS was considered sufficiently respectable for the 18-year-old Princess Elizabeth to join its Transport Corps, and *The Gentle Sex* offered further reassurance that life with the ATS was wholesome and worthwhile. The film follows its seven chosen women through their basic training. Gwen (Joan Gates) is a Cockney waitress; Joan (Barbara Waring) a teacher; Anne (Joyce Howard) a colonel's daughter; Erna (Lilli Palmer) a Czech refugee; Maggie (Rosamund John) a poor Glaswegian girl; Dot (Jean Gillie) a hairdresser; and Betty (Joan Greenwood) is a sheltered young woman who has never been away from home before. Anne, Maggie, Erna and Joan prove themselves on a long-distance lorry drive, while the others become fully integrated members of an anti-aircraft battery. The natural leadership one might have expected from the middle-class women fails to materialize. Betty is still a child who has to be coaxed and reassured; Joan is a sourpuss who gets her corporal's stripe but alienates the rest of the group; Anne is competent and popular but is sidetracked into a predictably tragic romance. Officers and sergeants are entirely peripheral and the group is bonded together by two contrasting working-class women. Maggie, constantly offering sweets and advice, is an old-fashioned girl who gives the group warmth and solidarity. Dot, though 'new-fangled with a roving eye', is allowed her good-time girl tendencies without condemnation and brings vitality and glamour to the group. She takes Betty under her wing and quickly slaps down the killjoy Joan, and even if Maggie is scandalized by her exotic nightie, the two women share a determination to enjoy their new experiences and together imbue the film with genial good humour.

Millions Like Us, in spite of its being the first film directed by Frank Launder and Sidney Gilliat (and the only one they jointly directed), is more sophisticated, a summation of a Gainsborough/Gaumont-British tradition marked by such films as Walter Forde's *Rome Express* (1932), Victor Saville's *Friday the Thirteenth* (1933) and Carol Reed's *Bank Holiday* (1937) which combine comedy with tragedy and realism with melodrama.[3] *Millions Like Us*, backed by the MoI and employing extensive location shooting at the Castle Bromwich aircraft factory, is usually presented as a prime example of a documentary/fiction fusion, but its strength comes from its well-cast characters and carefully structured script. The action centres on Celia Crowson (Patricia Roc), but her home life is fully established at the beginning of the film and her father and sister are brought back into the plot to provide vignettes of other areas of the Home Front. Celia's romance with a young airman, Fred Blake (Gordon Jackson), whom she marries shortly before he is shot down over Germany, is contrasted with another relationship between the blunt Northern foreman, Charlie Forbes (Eric Portman), and an upper-class girl, Jennifer Knowles (Anne Crawford), who adapts less easily than Celia to factory work.

Celia is no feminist icon – her horizons are firmly set on a steady husband, a nice home and two children – and Fred is equally ordinary. We watch their struggle to overcome their inarticulacy and take pleasure in the way in which they reciprocate each other's kindness and honesty. But the film avoids lapsing into sentimentality by showing the love affair of this unexceptional pair in the context of the wider struggle of the war and by paralleling it with the much more tempestuous relationship of Jennifer and Charlie. Jennifer, with her extravagant clothes and her cigarette holder, initially appears as the sort of upper-class caricature seen clogging the phone lines with her chatter in *Do It Now* (1939) or not being very serious about the war in *Old Mother Riley Joins Up*. But as she becomes integrated into the group and teases the dour foreman into a relationship, she becomes increasingly sympathetic. The doll-like Fred and Celia are like children playing at being adults, solemnly happy in the little world which they have created for themselves until it is cruelly shattered by the war. Charlie and Jennifer are more aware of the world and its pitfalls. Lying together on a hilltop, looking down on the town below, they talk about marriage. The previous sequence of the film concerns Fred's death and ends on a sombre shot of Celia standing by the window of the shabby room which she meant to transform into a home for them. To allow the ill-matched Jennifer and Charlie a harmonious resolution would detract from the significance of Celia's grief, but the aura of gloom needs to be dispelled by some glimpse of hope for the future.

Jennifer assures Charlie she can handle her rich parents and that they would approve of him, but he retorts that he might not approve of them. This is not just a matter of working-class arrogance: Charlie is a competent and efficient foreman in a big factory. Like Clifford Evans in *The Foreman Went to France*, he is sufficiently forward-looking to expect to move into a managerial position. A new man, he makes it clear that he wants no part of the upper-middle-class establishment held responsible for appeasement and the economic woes of the 1930s. He tells Jennifer that marriage between them would be 'not a scrap of use', pointing out that

'The world's roughly made up of two sorts of people, you're one sort and I'm the other. Oh, we're together now there's a war on, we need to be. But what's going to happen when it's over? Shall we go on like this or are we going to slide back? That's what I want to know. I'm not marrying you, Jenny, till I'm sure. I'm turning you down without even asking you.'

This is a less firm rejection than it sounds. Throughout the film their relationship has blossomed despite Charlie's antagonism. There is now a warm rapport between these two characters and the deferral of happiness until the end of the war is a penalty wartime lovers – in and out of films – often have to suffer.

The assertion of the need for a new society as a condition for future happiness emerges in Sidney Gilliat's two subsequent films: *Waterloo Road*, a back-street drama about spivs and marital infidelity, and *The Rake's Progress*, which looks back on the inter-war period with unregretful distrust. *Perfect Strangers*, made by Alexander Korda for MGM, is more indulgently optimistic about the future. Like *Waterloo Road*, it deals with the dangers to marriage of long wartime separations, and like *Millions Like Us*, it focuses on an ordinary lower-middle-class couple, but it has a different outlook to the Launder and Gilliat films.

Robert Donat and Deborah Kerr are cast as Robert and Cathy Wilson whose dreary and sickly lives are transformed by the war. The *Monthly Film Bulletin* was sceptical about the film's veracity:

The war sends Robert into the Navy, which cures his indigestion and makes him strong, brave and handsome, and Catherine into the W.R.N.S., which cures her cold and makes her glamorous. It is perhaps ungracious to wonder how many other weak digestions the Navy has ruined completely and how many Wrens have caught their death of cold.[4]

The film was a box-office success, but one can sympathize with those whose experience of war had been less sanguine than that of Robert and Cathy finding it irritating. Though Robert is shipwrecked and hospitalized, this seems more important for the opportunity it allows him to meet a nurse (Ann Todd), who has all the sensitivity and sophistication he thinks Cathy lacks, than for its illustration of the hazards of war. In *The Gentle Sex*, Dot tells the others that 'I think we might have quite a bit of fun.' The women become firm friends and share jokes and sorrows, but it is a tough life and fun is tempered by tragedy. The war is a dark presence and has to be treated seriously. *Perfect Strangers*, made when Germany had already been defeated (it was released in September 1945), looks at the war as an opportunity for regeneration and renewal and looks to the future with confidence. After a night spent in argument and recriminations, Robert returns to the flat to pick up his luggage and finds Cathy sitting in the window-seat looking out over bomb-damaged London. They are both tired but ready for reconciliation and he gently congratulates her on having the view she wanted but was denied by the surrounding high buildings. She bemoans the destruction and the years it will take to rebuild the city, but he reassures her, as the film ends on their embrace, 'what does that matter, we're young'.

In marked contrast to the populist appeal of *Millions Like Us*, *The Gentle Sex* and *Perfect Stranger*, Vernon Sewell's *The World Owes Me a Living*, made at British National after the departure of John Baxter, has a resolutely upper-middle-class viewpoint. It looks back on the inter-war period from the perspective of a group of ex-First World War flyers who struggle to make a living with their flying circus because the RAF hasn't room for them and the alternative is selling vacuum cleaners. It is a clumsy film with little of the sophistication of David Lean's *This Happy Breed* or Sidney Gilliat's *The Rake's Progress*, which also look back at the inter-war period. However, it offers an insight into a hidden world of jaundiced, hedonistic ex-officers and includes two strikingly unusual female characters. Sonia Dresdel's Eve Heatherley initially appears to be a femme fatale. There are hints at a previous unsatisfactory relationship between her and Paul (David Farrar), the group's leader, who tries to warn her off from decent, straightforward Jack Graves (Jack Livesey). She marries him none the less, and then seems to start an affair with the weak, resentful Jerry (Anthony Hawtrey). When she is struck down by a fatal illness, the two men fight over her memory. Jerry insists that Eve was not his mistress but a supportive friend: the reason he is distressed by her death is that she was the only person who was interested in his ideas and did not think of him as a crank and a failure. Jack himself now becomes interested in Jerry's ideas and recognizes that his scheme for using gliders for an airborne invasion is practical and feasible. He persuades the RAF to back their research and the group are rehabilitated as war clouds gather. However, this

The World Owes Me a Living: Moira (Judy Campbell) ready for flying lessons and romance with Paul Collyer (David Farrar). Supplied by BFI Stills, © courtesy of British National.

interferes with the plans of the other main female character, Moira Barrett (Judy Campbell).[5]

Moira, like Lucy Armitage in *Convoy*, is an independent-minded woman. She has been employing Paul as a flying instructor to improve her skills enough for her to fly across the Atlantic. She is richer, and better adjusted to society, than the men, but the onset of war leaves her stranded. The glider flight they have planned is frowned upon by the Air Ministry as it will attract publicity to what is now a military secret, and all the men in any case are being drafted into the RAF. Paul, at last in secure employment, feels able to ask her to marry him, but she tells him she doesn't want to talk about that now:

> 'Can't you understand how I feel? I'm never allowed to do anything! You talked me out of my first flight and now, after all the fuss and excitement and preparation, this one falls through too. It's all very fine, you've got a job, Jack's got a job, Chuck's got a job, Jerry's got a job. What about me!'

Paul replies: 'But darling, I'm offering you a job. Marry me.' She throws a vase of flowers at him, after which the film cuts back to where it started, with Paul, in hospital after a flying accident, struggling to recognize Moira. He asks her again if she will marry him, but his memory is obviously still faulty, for when she goes out into the waiting room she is greeted by two children eager to see their father. Paul's assumptions about the place of women look absurdly patronizing to modern eyes, but during the war most women regarded the role they were playing in factories and the armed services as temporary; their real job was to marry, bring up children and run a home.[6]

Love in the Scept'red Isle

War severely disrupted family life and eroded normal rules of behaviour. The possibility of sudden death created an atmosphere where romance flowered quickly. There was an increase in unplanned pregnancies, and though many of these were legitimized by marriage, the number of illegitimate births soared.[7] The Nazi occupation of Europe led to a flood of French, Belgian, Czech, Polish and Dutch servicemen into Britain. Problems with language were more than compensated for by the glamour of their cause, and the Poles in particular acquired a reputation as womanizers. From mid-1942 they were joined by large numbers of American GIs in the build-up to the Allied invasion of France. By spring 1944 there were close to one and a half million Americans in Britain. They were better paid and better dressed than their British counterparts, and were kept well supplied with cigarettes, sweets, nylons and condoms, giving them an unfair competitive advantage in attracting the attention of British women. Norman Longmate explains the resentment they aroused among British servicemen:

> Until the GIs began to arrive in 1942 British soldiers had regarded squalid conditions, petty tyranny, coarse clothes, poverty-stricken dependants and an insultingly low rate of pay as the inevitable consequence of being unlucky enough to be called up. The arrival of the Americans proved that none of this was necessary, and though the real culprits were the British Government, it was easier to blame the Americans for being better off. (Longmate, 1975, p. 101)

The immediate attraction of the GIs was their glamour – a combination of the escape from austerity they seemed to offer and the association of Americans with Hollywood films – but it was sustained by mutual appreciation. According to a woman working in an aircraft factory in Leicester:

'A British soldier would take a girl for a drink, bore her to death talking about cars or sport, etc. If he saw any "mates" he abandoned the girl except to buy her a drink now and then until it was time to go home. With the GIs it was very different. The GI would buy me a drink and entertain me as though I was the only person in the room.' (Quoted in Longmate, 1975, p. 257)

There was a less pleasant side to the story – abortions, illegitimate children, and an increase in prostitution and venereal disease – which can be glimpsed in post-war films like *Good Time Girl* (David Macdonald, 1948), but films made during the war are diplomatically positive. They celebrate English society and values by presenting them through bemused but increasingly admiring foreign eyes, and competition over women is handled warily. There is a stress on friendship rather than passion between foreign men and British women; only rarely are British men displaced, and where they are they react with stoicism and good humour. Some Americans are brash and tactless (though generally good-hearted), but they are balanced against more important characters who are kindly, considerate and friendly. Not until *Yanks* in 1978 does an American win a working-class Englishwoman away from her British Army boyfriend and not until *The Affair* in 1995 is a sexual relationship between an Englishwoman and a black GI shown.

In *A Canterbury Tale*, a land girl, Alison Smith (Sheila Sim), teams up with a GI, Sergeant Bob Johnson (Sergeant John Sweet), and an English sergeant, Peter Gibbs (Dennis Price), to prove that the man who threw glue in her hair is the local magistrate, Thomas Colpeper (Eric Portman). In a more conventional film, Alison might have had to fight off the rival claims of the British and American sergeants until matters were resolved by the return of the fiancé whom she thought was dead. Instead, Pressburger deflects the film into more mystical concerns, leaving Alison, Bob and Peter to collaborate with asexual chumminess. Bob's incomprehension about English customs provides an amusing undercurrent and his status as an English-speaking outsider allows him to cross class and cultural barriers with impunity. At the smithy, for example, where Alison's ignorance of such things as felly joints is gently mocked, Bob – brought up among the forests of Oregon – is warmly accepted as a man who understands country crafts and he is invited to dinner with the blacksmith (Edward Rigby). The film is inclusive enough to allow Bob serious

160

consideration, but it is not his point of view that dominates the film. He remains a visitor with an essentially superficial view of the English traditions Colpeper attempts to impart.[8]

In *The Way to the Stars*, English values are reasserted in a context tantamount to invasion. The RAF Blenheim squadron around which the first half of the film centres is packed off to Egypt to make way for Americans in their much more powerful Flying Fortresses. Toddy (Rosamund John), whose British husband is killed in the first half of the film, is courted by Johnny Hollis (Douglass Montgomery) in the second. Anglo-American romance figures heavily, but conflict is superficial and easily overcome. The brash American played by Bonar Colleano dates the decreasingly shy girl whom Peter Penrose (John Mills) has backed away from marrying, but for her he is never more than a lively distraction. When Peter has come to terms with the prospect of arbitrary death she is there waiting for him, unsullied by infidelity. The relationship between Johnny Hollis and Toddy is much deeper but it is founded on friendship rather than passion. Johnny plays with the widowed Toddy's baby and eagerly shows her photographs of his own wife and children. Towards the end, there are indications that, for Johnny, the line between friendship and love has begun to dissolve – he turns down the opportunity to return to America and his reasons seem more to do with Toddy than with his expressed wish not to desert his crew. This looming romantic dilemma, however, is avoided when he sacrifices his life keeping his plane going long enough for his crew to bale out and for him to crash it beyond the perimeters of the village.

John Patterson (Dean Jagger) in *I Live in Grosvenor Square* is, like Johnny Hollis, a quiet, amiable American airforceman who forms a close attachment to an Englishwoman and dies before they can settle down together. If *Millions Like Us* deals with one sort of people – the ordinary, hard-working people of Britain, adapting stoically to war – *I Live in Grosvenor Square* deals with the other sort. However, as refracted through the eyes of John and his loud-mouthed sidekick, Benjie Greenburg (Elliott Arluck), billeted in Mayfair while they recuperate, they are equally lovable, courageous and good-natured. The Duke of Exmoor (Robert Morley) is a friendly old soul who enjoys being called 'Pop' and invites the two Americans back to his country retreat. There they meet Major David Bruce (Rex Harrison), who has already befriended John and entertained him at his West End club, and Lady Pat Fairfax (Anna Neagle), the Duke's granddaughter.

Lady Pat is initially frosty, aware of the Americans' dismissal of her and David (her childhood sweetheart) as idle dilettantes. But once misunderstandings are cleared up – she is in the WAAF, David heads a commando unit – she and John become attracted to each other. Complications set in, however, and by the time they are resolved, John is back on active service and sacrifices his life crashing his plane safely clear of Exmoor village church. The Englishman loses out in direct competition over a woman but there are mitigating circumstances. Not only is the American the underdog, competing against a richer and more sophisticated man, but when he realizes the depth of David's feelings for Pat, he stops seeing her. It is only the intervention of the Duke, and of David himself, that brings the lovers back together. Also, the love affair is part of a wider pattern which shows the upper classes adapting to a rapidly changing society where nothing can be taken for granted. Just as David has to fight for, and loses, the woman he had assumed he would marry, he also has to fight a tough by-election campaign for the parliamentary seat his family has held for three hundred years – and loses to an anti-government radical.

I Live in Grosvenor Square, where kindly aristocrats welcome ordinary Americans into their stately homes and clubs in a way which the English class system ensured was impossible for them to do with their fellow countrymen, offers a dream of benevolence which appealed to audiences. Wilcox followed up its success with his Mayfair cycle – *Piccadilly Incident, The Courtneys of Curzon Street, Spring in Park Lane* and *Maytime in Mayfair* – old-fashioned romantic melodramas about princes and showgirls, fine ladies and enterprising commoners, rejuvenated by the incorporation of Americans, the war and other topical events. They share an indulgent affection for the English upper classes with Anthony Asquith's *The Demi-Paradise* and Harold French's *English without Tears* (in which an upper-class woman forms a relationship with, respectively, a Russian and the family butler).

Both films star Penelope Dudley Ward, whose mother had been the mistress of the Duke of Windsor until she was superseded by Wallis Simpson.[9] Like Asquith, she was very familiar with the corridors of power and seems to have had no intention of spending much of her life on the stages of Denham and Pinewood. Her earlier roles – as the hysterically spoilt rich girl Toppy Leroy in *The Citadel* (King Vidor, 1938), as the girl who drives David Cranford to his ship and gives him a passionate farewell kiss in *Convoy*, and as the new recruit to the naval officers' wives' club in *In Which We Serve* – were conventional but none the less stylish. In *The Demi-Paradise* and *English without Tears* she plays the type of posh young woman who passes from asexual adolescence to eligible marriage partner that Jane Baxter (in *Ships with Wings*), Carla Lehman (in *Sailors Three, Cottage to*

Love across the class barriers. Joan Heseltine (Penelope Dudley Ward) and her butler, Gilbey (Michael Wilding), enjoy the food of love in *English without Tears*. Supplied by BFI Stills, © courtesy of Carlton International.

Let and *Flying Fortress*) and Joyce Howard (in *The Common Touch*, *The Gentle Sex* and *They Met in the Dark*) often played. But Ward, a thin tomboy who might have been Joyce Grenfell's prettier younger sister, brings a whiff of aristocratic authenticity. With her vivacity and wry humour it is not difficult to believe in the revolutions she sets off in the hearts of Laurence Olivier's pompous Russian Stakhanovite and Michael Wilding's solemn butler (or to understand why, in real life, Carol Reed deserted the coolly beautiful Diana Wynyard for her). Without surrendering anything in the way of femininity or aristocratic assurance, she makes androgynous wartime comradeship seem exciting and love and friendship natural allies.

I Live in Grosvenor Square is a melodrama: we are meant to take Lady Pat's divided heart seriously and the man she chooses dies tragically. *The Demi-Paradise* and *English without Tears*, are romantic comedies where broken hearts can be easily mended and – even if there is a war on – nobody has to die. In *English without Tears*, Joan Heseltine (Ward), the niece of Lady Beauclerk (Margaret Rutherford), confesses to her aunt's butler, Tom Gilbey (Wilding), on the eve of his call-up, that she loves him. Gilbey, a stickler for form, tells her that such a relationship between a lady and a butler is impossible. Two years later he returns, now a second lieutenant and thus a gentleman, and proposes to her. But Joan has grown up and knows thousands of second lieutenants and he has to compete with a bevy of foreign officers headed by the Polish Felix Demborski (Albert Lieven) and the French François de Freycinet (Claude Dauphin). Their rivalry is a friendly one, and it ends up with the three men getting very drunk together and Joan joining the ATS in disgust. The situation is only resolved by the spurned ex-butler becoming a tyrannical major and bullying Joan when she comes under his command, thus rekindling her love. This is not Terence Rattigan at his most sophisticated, but the picture which eventually materializes, of a cosmopolitan society nourished by the eccentric Lady Beauclerk and invigorated by her niece, is endearing.

In *The Demi-Paradise*, a Russian engineer, Ivan Kouznetsoff (Olivier), comes to England in 1939. He finds it wet and unfriendly until his rescue by Ann Tisdall (Ward), whose father and grandfather run the shipbuilding company he has come to place an order with. Ivan finds many of his first impressions contradicted by English warmth, efficiency and hospitality and even goes so far as to propose to Ann. But he discovers that, infuriated by his patronizing assumptions, she has deliberately toyed with his affections and she derisively dismisses his offer. Sadder but wiser, he returns to Russia, while Ann, now aware that she feels much more deeply for him than she realized, is unable to redeem the situation.

In 1941, with the ship almost completed and the revolutionary propeller Ivan has designed giving trouble, he returns and finds himself welcomed as an old friend. Mirroring the disastrous evening of his proposal, Ann and Ivan go to a West End revue (where he is again bemused by the peculiar English humour of Leslie Henson) and Ann tells him that she loves him. But Ivan, having failed to solve the problems with the propeller, is preparing to return to Russia to face the consequences and is too depressed to do more than sadly kiss her hand. After she leaves him in a railway buffet, her love and faith in him combine with a Southern Railways cup of tea to give him the inspiration he needs to solve the problem. Special efforts are made by all the workers to cast and fit the propeller, Ivan makes a speech telling the English what a wonderful race they are and Ann launches the ship.

The story is told as a flashback by Ivan to two British sailors in an icy Russian port and there is nothing to indicate that Ann is with him. But the film is less concerned that its lovers live together happily

English pageantry: Christie (Guy Middleton) as Apollo in *The Demi-Paradise*.
Supplied by Flashbacks, © courtesy of Carlton International.

ever after than that misunderstandings are banished and Anglo-
Russian harmony prevails. On his first visit, Ivan discovered that the
bumbling, lazy bosses who seemed only peripherally interested in
running the shipyard were in fact efficient, practical and hard-
working men with a strong sense of duty and commitment. But the
women – not only Ann, but the maiden aunt (Edie Martin) who

fears him as a bloodthirsty revolutionary, and the ladies (spearheaded by Margaret Rutherford and Joyce Grenfell) who run the town pageant – are beyond his comprehension. On his second visit, Ann, whom he had thought perfidious and false, turns out to be loyal and true, Aunt Midge becomes the first person to welcome him as an ally when the Germans invade Russia, and the organizers of the archaic pageant raise £1000 to help the people of his home town.

Asquith warmly endorses Anglo-Russian co-operation but *The Demi-Paradise* – as its title implies – is about England. As in *I Live in Grosvenor Square*, the fact that we see England through foreign eyes is used as an excuse for self-congratulation and – as in *English without Tears* – there is no hint that the ruling classes are anything other than well-mannered, wise and tolerant. Asquith understands his milieu thoroughly and doesn't bother to fawn on his upper-class eccentrics in the way that Wilcox does, but all three films show the upper classes adapting with humour and democratic pragmatism to the changes wrought by the war and their dominant attitude is one of affection for what remains of the old order rather than enthusiasm for a new one.

The Lure of the Countryside

The English countryside assumed special importance during the war. J. B. Priestley, in his *English Journey* of 1933, had dismissed Old England, 'the country of the cathedrals and minsters, and manor houses and inns, of Parson and Squire; guide-book and quaint highways and byways', as 'a country to lounge about in; for a tourist who can afford to pay a fairly stiff price for a poorish dinner, an inconvenient bedroom and lukewarm water in a small brass jug' (Priestley, 1979, p. 372). But in June 1940, after a night with his rural neighbours of the Local Defence Volunteers, he saw things differently:

> I felt up there a powerful and rewarding sense of community; and with it too a feeling of deep continuity. There we were, ploughman and parson, shepherd and clerk, turning out at night, as our forefathers had often done before us, to keep watch and ward over the sleeping English hills and fields and homesteads. (Priestley, 1940, p. 12)

The heavy reliance on domestic agriculture now that the sea lanes were endangered by German raiders, and the increased awareness of

166

national identity brought about by the threat of invasion, awakened new interest in the countryside. The infiltration by land girls and evacuees of the rural population and the scattering of aerodromes and army bases across the countryside meant that it was opened up to public scrutiny. Angus Calder counters the idea that what was seen was necessarily idyllic: 'As evacuated schoolteachers found, the more picturesque parts of Britain were inhabited by increasingly demoralised, and often remarkably incestuous communities of near paupers' (Calder, 1971, p. 484). The declining fortunes of British agriculture in the face of cheap foreign imports had led to stagnation in the countryside since 1918 but war provoked an agricultural revolution. The number of tractors, for example, increased from 56,000 in 1939 to 253,000 in January 1946, and generations of neglect were swiftly remedied (Calder, 1971, p. 488).

British film-makers took some time to get over their suspicions that the countryside was backward and slightly sinister. *Poison Pen*, for example, directed by Austrian exile Paul Stein, and released in July 1939, shows a village community degenerating into vindictive spite under the onslaught of poison pen letters written by the vicar's sister (Flora Robson), who has been driven mad by a life wasted 'taking slops to senile old fools' and 'talking pious drivel to doters year in year out'. In MGM-British's *Busman's Honeymoon* (Arthur Woods, 1940), things are not very much better. Lord Peter Wimsey (Robert Montgomery) buys his bride, Harriet Vane (Constance Cummings), the country cottage in which she had spent her childhood. They arrive to find the previous owner has been murdered and that all the locals are either mad, bad or dangerous to know. Cummings doesn't fare much better with the English village she visits in David Macdonald's *This England*. This seems like a community fully adjusted to the needs of war, but while sheltering from a bombing raid, two of the locals, Appleyard (Emlyn Williams) and Rookeby (John Clements), take her through the village's history and present a gloomy pageant of 'this sticky, clinging, damnable creeper of an English past'.

Cavalcanti's *Went the Day Well?* acts as a fulcrum between old and new attitudes towards the countryside. The setting is a picturesque Buckinghamshire village with thatched cottages, but it is by no means cut off from the war: a land girl delivers the milk and the narrow high street is soon clogged with military trucks which, as it turns out, carry German soldiers who occupy the village. Power and influence seem to stem from the vicar, the lady of the manor and the organizer of the Home Guard, Oliver Wilsford (Leslie Banks), who acts like a country squire but is in fact a German agent. In the desperate situation that develops, both sides act with savagery. The Germans

167

shoot the aged vicar when he tries to ring the church bell and gun down the Home Guard as they cycle back to the village. The postmistress throws pepper in the eyes of a German soldier, then hacks him to death with an axe. But the film's most dramatic moment, for which Cavalcanti makes unusual use of slow motion, is when Nora Ashton, the vicar's daughter, shoots Oliver Wilsford. Wilsford has been introduced as a genial character who seems to command the respect of the village and something more than respect from Nora (Valerie Taylor). It is soon revealed that he is a traitor, but he continues to fool the villagers, calming Nora's suspicions when she puts together clues revealing oddly un-British characteristics about the soldiers, discouraging effective resistance and foiling an escape bid. By the time Nora shoots him, she has certain proof of his treachery. But the only person who shares this knowledge – the lady of the manor – is killed protecting the children and we might wonder whether Nora will be believed, or whether she will be treated as a vengeful spinster who had more personal reasons for shooting Wilsford.[10]

Sinister overtones also haunt *A Canterbury Tale*. Antonia Lant claims that

> The film marks female sexuality as strange and insalubrious, somehow activated by the blackout, emerging from it, through both the noirish introductory shot of Alison as femme fatale, silhouetted and wreathed in smoke, stamping out her cigarette, and through the 'glueman' plot. (Lant, 1991, p. 209)

Land girl Alison's clear-eyed honesty and pert girlishness quickly dissolve any aura of sexual threat surrounding these first images, but 'the glueman' plot remains puzzling and disturbing. Colpeper throws glue in women's hair in the blackout to discourage them from going out at night with men. This keeps them faithful to their absent boyfriends and husbands and gives the men stationed in the area so little to do that they attend his local history lectures. For C. A. Lejeune this was not the way an English country gentleman ought to behave:

> This fellow may be a mystagogue, with the love of England in his blood, but he is also plainly a crackpot of a rather unpleasant type with bees in the bonnet and bluebottles in the belfry. Only a psychiatrist, I imagine, would be deeply interested in his behaviour.[11]

Colpeper's glue-throwing cannot entirely be dismissed as a Maguffin. To reverse Lant's analysis, it marks male sexuality as dangerous and strange. Hardly a flicker of flirtation passes between Alison and either Peter or Bob, but the four sequences in which she encounters Colpeper are highly emotionally charged. With her hair still wet from attempting to wash away the glue, she is interviewed by Colpeper, who tells her that he refuses to employ women on the land. Uncowed, she insists that she will find other work in the neighbourhood. At Colpeper's crowded slide show, the atmospheric lighting on her and Colpeper's faces mark them out as the two people in the room in tune with his theme of the mystical continuity of the English landscape and – though she continues to work with Bob and Peter to prove he is the glueman – they shift from being adversaries closer to becoming allies.

On a hillside, Alison hears voices; Colpeper rises from the grass to assure her that he hears the same sounds. Alone in the long grass with 'the glueman' there is a frisson of danger, but Alison's clarity and steadfastness seem to banish Colpeper's misogyny and turn him from black to white magician. As they lean in to each other they look as much like a couple as Jennifer and Charlie on their hillside in *Millions Like Us*; and there is a further echo when Colpeper queries Alison's fiancé's father's attitude to her: ' "Good family", "shopgirl", rather dilapidated phrases for wartime.' In their final scene together, Alison goes to Canterbury to reclaim the caravan that she stayed in with her fiancé while he was excavating the old pilgrim's road. She finds it infested with moths and, for the only time in the film, becomes emotionally distraught. Colpeper appears and offers solace. His comment, 'I don't want to hurt your feelings but there's something impermanent about a caravan, everything on wheels must be on the move sooner or later', seems to answer her wish when she first sees his house (not knowing it is his): 'What wouldn't I give to grow old in a place like that.' But this is another impossible romance. The garage-owner rushes in to tell her that her fiancé is alive after all, and Colpeper slips silently away.

A Canterbury Tale, muddled though it might be, is the most ambitious and original of the films which explore the English countryside. In *Poison Pen*, superstition and ignorance disrupt the community; in *Went the Day Well?*, aggression is directed outwards towards the enemy (though this is complicated by the treacherous role played by Wilsford); in *Busman's Honeymoon*, mysteries are dispelled by rational and sophisticated town-dwellers. But in *A Canterbury Tale*, mysticism and pre-rational thought are shown to be potent and valuable – the source of blessings as well as curses.

Great Day, made by Lance Comfort for RKO, has superficial similarities with *A Canterbury Tale*. It is set in a similar rural community and

photographed by Powell's cinematographer, Ernest Hillier; Eric Portman again plays an odd misfit who feels passionately about the
English countryside, and Sheila Sim plays another land girl.[12] This
time they are father and daughter, Captain and Margaret Ellis, and
Mrs Ellis is played by Flora Robson. In contrast to her role in *Poison
Pen*, she is genuinely supportive of the village community and her
troubles stem from her husband, a First World War soldier who has
never come to terms with peacetime society and finds it even more
difficult to adjust to a new war where his services are not required.
As Sue Harper points out, *Great Day* makes a strong argument 'for the
vigour, inventiveness and communality of women', whereas the men
'are presented as more emotionally vulnerable and dependent' (Harper, 1996, p. 209). There is one striking sequence in which Margaret,
after a night sorting out her romantic problems, finds her father by a
lake in the early hours of the morning and averts his suicide. But for
most of the film Captain Ellis provokes distrust and unease rather
than sympathy. The situation of *Poison Pen* is reversed. Even though
they have an embittered spinster in their midst (the sister of the
farmer for whom Margaret works, who fears she will marry him and
usurp her position), the women work together harmoniously to
revitalize the community and support the war effort. The film ends
on a celebratory note with a reception organized by the Women's
Institute for Eleanor Roosevelt, but stability seems precarious while
men like Captain Ellis, gnawed by anxiety and dissatisfaction, remain
excluded. A cosier view of the countryside emerges in Two Cities'
rural comedies, *Tawny Pipit* and *Don't Take It to Heart*, though their
pastoral delights are tinged by a mild radicalism.

English without Tears begins with Lady Beauclerk and her entourage
travelling to Geneva to persuade the League of Nations to set up
sanctuaries for migrating British birds. Her proposal is misunderstood
as imperial aggrandizement, and once war breaks out she switches
her efforts to providing sanctuary for anti-Nazi exiles. But the British
affection for birds is taken up in *Tawny Pipit*. A recuperating airman,
Jimmy (Niall MacGinnis), and his nurse, Hazel (Rosamund John),
discover a pair of pipits nesting in a meadow near the village of
Lipsbury Lea. They call in Hazel's ornithologist uncle (Brefni O'Rorke)
and gain the support of a couple of evacuees, the vicar and the local
gentleman, Colonel Barton-Barrington (Bernard Miles). They are a
less self-consciously ordinary couple than Fred and Celia in *Millions
Like Us*, but their unstuffy classlessness makes them seem harbingers
of the new society. Like Colonel Blimp, Barton-Barrington is a
likeable fuddy-duddy who has to come to terms with the fact that
his power and influence have faded; and like Captain Ellis, he is a

veteran of the First World War, and holds quaint ideas about fighting the Hun. But he is also adaptable and approachable. His address to the village about the pipits sets the tone for the film:

> 'Now then, this love of animals and of nature has always been part and parcel of the British way of life and it's going to go on being. Now we've welcomed to our country thousands of foreigners at one time or another, French, Dutch, Poles, Czechs and so on, and a lot of them are jolly decent people, and anyway they can't help being foreigners. Well, that's what these little pipits are, you see. And we're jolly well going to see that they get fair play or we shall want to know the reason why. Now we've heard a great deal about the differences between Nazism and democracy, but in my opinion the big difference between ourselves and the Hun is that the Hun doesn't know the meaning of "play the game" and he never did and he never will. What we mean to give these little pipits is fair play and a square deal and no hitting below the belt.'

Although this speech is a ragbag of clichés, the way in which they are strung together with a knowing acknowledgement of their absurdity is therapeutic and reassuring. The hospitality offered to the pipits is extended to a visiting Russian sniper to whom the Colonel donates a rifle with a telescopic sight. As in *The Demi-Paradise*, the film captures something of the enthusiastic support for Russia that swept through Britain. In February 1943 this euphoria had climaxed with a spectacular pageant organized by Basil Dean at the Albert Hall:

> Two narrators, Ralph Richardson as the Spokesman and Sybil Thorndike as the Spokeswoman, were installed in two steel towers, placed at either side of the orchestral platform. Cloaked and helmeted all in gold they make impressive figures as they summon detachments from the nation's war effort to enter the arena: coalminers with their safety lamps, transport drivers in white coats, firemen, munition and railway workers. . . . Some of the detachments as they enter the arena raise their clenched fists in Communist salute, shouting 'Russia'. (Dean, 1973, pp. 284–5)

The Cold War almost obliterated the memory of such events, and there is a refreshing incongruity about the intrusion of schoolchildren singing the Internationale and land girls expressing their envy and admiration for a Russian sniper in a gentle rural comedy.

Don't Take It to Heart – like *The Flemish Farm*, produced by Sydney Box and written and directed by Jeffrey Dell – comes closest to Calder's vision of a countryside populated by incestuous paupers.

Everyone in the village of Chaunduyt is from one branch or another of the Bucket (or Buquet) family, and their main activity seems to be poaching and drinking rough cider. Plagued by a bald and aggressive incomer, Pike (Alfred Drayton), who wants to prosecute them for poaching and plough up their cricket pitch, they are galvanized into action by a radical young lawyer, Peter Hayward (Richard Greene), and Mary (Patricia Medina), the socialist lady of the manor.

Here, the old order is so decayed that the Earl of Chaunduyt (Brefni O'Rorke) is only too pleased to change places with Harry Bucket the poacher (Wylie Watson) when a mischievous ghost reveals that the line of succession was switched a few hundred years ago and that Harry is the real lord. Lady Mary is equally keen to ditch her aristocratic heritage and no longer feels compelled by her egalitarian principles to pursue her childhood sweetheart, George Bucket (who has anyway begun an incestuous relationship with one of the village girls), now his father is an earl. Harry points the way forward, muddling up his kings and queens during his guided tour but turning the run-down stately home into a rudimentary theme park offering the public postcards, cream teas and boat trips on the lake. It is left to his cousin, Alfred Bucket (Edward Rigby), the butler, to lament the passing of the of the old order, of the lavish days when the Chaunduyts ran 'a stable of thirty-five hunters down here and seventeen chorus girls in Town'.[13] He is acutely aware of the real casualties of this decline:

'The funny thing is, it isn't his lordship who feels it. When he heard it, he laughed. No, it's me and my sort, all the butlers and valets and footmen who waited on them and looked after them and bowed and scraped and milorded them. We're the ones, no one will have any use for us.'

Passion and Loss

Loneliness, tragedy, isolation, and the ever-present prospect of death led during the war to introversion and fantasy, as well as a desire for closeness and communality. As far as film was concerned, this was a need supplied by such Hollywood weepies as *Gone with the Wind* (Victor Fleming, 1939) and *Mrs Miniver*, and musical extravaganzas like *Yankee Doodle Dandy* (Michael Curtiz, 1942) and *Hollywood Canteen* (Delmer Daves, 1944), but there was also a potent and popular strand of British fantasy cinema. In Brian Desmond Hurst's *Dangerous Moonlight*, for example, an American reporter, Carole Peters (Sally

Gray), comes across a Polish airman, Stefan Radetzky (Anton Wal-brook), playing a piano in a bombed-out building in Warsaw. They are parted, but he eventually escapes to America where they are reunited, and she encourages him to play concerts publicizing and raising money for the Polish cause. They fall in love and marry, but – like such Hollywood exiles as David Niven, Laurence Olivier and Anna Neagle – he itches for a more active role in the struggle and goes to Britain to fight with the RAF. His wife thinks this is suicidally stupid and, by the time she has come round to his point of view, he has lost his memory in a plane crash. She encourages him to play the 'Warsaw Concerto', composed from his memories of their first meeting; this restores his memory and they begin their life again. The way in which the film deals with the combustible nature of relationships begun in dramatic and dangerous surroundings, and the lush and romantic way the story is told, provided a template for the melo-dramas that dominated the box-office from 1943 onwards.

With the exception of *Love Story*, and the framing story of *The Man in Grey*, Gainsborough's melodrama cycle ignores the war, but their star-crossed lovers torn apart by conflicting demands are subject to the same burdens of sacrifice and separation as the protagonists of war films. By 1944, when *Love Story* was released, the war was beginning to recede and – albeit obliquely – the problems of peace-time adjustment were beginning to emerge. In *Dangerous Moonlight*, Stefan's war wounds are a convenient way of displaying his heroism and providing a mechanism for bringing together the estranged lovers; in *Love Story*, the injuries Kit (Stewart Granger) has suffered are invisible to the naked eye but they cast a dark cloud over his future. He appears to be a coward and a skiver (as Granger would be in his next film, *Waterloo Road*), leading a carefree, womanizing life in Cornwall, well away from the war. In fact, he is a brave RAF pilot who is going blind because of the injury he suffered giving his crew enough time to bail out from a burning aircraft. He refuses to confide in anyone except his childhood friend Judy (Patricia Roc) because he cannot stand the thought of being pitied. His deception is neatly matched by that of the heroine, Lissa (Margaret Lockwood), a concert pianist who has been told she has only a few months to live and has come to Cornwall for a moment of relaxation before dying.

Numerous misunderstandings and romantic complications caused by the tough, chain-smoking Judy (a remarkable reversal of Roc's role in *Millions Like Us*) mean that the relationship between Kit and Lissa is a turbulent one. Judy is happy for Kit to go blind (rather than risk the operation which will kill or cure him), knowing that her only chance to hold him is by making him dependent on her. But Lissa's altruism and true love eventually win through, Kit's sight is restored, and only her terminal illness remains a threat to their happiness. Kit universalizes their situation to that of lovers everywhere threatened by the war, telling Lissa:

'Happiness such as we can have is worth grasping even if it's only for a day, an hour. If you can stand on the highest peak for one moment, you have what most people strive in vain for all their lives. . . . You say you've only a few months. Well how long has anyone in the world? How long have I? [He has rejoined the RAF.] A month? A year? Well perhaps I'll get away with it altogether. And so may you. But we're all living dangerously, there isn't any certainty any more. Just today and the hope of tomorrow.'

Leslie Arliss, the director of *The Man in Grey, Love Story* and *The Wicked Lady*, deliberately defied the tendency towards restraint, attacking diffidence and insisting on the importance of allowing characters 'to express their feelings freely in films without any embarrassment either to themselves or to their audiences'.[14] Audiences responded positively, but the critics were embarrassed. Isobel Quigley in *Time and Tide* found Kit and Lissa's free flow of emotion especially painful. She questioned Gainsborough's reason for making *Love Story*, with its 'puppets tortured by whimsy. . . . It's simpering, it's mawkish, it makes one squirm in one's fauteuil.'[15] But critics were not wholly immune to romanticism. C. A. Lejeune, in the 'Film-Goer's Diary' appended to *Red Roses Every Night*, wasted little time on realism and war films and insisted: 'we wanted action, movement, colour, music, comedy – some sort of proxy release from our pent-up emotions' (Morgan, 1948, p. 69). For many of the critics it was less a matter of realism or tinsel than the tastefulness and quality of the tinsel. Had *Love Story* been made with Rosamund John, Robert Donat and Peggy Ashcroft (the type of actors favoured by Korda or Two Cities), it would have been a much more acceptable film. *The Seventh Veil*, equally lush and melodramatic but starring Ann Todd and James Mason, won guarded approval from the critics and – though they are embellished by theatrical craftsmanship and concentrate on an exclusively middle-class world – films like *The Way to the Stars* and *Brief Encounter* address similar issues of passion and loss. Films that mixed issues of social concern with melodramatic romance provided a bridge between the quality films praised by the critics and the middle-brow melodramas upon which the critics heaped their obloquy.

The Lamp Still Burns ostensibly explores the conflict between love and duty. Leslie Howard, the film's producer, was shot down on a flight from Lisbon before it was completed and, although he had left the direction of the film to Maurice Elvey, he might have been expected to shape it firmly during post-production. As it is, *The Lamp Still Burns* lurches between a lush romance and a critique of the harsh regime suffered by nurses in pre-NHS hospitals.[16] Rosamund John plays Hilary Clarke, a proto-feminist architect who, after a road accident involving her office boy, decides to become a nurse. Her change of direction seems also to have been influenced by the disturbance set up by a clash with one of her clients, the arrogantly masculine Larry Rains (Stewart Granger). Rains seems equally unsettled by the encounter: when, in her capacity as nurse, she visits the sickbay she designed for his factory, he seems more interested in her than in the celebrity violinist he is engaged to. An explosion results in Rains and his fiancée going to the hospital, and, delirious after an operation, he declares his love for Hilary. These passionate events are paralleled by Hilary's mundane attempts to come to terms with the arduous training and petty rules and restrictions involved in becoming a nurse. In the book on which the film is based, Monica Dickens' *One Pair of Feet*, the new nurse becomes so frustrated at the tyrannical way in which the hospital is run that she gives up her vocation and takes a job in a munitions factory. However, this was not a particularly apt propaganda message for a major film to convey, and Elvey, Howard and their writers struggle hard to squeeze the plea for reform entailed in the book into a more acceptable form.

After an emotional Christmas Day in which Hilary insists that Larry patch things up with his fiancée (who in turn tells him she would rather go back to her violin than be a consolation prize for the women he really loves), she shares a bottle of beer with a young doctor, argues with the matron and is dismissed from the service. A disciplinary hearing allows her to plead her case, but she knows that Larry – who is now on the Board after making a financial gift to the hospital – loves her and is free to marry. If she wins her appeal she can continue with the rather grim life of a nurse; if she fails, she can marry a rich man. She makes a passionate speech and wins her case and Larry, doggedly backing her, tells her that 'one day you're going to have a job and a home'. He promises to campaign for a health service where women do not have to choose between marriage and their career. In the circumstances, it is not a bad solution. But in ameliorating the critique of hospital conditions, Hilary's rebellion is made to seem querulous, and her romantic self-sacrifice unnecessary when she could usefully continue her career as an architect designing medical centres.

Piccadilly Incident is more darkly pessimistic in its combination of a legal wrangle over the rights of children born to unwittingly bigamous parents and a tangled tale of romantic love. The social situation of *I Live in Grosvenor Square* is reversed in *Piccadilly Incident*, with Anna Neagle playing Diana 'Sunshine' Fraser, a showgirl turned Wren who bumps into a baronet, Alan Pearson (Michael Wilding), in the blackout. They marry on Diana's 72-hour leave before she is sent to Singapore. When the island is evacuated, she is shipwrecked and reported lost at sea. Alan, after a suitable period of grieving, finds solace with a friendly American women. In fact, marooned on a desert island with four randy sailors, Diana and her friend Sally (Brenda Bruce) are struggling valiantly to save themselves for their men back home. As Sally wearily complains, comforting Diana when she returns dishevelled after a tussle on the moonlit beach: 'If the allies had fought for democracy as hard as we have to fight for our honour, the war would have been over in a month.' Frustration leads to a desperate attempt to escape the island, and eventual rescue and return. But for Diana there is no joyful reunion. Alan has remarried and now has a child. Distraught, she visits her father-in-law, a judge played by A. E. Matthews (whose earlier incarnations included the customs officer who was reluctant to allow Theo Kretschmar-Schuldorff into Britain in *The Life and Death of Colonel Blimp*, and the selfish, misanthropic old lord in *They Came to a City*). Although he is kindly and diplomatic, his priorities are stability, respectability and the smooth transition of property and titles – all of which Diana's return threatens. He gloomily commiserates with her, pointing out how happy Alan is with his new wife, what a long time it is since her whirlwind romance with him and what problems her existence causes the child – who will now be declared illegitimate and be unable to inherit the family title. It is a timely reminder that the old order, if shabby and in retreat, still had sharp teeth and would fight fiercely to retain its property and values.

Diana tries to do the decent thing, finding Alan and telling him that she has been having a jolly time with a sailor on a desert island for the last few years and it is a good thing he is married to someone else. He doesn't believe her, and when she is mortally wounded in a bomb attack, she confesses that she lied and has never stopped loving him. No doubt this is the tidiest solution (though, ironically, not of the inheritance issue, as the child's legitimacy cannot be backdated), but it is none the less a bleak one. In 1947 Wilcox lashed out at what he considered the morbid tendencies of his fellow producers, advocating 'what one might call open pictures, happy unclouded pictures' rather than 'sadism, abnormality and psycho-analysis'.[17] But the war left a legacy of trauma, gloom and exhaustion which scarred post-war societies and burst through into films despite the intentions of an increasingly conventional and conformist industry to concentrate on happy people living smooth, untroubled lives. Even Wilcox and Neagle, after the froth of *Spring in Park Lane* and *Maytime in Mayfair*, were to plunge back again into the murky depths with *Odette* in 1950.

NOTES

1 'Almost a fifth of all adult women did not marry between 1921 and 1939' (Summerfield, 1984, p. 13). Taylor (1983), p. 177, points out that war losses have to be balanced against emigration – mainly of young single men – which was running at 300,000 a year before 1914. But the war also left one and a half million men permanently damaged by poison gas, war wounds and shell-shock. Those men who were married were likely to be dependent on their wives and to die prematurely, those who were not would be an unappealing prospect as partners.

2 For the troubled production history of the film, see Brunel (1949), pp. 192–4. Brunel, whose career at last seemed to be picking up after a long period in the doldrums, began directing the film at a small studio in Highbury, north London, but he found it difficult to get satisfactory results in the cramped conditions. When Howard took over as director, he insisted that production be restarted at Denham.

3 Gilliat wrote the script for *Rome Express* and collaborated with Ian Dalrymple, Angus MacPhail and Emlyn Williams on the script of *Friday the Thirteenth*. Frank Launder was script editor on *Bank Holiday*.

4 *Monthly Film Bulletin*, September 1945, p. 106.

5 After *Convoy*, Judy Campbell played Doris, the stuck-up barmaid of the Shakespeare in *Saloon Bar*, and a crime reporter who teams up with a writer of detective thrillers to solve the murder in *East of Piccadilly* (Harold Huth, 1942).

6 It was a view shared by a number of talented actresses: Judy Campbell continued an active and successful career, but Penelope Dudley Ward married Carol Reed and made no further films after *English without Tears*; Valerie Hobson and Rosamund John both married politicians (John Profumo and John Silkin, respectively); and Sheila Sim married Richard Attenborough. By the mid-1950s all of them had given up acting.

7 According to Costello (1986), p. 14, illegitimate births rose from 4.4 per cent in 1939 to 8.9 per cent in 1945. Divorce went up from 5.75 per cent in 1939 to 10.5 per cent in 1945.

8 For its American release in 1949, *A Canterbury Tale* was drastically reorganized to make Bob the central character and a newly shot prologue was added in which he attempts to explain his experiences in England to the girl who is now his wife. See Lant (1991), pp. 197–219.

9 Nicholas Wapshott's description of the first meeting of Freda Dudley Ward and the future Edward VIII reads very like the opening sequence of Wilcox's *Piccadilly Incident*: 'walking through Belgrave Square one

evening during the First World War, the maroons went up announcing an air raid. She made for the open front door of a house in the square and was invited down to the basement for shelter. In the semi-darkness Freda met and spoke to a man who, it transpired, was the Prince of Wales. He asked Freda to stay for the rest of the party which had been interrupted by the bombing. They danced until the early hours and their intimate friendship lasted for the next sixteen years' (Wapshott, 1990, p. 147).

10 The German commander insists that Nora be confined with Mrs Fraser and the children because 'she might become hysterical' (she has just seen her aged father gunned down so she has good reason to be upset). Valerie Taylor made few subsequent appearances in films, though she turns up as the severe, crabbed beauty salon owner Madame Denise, in Polanski's *Repulsion* (1964).

11 *Observer*, 14 May 1944.

12 Chillingbourne is a combination of the village of Chilham and the town of Sittingbourne.

13 If one follows the genealogy seriously, Harry is in fact Alfred's great-uncle.

14 Publicity material on 'Studio Personalities' (BFI microfiche, *Love Story*).

15 *Time and Tide*, 14 October 1944.

16 Two of the leading players in *The Lamp Still Burns* – Stewart Granger and Cathleen Nesbitt – were to appear the following year in similar but more full-blooded roles in Asquith's *Fanny by Gaslight* (with Phyllis Calvert providing a feisty substitute for Rosamund John).

17 *Kinematograph Weekly*, 18 December 1947, p. 18.

7

Tigers in the Smoke:
Dark Legacies of the War

A Dorset housewife went walking down the garden path with
Hitler, who promised her some nice plants. That same night
her best friend dreamed she was in bed with Hitler 'who had
his boots on'. . . . Mutual respect was usual in these nocturnal
relationships, as again with an Essex widow (69) who was
anxiously 'trying to tidy up a room . . . because I felt Hitler
was possibly coming'. (Tom Harrisson, 1976, p. 320)

S
ome of the best-remembered war films come from the last
period of the war – *San Demetrio London*, *Western Approaches*,
The Way Ahead, *The True Glory* – but the trend in feature film
production was towards costume films, comic fantasies and contemporary melodramas. From 1945 onwards, melodrama and nostalgia
seeped into war films like Asquith's *The Way to the Stars*, Dearden and
Relph's *The Captive Heart* and *Frieda*, and Wilcox's *I Live in Grosvenor
Square* and *Piccadilly Incident*. Grimmer and more realistic films like
The Small Back Room and *Against the Wind* fared less well at the box-
office. However, the turn away from the war was a temporary one,
and masked an enduring fascination which was to haunt the following decade.

The Problems of Peace

Joy at the ending of the war was soon dampened by the legacy left
by six years of death and destruction. Britain came out of the war

with external disinvestment amounting to four thousand million
pounds; with her shipping, an important source of invisible exports,
reduced by thirty per cent; with her civilian industries physically

179

run down after six years of war and her visible exports running at no more than four-tenths of her pre-war level; with 355,000 of her citizens dead by enemy action at home or abroad. (Calder, 1971, p. 677)

Returning servicemen were unlikely to find homes fit for heroes to live in. Three-quarters of a million dwellings had been destroyed or severely damaged by bombing and few resources had been diverted from the war effort into rebuilding and repair (Addison, 1985, p. 56). Shortages meant that clothes, petrol and many foodstuffs continued to be rationed until the early 1950s. Demobilization was carried out more smoothly, fairly and quickly than after the First World War, and though there were mutinies by impatient airmen at RAF bases in India and the Middle East, this was a less worrying phenomenon than the 20,000 deserters on the loose in Britain. Unable to go into legitimate employment and without ration books, they were easily recruited to serve the flourishing black market.

The conflicting legacies of altruism and violence, community spirit and individual enterprise, lawlessness and integrity fought for prominence in post-war Britain. As Harry Hopkins explains:

There existed side by side, often overlapping in baffling fashion, an England of 'Plain living and high thinking', and an England of high living and distinctly low thinking, an England of 'Reality' and an England of 'Escape', the England of Sir Stafford Cripps, of equality of sacrifice and the export drive, and the England of the black market restaurant, the expense account, and Mr Sidney Stanley, 'the Pole of Park Lane'. (Hopkins, 1963, p. 97)

Cinema provided a forum for the playing out of these contradictions, leavening a diet of innocuous comedies and celebrations of heroism with a darker strand of melodramas, horror and crime films. Films about the war were few in number until 1950, but after the success of *The Wooden Horse* and *Odette* they became a popular staple of British cinema. Though they have been dismissed by some critics as formulaic and simple-mindedly patriotic, they often incorporate elements of trauma and disturbance.[1]

Formidable though the problems of peace might have been, they were unlikely to daunt a community which had survived six years of war, and the Labour government elected in July 1945 proceeded with the implementation of a welfare state and the nationalization of creakingly inefficient industries. In Europe, where the ravages of war had been more severe, chaos and famine threatened. Victims of the

Nazis attempted to struggle back to their homelands; Germans who had settled in Poland, Czechoslovakia, East Prussia and the Baltic States were driven out. Camps for displaced persons peppered the Continent.

Not many British films concern themselves with the international situation, but in the late 1940s Gainsborough's *The Lost People* and *Portrait from Life* and Ealing's *Frieda* – all with the young Swedish actress Mai Zetterling – dealt with the fate of displaced persons and examined British attitudes to post-war Germany.[2] *The Lost People* was exactly the type of worthwhile, humanist project which appealed to Sydney and Muriel Box – a Brechtian epic drama set in a German theatre commandeered as a dispersal centre – but its production was plagued by difficulties.[3] A large cast, a low budget and an inappropriate director proved a fatal combination and much of the film had to be reshot by Muriel Box before it could be released. The studio sets, the heavy reliance on dialogue, and the subordination of relationships between the characters to a didactic message make it seem more like a 1950s television play than a commercial feature film, and one gets little sense of the reality of life in war-torn Europe. The sergeant major (William Hartnell) tells Captain Ridley (Dennis Price): 'You need to be a cross between a lion-tamer and King Solomon to sort this little lot out', but Ridley settles conflicts like a firm but fair scoutmaster. Threats to his authority are defused by a bubonic plague scare and the murder of an innocent girl, which he uses as illustrations of what might happen if British common sense were to be overthrown.

Zetterling plays the gamine Lily, whose streetwise cynicism is dissolved by the earnest affection of the honest, selfless Jan (Richard Attenborough). The couple represent a utopian hope for new life and future happiness. After a chaste night together, Ridley arranges their wedding. But the film is more concerned with ramming home its message – the need for everyone to overcome their prejudices and work together – than with the fate of its individual characters, and Lily is arbitrarily killed off.

The other romantic relationship is between Ridley and Marie (Siobhan McKenna), a Franco-Irish communist. She is an anti-British troublemaker, determined the refugees should run the camp themselves and that those suspected of collaboration be denied food. But, like Lily, she is charmed by a man who is kind and generous towards her without wanting sexual favours in return. Their relationship is potentially fascinating, but it is dampened by Ridley's urbane asexuality: when asked why he has not kissed her he replies, 'Well to tell you the truth, it never really occurred to me'. Emotionally stillborn though the film is, the questioning of British good intentions and the linking of communism with anti-Nazi liberation gives it a surprisingly unhysterical tone at a time when the Iron Curtain had fallen and the Berlin airlift was taking place.

Portrait from Life, Terence Fisher's first film, is a more skilful affair, though it steers clear of political issues. A British officer (Guy Rolfe) with the Army of Occupation trawls through the camps for displaced persons in Germany in search of Hildegarde (Zetterling), a beautiful girl whose portrait he has seen while on leave in London. When he finds her, she seems to be fully integrated into a German family. Careful detective work reveals, however, that her supposed parents are a leading Nazi and his mistress who have taken advantage of her amnesia to give credence to their forged identity. The real father, to whom she is restored, is an Austrian-Jewish professor living in London. The way in which Herbert Lom's suave Nazi acts like Baron Frankenstein in remoulding the girl to help him create a new life for himself makes *Portrait from Life* a fascinating precursor of Fisher's horror films, and as with Dracula and Frankenstein, the moral issues are clear-cut. The question of whether the sweet and innocent Hildegarde is a good German does not arise. We know, even when she does not, that she is someone other than who she seems. It will eventually be revealed that she is a Jew whose life has been so blighted by the Nazis that she has had to block out the past. Things were much murkier in the film which introduced Zetterling to British audiences, Basil Dearden's *Frieda*.

In *The Black Record*, a series of broadcasts made for the Overseas Service of the BBC in 1940, Lord Vansittart had argued that the Nazis were a new variation on Germany's militaristic culture; it was not an evil elite but the whole German population who were guilty of the war. Vansittart, a long-time ally of Churchill's and a violent opponent of appeasement, found support for his view on the left as well as on the right of the political spectrum. Hugh Dalton snapped him up from his nebulous post as Chief Diplomatic Adviser to the government and made him a Special Adviser to SOE; and Nell, the exponent of the 'all Germans are guilty' viewpoint in *Frieda*, is a Labour MP. However, 'Vansittartism' was never universally accepted. During the war, films like *Pastor Hall*, *49th Parallel* and *Freedom Radio* had striven – with official backing – to differentiate between good Germans and Nazis, and fervent anti-Nazis like J. B. Priestley were willing to acknowledge a 'bright face' as well as a 'dark face' to Germany. If the bright face, 'which speaks to us of beautiful music, profound philosophy, Gothic romance, young men and maidens wandering through the enchanted forests', had been eclipsed by the horrors of Nazism, the same thing could happen in Britain or anywhere else (Priestley, 1940, p. 17). One did not have to be German to be a Nazi; hence the danger of fifth columnists. Once the war was over, the need to rediscover good Germans – to clean up Germany's bright face – became paramount. In the new world order Germany might be the defeated enemy, but it also acted as an essential buffer between the West and the vastly expanded Soviet empire.

In *Frieda*, a British airman, Robert Dawson (David Farrar), returns home to his small country town with his new bride, Frieda Mannsfeld (Zetterling), a German nurse who helped him escape from a prisoner of war camp. He calms her apprehensions by assuring her that the people of Denfield will welcome her with open arms. However, the local children label her 'Lily the Werewolf', Robert's family act towards her with cold disapproval and the only person to offer support is his widowed sister-in-law Judy (Glynis Johns), who appears anxious to contradict the impression that she herself expected to marry him.

Posters advertising the film asked audiences: 'Could you love Frieda?' 'Would you take Frieda into your home?' As Frieda is gentle and kind (and played by a Swede rather than a German), the question is unfairly loaded. Nevertheless, the question of her guilt as a German is dealt with seriously. Nazi atrocities, such as the massacre at Lidice in reprisal for the assassination of Reinhard Heydrich, had provoked widespread revulsion, but the full horror of the Holocaust only became known with the liberation of the concentration camps. Frieda has to face up to what has been done by her country, having her pleasant evening at the pictures turned into a nightmare when the newsreel shows images of conditions at Belsen; and having to confront the Nazi heritage in the form of her brother (Albert Lieven), who is unrepentant about the past and eager for a new war.

The most ambiguous figure in the film is David's Aunt Nell (Flora Robson), whose 'undomesticated femininity' enables her to share a pint with the men in the pub and get herself elected to Parliament. Brunsdon and Moseley (1997) pair her with Rikky, Frieda's Nazi brother, in that both of them believe there is something inherent in the German soul which makes Germans all essentially the same.[4] Nell is not prepared to absolve Frieda from the collective guilt, and says as much in her election speech. Frieda, belying Terry Lovell's description of her as 'a patient, long-suffering, almost masochistic victim' (Lovell, 1984, p. 32), confronts Nell with the logical consequences of her attitude: 'Then it does not matter what I am myself? If I do right or wrong? If my heart is good or bad? I am a German, that is all that counts.' Her answer is evasive, assuring Frieda that

The looming nightmare: Frieda (Mai Zetterling), Robert (David Farrar) and Nell (Flora Robson) in *Frieda*. Supplied by Flashbacks, © courtesy of Canal + Image.

once the war is over nine out of ten people will accept her. But when Frieda presses her, she admits that she is one of the one in ten who will not. She acts as a lightning conductor, expressing views about the Germans which would not have been uncommon in the aftermath of the war. Unlike Rikky, the fanatic driven by irrational zeal, Nell expresses her views thoughtfully and carefully, and by the end of the film she accepts she was wrong: 'No matter who they are, no matter what they've done, you can't treat human beings as though they were less than human without becoming less than human yourself.'[5]

In *Love Story* and *The Wicked Lady*, two women (in the former, Patricia Roc's Judy and Margaret Lockwood's Lissa; in the latter, Roc's Caroline and Lockwood's Barbara) compete with each other for a man. There is an element of friendship between the women, but it is ruthlessly subordinated to the aim of romantic conquest. In *Frieda* the opposite happens. The friendship between Judy and Frieda is genuine – a rapport expressed in looks and gestures, mirroring and resemblances – and they instinctively understand each other. When

Robert shows his affinity for Judy by helping her with a jigsaw puzzle, she leaves the room, aware of the threat she poses, and Frieda, unsettled, asks Robert to postpone their wedding. While Judy is in London with Nell, Robert and Frieda's romance blossoms. When Judy returns, the chimera of her natural partnership with Robert has vanished. At the Christmas Eve dance, the band plays 'Love Steals Your Heart' (the song which symbolizes the undying love of Ralph and Caroline in *The Wicked Lady*) while they spend a moment alone together, but Robert's thoughts are now with Frieda. Within the film's essentially pragmatic world this is no tragedy. Judy exchanges the possibility of an almost incestuous romance with a man who would have been a substitute for his dead brother for the friendship and gratitude of a couple she has helped bring together.

Terry Lovell (1984) and Charlotte Brunsdon and Rachel Moseley (1997) stress the physical similarity between Frieda and Judy. Lovell insists that 'To legitimate her formal position as successor to the place which seems rightfully to belong to Judy, Frieda must show that she is "really" like Judy and to that extent fit to replace her' (Lovell, 1984, p. 32). But this underestimates both the ambition and the conservatism of the film. There is no evidence that Judy adores Robert and enjoys housework; on the contrary, like the independent-minded women played by Penelope Dudley Ward and Judy Campbell, she is assertive and practical beyond the confines of home. She deals firmly with the bureaucrat who seems reluctant to allow Frieda a ration book and takes efficient charge of Nell's parliamentary diary. What she would offer Robert is the sort of affable, equal relationship that Lady Pat shares with David Bruce in *I Live in Grosvenor Square* and which she rejects in favour of more exotic romance with an American. Frieda represents a more nurturing, domesticated femininity, which Robert doesn't quite know how to handle, but she also remains obstinately German. When she is most happy, most integrated into the rural community – riding on a hay wain past thatched English cottages, coming out from the jolly, fraternal Christmas party – she breaks out into German song. Her looks, her humanist concern, her quiet intensity, even the way in which she throws herself into the rushing stream when the man she loves rejects her, associate her with German romanticism, with the bright face of Germany which had been eclipsed by Hitler's dark shadow.

Charles Barr claims that Robert acts sadistically towards Frieda. Most of the evidence he adduces is faulty. It is Frieda, not Robert, who insists on separate bedrooms, a second marriage and an interval before it takes place; Frieda, not Robert, who insists on staying to listen to Nell's election speech and watch the painful concentration camp newsreel (Barr, 1977, pp. 75–6). None the less, the iconography of the film supports Barr's perceptions, and American psychologists Nathan Leites and Martha Wolfenstein saw *Frieda* as part of a group of British films sharing common characteristics:

> British films in contrast to both American and French tend to see women more as possible victims of men's violence or betrayal. Correspondingly they give more emphasis to the dual potentialities of men, as attackers or rescuers. . . . The cautionary images of the beautiful girl found strangled in the park, of a girl about to jump off a moonlit bridge because she is driven to distraction by a violent and moody man, or simply of a beautiful blond head bowed in suffering, are recurrent motifs in British films. (Leites and Wolfenstein, 1950, p. 23)

But Robert's power seems fettered by the subtle alliance of Frieda and Judy.[6] Farrar's performances in *The World Owes Me a Living*, *Frieda*, *Black Narcissus*, *The Small Back Room* and *Cage of Gold* are all marked by a vigorous, surly masculinity. Only in the last film of this quintet is he malevolent, but there is a brooding undercurrent of violence in his persona which makes him seem dangerous. If Frieda is less formidable than the strong women played by Judy Campbell, Deborah Kerr and Kathleen Byron whom Farrar confronts in the other films, she is nevertheless part of a network of women – Judy, Nell, Bob's mother, even Edith the housekeeper – who dominate the film. Barr's misconception of Robert as sadistic is understandable: to see this big, energetic man moving uncomfortably in the delicate female world creates an undercurrent of tension which is only finally dissipated in the brutal fight between David and Rikky, and Frieda's dramatic suicide bid.

Unsettled Servicemen

Andrew Spicer notes that during the war a number of articles were published in the *Lancet* and the *British Medical Journal* about the problem of 'war neuroses', and documentaries such as *A Soldier Comes Home* (1946) and pamphlets like Mass Observation's *The Journey Home* (1944) alerted the public to the sort of problems returning ex-servicemen were likely to pose (Spicer, 2001, ch. 8, 'Damaged men').

Mass Observation reported 'a fear of purposelessness':

wartime values of communal effort, and working for an end beyond self and employer, are widely expected to vanish with the peace. Unable to feel assured of their future as members of a purposeful community, many are thinking in terms of private adventurism or escape, so accentuating the potential conflict between wartime co-operation and post-war 'selfishness'. (Mass Observation, 1944, p. 116)[7]

These concerns manifested themselves in the immediate post-war period in such films as *Mine Own Executioner*, with Kieron Moore as a war hero who has been turned dangerously psychotic by his war experience, and in the numerous films about deserters and men who turn to crime because they are unable to readjust to peacetime society.

In Cavalcanti's *They Made Me a Fugitive*, Clem Morgan (Trevor Howard) is an ex-flyer so bored with civilian life that he allows the toss of a coin to determine whether or not he will throw in his lot with a bunch of black-market racketeers. In *The Flamingo Affair*, an ex-commando captain, Dick Tarleton (Denis Webb), is tempted into a web of intrigue and crime by a glittering femme fatale. In *Night Beat*, two ex-commandos who have returned from Burma join the police force, and while one (Hector Ross) sticks to the straight and narrow, the other (Ronald Howard) quickly gets bored and involves himself with spivs and loose women. In *Good Time Girl* (David Macdonald, 1948), Gwen Rawlings (Jean Kent) falls into her deepest pit of degradation when she joins up with a couple of American deserters (Bonar Colleano and Hugh McDermott), who cosh the motorist she lures into their trap so brutally that he dies.

Sight and Sound reviewer Arthur Vesselo complained that *They Made Me a Fugitive* and films of a similar ilk were guilty of a 'morbid burrowing'. Such films seemed to echo the German Expressionist cinema of the 1920s and were seen as worrying symptoms of a disturbed society. Despite dealing with indigenously British issues, they 'have nevertheless an unpleasant undertone, a parade of frustrated violence, an inversion and disordering of moral values, a groping into the grimier recesses of the mind, which are unhealthy symptoms of the same kind of illness'.[8] Cavalcanti had shown some interest in morbid themes in the two supernatural films he produced at Ealing, *The Halfway House* (Basil Dearden, 1944) and *Dead of Night* (Basil Dearden/Robert Hamer/Charles Crichton/Cavalcanti, 1945). But the episode that he directed – the ventriloquist's dummy story in *Dead of Night* – has a dark sense of fun and a pleasure in odd juxtapositions which might seem closer to Surrealism than Expressionism.

In *They Made Me a Fugitive*, as in *Went the Day Well?*, there are semi-comic elements (for example, the Valhalla funeral parlour which is used as a front by the criminal gang, with illicit goods being carted around in coffins), and it is the vitality of this low-life milieu rather than its sordidness or degradation which seems to attract Cavalcanti. But once again there is savagery, cruelty and a willingness to go past the boundaries of acceptable behaviour into uncomfortable areas beyond, and Vesselo detects a sardonic pessimism which character-ized American thrillers and melodramas that were subsequently labelled *film noir*.[9]

Noirish elements are also apparent in Ralph Thomas's *The Clouded Yellow*, produced by Betty Box. Trevor Howard plays Major David Summers, an SIS agent who, having fouled up his last mission, is discarded as a burnt-out wreck. He takes a job in a country house, cataloguing a butterfly collection. His employer, Nicholas Fenton (Barry Jones), is sympathetic – 'Convalescence of the mind. Peace. That's what we all strive for, don't we.' And in turn David supports Fenton's disturbed niece, Sophie (Jean Simmons). She is isolated and unhappy and her aunt (Sonia Dresdel) takes pains to make her believe she is mad, but David assures her he understands her depression:

> 'I know what it's like to be alone. I know what despair can feel like too. Even the sun looks grey. And self-pity's such a dreary thing that you despise yourself and wonder whether it matters if you go on living or not.'

Helping her seems to banish David's own shadows, but their happi-ness is threatened by the murder of a loutish womanizer (Maxwell Reed), for which Sophie is the main suspect. David persuades her to go on the run with him and, though his boss at SIS proves treacher-ous, he is able to evade capture by using his secret agent contacts and skills. As in *They Made Me a Fugitive*, the film ends with the real murderer falling to his death without telling the police the true story, but the outlook is less gloomy. In *They Made Me a Fugitive*, Clem Morgan has spent bitter years imprisoned on Dartmoor and expects to go back there. A not unsympathetic policeman tells him he can submit his case to the Home Secretary if there is any fresh evidence, but he is not optimistic. In *The Clouded Yellow*, David and Sophie have proved their resourcefulness and resilience on the run in Newcastle, the Lake District and Liverpool and found help and support – particu-larly from the Jewish couple whom David had helped escape Nazi clutches during the war. Thus, they have recovered their sanity and

188

self-respect. Although they are under arrest, it seems likely they will clear their names and build a new life together.

Apart from the American deserters in *Good Time Girl*, all these maladjusted characters are redeemable, but ex-servicemen turned completely bad appear in two films at the end of the decade – Lance Comfort's *Silent Dust* and Basil Dearden's *Cage of Gold*. Both are well-heeled officers for whom ample opportunities would be available in peacetime society and their downfall is blamed on personal weakness rather than on an unjust or ungrateful society.

Nigel Patrick's Simon Rawley in *Silent Dust* is introduced as a dead hero, for whom his rich, blind father (Stephen Murray) has built a memorial pavilion. But on the eve of the ceremony to mark its opening, he reappears, dishevelled and scarred, and turns out to be a coward, a sadist and a murderer. David Farrar's Bill Glennon in *Cage of Gold* is less obviously evil. He is a wing commander with a good war record and might be considered the same sort of restless adventurer as Clem Morgan in *They Made Me a Fugitive*. But whereas Morgan develops into a satisfactory hero – a daredevil tempted into wrongdoing, but paying a disproportionately heavy price for his folly – Glennon becomes the film's villain, a cruel wastrel who exploits women in his search for an easy life. In *They Made Me a Fugitive*, our sympathies naturally lie with Morgan in his conflict with the sadistic and immoral gangster, Narcy (Griffith Jones); but Glennon's glossy charisma is contrasted unfavourably with the dull but sincere altruism of Alan Kearn (James Donald), a doctor who turns down a career in Harley Street to work within the newly established National Health Service. Kearn comforts and marries the woman (Jean Simmons) whom Glennon has abandoned and tries to protect her from the police when he suspects she has murdered him. Glennon, like Rawley, is killed by someone he has wronged. Time and sympathy seemed to be running out for those unwilling or unable to adjust to the rules of peacetime society.

The characters in these films are disrupted and maladjusted, but they are not psychologically disturbed.[10] The only film to be centrally concerned with someone seriously traumatized by the war is *Mine Own Executioner*, directed by Anthony Kimmins, from a novel by Nigel Balchin. Burgess Meredith plays Felix Milne, a non-medically trained psychologist whose professional life is disrupted by irritation with his scatty wife (Dulcie Gray) and attraction for a more glamorous woman (Christine Norden). This has disastrous consequences. One of his patients, Adam Lucien (Kieron Moore), has been unbalanced by his experiences in a Japanese prisoner of war camp and is potentially murderous. While Felix is out wining and dining with the other

Cage of Gold: The unreliable airman: Bill Glennon (David Farrar) charms his way back into the affections of Judith (Jean Simmons), who ought to have learnt her lesson the first time. Supplied by BFI Stills, © courtesy of Canal + Image.

woman, Adam relapses into psychosis, returns home and strangles his wife. The film meanders into areas not normally explored in British films – medical ethics, the treatment of psychological disorder, the disruptive effect of sexual allure on a companionate marriage – but splitting maladjustment between psychologist and patient means that neither is dealt with satisfactorily: Felix is irresponsibly indulgent and Adam's psychological problems are never fully explained.

The Small Back Room, adapted by Emeric Pressburger from another of Balchin's novels and directed by Michael Powell, is more cogent. Sammy Rice (David Farrar) is a bomb disposal expert who has had his foot blown off and the film dwells on his battle with constant pain and with the whisky which is the only thing that effectively alleviates it. Like Stewart Granger's Kit in *Love Story*, he is sensitive about his impairment, but whereas Kit wards off pity with a breezy charm, Sammy protects himself by being grumpy, bad-tempered and self-destructive. Unlike *Mine Own Executioner*, *The Small Back Room* is set during the war, but in marked contrast to the wartime films, it shows

190

the war effort as bedevilled by cynicism, vanity and personal ambition. In a society run on Machiavellian rather than on benevolent lines, Sammy's pain is a mark of his integrity, ensuring that his values remain undistorted by material considerations.

Like Felix, he relies heavily on a patient, loving woman (his fiancée Susan, played by Kathleen Byron). Felix cannot hold back from philandering, and needs the chastening experience of Adam Lucien's death to bring him to his senses. Sammy is blankly indifferent to other women, and though it is ostensibly his tin foot which troubles him, he wrestles with inner demons. Thus the long final section where he defuses a bomb on a stony, deserted beach serves as a sort of exorcism, fitting him once again for normal life.[11]

Post-war malaise darkened resistance films like *Against the Wind* and *Odette*, and although most 1950s films are brighter, concentrating on glory rather than trauma, a handful of films turn their back on the prevailing optimism and cast a dark shadow.

The Legacy of the War

Jacques Tourneur's *Circle of Danger* and Guy Hamilton's *The Intruder* are both structured around the investigation of a mystery with its roots in the war. In Tourneur's film, an American, Clay Douglas (Ray Milland), seeks an explanation for the suspicious death of his younger brother during a commando raid. He traces officers and men of his brother's British platoon, which allows the film the opportunity to visit various parts of Britain – Welsh coalmines, the Scottish Highlands, Covent Garden market, the Thames at Shepperton, Richmond Park – and meet a cross-section of the population. None of them are very helpful or revealing. One of them, Sholto Lewis (Marius Goring), a fey choreographer who arouses the red-blooded Douglas's contempt, is hostile and evasive. Douglas's investigation is complicated by his rivalry with the platoon's taciturn commander, Hamish McArran (Hugh Sinclair), for the affections of a writer and illustrator of children's books, Elspeth Graham (Patricia Roc). The American gets the girl, but the revelation of the film's mystery – that the young American volunteer was shot in the back of the head by his British officer because his gung-ho bravado jeopardized the success of the mission – makes Hamish's concession over Elspeth look like a gift of atonement rather than a defeat.

In *The Intruder*, the subject of the investigation is still alive and the quest for the truth comes from within the group. Wolf Merton (Jack Hawkins), an ex-tank commander, comes home after a game of golf to find his house being burgled by Ginger Edwards (Michael Medwin), one of his wartime squadron. He coaxes the bitter and suspicious Ginger into talking, but when the doorbell rings he assumes Merton has betrayed him and runs off. Puzzled and disturbed, Merton determines to trace Ginger and find out what turned a good soldier into a thief. As in *Circle of Danger*, a number of not wholly reliable witnesses fill in the story, but *The Intruder* eschews romance almost entirely and returns to the war in a series of vivid flashbacks. It is revealed that Ginger was a particularly courageous and popular soldier who has been turned to the bad after being given a heavy prison sentence for accidentally killing the bullying uncle who caused the death of his young brother. His fate is juxtaposed with that of two other members of the squad whom Merton calls upon.

John Summers (George Cole) is a Covent Garden trader. In his flashback we see him promoted out of the ranks and being mystified and humiliated by the rituals of the officers' mess. Ginger feels sorry for him and they get very drunk together. Merton understands the situation and refuses to reprimand Summers or to allow him to resign his commission. Summers uses the episode to explain why he has not kept in touch with Ginger, but Merton is not taken in. The bonds between the two men are not likely to have been broken so easily and Summers is hiding Ginger in the cellar. Summers' reversion to his working-class origins might be seen as a reassurance that the class system has survived the war intact. But in a film which harks back to wartime solidarity, the fact that Summers lies to protect Ginger is favourably contrasted with the behaviour of the middle-class Captain Pirry.

Pirry (Dennis Price) has become a businessman and is shown to be supercilious and devious. Unlike Merton, his commanding officer, he has retained his military title and is trading off a spurious wartime record. In Summers' flashback we see him acting as a snob and a sneak, and the flashback Merton drifts into as he is kept waiting in the outer office reveals him as a coward. Reluctantly pushing forward into enemy territory, the tank Pirry commands is hit and catches fire. Panic-stricken, he runs for it, leaving Ginger to drag out a wounded man before the tank bursts into flames. Aware now that Merton, as well as Ginger, knows of his cowardice, Pirry tips off the police to follow Merton in the expectation that he will eventually lead them to him.

Merton does finally catch up with Ginger and gives him a severe talking to about the need to take one's punishment. But such rhetoric now means nothing to him. Like Clem Morgan in *They Made Me a Fugitive*, he is embittered by his experience of the brutality and arbitrary injustice of the British legal situation. Cornered by the police, he prefers to take any chance rather than give himself up. Merton, caught between the desperation of a hunted man and the implacable force of the law, has to decide which side he is on. His solution is to revert to the flexible morality of wartime: he lies to the police and covers Ginger's escape. To his surprise, Ginger subsequently gives himself up. Merton's gesture of solidarity has restored his faith and made it possible for him to be reintegrated back into society. The warmth of the reconciliation between Merton and Ginger makes the ending less downbeat than that of *They Made Me a Fugitive*, where Morgan involuntarily returns to prison to serve out his unjust sentence. But the film sounds a note of warning on how easily wartime ideals could become corroded and forgotten.

The Ship That Died of Shame is more anxious about wartime virtues becoming peacetime threats. The film begins in the war with Bill Randall (George Baker), the captain of a motor gunboat, having an exhilarating time carrying out hit-and-run raids in coastal waters. The mood darkens when his newly wed wife, Helen (Virginia McKenna), is killed by a stray German bomb, and the malaise continues into peacetime. Randall fails to establish his own shipbuilding business and his plea to be taken back in his old job falls on deaf ears. Drinking in the depressing surroundings of the Coastal Services Club, he bumps into his wartime second-in-command, George Hoskins (Richard Attenborough), who is flush with money and obviously doing well. Randall welcomes Hoskins' proposal to rescue their old ship from the breaker's yard and stifles his scruples about the sort of smuggling activity in which Hoskins is involved. With the help of a third member of the crew, the coxswain Birdie Dick (Bill Owen), Randall makes the ship seaworthy. But as the unsavouriness of the tasks undertaken increases, the ship performs less and less willingly. The relationship between the three men degenerates and the ship destroys itself on the rocks.

Jim Cook argues that *The Ship That Died of Shame* 'is an exemplary film of its time, not only activating memories but, through its narrative structure, constructing and expressing a striking critique of such nostalgia and the drives which fuel it' (Cook, 1986, p. 362). Tim O'Sullivan argues precisely the opposite, that the film offers 'a nostalgic view of wartime operations and the male comradeship involved, as a situation based on a clear and desirable order, on a harmony and moral purpose which underpinned the danger, spirit of adventure and thrills of active service' (O'Sullivan, 1997, p. 173). Both views are plausible. Dearden and Relph's moral message dwells on the necessity to abjure the past and come to terms with the present. But, in contrast to the flashbacks in *The Intruder*, which show war as bloody

Haunted by memories of the war: Hoskins (Richard Attenborough) and Randall (George Baker) in *The Ship That Died of Shame*. Supplied by British Cinema and Television Research Group Archive, De Montfort University, © courtesy of Canal + Image.

and dangerous, the wartime sequences in *The Ship That Died of Shame* – apart from Randall's grim discovery of his wife's death – are thrilling and exciting, while the peacetime world is unappetisingly grim.

Nicholas Pronay asserts that the war films made between 1945 and 1960 'allowed the people in the audience to re-live vicariously their experiences, the fears, guilt and dilemmas of their own particular war; and to catharsise psychological sores still festering' (Pronay, 1988, p. 51). There is no evidence to show that *Reach for the Sky* or *The Dam Busters* made RAF fighter and bomber crews feel better about the loss of their colleagues or their own injuries, or that SOE agents were particularly soothed and reassured by watching *Odette* or *Carve Her Name with Pride*. Prisoner of war camp films such as *The Wooden Horse* and *The Colditz Story* might have pleased the tiny minority of prisoners who attempted to escape, but they were unlikely to have been cathartic for the great majority who had no opportunity or inclination to do so. The aspect of the war which affected most people's lives – the Blitz – was not touched on in the films of the

1950s, and the operation which involved the greatest number of British troops, the invasion of Europe, had to wait for the American-backed epic *The Longest Day* (Andrew Marton, Ken Annakin and Bernhard Wicki) in 1962. In the proper sense of a tragedy which purges through shock and pity, few of the war films of the 1950s can be regarded as cathartic and their appeal to contemporary audiences lies in their confirmation of the idea that it was British courage and enterprise that won the war.

The Ship That Died of Shame – like the other film based on a story by Nicholas Monsarrat, *The Cruel Sea* – is concerned less with victory or heroism than with the overwhelming experience of the war on men's lives (women hardly figure in the film). In both films there is a regretful farewell to the comradeship and purposefulness of the war. *The Cruel Sea* looks forward to ease and comfort after the hardship of the war. *The Ship That Died of Shame* shows how seedy peacetime society has turned out to be; but the attempt to recapture the excitement and common purpose of the war years is shown to be a false trail. Bill Randall faces up to his festering psychological scars and exorcizes them. Nostalgia beckons but has to be purged.

Tiger in the Smoke is more straightforwardly eager to banish the past. It begins with the plans for a society lady's wedding being disrupted by the apparent return from the dead of her husband, thought to have been killed in the war. Major Elkin, an Anglo-French commando officer whom Meg (Muriel Pavlow) married when she was very young, turns out to be dead after all. Unlike Simon Rawley in *Silent Dust* or Bill Glennon in *Cage of Gold*, his legacy is a benevolent one: treasure from his ancestral home in Brittany as a wedding gift to whoever steps into his shoes. But before the affluent upper-middle-class couple can receive their benediction – a priceless carved wooden Madonna – they have to endure a campaign of terror waged by Elkin's old platoon, who imagine the treasure as gold and silver and regard it as their just recompense for the misfortune and neglect visited upon them by an ungrateful peacetime society.

Raymond Durgnat notes that the opening sequence 'with its street-band of wretched and embittered ex-servicemen tramping through London fogs, dogging the city gent with scrannel music' presents 'a world "possessed" by the equal and complementary evils of unaware complacency and craven spite' (Durgnat, 1970, p. 240). The sourness of relations between stuffy representatives of the middle-class and working-class characters who are depraved or degraded gives the film an unusual edginess. For most of its duration, the heroine, Meg, is on the verge of hysteria, and Levett (Donald Sinden), her future husband, is bound and gagged.

Traces of evil left by the war: Meg (Muriel Pavlow) looks on as Havoc (Tony Wright) searches for secret documents in *Tiger in the Smoke*. Supplied by Flashbacks, © courtesy of Carlton International.

The ex-servicemen turned buskers appear like apparitions in the fog. They are nightmarish figures, but once we see them properly they are exposed as pathetic wrecks of men, irreparably damaged by their wartime experiences. Their leader, the psychopathic Jack Havoc (Tony Wright), who breaks out of jail and commits cold-blooded murder, is much more of a threat. The police chief regards him as the incarnation of evil; Meg thinks she sees dark wings as he jumps from a high window; and her father, the canon, confronts him as the anti-Christ when he discovers him marauding though his church.

Tony Wright hardly manages to make Havoc more than a bland spiv (Beatrice Varley as his mother is a much more frightening distillation of spritely malice), and at the end of the film he is shown to be a coward. With Havoc ignominiously hauled away, strapped to a stretcher, and the buskers dead, dispersed or arrested, it seems that the fog of the past can be banished, the ghosts of war exorcized. But anarchic working-class forces released by the war still seem to linger and the middle-class world represented by Meg and her family has been shaken to its foundations.

Intimations of the Macabre

For Roy Armes, *The Man Who Never Was* is typical of 1950s war films, where 'The prevalent officer world is one of hard work, quiet confidence and stiff-upper-lip understatement, and the other ranks all know their place and are jolly good chaps really' (Armes, 1978, p. 178). In fact, the film has a macabre quality at odds with Armes' impression of cosy blandness. When Ewen Montagu (Clifton Webb) first proposes using a document-laden dead body to fool the Germans about the invasion of Sicily, he is told it is an outrageous, disgusting, preposterous idea – and to investigate its feasibility. The trawl through hospitals and mortuaries for the right sort of body, the need to persuade a bereaved parent that his son can serve his country even when dead, the technicalities of preservation and decay, allow disturbing currents only glimpsed in most 1950s war films to rise to the surface.

The script by Nigel Balchin sticks to a tight plot which allows no digressions, but one might expect his meticulously constructed box of tricks to be thrown out of kilter by the casting of two American stars. Webb, best known as the decadent villain of Otto Preminger's *Laura* (1944), adopts an appropriately sardonic tone for Montagu; Gloria Grahame, as a frothy American chatterbox, fits less easily into the upper-class English world, but her character flares into life in two bravura sequences.

The plot involves dumping a dead body on the Spanish shore with confidential letters indicating that the Allied invasion will be launched on Sardinia rather than Sicily. To help give the corpse a convincing identity, he also carries bills, membership cards and a love letter from his fiancée. Pam (Josephine Griffin), a pretty English Wren who is acting as Montagu's assistant, is asked to write the letter but, not having been in love herself, she is stilted and unconvincing. It is her flatmate, Lucy (Grahame), an avowed hedonist who doesn't believe in getting involved too deeply, who steps into the breach. She has allowed her RAF boyfriend to buy her a ring, and she takes over the writing of the letter as a means of pouring out her confused feelings.

Chickens come home to roost when the Germans send O'Reilly (Stephen Boyd), a frighteningly plausible Irish spy, to check on the identity of the dead man. British obtuseness ensures that his tailor and his club reveal nothing useful, so O'Reilly tries to contact the writer of the passionate love letter. He confronts Pam, who stalls indecisively until Lucy arrives, drunk and bemused having learnt that her fiancé has been killed in action. She knows little of the operation for which the letter has been used and, as O'Reilly is sharp and persistent, it looks likely that she will blow the whole scheme. However, she instinctively divines what is going on and switches the grief she feels about her fiancé into a paean of loss for the dead courier. This extraordinarily deft piece of acting convinces O'Reilly that the dead man and his letters are genuine, but it also serves as a eulogy for the young men of the RAF with whom Lucy has emotionally entangled herself and for the anonymous man whose body has been used so deviously.

Like *The Man Who Never Was*, Carol Reed's *The Key* is intriguingly macabre. Stella (Sophia Loren) shelters and succours a succession of war-weary tugboat captains who are never quite sure whether she is a goddess or a whore, an island of love in the cold, cruel world or a siren leading them on to their doom. In several films, from *The Way to the Stars* onwards, men find it difficult combining the tenderness of a love relationship with the need to steel oneself for death. *The Key* dwells more misanthropically on fear. Constant exposure to mortal danger has a corrosive effect on men which leads to their disintegration and consequent death. Stella's ability to discern the stages of this process makes her something of a witch, but it also fills her with a despairing quietude.

Her current lover, Chris (Trevor Howard), tries to be hardbitten and cheerful but he knows his fate is sealed and passes the key (to the flat and to Stella) on to an eligible successor, David Rose (William Holden). Rose, an American fresh to the struggle, is less haunted by the shadow of death and Stella begins to wake from her zombie-like state. At this point, with the ghost of Stella's previous lover banished and Rose dispelling the doom clouds, the film appears to shed its allegorical pretensions and turn into a romance. The stakes are upped when Rose is sent out to rescue an American freighter which is ignoring safety precautions and openly broadcasting its position. Rationally, he knows that his chances of survival are minimal and he passes on the key. Rose's tug is sunk but he is picked up. When he returns to the flat he finds Stella gone – disgusted at Rose's lack of faith, she has shaken off her somnambulism and left to start a new life. He rushes to the railway station, only to see her train pulling out.

At the end of *The Third Man*, a breathtakingly long-held shot allows Anna (Alida Valli) to walk along a cemetery avenue and straight past Holly Martins, brusquely demolishing his hopes of a future relationship. It is an unhappy end, but like the strings pulling up the sails of a ship in a bottle it jerks everything into place. The end of *The Key* has the opposite effect: David Rose missing Stella's train merely looks like bad timing, exposing the film's inconsistencies and robbing the lovers' relationship of meaning and significance. The carefully built-up atmosphere, the enigmatic acting, the profound themes, dissolve into banality.

Fighting a Dirty War

Towards the end of the 1950s, films began to emerge that, if not actually questioning the need to fight, dwelt more on the futility and viciousness of war than on the opportunities for heroism. Films like *The Way to the Stars* and *The Cruel Sea* are very moving in their portrayal of loss, but the context is one of necessary struggle. From *The Bridge on the River Kwai* onwards, the moral dilemmas are more confusing and the answers less clear-cut.

Two films at the end of the 1950s, Anthony Asquith's *Orders to Kill* and Jack Lee's *Circle of Deception*, delve particularly deeply into moral issues. Both concern young men sent to France on missions to do with the resistance. Gene Summers (Paul Massie), in *Orders to Kill*, is a grounded USAF pilot who, instead of being given the sort of desk job he might have expected, is recruited by an intelligence organization – presumably the OSS (Office of Strategic Services – predecessor of the CIA). His first mission is to kill a French resistance worker, Marcel Lafitte, who is thought to have turned informer. In *Circle of Deception*, Paul Raine (Bradford Dillman), a Canadian who has not yet seen active service, is trained by SOE and sent to join a resistance circuit in the Pas de Calais with badly needed explosives detonators and orders to carry out sabotage operations in preparation for the expected invasion. His superior knows that the circuit has been broken up and is now controlled by German intelligence – and, of course, that the invasion will be in Normandy, not in northern France. He cold-bloodedly calculates that Raine will fall into German hands and, when tortured, will pass on vital misinformation.

In both films the men in control are liars and cynics. In *Orders to Kill*, Kimball (John Crawford) decides to send Summers to France because his mother is a friend of the general and he might be uncomfortable to have around the office. Rawson (Harry Andrews), in *Circle of Deception*, is a much more formidable figure. Having settled on Raine, he does not hesitate to exploit his patriotic enthusiasm or his sexual attraction to Lucy (Suzy Parker), his female assistant. He traps him irrevocably by neutralizing the poison capsule which would have allowed him to escape from endless torture. Andrews is excellent at playing stern, tough, yet kindly elder men (as in *Ice Cold in*

Alex), but here he makes no attempt to make his character pleasant or sympathetic. Dubious of the value of the psychological profiling tests he is advised to use in selecting a candidate for the mission, he anonymously fills one in himself. The report that comes back suggests he is cold, manipulative and unscrupulous. Without a trace of embarrassment he recognizes its accuracy and is converted to the efficacy of the tests. Morality for Rawson is a matter of logistics. If the Germans can be persuaded that the Allied invasion will be directed at the Pas de Calais, rather than Normandy, then tens of thousands of lives might be saved.[12] As he tells Lucy when she challenges their right to treat a good man so unfairly:

> 'Fair? Fair? What do you think war is? A game of tennis? Is it fair to plan an attack knowing that a lot of your men are going to be killed? If you're going to win a war attacks have to be made and someone has to take the responsibility of planning them.'[13]

The mission in *Orders to Kill* is more mundane but less plausible. The evidence against Lafitte is conjectural and the obligation on Summers, an inexperienced agent, to kill him seems unreasonable. The plot is made to work by the spellbinding performances Asquith coaxes from Leslie French as Lafitte and Irene Worth as Summers' French contact, Léonie. Lafitte exudes honesty and kindness, and his demise is all the more tragic for the help and support he gives the nervous Summers with his mission. Léonie is a sophisticated, sexually alluring older woman and – despite her impeccable morality – behaves like a femme fatale in a *film noir*, urging the young protagonist to murder an innocent man.

When Summers meets Lafitte, his resolve crumbles. This kind, bespectacled, generous and sentimental man doesn't seem like a traitor. His vulnerability is accentuated in a sequence where he invites Summers into his home. Madame Lafitte is cautious, unfriendly, constantly on the watch for the troubles her husband's childlike trustingness might get him into. His daughter, Morrisette, is plain and bespectacled like her father (she was cast as one of the Ugly Sisters in her convent school's production of *Cinderella*), but she loves dancing. In an ironic echo of the sequence in *The Way to the Stars*, where the teenage Jean Simmons entrances a packed ballroom, singing, 'Let him go, let him tarry', Morrisette insists on performing an ungainly dance. It has the opposite effect. Summers, distracted by the argument going on in the next room between Lafitte and his wife, virtually ignores her. Even so, the girl takes no offence and when, after the war is over, he returns to make financial recompense for murdering her father, she welcomes him as a friend.

Summers grows to like and trust Lafitte, and he confronts Léonie with his reasons for doubting his guilt, including the sentimental one which he expects her, as a woman, to understand, that he is devoted to his cat. She listens patiently and then delivers a furious diatribe:

> 'Dozens of Frenchmen have risked their lives receiving and guiding and hiding and clothing you, only to have you go to pieces because of a stinking cat that should have been carved up and eaten months ago. Himmler likes cats, Goering likes pictures, Hitler likes music, Goebbels is a wonderful father – what of it?'

She goes on to ask him whether he thought of the innocent people, the women and children – and cats – that he had killed on his bombing missions. She is utterly convincing and, chastened, he goes off to do something evil and wrong.[14]

Circle of Deception, the last film made by Jack Lee before he gave up on British cinema and emigrated to Australia, features a young American couple, Bradford Dillman and Suzy Parker, in the leading roles. The film might have had greater resonance had it taken a chance on emerging British actors – Oliver Reed and Susannah York, for example – but Dillman and Parker have an innocent placidity which makes them seem like obedient children to Andrews' monstrous father figure in a Freudian family plot.

In both *Orders to Kill* and *Circle of Deception*, the lead man goes to pieces after completing his mission. Raine, living among the low-life of Tangiers, is cured by the cathartic act of telling his story and having it reinterpreted by the woman whom he assumes despises him, but who feels guilt for her part in the deception played on him. Ironically, the Machiavellian manipulation to which he has been subjected is easier for him to deal with than the belief that he cracked and betrayed his trust. Summers' recuperation is more protracted. After the murder and the – coincidental – arrest of Léonie, a phantasmagoric montage sequence shows him drinking himself into degradation (using the money he stole from Lafitte to conceal the motive for his murder). Picked up and dried out by the American military authorities after the war, he extracts confirmation of the innocence of the man he has killed and returns to Paris to find Madame Lafitte and Morrisette. He gains a sort of redemption in *not* burdening them with the truth about the murder, assuring them of the heroic nature of Lafitte's actions (as a good resistance worker he had told them nothing of that side of his life) and relieving their poverty with a pension from his own accumulated back pay.

John Ramsden argues that

post-war films reinterpreted the Second World War experience in such a cosily reassuring way that by about 1960 it was safe material even for comedians on the BBC [and he quotes a Tony Hancock spoof of a POW camp drama]. From there it was an easy road downhill to *'Allo 'Allo, Dad's Army*, and *It Ain't Half Hot Mum*. (Ramsden, 1998, p. 62)

In an otherwise perceptive essay, this is a disappointing return to orthodoxy. Films that celebrate British wartime exploits – from *Angels One Five* at the beginning of the decade to *Sea of Sand* at the end – face up to the sadness and waste of war at least as much as they celebrate its glory and excitement. Such films work hard to contain worries and traumas about the war, presenting it as a just and necessary conflict, but beneath the stiff-upper-lip bravery was an awareness that the war had been a traumatic experience leaving psychological as well as physical scars.

NOTES

1 It needs to be borne in mind that many of the more popular British war films were reissued in the late 1940s, particularly during the embargo which Hollywood imposed on the import of its films (in response to the government's attempt to impose an import duty) between August 1947 and March 1948.
2 Other films dealing with the aftermath of war include Humphrey Jennings' 19-minute documentary *A Defeated People* (1945), Luigi Zampa's *Children of Chance* (1949), Charles Crichton's *The Divided Heart* (1954), and J. Lee Thompson's *Before Winter Comes* (1969).
3 See 'Sydney and Muriel Box's diary', in the Sydney and Muriel Box Special Collection, BFI Library, for the production difficulties of *The Lost People*. One can surmise that Bernard Knowles, a brilliant cinematographer but a less successful director of actors, was unsuited to such a dialogue-driven project. Muriel Box does not appear to have been credited for her contribution, but her experience with the film made it possible for her to launch a career as a director.
4 Brunsdon and Moseley's (1997) exploration of the film's attitude towards Nell's 'undomesticated femininity' would be a useful starting-point for an examination of Flora Robson's screen persona and how it is manifested in films like *Poison Pen, Great Day* and *Holiday Camp*.
5 Dearden and Relph employ a similar strategy with Learoyd (Michael

202

Craig), the racist policeman in *Sapphire* (1959), who, by the end of the film has modified his views sufficiently to want to shake Sapphire's black brother by the hand.

6 Lovell dismisses Robert as 'hollow and lifeless' with a 'frigid British soul' (Lovell, 1984, p. 33).

7 The series of documentaries made for Channel 4 in 1998 about shell shock confirmed that many ex-servicemen did indeed find it difficult to overcome traumatic experiences endured during the war. See also, for example, Mark Rowe, 'Veterans of WW2 still in trauma', *Independent on Sunday*, 7 November 1999; Tony Heath, 'We who are left grow old, but the horror of war lingers', *Independent on Sunday*, 14 November 1999.

8 Arthur Vesselo, 'The quarter in Britain', *Sight and Sound*, Autumn 1947, vol. 16, no. 63, p. 120.

9 Cavalcanti, like Clem Morgan, spurned respectability and went for the dangerous option. After two more British films, *For Them That Trespass* and *The First Gentleman* (both 1948), he returned to Brazil, where his attempts to build a domestic film industry were stymied by governments suspicious of his radical ideas.

10 There is something seriously wrong in the relationship between Simon and his father in *Silent Dust*, but this obviously pre-dates the war; and within the film Simon is dismissed as a worthless coward whose death at his father's hands is well deserved.

11 The relationship between Sammy and Susan is all the more effective for its contrast with the infatuation of Sister Ruth (Kathleen Byron) with Mr Dean (Farrar), which pushes her over the edge into madness in *Black Narcissus*.

12 Francis Suttill, organizer of an extensive resistance circuit centred on Paris which had been penetrated by the Sicherheitsdienst, returned to England in May 1943, and had a personal audience with Churchill before being sent back to be arrested. What Suttill and his fellow agents in the Prosper circuit were expected to reveal was an invasion date for 1943 (September, in the Pas de Calais), which it was hoped – over-optimistically – would impel the Germans to withdraw troops from the Eastern front and relieve pressure on the Russians. See Marshall (1988), p. 161, for Suttill and Churchill.

13 It is interesting to compare Rawson's implacable realism with the attitude of Canada Mackendrick (Alan Ladd) in *The Red Beret*. A one-time officer, he prefers to serve in the ranks rather than take on once again the awesome responsibility for other men's lives.

14 Summary execution of alleged collaborators was a commonplace in the months following the liberation of France, but proving someone a traitor during the occupation was not easily done. Double agents Roger Bardet and Henri Déricourt continually faced out their accusers (including each other, as Bardet's connections were with the Abwehr – the German military intelligence – and Déricourt's with its deadly rival, the SS-controlled Sicherheitsdienst). See Foot (1966) for Bardet; Marshall (1988) for Déricourt.

8

Reliving Past Glories:
The Heyday of the British War Film

Sister came in and said my wife had arrived. I was well
enough to worry about her seeing me as I was: my hands,
forearms, and legs were encased in dried tannic acid; my face
was treated in the same way, and I peered through slits in the
mask. I heard footsteps approaching the bed, and then saw
my wife standing gazing down at me. She flushed a little and
said, 'What on earth have you been doing to yourself, darling?' 'Had a row with a German', I replied.[1]

The 1950s were a period of prosperity and full employment.
Wage levels rose faster than prices and the 1944 Education Act
opened up educational opportunities and encouraged a degree
of social mobility. But if most people had 'never had it so good', they
did not take prosperity for granted. Respectability, caution, and a
ferocious defence of pay differentials and skill demarcations marked
the 1950s; and beneath the surface lurked a conflict between the
desire to enjoy the pleasures of peace and a remembrance of the
drama and excitement of the war.

The Second World War, like most wars, was fought by very young
men (the average age of Battle of Britain pilots was 21), and for those
who survived it was likely to be the most traumatic and intense
period of their lives. War films allowed an opportunity of reliving and
coming to terms with that experience. Ian McEwan recalls that
'although I was born three years after the war ended, it was a living
presence throughout my childhood. Sometimes I found it hard to
believe that I had not been alive in the summer of 1940' (McEwan,
1982, pp. 15–16). A generation grew up in the 1950s surrounded by
bombed building sites and memories of the war. Ordinary adults –
insurance agents, window cleaners, schoolteachers – hinted at dark
deeds and fabulous adventures in the desert, or in the jungle, or on

the beaches of Normandy, though there was little boasting of heroism or graphic description of the horrors of war. For those too young to have experienced it, the war was an endless subject of excitement and adventure – the blackout, the Blitz, the resistance movements, the glories of aerial combat and naval endeavour. During a period in which a generation gap began to open up between parents and children, war films were one of the few things that fathers could enthusiastically share with their sons.

The reliance on memoirs written by articulate middle-class officers, the reconstruction of highly organized campaigns and missions, and the removal of the necessity of showing everybody pulling together displaced the populism of the wartime films. In *Reach for the Sky*, for example, working-class characters exist only to polish shoes and start engines, and the waitress who captures Douglas Bader's heart turns out to be a wing commander's daughter in mufti. But if 1950s war films are skewed towards the middle class, their emphasis on courage and personal heroism meant that issues around class tended to be submerged. The concentration on active service and the use of actors like Jack Hawkins and Kenneth More, whose gritty or breezy professionalism was less alienating than the clipped suavity of Clive Brook or Noël Coward, steered the films away from the dangerous waters of class and made them acceptable to working-class men and boys.

According to Neil Rattigan, 1950s war films were a 'reflection of the last ditch effort by the dominant class to maintain its hegemony by re-writing the history of the celluloid war in its own favour' (Rattigan, 1994b, p. 150). But the prestige and box-office success of a handful of films – *The Cruel Sea*, *The Colditz Story*, *The Dam Busters*, *Reach for the Sky*, *The Battle of the River Plate* and *Sink the Bismarck!* – has left a misleading impression of uniformity. Lewis Gilbert, who made *Reach for the Sky* and *Sink the Bismarck!*, was also responsible for *The Sea Shall Not Have Them*, *Carve Her Name with Pride* and *Light Up the Sky*, which are dominated by characters of much more humble origins. And although the egalitarianism of the war years was gradually eroded, more impudent, irreverent attitudes began creeping in towards the end of the decade.

War films were the mainstay of the British film industry in the 1950s. *The Dam Busters* and *Reach for the Sky* were the top box-office films of 1955 and 1956 respectively, and *The Cruel Sea*, *The Battle of the River Plate*, *The Bridge on the River Kwai* and *Sink the Bismarck!* were equally successful. They share common themes, actors and a visual style and promote similar ideological messages, but they are less formula-bound than one might suppose and as such are not easily categorized.

Categorizing 1950s War Films

Andy Medhurst, reassessing British war films of the 1950s, divides them into the combat film, which depicts 'a small group of active servicemen engaged in a particular military operation'; the anti-war film, 'which differs in ideology of approach rather than in subject matter from the combat film'; and the Home Front film, 'which deals with the effects of a war, being waged elsewhere, on one of the participant countries' (Medhurst, 1984, p. 35). But as there are very few anti-war or Home Front films in the 1950s, this doesn't take us very far. Nicholas Pronay classifies post-war war films more boldly, dividing them into numerous thematic categories such as 'doomed love that springs up between enemies', 'soldiers given up for dead returning unexpectedly', and 'subversive and psychological warfare' (Pronay, 1988, pp. 43, 46). This gives an indication of the wide range of films made about the war, but Pronay's fragmented groups make comparison between films difficult.

British cinema has not traditionally been regarded as a cinema of auteurs, but since the 1980s directors like Michael Powell, Lindsay Anderson, Basil Dearden, J. Lee Thompson, John and Roy Boulting and even Lance Comfort have been dragged from obscurity to join a small pantheon topped by Sir Carol Reed and Sir David Lean. Most important directors had at least one crack at a war film in the 1950s but the reliance on real people and real events, or on novels and plays based on real people and events, acted as a curb on directorial flamboyance. However, it is possible to tentatively group together three tendencies, focusing them around the most prolific directors of war films in the 1950s: Jack Lee, Ralph Thomas and Lewis Gilbert.

Jack Lee, who made *The Wooden Horse*, *A Town Like Alice* and *Circle of Deception*, came directly out of wartime documentary and his films can be coupled with Philip Leacock's *Appointment in London* and Charles Frend's *The Cruel Sea*, which are also heavily influenced by the documentary tradition. One might also include in this group Ken Annakin's *Landfall* and Bob Compton Bennett's *Gift Horse*, which retain vestiges of wartime populism, though in Bennett's film this is confined to the sympathetic representation of Dripper Daniels (Richard Attenborough), a bolshie trade union organizer who eventually realizes that his captain is fair-minded and worthy of loyalty.

In *Landfall*, class harmonization is more central to the film. Rick (Michael Denison), an upper-middle-class flight lieutenant, falls for Mona (Patricia Plunkett), a working-class barmaid whose parents run a small shop. She is very conscious of the class divide between them, but when Rick is accused of attacking a British submarine in mistake for a U-boat, Mona confronts the admiral with the evidence which will clear his name. She also encounters the admiral's wife, who convinces her that she will be an asset rather than a liability to an officer who might one day be an air marshal, and the rift between them is healed. It is a pleasing view of class harmony, given some plausibility by the solid decency of the two central characters, which really does seem to transcend their different backgrounds, but it was a vision which had faded by the early 1950s.

The war films made by Ralph Thomas – *Appointment with Venus, Above Us the Waves, Conspiracy of Hearts* and *The Wind Cannot Read* – share a number of characteristics with Powell and Pressburger's *The Battle of the River Plate* and *Ill Met by Moonlight*. Dominated as it is by Dirk Bogarde (who had achieved stardom in Thomas's *Doctor in the House* and reappears in *The Wind Cannot Read*), *Ill Met by Moonlight* seems a more appropriate project for Thomas than for Powell. *Conspiracy of Hearts*, in which a German princess (Lilli Palmer) who has become the Mother Superior of an Italian nunnery defies the German commandant of a concentration camp (Albert Lieven) by helping Jewish children to escape, uses ingredients one might expect to find in a Pressburger script. All these films have likeable German characters (except for *The Wind Cannot Read*, which is set in India), make good use of location settings, and are relatively untroubled in their attitudes towards heroism.

The third group, centring around Lewis Gilbert, represents the mainstream, though that mainstream is less class-bound and formulaic than one might expect. There are similarities between Gilbert's documentary-influenced *Albert RN* and *The Sea Shall Not Have Them*, and between his two film biographies, *Reach for the Sky* and *Carve Her Name with Pride*. But the fact that he ended the decade with two films as different in style and ethos as *Sink the Bismarck!* and *Light Up the Sky* illustrates how faint the authorial voice tends to be in 1950s war films.[2] Gilbert, like Terence Young, Guy Hamilton and John Guillermin, went on to direct James Bond films, and Hamilton's *The Intruder* and *The Colditz Story* and Guillermin's *I Was Monty's Double* are similar in style and ethos to the Gilbert films, though Young's *They Were Not Divided, The Red Beret* and *No Time to Die* veered towards a more Americanized style. One can imagine that if Gilbert, Guillermin or Hamilton had been entrusted with key films like *The Dam Busters* or *Dunkirk*, the results would not have been very different.

One of the factors that makes for uniformity in 1950s war films is their domination by a regular corps of actors: Jack Hawkins, John

Mills, Dirk Bogarde, Kenneth More, Richard Todd, Trevor Howard, Leo Genn and Anthony Steel in the starring roles; Richard Attenborough, John Gregson, Harry Andrews, Anthony Quayle, Bernard Lee and Bryan Forbes offering solid support; and the ubiquitous Sam Kydd popping up regularly as an erk, a sentry, a radio operator or the reliable backbone of a commando squad. Each of the stars brought a distinct personality to their films and they are less interchangeable than the directors, but their personas were not entirely fixed.

Kenneth More is best remembered for his depiction of Douglas Bader in *Reach for the Sky*, but a year earlier he had played the feckless Freddie Page in *The Deep Blue Sea* and his earlier roles had included an unscrupulous SIS agent in *The Clouded Yellow* and a pacifist painter in *Appointment with Venus*. John Mills retained his ability to switch between working-class and officer roles. After his competent but predictable impersonation of the escapee Pat Reid in *The Colditz Story*, and his reworking of the submarine captain from *We Dive at Dawn* for *Above Us the Waves*, he opted for less conventional roles. Captain Anson in *Ice Cold in Alex* is flaky, battle-fatigued and dependent on alcohol to hold his nerve together; Tubby Binns in *Dunkirk*, though in some ways a reversion to Shortie Blake from *In Which We Serve*, has to assume an unwelcome position of responsibility and is edgy and troubled.[3]

Richard Todd, Leo Genn and Anthony Steel have a narrower range and their stardom hardly survived the 1950s. However, Todd's unflappable orthodoxy is modulated into a priggishness which needs to be humanized in *The Hasty Heart*; an intolerance which blinds him to what is going on in *Danger Within*; and an excuse for inadequate leadership in *The Long and the Short and the Tall*. Similarly, Steel's good-natured reliability turns belligerent when he's put under pressure in *The Wooden Horse*. Jack Hawkins plays no-nonsense commander roles in *Angels One Five*, *The Intruder*, *The Cruel Sea* and *The Malta Story*, but his performances are always cleverly nuanced and his later roles, in *The Bridge on the River Kwai* and *The League of Gentlemen*, erode the image of self-sufficient masculinity.

Trevor Howard played likeable, if angst-ridden characters in *Odette* and *The Clouded Yellow*, but in *Gift Horse*, *The Cockleshell Heroes* and *The Key*, he was cast in a succession of misanthropic roles which become progressively more disturbing. Commander Fraser in *Gift Horse* is bitter because he has failed to rise in the naval hierarchy, but his troubles are due to a single unfair judgement made many years ago and are at least partially righted in the film. Captain Thompson in *The Cockleshell Heroes* is a sour, cussed disciplinarian and his failure to prosper seems rooted in his personality. He finds a sympathetic partner in José Ferrer's Major Stringer, a pipe-smoking intellectual, prepared to listen and learn from his choleric criticism, but salvation comes at the cost of being shot by a German firing squad. Captain Ford in *The Key* is much friendlier, but there is a grating sense of hysteria underlying the jollity, and his death comes as a blessed relief.

One might have expected Dirk Bogarde, as a gay actor, to have presented the war film with more problems, but in his best roles there is a depth and subtlety which makes him a more complex and interesting figure than more stolidly masculine types. His romantic relationships with women are fluid and emotional compared to the inhibited romances engaged in by, for example, Kenneth More in *Reach for the Sky* and *Sink the Bismarck!*, though they tend to be cerebral and sanitized. Eve Canyon (Dinah Sheridan), in *Appointment in London*, is the sort of independently minded upper-class English-woman who prefers a wryly diffident good companion to someone who might make obtrusive emotional demands on her; and Suzuki San (Yoko Tani), in *The Wind Cannot Read*, is an adorable clockwork doll who knows that her terminal illness will ensure she runs down before she becomes an embarrassment to her English husband.

Todd and Hawkins are rarely allowed near a woman in their war films, and the steamy scenes between John Mills and Sylvia Syms, in *Ice Cold in Alex*, which he found 'a sheer relief' after years of only being allowed to give women 'polite pecks on the cheeks between battles', finished up on the cutting room floor (Mills, 1980, p. 231). Heterosexual romance hardly intrudes into many war films, and where it is absent, masculinity often comes under closer scrutiny. Bogarde's depictions of Patrick Leigh Fermor in *Ill Met by Moonlight* and Sergeant Major Charles Coward in *The Password Is Courage* are both studies of heroic masculinity, but they are both well-known war heroes and operate in a *Boy's Own Paper* world of simple values. Lewis Milestone's *They Who Dare* is more willing to dismantle and examine the components of heroism.

From the opening sequence, when a fresh-faced SAS lieutenant's date in a Cairo bar turns out to be Bogarde's debonair Lieutenant Graham, it is apparent that his character is part of what Costello calls 'the homosexual military elite' (1986, p. 168).[4] This is partially masked by his romancing of a languidly sexy hostess (who taunts his young companion with the SAS motto 'they who dare, win'), but also by the fact that Graham is characterized by courage and daring rather than by weakness and effeminacy. A British Army study of sexual offenders claimed that the active military homosexual often exerted excessive authority 'to dominate the male group, obtain love, respect, and acknowledgement of his prowess. He must lead, cannot be led, and finds it intolerable to be in a passive position of obeying.'[5] Graham is too perceptive of his own faults to quite fit this stereotype; but his yearning for heroism in a situation which requires more than charisma and reckless bravery gives the film a sophistication and intelligence overlooked by contemporary reviewers.

The mission, to blow up enemy airfields on a Greek island, starts to go wrong at an early stage and tensions within the group – made up of mutually suspicious naval marines, army commandos and Greek partisans, and led by the two SAS officers – make things worse. The Greeks disobey orders, the marines (apart from Sam Kydd) grumble, and one of the commandos, Denholm Elliott's Sergeant Corcoran, a grammar-school intellectual who has turned down the chance of becoming an officer, makes increasingly outspoken criticisms of Graham's leadership. The key question, modulated over a number of episodes as the situation changes, is to what extent Graham's taste for danger is preventing him from abandoning a mission that can no longer be feasibly carried out. The problem of how much of a risk a leader should take with the lives of his men is a problem which crops up regularly (in *The Key* and in *Memphis Belle*, for example), but it is generally sidestepped by the need to obey orders, to ensure eventual survival, or make the necessary sacrifices that war demands. In *They Who Dare*, there are few external constraints – no one will blame them if they abandon the mission – and Graham's success in pulling off the operation is negated by his insistence on planting a bomb so near the guardhouse it raises the alarm. Bogarde's performance, as he churns over Graham's doubts and fears, guilts and regrets, builds up a multidimensional character. The film meanders in its early stages and rushes towards an unsatisfactory denouement, but the confrontation between Graham's daredevilry and Corcoran's furious insistence on his right not to unnecessarily endanger his life gives it a salutary complexity.[6]

Vital components though the actors are, 1950s war films are as little vehicles for particular stars as they are for the thematic obsessions and personal idiosyncrasies of directors. As a way of grouping films together, one has to fall back on a simple division between resistance and counter-espionage films, POW camp films, and films that deal with the RAF, the Royal Navy and the Army, though the latter two categories are complicated by the substantial numbers of films about special operations involving sea, air and land forces, and these, in turn, merge with films which focus upon undercover operations. A separate category is necessary for films that examine the war in the East, where the jungle terrain and the nature of the enemy unite such disparate films as *A Town Like Alice*, *The Bridge on the River Kwai* and *Yesterday's Enemy*. Finally, there are a sufficient number of comedies – *Private Angelo, Worm's Eye View, Hotel Sahara, Private's Progress, Operation Bullshine, Don't Panic Chaps, The Square Peg, Desert Mice* and *The Night We Dropped a Clanger* – to justify their own section. However, they are a very disparate bunch, and need to be considered alongside the service comedies such as *Carry On Sergeant* (Gerald Thomas, 1958) which proliferated in a society where young men had to undergo compulsory national service.[7]

The most interesting of the resistance films – *Odette* and *Carve Her Name with Pride, Orders to Kill* and *Circle of Deception* – have been dealt with in earlier chapters (see Chapters 4 and 7), but it is important to recognize that they are part of a larger group. Five films with a substantial American input – Hugo Fregonese's *Seven Thunders*, Robert Aldrich's *The Angry Hills*, Victor Vicas's *Count Five and Die*, Ray Milland's *The Safecracker* and André de Toth's *The Two-Headed Spy* – provide a context for the American influences on *Orders to Kill* and *Circle of Deception*. In *Seven Thunders*, the two central characters are played by Stephen Boyd and Tony Wright, who were cast as disturbingly cold-blooded villains in other 1950s films. A kindly doctor (James Robertson Justice) looks forward to his hundredth murder victim from among those desperate enough to believe he will help them escape; a girl is shot dead by a panic-stricken young German soldier; and the Old Port area of Marseilles is systematically demolished. Despite this, the film is resolutely optimistic. Conflict between the two escaped prisoners of war, an officer (Boyd) who is drawn into a sexual relationship with a French street waif (Anna Gaylor) and a teetotal NCO (Wright) anxious to return to his wife and children, is resolved in loyalty and mutual support; and while the city collapses around them they escape to freedom.

Fewer films parallel the activities of Odette Sansom and Violette Szabo. Vernon Sewell's *The Battle of the V1* reverts back to the resistance/adventure cycle of the war years, but without much enthusiasm, and is less interesting than two films made on the cusp of the 1960s, *Foxhole in Cairo* and *Operation Amsterdam*. *Foxhole in Cairo*, a poor cousin to *Circle of Deception*, is interesting primarily for its casting. On one side is James Robertson Justice (who had taught Summers how to murder someone silently in *Orders to Kill* and himself become a serial killer in *Seven Thunders*) as the head of counter-espionage in Cairo; Fenella Fielding as a Jewish Mata Hari; and Niall MacGinnis as her seedy but ruthless spymaster. On the other side is Albert Lieven, who had been playing Nazis since he was released from internment in 1941, as Rommel, and Michael Caine and Lee Montagu as German wireless operators. It is difficult to make much of an argument for the film's significance and profundity, but it is a good example of how, even with thin material, British war films of this period are likeably concise and enjoyable.

Operation Amsterdam has an even better ensemble cast, ranging from John Le Mesurier and Tony Britton to Malcolm Keen (whose career goes back to Hitchcock's silent films) and Eva Bartok, a Hungarian starlet who brings a touch of Continental passion to offset the reliability of the solid Dutch businessmen played by Peter Finch and Alexander Knox. In contrast to the studio-bound world of *Foxhole in Cairo*, director Michael McCarthy makes stylish use of locations and the film brilliantly evokes a semi-deserted Amsterdam in the uneasy last hours before the Nazis move in. The best comparison is with *The Foreman Went to France*. The epic quality of Charles Frend's film is missing, but there is still a fruitful adherence to realism and the virtues of doing the right thing in a situation where the structures and values of everyday life have been shattered by war.

Prisoner of War Films

Prisoner of war camps had appeared occasionally in films made during the war, but Jack Beddington of the MoI had requested producers not to deal with escapes in case this goaded the Germans into making conditions in the camps harsher. Max Greene's *The Man from Morocco* featured a group of Spanish Civil War survivors interned by the unsympathetic Vichy French authorities and Frank Launder's *Two Thousand Women* followed the fortunes of an assortment of British women caught in France by the rapid German victory and imprisoned. But the first film to deal with male British POWs did not emerge until the war was over.

In *The Captive Heart*, the representation of camaraderie and boredom and the devising of clandestine activities is convincingly presented, but there is no actual escape and there are frequent flashbacks to the home life of the prisoners. Whereas the 1950s POW camp films are almost exclusively male affairs, at the centre of *The Captive Heart* is a love story. A Czech soldier, Captain Karel Hasek (Michael Redgrave), assumes the identity of a British officer to avoid being shot by the Gestapo. When he is captured, his fellow prisoners become suspicious and he narrowly avoids being eliminated as an informer; but once his story is believed, his British colleagues rally round to conceal his identity from the Gestapo. This leads to a melodramatic romance as Hasek begins a correspondence with the wife of the man he is impersonating and – showing a tenderness and sensitivity her British husband obviously lacked – wins her love. The problem that the letters will be written in unfamiliar handwriting is brutally solved by smashing Hasek's right hand with a sledgehammer, giving him an excuse to write with his left. The eventual meeting between Hasek and the woman he has cruelly deceived and come to love (played by Rachel Kempson, Redgrave's wife) is handled in such a way that we can believe both her horror at what has happened and her rapid adjustment to the situation.

The Captive Heart devotes considerable attention to the working-class characters played by Jack Warner, Mervyn Johns and Jimmy Hanley, but subsequent POW camp films concentrated on middle-class officers. As Vincent Firth explains:

> The facts are that under the Geneva Convention, officer prisoners cannot be put to manual work. They therefore had all the time in the world to dream up escape plans, while Other Ranks were kept far too busy at work to have any energy left for digging tunnels. (Firth, 1977, p. 42)

The Wooden Horse, Albert RN, The Colditz Story and *Danger Within* also avoid the intriguing romantic problems of *The Captive Heart* and concentrate on the mechanics of escape. Jack Lee's meticulous attention to detail gives *The Wooden Horse* an admirable sense of integrity. The plan, to escape by digging a tunnel under a vaulting horse carried out into the exercise yard every day, looks implausible (despite being true), but Lee brings to bear his documentary training to demonstrate exactly how things are done. Details such as the careful way the entrance hole is covered over and the way in which the men are carried in the horse help us believe this could really happen.

Lee's realism is also apparent in the way in which minor, but significant emotions, like irritation and bad temper, seep into the film. The men sharing a hut with the escapees get fed up with having to do all the chores because their tunnelling colleagues have more important things to do. It serves as a useful reminder that not all POWs' lives revolved around escape. As Nicholas Pronay points out, British POWs

> were kept by the Germans in camps with model conditions (at least by German standards and until late 1944) in contrast to those in which Soviet, Polish or French prisoners tended to be held, and in fact successful escapes were very small in number. (Pronay, 1988, p. 46)

213

When POWs did escape, they could expect no help from the German population and even if they reached occupied countries where resistance groups were operating, there were problems getting in touch with them. Peter (Leo Genn) and John (Anthony Steel) use the horse to tunnel out of the camp and manage to get to the Baltic port of Lübeck, but the uncertainties and dangers of not knowing in whom they can trust (Frenchmen drafted in as forced labourers? Scandinavian seamen?) gnaws at the friendship of the two men and almost brings them to blows. All ends happily, but the problems involved in an escape bid are not glossed over.

Albert RN and *The Colditz Story*, which, like *The Wooden Horse*, are based on real-life memoirs, set the parameters of the British POW camp film, a sub-genre which has been particularly unkindly treated by film critics. Andy Medhurst dismisses *The Colditz Story* as typical of those films which use the war as a source for 'pure adventure stories' and complains that, after the gloomily atmospheric opening,

> all sense of threat is dissipated by reassuring British humour, and the tone of the film (a Billy Bunter story where Mr Quelch is a Nazi) is established. The war is just a backdrop for masculine high jinks, a stirring test of strength and ingenuity. (Medhurst, 1984, p. 35)

The sombre tone of the film's opening is dispersed less easily than Medhurst supposes, and the 'high jinks' are carefully set against more serious incidents.[8] There is little questioning of the escape ethos in *The Colditz Story* – hardly surprising in a film set in a camp for hardened escapees – but the way in which the film deals with a varied assortment of escapes is ingenious and effective.

The escapes in the early part of the film are handled in a light-hearted way, but their function is merely to highlight the lack of co-ordination between the various national groups. A serious, four-nations escape then follows, but it fails because of treachery within the camp. After punishment, recrimination and the exposure of the traitor, two snap escape attempts occur. The French – somewhat reluctantly – help to carry out a young British officer, Jimmy Winslow (Bryan Forbes), among discarded bedding. But, to the chagrin of the camp, he is caught within a few miles of the Swiss border and brought back.

It is only with the escape of the French athlete La Tour (Eugene Deckers) that the impregnability of Colditz is breached; and the ease with which he leapfrogs over the perimeter fence makes a mockery not only of the Germans' security precautions but of the meticulous planning and lack of results achieved by the Escape Committee. The final escape is British and successful, but director Guy Hamilton resists the temptation to turn it into a jingoistic triumph. An escape route is planned which will emerge not outside the prison walls, but in the building housing the German mess. The two escapees, disguised as German guards, will thus materialize without rousing suspicion and stroll out of the camp. It is the brainchild of a brooding Scots giant, Mac MacGill (Christopher Rhodes), who is made to realize that his own size and aggressiveness make him too well known to pass as a German. Depressed, he tries to emulate La Tour, but his escape over the wire is too slow and he is shot down. Just as the demoralized return of Jimmy Winslow is balanced by La Tour's spectacular leap for freedom, the exhilaration of the escape of Pat Reid (John Mills) and Harry Tyler (Lionel Jeffries) is dampened by the death of MacGill.

Critical reception of *The Colditz Story* at the time was mildly favourable, but Paul Dehn, the *Daily Mirror* critic who would go on to script *Orders to Kill* and *The Night of the Generals*, warned that, in praising the film, 'I hope I am deterring future producers from climbing a cinematic mountain which has now been conquered'.[9] Surprisingly, his advice was followed and there was no spate of Colditz follow-ups. Roy Baker's *The One That Got Away* turned the tables by telling the story of a German Luftwaffe pilot determined to escape from British POW camps; Ken Annakin's *Very Important Person* introduced an element of comedy; Andrew Stone's *The Password Is Courage* moved away from officers to the more unusual case of a persistent NCO escapee; David Lean's *The Bridge on the River Kwai* and Val Guest's *The Camp on Blood Island* depicted the very different conditions of life in Japanese POW camps. Thus, until *The Great Escape* (an American production despite its considerable British contingent), the only true successor to *The Colditz Story* was Don Chaffey's *Danger Within*, and even here there are significant differences.

In contrast to the grim citadel of Colditz, the prison camp of *Danger Within* is in sunny Italy which, with its bridge school, rugby team and amateur dramatics, has the atmosphere of a holiday camp.[10] But things are not quite as rosy as they seem. From the opening shot of an apparently dead man lying in the sand, who, after the titles have rolled, scratches his bum, yawns, looks up at a watch tower, and gets up, the film announces its interest in the deceptiveness of appearances. The neatly bearded deputy camp commander strolling around the camp is really a prisoner impersonating him; a shifty Greek prisoner, ostracized as an informer, is a British agent; the most zealous and intelligent of the escape team, Tony Long (William Franklyn), really is an informer. Captain Benucci (Peter Arne) scornfully dismisses the claims that he is so successful in foiling escape bids because he is being supplied with inside information, pointing out that the escapes are so amateurish that he hardly needs an informer to spot them. But this, too, is a deception and he is regularly informed of escape activities by Tony Long in letters supposedly written to his sweetheart.

Danger Within successfully unites what had become almost standard escape film elements – the tunnel collapse, the theatrical event covering an escape, the corruptible guard, the prisoners with endearing eccentricities – with a more thoroughgoing interrogation of the ethos of escape. The senior British officer (Bernard Lee) consistently refuses to be browbeaten by his escape officer (Richard Todd), and the escapees are regarded as trouble-making nuisances by many of the other prisoners. But when it looks as if the Italian surrender to the Allies will result not in the liberation of the camp but the removal of the prisoners to Germany, a wholesale escape plan swings into action. It is as if, in acknowledgement of all those POWs who made no attempt to escape, an exceptional situation has to be engineered to make escaping a noble and necessary enterprise.

The War in the Air

The Dam Busters and *Reach for the Sky* are such defining films for the representation of the Second World War in the 1950s that it comes as something of a surprise that apart from *Landfall*, set in Coastal Command and with an atypical emphasis on life outside the service, there were only two other RAF films made between 1945 and 1960. *Appointment in London*, like *The Dam Busters*, deals with bombers; *Angels One Five*, like *Reach for the Sky*, with fighters. Guy Gibson, the leader of the dam busters raid, and a rare example of a bomber pilot who switched back to bombers after leading a fighter squadron, recalled that all would-be pilots 'clamoured to be put on to single seaters' and 'hero worshipped the white-overalled Squadron-Crested youth who had just stepped down from a Spitfire'. But the high prestige of the fighter caused resentment during the war:

Even in the cities, the fighters seemed to have all the fun, walking off with the women and drinking the beer, mainly because their stations were always close to a town, while a bomber base is miles from anywhere. Naturally all this irked the boys of Bomber Command quite a lot. They began to take an active dislike to the flying-booted, scarf-flapping glamour boys; many a rude word was spoken between the two in practically every pub between Biggin Hill and Edinburgh. (Gibson, 1995, p. 94)[11]

Attempts to make films about fighters, however, seemed jinxed. Harry Watt was asked by the American producer Walter Wanger to make a follow-up to *Target for Tonight* around the activities of the Eagle Squadron, the force of American volunteer pilots flying with the RAF. But casualties were so high that continuity became impossible and the project was abandoned in favour of a Hollywood studio production.[12] Similarly, a film about a Spitfire squadron with a script by Frank Launder, which was to have been directed by Carol Reed as one of Gainsborough's productions for 20th Century-Fox, was abandoned when Fox announced it was making *A Yank in the RAF* in Hollywood. *The First of the Few*, Leslie Howard's biographical film about R. J. Mitchell, the designer of the Spitfire, has a prologue and an epilogue set during the Battle of Britain, which is also briefly glimpsed in *Dangerous Moonlight* and *Unpublished Story*, but fighter squadrons are surprisingly rare in wartime British cinema. The gentle, wounded, bird-loving pilot played by Niall MacGinnis in *Tawny Pipit*, and Anne's briefly glimpsed fighter pilot lover in *The Gentle Sex*, are never seen in action, and the Spitfire pilot played by John Mills in *Cottage to Let* is a fraud. Richard Attenborough's Jack Arnold switches from light bombers to night fighters (as Gibson did for a time) in *School for Secrets*, but he is a junior partner to the boffins trying out their radar devices.

Consequently, *Angels One Five* is the first film to be centrally concerned with the pilots who fought in the Battle of Britain. Even so, it is a relatively modest production. Most of the drama happens on the ground and the film concentrates on the mechanics of the control room rather than on the heroics of aerial combat. This was partly a matter of budgeting and resources – fighter aircraft, particularly the fabric-clad Hurricanes, led short lives and the aeroplanes used in the film had to be borrowed back from the Portuguese Air Force – but it was also an accurate reflection of Fighter Command strategy. The Battle of Britain was won by Air Chief Marshal Hugh Dowding's coldly realistic strategy of sending small groups of fighters, guided by information obtained by ground control, the radar network and the Observer Corps, to make accurate hit-and-run attacks on the huge fleets of bombers sent over by the Luftwaffe. Dowding was convinced that Britain would lose a war of attrition in which each side merely sought to shoot down the maximum number of enemy aircraft. He continually discouraged futile heroics and stressed that the main aim was to harry and destroy German bombers, not to indulge in dogfights with their fighter escorts.

The director of *Angels One Five*, George More O'Ferrall, had gained his experience not in the film studios or in documentary but in the very new field of television drama, and indeed the film has the virtues of a good television play. The characters are intimately observed, the dialogue is concise and convincing, and there are no lyrical interludes or bombastic visual *longueurs*. The emphasis, as in *The Way to the Stars*, is on quiet, underplayed heroism and the pain and sorrow brought by wartime death, but it is a less elegiac film. The metaphors – a glass of beer left by the squadron leader who will never return to drink it; the radio lapsing into silence as a plane goes into its death dive – are powerful, but they are less personal and more matter-of-fact. Emotions have cooled and the war can be looked back on more dispassionately. The plot is a conventional one of a priggish new recruit, 'Septic' Baird (John Gregson), gradually winning acceptance among his battle-wise colleagues, but the characters have an archetypal resonance, particularly Jack Hawkins' 'Tiger' Small, the stern but benevolent station commander, and Dulcie Gray's Nadine Clinton, who serves as mother, sister, sweetheart, wife to the young pilots. Septic's education includes a spell in the control room, which teaches him about the necessity of teamwork, and a romance which helps him become less self-centred. His death comes as a salutary reminder that even competent and well-integrated pilots sacrificed their lives in the Battle of Britain.[13]

Reach for the Sky, based on Paul Brickhill's best-selling biography of the legless air ace Douglas Bader, is a much bigger production and, in keeping with Bader's own attitude, a romance of the air rather than a control room drama. Kenneth More's performance is impressive, but the film suffers from being an over-reverential portrait of a controversial figure.[14] Having established Bader's reckless courage and dogged determination, the film proceeds to endorse his more dubious achievements as a strategist. Bader, backed by his Group Controller, Trafford Leigh-Mallory, advocated 'big wings' of five or more squadrons which would fight pitched battles with the Germans and act on their own initiative rather than under orders from ground control. This exacerbated an already bad relationship between Leigh-Mallory and his counterpart in No. 11 Group (which covered London and the South East, and thus bore the brunt of the fighting), Keith Park. A later biographer of Bader condemns Dowding's inability to stem what amounted to insubordination, commenting sternly that 'a Montgomery would have had Leigh-Mallory straight on to the retirement list, and Bader posted to a real front-line unit' (Burns, 1998,

p. 124). But Bader's belligerent approach fitted the myth of 'knights of the air', using skill and initiative to destroy an enemy who had proved unable to win superiority of the skies but was bringing death and destruction to the civilian population with its nightly bombing raids. Once the Battle of Britain was won, the political appeal of this myth made it expedient to sack Dowding, to move Leigh-Mallory to No. 11 Group and to make Bader into a national hero. But the 'big wing' strategy was not a success and the policy advocated by Bader and Leigh-Mallory of sending wings of fighter squadrons over France proved costly in terms of machines and men.

Appointment in London is to some extent a fictional sequel to Harry Watt's *Target for Tonight*, covering a later stage of the war when four-engined Lancasters had taken the place of Wellingtons and huge raids were carried out with pathfinder aircraft using flares to guide the bombers to their targets. It is also something of a dry run for *The Dam Busters*. Though there was little physical resemblance between Dirk Bogarde and Guy Gibson, Bogarde's character, Wing Commander Tim Mason, shares Gibson's insistence on the need for tight discipline and good practice, his care and concern for his crews, and his reluctance to give up active flying for a desk job, despite having flown many more missions than might be reasonably expected. Although the story comes from John Wooldridge, himself a distinguished flier, it shares with Gibson's book, *Enemy Coast Ahead*, such incidents as an improperly lodged bomb falling out of an aircraft before it takes off (though with less drastic results in the film), and the final raid is very like the one on which Gibson, as Master Bomber, was finally shot down. The romantic rivalries and psychological complexities are handled well enough, but Leacock's main achievement lies in the authenticity of his reconstruction of life in a bomber squadron during the height of the British night bombing offensive, and the 600-bomber raid on a German secret weapons establishment, with which the film ends, is chillingly impressive.

The Dam Busters channels heroism in more conventional directions, but structurally it is more adventurous.[15] Raymond Durgnat notes that 'the quiet, grey, subdued style' he thought typical of the Lewis Gilbert films is enlivened in *The Dam Busters* by R. C. Sherriff's scenario, with its 'bold, original architecture of disappointment, destruction and loss' (Durgnat, 1970, p. 130). In place of the romantic subplot of *Appointment in London*, *The Dam Busters* devotes half its time to Barnes Wallis and the development and testing of the bouncing bomb. The endlessly fascinating pictures of the bomb tests (most of them actuality footage) and Michael Redgrave's masterly characterization of Barnes Wallis give the film an eccentricity which balances out the more conventional depiction of the training and carrying out of the raid. Richard Todd's representation of Guy Gibson is stolid and inexpressive, but it is difficult to see how else he might have played him. Gibson had flown 173 sorties by the time of the dam busters raid and he was killed in action a year later. *Enemy Coast Ahead*, published two years after his death, reveals him as a gauche but by no means unsympathetic young man (he was 24 when he died), whose life revolved around parties and drinking bouts and brief interludes with a young wife when the pressures of flying allowed it. An insensitivity towards those living less extreme lives no doubt sometimes made him seem, as one sergeant fitter put it, 'a bumptious little bastard', but his heroism is unquestionable. Todd's Gibson is more measured and restrained. We hear nothing of a wife, and when he goes to a show his attention drifts from the chorus girls to the spotlights, which he realizes can be used as a means of measuring the dangerously low height at which they are being asked to fly.

The raid on the dams was successful (though the breaches were soon repaired), but the casualty rate was unacceptably high. Ten of the nineteen planes were lost, 56 of the 133 men were killed, and the squadron's consequent reputation as a 'suicide squadron' made recruitment difficult. More important, this sort of strategic bombing was considered futile by the head of Bomber Command, Air Marshal Sir Arthur Harris. Barnes Wallis's bouncing bomb was visually spectacular but his 10-ton 'Grand Slam' was considered more useful by Bomber Command. While the USAF developed long-range fighters to accompany its bombers on daylight precision bombing raids, the RAF concentrated its efforts on the night bombing of civilian targets, with dubiously impressive results.[16]

Naval Dramas

In the 1950s, more films dealt with the war at sea than any other aspect of the conflict. *Gift Horse* and *The Cruel Sea* feature ships on convoy escort duty (though *Gift Horse* culminates in a commando raid on St Nazaire docks). *The Battle of the River Plate* and *Sink the Bismarck!* look at the successful naval campaigns against German battleships. *The Key* covers the work of seagoing tugs sent to bring in crippled vessels separated from their convoys. *Above Us the Waves* deals with an attack by midget submarines on the battleship *Tirpitz*; *The Silent Enemy* with British naval divers countering the activities of Italian midget submarines; and *The Cockleshell Heroes* with Royal Marines sent on a canoe-borne mission to attach limpet mines to German ships in Bordeaux harbour.

Gift Horse, despite a resonant performance from Trevor Howard, made an unprepossessing start to the cycle.[17] It is as if the sense of failure which hangs around Howard's Commander Fraser has spread throughout the film, giving it a gloomy, broken-backed quality. Fraser has been unjustly accused of negligence and has suffered years of bitterness at an injustice which has ruined his career. He is given charge of one of the old four-funnelled destroyers which the United States agreed to pass on to Britain in return for allowing American bases to be set up in the West Indies and Newfoundland, but its unseaworthiness makes it more of a liability than an asset. Fraser eventually succeeds in sinking a U-boat and instilling a team spirit among the ship's raw and discontented crew, but the celebrations are marred by news of his 17-year-old son's death in action.

Fraser's tragedy-filled life makes him sympathetic to the troubles of his men: Dripper Daniels (Richard Attenborough), too proud to ask for what might be construed as a favour, is none the less whisked off to be with his mother when she is operated on for cancer; Flanagan (Sonny Tufts) is forgiven for having deserted his post when it is revealed that his wife and baby have been killed in a bombing raid on Exeter where he has sent them for safe keeping. But the film's echoes of wartime populism are faint and weary. Appropriately, the denouement comes when Fraser's ship is selected to be packed with explosives and rammed into the gates of St Nazaire docks.

The Cruel Sea, directed by Charles Frend, who had made *San Demetrio London* in the midst of the war, is even more grim and harrowing, but it has a cathartic energy denied *Gift Horse*. It reasserts Ealing's commitment to realism, but in contrast to the carefully balanced class divisions of *In Which We Serve* and the cheerful, everybody-pitching-in-together feel of *San Demetrio London*, *The Cruel Sea* is permeated by an air of middle-class professionalism. The one person who doesn't fit, Bennett (Stanley Baker), the First Officer – a secondhand car salesman before the war and the sort of bounder one wouldn't trust with one's sister – is got rid of by his two better-bred juniors, Lockhart (Donald Sinden) and Morell (Denholm Elliott). Petty officers are allowed a respectful presence and even a romance, but the film is dominated by Jack Hawkins' Commander Ericson.

As in *In Which We Serve*, the film begins with the captain taking charge of his ship, though here Ericson is a merchant seaman and his ship, the *Compass Rose*, a small, fast corvette. Ericson is much less paternalistic than his wartime predecessors; although he eventually builds up a strong relationship with Lockhart, he keeps a businesslike distance from both officers and men. His authority is momentarily challenged when, after depth charges are dropped which blow up a group of shipwrecked British sailors rather than the U-boat that lurked beneath them, one of his men mutinously shouts out 'murderer'. We are not expected to agree: his actions are carefully framed within a 'war is hell' context and the emphasis is on the agonizing decision Ericson has to make rather than the anonymous sailors in the water. In later films, such an act might betoken the cynical brutality of war, but here it is a moment of pathos and belies the charge of emotional aridity levelled at 1950s war films. Tortured by what he has done, Ericson gets very drunk to drown the pain. Three merchant ship captains he has rescued offer their commiserations and Lockhart (who had identified the submarine) tries to take the blame for the death of the men in the water. But Ericson, with tears streaming down his face, insists, 'No one murdered them. It's the war. The whole bloody war. We've just got to do these things and say our prayers at the end.' In his autobiography, Hawkins records how, having played the scene with great emotion, he was quietly taken aside by Michael Balcon and asked to redo it in the restrained style favoured by Ealing. Hawkins obliged, but the results were considered too formal and a third, intermediately emotional attempt was shot. In the end, however, Ealing had the good sense to use the original version and this moving denial of stiff-upper-lip restraint was allowed to remain (Hawkins, 1973, pp. 106–7).

This sequence is the film's emotional heart, but it takes place only one-third of the way through. After they finally sink a U-boat, there is a relaxation in the narrative drive and we see something of the domestic lives of Ericson's two lieutenants. Morell has a flashy wife (Moira Lister) who is obviously cheating on him. Lockhart is attracted to Julie Hallam (Virginia McKenna), a bright, intelligent Wren. Christine Geraghty complains that Lockhart and Julie's relationship 'is singularly bloodless' (Geraghty, 1984, p. 65). But this is a judgement based on 1980s, post-permissive standards. In comparison with, for example, the relationship between James Donald's cod-Canadian and the admiral's daughter (Joan Rice) he courts in *Gift Horse*, it is subtle and resonant. In both films there is a scene where the woman knows the man she loves is being sent somewhere even more dangerous than he supposes. Joan Rice is only able to register bottled-up concern; but McKenna's transformation of the trite 'Take care of yourself, won't you' with the rider 'I mean it – you see, I know where you're going' exposes the bleak reality that he is unlikely to return and justifies the carefulness with which they act towards each other.

Compass Rose is sunk and the oil-soaked survivors (including Ericson and Lockhart) are picked up. Ericson, still haunted by the dreadful cries of men trapped down below, takes command of a bigger ship and sinks another U-boat. It is war at its most bleak, but the growing friendship between Ericson and Lockhart gives meaning and purpose to it and prevents the film lapsing into nihilism. The other naval films share *The Cruel Sea*'s realist ethos, but they rely more upon dramatic incident and most of them are based on real events.

The Sea Shall Not Have Them is fiction, but it shares the documentary ethos of Charles Crichton's *For Those in Peril*. Both films are about the Air–Sea Rescue Service, and although in Gilbert's film action is focused on a boat rather than a plane, it is a boat run by a fire-eating flight sergeant (Nigel Patrick) with a deep loyalty to the RAF who considers his son's decision to join the Navy an act of betrayal. The main characters in *For Those in Peril* are two pilot officers (David Farrar and Ralph Michael), but *The Sea Shall Not Have Them*, contradicting the general trend in 1950s films, has a more populist ethos. On the rescue launch, things are very much run by the NCOs, and Anthony Steel's officer keeps a low profile. On the dinghy they are searching for there is an outbreak of class tension but it is easily calmed. Dirk Bogarde's edgy wireless operator is worried that he has jeopardized his chances of becoming an officer by being caught using RAF petrol for his old Morris and that his background as the son of a greengrocer from Luton will tell against him. But he is reassured by Air Commodore Waltby (Michael Redgrave), whose secret documents they have been flying home. Though he initially appears to be a stuffy representative of a privileged world, Waltby is revealed as a modest hero who has been behind enemy lines with the resistance, and that far from enjoying the advantages of birth, his father was a railway porter at Luton station.

The Battle of the River Plate and *Sink the Bismarck!* concentrate on major events of the naval war – the hunting down of the German battleships *Admiral Graf Spee* and *Bismarck*. The Battle of the River Plate had already been covered in *For Freedom*, but in 1940, with limited financial resources and a war going on, Gainsborough had to rely on models for its ships. Powell, through his production manager, John Brabourne (the son-in-law of Lord Mountbatten), was able to use real battleships and cruisers (including the New Zealand ship the *Achilles*, which had taken part in the action in 1939) and he revelled in the visual possibilities of showing the movement of big ships at sea. But as Kevin Macdonald notes: 'The script is a pale, cosmeticized reflection of the Archers' wartime work, with none of the novelty of form, character and theme that distinguishes Emeric's best work' (Macdonald, 1994, pp. 357–8). Pressburger borrows from *For Freedom* two devices for allowing us a viewpoint other than that of the officers on the British cruisers, but neither survive their transplanting very successfully.

Captain Dove, the skipper of one of the merchant ships sunk by the *Graf Spee*, is taken prisoner and we see through his eyes what is happening on the German battleship. In *For Freedom*, Dove plays himself with considerable wit and panache. In *The Battle of the River Plate*, he is played more ponderously by Bernard Lee, but he forms a much closer bond with the battleship's commander, Captain Langsdorff (Peter Finch). Langsdorff, another of Powell and Pressburger's good Germans, is the most interesting and sympathetic character in the film. But since he is glimpsed only obliquely through Dove's eyes, he is unable to become a proper protagonist and the film lacks a centre.

This is particularly apparent in the last act of the film, when the damaged *Graf Spee* seeks shelter in Montevideo, at the mouth of the River Plate. Pressburger reuses the device of an American radio reporter giving a harbourside commentary. In *For Freedom*, this ties in with the newsreel setting of the film; but in *The Battle of the River Plate*, the interesting dilemma has settled around Langsdorff and how he will respond to the necessity of leaving Montevideo to face a British force – whose strength he can only guess – with his ship insufficiently repaired to face them effectively. The harbourside commentator can shed no light here, and there is an inevitable sense of anticlimax when Langsdorff scuttles his ship rather than bringing her out for a decisive battle.

Sink the Bismarck!, despite coming four years later, looks like a reversion to the films of the early 1950s. It deals with a much more spectacular, exciting and decisive battle, but Gilbert centres the film in the Admiralty War Room. Captain Shepard (Kenneth More), a stiff disciplinarian who clearly does not approve of the informal regime of his predecessor, takes over just in time for the big battle. We learn that he is recovering from the shock of returning home after being shipwrecked to find his house destroyed and his wife dead. His only son is a Swordfish pilot on the *Ark Royal*, and after Shepard orders the carrier to join the pursuit of the *Bismarck*, his son's plane is reported missing. The sinking of the *Bismarck* becomes Shepard's personal crusade and victory helps bring about his re-entry into life. The other humanizing factor is the influence of a beautiful, loyal and tactful assistant. Dana Wynter's Anne Davis almost equals Sophia Loren's Stella in *The Key* in her seraphic solicitude, but whereas Stella is slightly sinister, Anne is just a very nice girl who always knows what to do and what to say. Both the romance and the conduct of the battle are very formal, but More succeeds in conveying the impression of a man who has shrunk into himself, and his gradual opening up – the turning point is when he cries – is interesting and moving.

Gilbert's Germans ('We are faster, we are unsinkable, we are German') are more stereotyped and less sympathetic than Powell and Pressburger's, but the stakes are much higher. *Graf Spee*'s shark-like attacks on unarmed merchantmen are mitigated by the chivalrous way in which Langsdorff treats survivors. *Bismarck*'s sinking of the *Hood*, with the loss of all but three of her 1500 men, sets up an atavistic desire for revenge, and Karel Stepanek's preposterously arrogant Admiral Lutjens presents a good target.

Above Us the Waves, *The Cockleshell Heroes* and *The Silent Enemy* all concentrate on small-scale, specialist operations and place the emphasis on camaraderie and the interdependence of a highly trained team of men. The story of *Above Us the Waves* concerns the successful attack on the *Tirpitz* in a Norwegian fjord. It is exciting and dangerous, but it provides little in the way of dramatic conflict between the characters, and the cramped space of a midget submarine allows little opportunity for the visual splendour displayed in an outdoor drama like *The Battle of the River Plate*. Ralph Thomas devotes time to the recruitment and training of the submarine teams and an unsuccessful first operation, but it is with the attack on the *Tirpitz* that the film comes alive. By this time, the characters are well established and easily recognized, and we care about their fate. Consequently, he is able to cut between the three crews in their identical crafts without confusion and to maintain our interest in their long sojourn under the sea. As in *Gift Horse*, *The Cockleshell Heroes* and *The Bridge on the River Kwai*, the charges are successfully placed, but there is a delay while we wait to see if they will go off. In each of these films it makes for an effective climax, but *Above Us the Waves* is particularly successful in combining the thrill of a destructive explosion with an acknowledgement of the waste and sacrifice of war. The suspense over whether or not the mines will explode is complicated by the fact that two of the three midget submarine crews have been caught and are on board the *Tirpitz* themselves; and the victory of the successful mission is overshadowed by the self-destruction of the third submarine as it attempts to surface.

The Cockleshell Heroes is the best of the ambitious Technicolor films made by American expatriates Irving Allen and Cubby Broccoli for Columbia. They had celebrated the achievements of British paratroopers in *The Red Beret* and attempted to emulate their success by turning to the Royal Marines. Fortunately, the script is much better. The enterprise – to sail in canoes 40 miles down a heavily guarded river to plant limpet mines on German ships moored in the harbour of Bordeaux – seems highly improbable (though it is based on real events), but the conflict between the hardbitten professional (Trevor Howard's Thompson) and the amiable amateur (José Ferrer's Stringer) is fruitful and convincing. The failure of Stringer's democratic methods and his adoption of Thompson's despotic ones might seem to betoken a reactionary stress on the need for discipline and blind obedience, but this is not really how the film works. Thompson's castigation of Stringer's failure to provide firm and definite leadership is a salutary jolt to his easy-going optimism, but it is Thompson's attitude which is radically transformed. He moves from a position of deep scepticism to such wholehearted commitment that he is able to go on the mission himself and ensure its success, albeit at the cost of his own life.

There is a similar introduction of a disciplinarian, Chief Petty Officer Thorpe (Sid James), in *The Silent Enemy*, but his presence is entirely benign. He acts like a mother figure to the scruffy and informal naval divers, keeping the house clean, waking them up in time and making sure they keep themselves tidy enough to stay out of trouble. When Commander Crabbe (Laurence Harvey) needs to carry out an operation for which he knows he will not be given permission (blowing up the Italian midget submarine mother-ship in neutral waters), it is CPO Thorpe, wily in the ways of bending the rules, who comes up with a solution.[18] The hazard of underwater warfare creates its own set of values. Respect is shown for the brave and resourceful Italians, despite the havoc they wreak, and Crabbe is treated with deference by his men because of his courage and initiative rather than his rank. His embarrassed and exasperated response to their congratulations on being awarded the George Cross, 'You all deserve the ruddy medal', is an assertion that it is the team rather than a single gallant individual which is responsible for their achievements.

The Ground War

Films that focus on the Army are more of a mixed bag than ones which deal with the other services. Brian Desmond Hurst's *Theirs Is the Glory*, a semi-documentary reconstruction of the Battle of Arnhem, still operates within the parameters of a People's War, but in

Terence Young's *They Were Not Divided*, made four years later, the emphasis is on upper-middle-class officers. An Englishman, Philip Hamilton (Edward Underdown), an Irishman, Smoke O'Connor (Michael Brennan), and an American, David Morgan (Ralph Clanton), join the Welsh Guards. Philip and David, who are both gentlemen, become officers, but Smoke is a comic Irishman, only fit to be an NCO. In the protracted period before they are sent into action, Smoke paints and repaints their tanks, while Philip is able to spend time with his wife, and David falls in love with a woman he meets swimming naked in a woodland pool. These romantic interludes make one yearn for the economy and restraint shown by Lockhart and Julie in *The Cruel Sea*. However, the action sequences in France, Belgium and Holland, though long delayed, are very effective. Like Hurst in *Theirs Is the Glory*, Young uses a combination of actuality footage and realistic reconstruction. There are no false heroics, and although the ending, with the British and American flags on Philip's and David's graves tilting towards each other, is contrived, it is a small price to pay for the film's authentic representation of tank warfare.

Surprisingly, a return to the subject of the European war did not happen until the end of the decade, when *Dunkirk* and the Anglo-American film *The Longest Day* recreated the evacuation and long-awaited re-invasion of France by Allied forces. Terence Young's subsequent two war films, which are both disappointing, concentrate on North Africa and the desert war. *The Red Beret*, a homage to British paratroopers, displays impressive Technicolor action sequences, but the story is trite. Canada Mackendrick (Alan Ladd) is another American who has joined the British Army while the United States is still neutral. Despite his expertise and leadership qualities, he refuses to take a commission. His love affair with a parachute packer (Susan Stephen), who seems unsure whether she is supposed to be British or American, is embarrassingly stilted. And when he reveals his secret sorrow – he was once an officer in the American Army and had to make a decision which caused the death of one of his men – it is not traumatic enough to justify his actions. *No Time to Die* wisely devotes less time to romance, but the interaction among its small group of characters caught up in the desert war is much less accomplished than in Guy Green's *Sea of Sand* and J. Lee Thompson's *Ice Cold in Alex*.[19]

Sea of Sand bears a slight resemblance to *Angels One Five*, with John Gregson once again joining a band of experienced fighters who have little time for the rules and regulations that he holds important.[20] Captain Williams, however, is older and wiser, a regular army officer

United in the common struggle: disciplinarian Captain Williams (John Gregson) and maverick Captain Cotton (Michael Craig) in *Sea of Sand*. Supplied by British Cinema and Television Research Group Archive, De Montfort University, © courtesy of Carlton International.

who holds doggedly to his views, and in contrast to Captain Thompson in *The Cockleshell Heroes*, his attitude towards discipline is not fuelled by cynicism or disillusion. Williams is a happily married man with a young son and he enjoys soldiering. His rival, Captain Cotton (Michael Craig), dresses like a brigand, doesn't require his men to call him sir, and insists that officers muck in with the men when a truck gets bogged down and has to be dug out. In contrast to Williams, his marriage has collapsed and, despite the fact that he is an architect rather than a soldier by profession, his life revolves around the war. In *The Cockleshell Heroes*, the disciplinarian Thompson wins the argument but it is the nonchalant Major Stringer who lives to tell the tale. Similarly, in *Sea of Sand* it is Williams who dies, but by this time the differences between him and Cotton have been shown to be a matter of style rather than substance and the two men have become almost interchangeable in their bravery, endurance and concern for their men.

It is one of the strengths of Robert Westerby's script that the characters are psychologically complex enough to surprise the audience and the other characters by their actions. Wiliams, having broken down on a road used by German military vehicles, displays a hitherto unsuspected fluency in German to get himself out of a tight spot. Cotton admits to a satisfying exhilaration in getting the squad to its destination, and his remorse at Williams' death reveals his secret admiration for the calm, orderly life of the other man. Brody (Richard Attenborough), a disreputable, rule-breaking driver, turns his waywardness to good effect by spitting brandy in the face of a German soldier who has ambushed them. *Sea of Sand* is a small-scale production, but like other late 1950s films, such as *Danger Within* and *The Silent Enemy*, it demonstrates a refreshing irreverence and vitality. Bravery is celebrated, sacrifice and death regretted, but there is also a recognition of the excitement and comradeship of war.

In *Ice Cold in Alex*, tensions within the group are more important than conflict with the enemy, and these are subsumed in a common struggle against the desert. Captain Anson (John Mills) and Sergeant Major Pugh (Harry Andrews) retreat before Rommel's advancing army in a battered ambulance with two nurses (Sylvia Syms and Diane Clare) and pick up a South African, Captain Van Der Peol (Anthony Quayle) on the long trek through the desert to Alexandria. Anson is battle-fatigued and drinks to hold himself together; Van Der Peol is stronger, more determined and resourceful and is revealed to be a German spy.

One nurse is killed; the other, Syms's Diana Murdoch, causes the ambulance to slip back down a steep incline. None the less, Diana, like Anna (Eva Bartok) in *Operation Amsterdam*, is an active female presence rather than a passive object of desire. She holds the group together, healing Anson's neuroses and making possible the co-operation between the men which ensures their survival. Their battle for survival in a hostile environment gives the film an epic quality and justifies a suspension of national rivalry which is practical rather than sentimental. Van Der Peol is arrested when they get to Alexandria but not before he has had his ice-cold lager, and his British comrades ensure that he is treated as a POW rather than shot as a spy.[21]

The War in the East

The retreat from Dunkirk, ignominious though it was, had its heroic and glorious aspects. The surrender of Singapore to the Japanese was a national humiliation which cinema audiences were unlikely to want to dwell upon. *Burma Victory* celebrated what had become almost a forgotten war, *Piccadilly Incident* makes clever use of the fall of Singapore to cause a tragic separation between its lovers, and *The Hasty Heart* begins in the Burmese jungle, where McLachlan (Richard Todd) is wounded and taken to the hospital compound where most of the action is set. But it was not until the 1950s that the war in the East was properly explored. Seven films – *The Purple Plain*, *A Town Like Alice*, *Sea Wife*, *The Bridge on the River Kwai*, *The Wind Cannot Read*, *The Camp on Blood Island* and *Yesterday's Enemy* – were released between 1954 and 1959, and were soon followed by *The Long and the Short and the Tall* and *The Secret of Blood Island*. After that there was nothing more until Nagisa Oshima's *Merry Christmas, Mr Lawrence* in 1983.

The Bridge on the River Kwai, unlike *The Cruel Sea* and *The Dam Busters*, managed to attract American as well as British audiences, but to do so it had to introduce an American character who has no proper dramatic function and turn its British characters into caricatures. Alec Guinness's Colonel Nicholson is an army officer whose reliance on rules and regulations leads him to an act of collaboration. Nicholson is almost endearingly wrong-headed, but his stupidity infects everybody else in the camp except for the escapees – who make an early exit – and the doctor, Clipton (James Donald), who protests ineffectually. Officers and men quickly swallow their surprise that Nicholson wants to build a bridge which will be a monument to British initiative and enterprise and they enthusiastically put their backs into it. The Japanese are incapable of even positioning the bridge in the right place and, until Nicholson intervenes, allow the British prisoners to indulge in skiving and sabotage. Nicholson's view, that British soldiers are happy and contented only when subjected to strict discipline and a rigid code of conduct, is never challenged. Effective opposition to a paternalism which has merged into treacherous collaboration has to come from outside – from Shears (William Holden), the American sailor who escapes from the camp and reluctantly returns to help blow up the bridge, and Warden (Jack Hawkins), a gung-ho British commando officer. Unfortunately, both men trail histories which don't fit their characters (Warden taught Oriental languages at Cambridge, Shears is an ordinary seaman who has been masquerading as a naval commander), and they are accompanied by four Siamese women who look like competitors in a beauty contest. The ending, exciting though it is, sacrifices a clash of values for Grand Guignol. Nicholson and Saito, the camp commander, follow the cables linking the detonator to the explosive charges and, when fired on from above by Warden, Nicholson staggers and falls on the detonator, blowing up the bridge.[22]

The Camp on Blood Island is shot in black-and-white and thus less lavish than *The Bridge on the River Kwai*, but its story – the attempt to conceal from the camp commander that Japan has surrendered in order to prevent him massacring all the prisoners – is good, and like Val Guest's second Far Eastern film, *Yesterday's Enemy*, it doesn't shy away either from brutality or from difficult moral choices. The dilemma is comparable with that in *Danger Within*, but the implications are more serious. *Danger Within* has its stark moments – in particular, the cold-blooded gunning down of the likeable trio of escapees played by Michael Wilding, Peter Jones and Donald Houston – but conditions of life are generally pleasant and easy. A transfer from an Italian to a German camp might be intensely disappointing to those hoping for liberation, but for these British POWs it ought not to be life-threatening. The choices in *The Camp on Blood Island* are narrowed down to hazardous escape into impenetrable jungle; death by starvation, beating or organized massacre; or a desperate attempt at insurrection.

The moral issues are more nebulous in Robert Parish's *The Purple Plain*, Bob McNaught's *Sea Wife* and Ralph Thomas's *The Wind Cannot Read*, and any suffering is balanced by romance. *Sea Wife* dissipates the tensions it sets up among the survivors of a liner torpedoed by a Japanese submarine, allowing its most sympathetic character (played by the black calypso-singer Cy Grant) to be eaten by a shark and the nun (Joan Collins), whose sexuality unsettles her male companions, to return serenely to the bosom of the Church. *The Purple Plain*, regardless of its Technicolor and its Hollywood director and star, is a modest, restrained film. Its only moments of excess are when Forrester (Gregory Peck), the troubled protagonist, lapses into dark dreams which have haunted him since his newly-wed wife was killed in a bombing raid. When he is marooned in the jungle with Blore (Maurice Denham), an unrealistically optimistic non-combatant, and an injured navigator (Lyndon Brook), he gets on with the impossible task of carrying his colleague to safety without making a fuss.[23] The romance between Forrester and Anna (Win Min Than), a Burmese woman who seems able to understand and soothe his troubled mind, is a low-key affair, ignited when she gives him a ruby to signify he has won her heart and brought to a satisfactory consummation when, after a horrendous trek through the jungle, he lies down next to her sleeping form.

The Wind Cannot Read is much more grandiloquent, a gaudy

travelogue with an exotic and tragic romance at its heart. Whereas Forrester's restraint barely allows him a brief hug with Anna, Michael Quinn (Dirk Bogarde) courts and secretly marries his Japanese language teacher, Suzuki San (Yoko Tani), with unconcealed and eagerly reciprocated devotion. Most of the action takes place in India, in lushly idyllic settings, and Quinn's capture and torture by the Japanese is merely a device to keep the lovers apart. Although he has been strung up by his wrists in the midday sun, as soon as he realizes his wife is dangerously ill, he hurtles off into the jungle as easily and impulsively as La Tour in *The Colditz Story* clears the high wire fence.

Despite their differences, both films balance brutal Japanese militarism with the softer, caring qualities represented by Oriental women. The Brigadier embarrasses the modest Suzuki San by announcing that she 'shows us all the finest qualities of the Japanese people', though he advises Quinn that anything more public than a low-key affair would lead to his being whisked off to the front line. The Japanese are never seen in *The Purple Plain*, but there is a strong emphasis on the benefits of an Eastern way of life, where emotion is openly expressed rather than buried deep within. It is Anna's harmony and tranquillity which restore Forrester to wholeness and make it possible for him to survive his ordeal in the jungle and return to her.[24] The friendship between them is encouraged by both the doctor (Bernard Lee) and the missionary (Brenda de Banzie), and there is no indication that their marriage would be seen as inappropriate.

A Town Like Alice, like *Landfall* adapted from a novel by Nevil Shute, follows the epic pattern of Pat Jackson's *Western Approaches* and Harry Watt's *The Overlanders*, but, unusually for the 1950s, it concentrates on a group of women. Virginia McKenna's Jean Paget is as intrepid as Violette Szabo or Odette Sanson, but her elevation to heroism comes from an unmelodramatic series of accidents. When she stops to answer a ringing phone, she gets roped into helping her boss's wife and children, thus missing her chance of evacuation. She becomes the leader of a group of women forced to tramp through the Malayan jungle in search of a POW camp which will take them in because her level-headed common sense is necessary for their survival. Forrester in *The Purple Plain*, Shears in *The Bridge on the River Kwai*, Quinn in *The Wind Cannot Read* all endure difficult treks through hostile Far Eastern terrain, but the trek is the central core of *A Town Like Alice*.

Unlike most epic journeys – the trek across the desert to Alexandria in *Ice Cold in Alex*, for example – this one is futile and circular. None of the prison camps are prepared to take in the women and they are passed on like an unwanted parcel. The monotony of their ordeal is enlivened by a romance between Jean and the Australian Joe Harman (Peter Finch), another cross-cultural relationship fuelled by curiosity and exoticism as well as by shared hardship and friendliness. His reckless bravado in stealing a chicken for the women brings down nemesis on his head and leads to his crucifixion and, we are led to assume, death. But his stoical endurance is respected by the Japanese camp commander – confirming that the Japanese, though harsh, are not monsters – and he survives to meet up with her after the war in Alice Springs.

It is not the romance, but a rapprochement between the women, the Japanese invaders and the local Malays, which puts an end to the trek. For the Japanese, the women are an embarrassing problem they would rather forget about, and as they pose no threat, their guard is reduced to one old man who becomes so weak that the women have to help him. When he dies, there is no one to oversee their progress and they turn to the Malay villagers for a solution. Jean has already signalled her willingness to abandon the division between the colonizers and the colonized when she discards her tattered clothes for Oriental dress, and there is an unforced resolution to the women's journey when they persuade the villagers to let them work alongside them in the paddy fields. The villagers' presumption that white women are useless parasites is so obviously disproved by this tough bunch of survivors that there is no need for sentimentality and pity; these women will be hard and productive workers. A loss of power and status is more than compensated for by a pride in equality and self-sufficiency.

Reassessing 1950s War Films

What is striking about 1950s war films is not the success of a particular cycle of films – POW camp films, stiff-upper-lip naval dramas, heroic RAF films, tales of the resistance, commando raid action pictures – but the success of a wide spectrum of different types of war films and the very low rate of failure. Despite the competition of over 300 American films a year, a remarkable number of British war films were included in the top box-office films each year, and few were expensive flops. The public's taste ranged from the restraint of *Angels One Five* to the Technicolor splendour of *The Red Beret*; from the grimly uncompromising vision of *The Cruel Sea* to the romantic daredevilry of *Reach for the Sky*; from the gentlemanly heroics of *The Battle of the River Plate* to the visceral brutality of *The Camp on Blood Island*. The popularity of British as against American war films in the

1950s indicates that it was the myths around Britain's achievement in the Second World War rather than a celebration of war as such that attracted audiences. Few of the films can be accused of romanticizing or glamorizing war, and the predominant tone is one of subdued realism – the stiff-upper-lip ethos acting as a convenient shorthand for necessarily suppressed pain, bitterness and fear.

After the Suez crisis of 1956, film critics began to complain of British cinema's unwillingness to forget the war, and in the 1960s, attitudes changed radically, particularly among young people who objected to the stockpiling of nuclear weapons and the Vietnam War. As film studies developed as a discipline, Second World War films came to be seen as one of the least redeemable areas of British cinema.[25] Clyde Jeavons attributed the popularity of war films in the 1950s to nostalgia and the tendency to look back to past glories rather than face the problems of the present (Jeavons, 1974, p. 188). Roy Armes considered that 1950s war films offered 'strong evidence of a reaction against contemporary social change, a nostalgia for the fixed hierarchical society of the armed services and the firm, unquestioned virtues (fortitude, loyalty, courage) of the war period'. He dismisses them as 'archaic memories of a self-deluding era's retreat into a cosy never-never land' (Armes, 1978, p. 179).[26]

The 1980s saw the tide turn and the beginning of a gradual rehabilitation. Andy Medhurst attempted to rescue *Angels One Five*, *The Cruel Sea* and *The Dam Busters* from 'the realms of the formally conservative and the ideologically irredeemable', recasting them 'as films about repression, rather than as hopelessly repressed films' (Medhurst, 1984, pp. 35, 38). Christine Geraghty, writing in the same collection of essays as Medhurst, argued that war films, in their concern with how men should behave in extreme situations, offered a guide to appropriate forms of masculinity. She stressed the change from wartime films which celebrated the participation of ordinary people in a People's War, to 1950s war films, which explored the dilemmas faced by exceptionally heroic men:

> The leading men in the films are no longer ordinary individuals but men who are marked out as heroic: Bader (Kenneth More) in *Reach for the Sky*, Ericson (Jack Hawkins) in *The Cruel Sea*, even Wallis (Michael Redgrave) in *The Dam Busters*, are set apart from the rest by their exceptional courage and commitment. (Geraghty, 1984, p. 65).

These men are heroes because they wrestle with and overcome their doubts and fears. Key moments in post-war films, for example

Ericson's decision to sacrifice the shipwrecked sailors for a crack at the U-boat which he thinks lurks below them in *The Cruel Sea*, test the protagonist's resolve almost to breaking point. Their stiff-upper-lip stoicism is achieved at considerable cost:

> The necessity of denying fear seems to involve a denial of other feelings, including love and sexual attraction. Sexual love, which is domesticated in the wartime films through courtship and marriage, becomes marginal. Unable to admit to feelings, the heroes of the war films can scarcely articulate emotion, let alone act on it, and what pleasure they have seems to come from their skill with and control over machines. The heroes of these films abandon the private sphere of sexuality to those who are too weak to resist it. (Geraghty, 1984, p. 66)

Geraghty underestimates the ability of wartime heroes to articulate their emotions. Ericson cries, Shepard cries, Barnes Wallis becomes deeply distressed when he realizes how many bombers will not return. Philip Hamilton in *They Were Not Divided* and Douglas Bader in *Reach for the Sky* are married to chummy, loyal, but by no means sexless wives. The restrained behaviour of Lockhart, or Forrester, or Tim Mason is not caused by repression or emotional inarticulacy. They are adepts at a language which uses small gestures and veiled words to convey passion without exposing it to the public gaze.

Three further essays followed, by Nicholas Pronay (1988), John Ramsden (1998) and James Chapman (1998a): all of them erudite, useful and perceptive, all of them drawing back from any general revaluation. This is partly a matter of numbers. Pronay lists 85 war films made between 1946 and 1959, but he offers detailed analysis only of *The Bridge on the River Kwai*. Reliance on plot synopses reduces films to uniformity and smoothes over their differences. I have been unable to track down a handful of films that sound interesting – *But Not in Vain*, *The Two-Headed Spy*, *The Angry Hills* and *Count Five and Die*, for example – but on the evidence of the large numbers of films I have seen, the charges Roy Armes makes of a reaction against social change, a nostalgia for fixed hierarchical values and a retreat into a 'cosy never-never land' seem entirely misconceived.

It would be odd if a series of events as cataclysmic as the Second World War did not reverberate long after they were over. The danger, excitement, sadness, death and horror of the war had either to be deeply repressed or to find appropriate outlets. It is to the credit of British cinema (and of the society it grew out of) that so few of the films made in the key period between 1945 and 1960 were exploitative and xenophobic, and how many of them are enlightening, honourable and moving.

NOTES

1 RAF casualty, 'I had a row with a German', in Narracott (1947).
2 Gilbert worked with the US Air Corps film unit during the war and cut his teeth on such documentaries as *Sailors Do Care* and *Arctic Harvester*.
3 Mills' private detective in *The End of the Affair* might be regarded as an inappropriately Dickensian caricature, but his appearances are enjoyable interludes in an otherwise very glum film.
4 According to Costello (1986, p. 168), the Shepheard's Hotel in Cairo was 'the favourite gathering place for the officers of Colonel Stirling's Long Range Desert Group', and 'the rendezvous for a wide circle of the homosexual military elite'.
5 The quotation is from Costello (1986, p. 162). Unfortunately, he doesn't give details of the 'British Army study of sexual offenders', unless it is included in the *Report on the State of the Public Health during Six Years of War: Report of the Chief Medical Officer* (London: HMSO, 1946).
6 See Bogarde (1978), p. 136, for the production of *They Who Dare*. Bogarde enjoyed working with Milestone (the director of *All Quiet on the Western Front* (1930)), but admits they were never able to get the script right.
7 National Service was phased out after 1959. Service comedy also penetrated television, most notably in *The Army Game*, which ran for 153 episodes between 1957 and 1962.
8 Guy Hamilton, interviewed in *A Very British War Movie* (tx. Channel 4, December 1999), talks about the Colditz prisoners being like 'naughty schoolchildren', but he stresses the heroism and ingenuity of the escapees and the efforts made to represent both events and settings accurately. Colditz Castle was in what was then East Germany and totally inaccessible. It was reconstructed – as accurately as possible from old photographs – at Shepperton. For the events on which the film was based – including the escape of 'Jimmy Winslow' (Peter Allan) – see the three-part Channel 4 series *Escape from Colditz* (tx. March 2000).
9 *Daily Mirror*, 21 January 1955.
10 According to the Australian character actor Vincent Ball, the camp for *Danger Within* was built near Gerrards Cross in Buckinghamshire (McFarlane, 1997, p. 55).
11 Gibson was killed in 1944; *Enemy Coast Ahead* was first published in 1946.
12 *Eagle Squadron* (Arthur Lubin) was made for Universal in 1942. *A Yank in the RAF* (1941) was directed by Henry King and starred Tyrone Power.
13 Gregson's characters seem marked by death. The midget submarine that he commands in *Above Us the Waves* is the one which blows itself up; in

Sea of Sand, he draws the fire of a German armoured car to save the survivors of his platoon.

14 According to Lewis Gilbert, 'More knew that we were walking a tightrope in portraying a story of a man without legs'. Quoted by Alan T. Sutherland, NFT Programme Note for 'Disablement in Film' season.

15 Josh Billings lists *Appointment in London* as one of British Lion's 'other winners', along with *The Intruder*, though he puts them behind Lewis Gilbert's *Cosh Boy* and doesn't include them in the national money-makers. 'Gold spinners of 1953', *Kinematograph Weekly*, 17 December 1953, p. 10.

16 According to Taylor (1983), 25,000 died in the Dresden fire storm; the Germans claimed a quarter of a million at the time; Calder (1971) gives a figure of 135,000, but Taylor's more modest figure is horrific enough.

17 *Gift Horse* was a modest commercial success: Josh Billings mentions it as one of the 'other notable attractions' of 1952. *Kinematograph Weekly*, 18 December 1952, p. 10. Roy Baker's *Morning Departure* (1950), about an attempt to rescue a submarine stuck on the bottom of the sea, preceded *Gift Horse*, but it is not set in wartime.

18 Ironically, the admiral is played by John Clements, whose characters had committed far more serious misdemeanours in *Convoy* and *Ships with Wings*.

19 There is a third film which belongs here, Hammer's *The Steel Bayonet*, which has a likeable array of grumbling soldiers who come to grisly ends (Michael Ripper having his guts shot away as he tries to give his officer a cup of tea; Robert Brown incinerated by a flame-thrower as he foolishly returns to help the same officer), but its setting looks less like Tunisia than the wastelands of Essex.

20 *Sea of Sand* was made for the independent company Tempean, set up by Robert Baker and Monty Berman, who had met while serving with the Army Film Unit in North Africa. The film was shot in Tripoli.

21 See Chibnall (2000) for a more detailed analysis of *Ice Cold in Alex*; and *A Very British War Movie* (tx. Channel 4, December 1999) for illuminating interviews with Sylvia Syms and J. Lee Thompson.

22 See BBC's *Timewatch: The Real Bridge on the River Kwai* (tx. March 2000) for a fascinating account of the building of the bridge and of the soldier on whom Nicholson was (inaccurately and unfairly) based, Colonel Philip Toosey.

23 As with *The Cruel Sea*, the script for *The Purple Plain* is by Eric Ambler.

24 Anna possesses, as well as her Eastern qualities, the intelligence, beauty, good sense and staunch loyalty that Muriel Pavlow and Virginia McKenna embody in Englishwomen. Pavlow manages to play, with surprising conviction, a working-class Maltese woman whom an archaeologist-turned-airman played by Alec Guinness wants to marry in *The Malta Story*. He counters her protestations that she would never be able to become an English gentlewoman by pointing out that he wants a wife who will rough it with him on archaeological digs in exotic locations.

25 See Chapman (1998a) for the attitudes of critics like William Whitebait in the *New Statesman* and Leslie Mallory in the *News Chronicle*. Chapman

also offers intelligent explanations why critical neglect of Second World War films has continued. .

26 Durgnat's attitude to post-1945 war films is less dismissive and more perceptive, but his was a voice crying in the wilderness (Durgnat, 1970, pp. 83–92).

9

Fallout: The Enduring Fascination of the Second World War

And we talked of girls and dropping bombs on Rome,
And thought of the quiet dead and the loud celebrities
Exhorting us to slaughter, and the herded refugees . . .
(Alun Lewis, 'All Day It Has Rained')[1]

The 1950s might be seen as the heyday of the British Second World War film, but its long decline has been distinguished by odd revivals and lingering Indian summers. An extraordinary range of films has been made about the war, from painstaking, spectacular re-creations such as *Battle of Britain* and *A Bridge Too Far*, to sharp, sour critiques like *Licking Hitler*, or sunny, unassuming comedies like *Dad's Army*. One can note, however, a clear break at the end of the 1970s when there was a shift in narrative emphasis from violent action to intimate romance and a greater willingness to question received myths about the war. But it would be wrong to assume that the films of the 1960s and 1970s were simple-minded combat films.

No More Heroes

Films made during the 1960s continued to deal with POW camp escapes, RAF missions and commando raids, but changes in the style and ethos of the industry sometimes made for odd distortions of the familiar formulas. Philip Leacock's *The War Lover*, released in 1962, like his *Appointment in London*, made ten years earlier, is a black and white film which centres on the pilot of a heavy bomber and ends with the re-creation of a bombing raid over Germany. But the two films contrast radically in their treatment of heroism and romance. Wing Commander Tim Mason (Dirk Bogarde), in *Appointment in*

London, is a gentlemanly disciplinarian who has flown more than his share of missions and is soon to be grounded. His obstinacy in completing his tour of duty has more to do with a sense of shared responsibility than with any need to prove his personal heroism. In a revealing moment, he confesses to feeling guilty about the death of a young pilot, Greeno (Bryan Forbes), whom he had reprimanded for making phone calls which breached security, thus setting him off on a cycle of moodiness and depression which led directly to his death. He now knows that the calls were to the wife Greeno had not dared admit to because of Mason's disapproval of married men flying, and we expect him to regret being harsh and uncompromising. In fact, the reverse is the case: he feels he has been too lax, allowing the men to drift into relying on luck and instinct rather than on their discipline and training. Later, Mason risks court martial himself by disobeying orders to fly a last mission, but this can be construed as a necessary bolstering of morale for a crew badly shaken by a near fatal accident before take-off.

Though Mason's life is dominated by his job, he finds brief moments for romance with a WAAF intelligence officer, Eve Canyon (Dinah Sheridan). His rival, an American liaison officer (William Sylvester), has more time and money to lavish on her, but Eve unhesitatingly plumps for the Englishman. There is a natural fit between the pair which obviates the need for words of love and, though sexual contact hardly goes further than Eve taking off her hat, they are firmly and convincingly committed to each other. Mason gets the girl and proves himself a hero, but he does both with a diffidence which precludes questions about either his courage or his masculinity.

Group Captain Buzz Rickson (Steve McQueen), in *The War Lover*, is a boastful womanizer who disdains and ignores air force discipline. He is obsessed by sexual conquest, addicted to the dangers of war and gets an orgasmic satisfaction from dropping bombs. Mason presents a world-weary decency and an acknowledgement of the need for thorough training and good morale as prerequisites of military valour. Rickson shows less pleasant qualities – ruthlessness and a strong instinct for self-preservation – as necessary for survival. He risks the lives of his Flying Fortress crew, performing dangerous aerobatics in protest at being made to fly a mission which involves the dropping of propaganda leaflets rather than bombs. He complains about the competence and mental stability of his navigator because he takes a personal dislike to him. He tries to steal the girl of his room-mate and co-pilot, Bolland (Robert Wagner). But in all these cases, there is a degree of justification for his bad behaviour, and throughout most of the film, McQueen and Leacock resist the temptation to demonize Rickson or to make him redeemably cute.

However, Philip Leacock is less assured in these troubled waters than he had been with the certainties of the 1950s. Daphne, the modern, sexual woman played by Shirley Ann Field, acts with zombie-like strangeness and her encounters with Rickson are uncomfortably contrived. At the end of *Appointment in London*, Mason has to take over the role of the master bomber to ensure the success of a major raid. It is an uncomplicated case of the hero stepping into the breach to save the day, but it is totally convincing. During the final raid in *The War Lover*, Rickson disintegrates and, after his crew have bailed out, he crashes his plane into the white cliffs of Dover. It is plausible enough that his instincts should be blunted by a sleepless night, but his failed seduction of Daphne seems an inadequate reason for him to will his own destruction. The impression that the film is turning its back on the disturbing issues it has raised is reinforced by the epilogue where, after Rickson crashes, Bolland and Daphne wander hand in hand though the back-projected quadrangles of Cambridge. What had started as a bold attempt to re-examine 'the fine line that separates the hero from the psychopath' limps uncertainly back to the conventions it had sought to question.

The most consistent producer of war films in the 1960s was the American Mirisch Corporation, which made *633 Squadron*, *Hell Boats*, *Attack on the Iron Coast*, *Submarine X-1* and *Mosquito Squadron*.[2] Its two RAF films – *633 Squadron* and *Mosquito Squadron* – are clumsier and less sophisticated than *The War Lover*, but their impressive flying sequences and attempt to update wartime myths make them worthy of consideration. Both films take *The Dam Busters* as their model, concentrating on the training and accomplishment of a strategically vital but very hazardous bombing raid. But in place of Barnes Wallis and the bouncing bomb, they substitute subplots about resistance groups preparing the ground for the raid and involve the mission leader in a romantic relationship.[3]

Both films are sceptical about heroism and bitter about the costs of such operations. Wing Commander Roy Grant (Cliff Robertson), in *633 Squadron*, is a veteran of the Eagle Squadron, made up of American volunteers who fought with the RAF before America entered the war, but any idealism he once had has disappeared. His misgivings about the mission – an attempt to destroy a rocket fuel factory in Norway by causing it to be buried under an avalanche – are justified. The factory is destroyed, but all ten of 633 Squadron's Mosquitoes crash or are shot down, and Roy ends the film dazed and wounded in a Norwegian field. With such high casualties, the air vice marshal's comment – 'You can't kill a squadron' – seems like empty bombast.

Squadron Leader Quint Munroe (David McCallum), in *Mosquito Squadron*, is glum to the point of misanthropy and burdened with a callously jovial air commodore (Charles Gray), who makes Harry Andrews' air vice marshal in *633 Squadron* seem a model of sensitivity. Munroe also accomplishes his mission – the bombing of a chateau in France where a V3 weapon is being developed – at the cost of all his aircraft, but the film ends less indeterminately with the resistance ensuring his escape back to England.[4]

Andy Medhurst argues that in the 1950s heterosexual relations 'block and deflect the ideological project of the war film', while love between men propels it forward (Medhurst, 1984, p. 37). It is a generalization which underestimates the civilizing and buttressing function of women in many of the films, but it raises the issue of how more developed relationships between men and women fit into war films primarily concerned with heroic action. Both *633 Squadron* and *Mosquito Squadron* link their romances firmly with the mission. In the former, Roy becomes involved with Hilde (Maria Perschy), the sister of the Norwegian resistance leader Erik Bergman (George Chakiris), who has been helping him plan the operation. When Erik returns to Norway and is captured, Roy is instructed to bomb the Gestapo building in which he is being held before he can be made to reveal the secrets of the mission. As Hilde is very attached to Erik – the last surviving member of her family – Roy is apprehensive about how the fact that he has effectively murdered him will affect their relationship. Unfortunately, the opportunity this opens up for exploring the sort of moral issues which animate *Orders to Kill* and *Circle of Deception* is ignored. We see the cruelly tortured Erik inadvertently telling what he knows before being bombed into oblivion along with his persecutors, and Hilde, far from objecting, thanks Roy for putting him out of his misery.

In *Mosquito Squadron*, Quint Munroe's romance is more complex, but the conventions it relies on are those of Victorian melodrama. Quint is (technically at least) a Canadian, who has been brought up by an English couple after his parents are killed in an accident, and their own son, Scotty, is his best friend, room-mate and squadron leader. In the opening moments of the film, Scotty is shot down in flames and presumed dead. Quint is reluctantly drawn into a relationship with Scotty's wife, Beth (Suzanne Neve). Like Peter Penrose, Tim Mason and Roy Grant, he disapproves of serious relationships between women and active flyers and faces the additional hurdle of guilt about stepping into Scotty's shoes. Just as he is beginning to overcome his scruples, he learns that Scotty is still alive. A German raid on the airfield ends with a reel of film being dropped which shows RAF POWs – a dazed-looking Scotty among them – being brought into the chateau. Their lives will be forfeited if the raid goes ahead.

In contrast to *633 Squadron*, where a potentially difficult moral choice is glibly defused, the solution Quint devises intensifies his own conflicts. He proposes to use bouncing bombs to breach the chateau walls, thus enabling the local resistance fighters to rescue the POWs before the chateau is bombed. But if he succeeds in saving Scotty, he will have to cede Beth and revert to living in the shadow of his 'brother'. In the event, Scotty, who has lost his memory, sacrifices himself, eliminating a tank which is impeding their escape, and Quint, having tried as far as possible to do the decent thing, feels justified in welcoming Beth's embrace when he returns. Too much else is going on for their relationship to be explored in any depth, but Quint's decision to withhold what he knows about Scotty's fate is based on a considered sensitivity rather than evasion. As in *Orders to Kill*, there is an awareness that truth is a burden that can hamper and hinder the process of carrying on and building a new life.

The way in which these two films explore heroism, death and romance sheds a retrospectively revealing light on the supposed stiff-upper-lip restraint of earlier films. The romances between Roy and Hilde, Beth and Quint are less deep, less passionate, less emotional than those between Toddy and Johnny Hollis in *The Way to the Stars* and Eve and Tim Mason in *Appointment in London*. In *The War Lover*, Daphne and Bolland get to take off their clothes and go to bed together, but in the Mirisch films, romance is signified by soft music and walks in the countryside. There are faint intimations of poignancy in Hilde's protective concern for Roy and Erik, men haunted by the shadow of death; and Beth, a confident middle-class English-woman with sure instincts for what she wants, is allowed some boldness in wanting to forget her dead husband and begin a new life with another man. (In fact, it is possible to see the relationship between Quint and Beth as taking up the thread of what might have happened between Robert and Judy in *Frieda* had he not returned with a German bride.) But despite the permissive climate of the 1960s, the war film remained dogged by inhibition and restraint. Generic conventions were at odds with the loosening of taboos about sexual passion and the films teeter uncertainly around sexual issues. Not until the end of the 1970s (in *Licking Hitler*, *Hanover Street* and *Yanks*) did the Second World War film adapt sufficiently to allow explicitly sexual relationships.

The other Mirisch films retread familiar paths. *Submarine X-1*, in its account of a midget submarine attack on a German battleship, is less sophisticated in its use of suspense, character interaction and settings than *Above Us the Waves*. *Attack on the Iron Coast*, like *Gift Horse*, deals with the sabotage of the St Nazaire naval base, but is plagued by turgidly wooden acting and a one-dimensional script. In *Gift Horse*, Trevor Howard's embittered naval commander, unfairly treated by a cliquish and short-sighted naval hierarchy, becomes increasingly sympathetic; in *Attack on the Iron Coast*, the blustering American major, played by Lloyd Bridges, thoroughly deserves his reputation as a pig-headed incompetent. The impression of treading water is also evident in those films that deal with prisoners of war. Andrew Stone's *The Password Is Courage* concentrates on ordinary soldiers rather than officers and, as Sergeant Major Charlie Coward (Dirk Bogarde) spends as much time outside the camps as in them, the film avoids the claustrophobic world of *The Wooden Horse*, *The Colditz Story* and *Danger Within*. But its lightweight quality makes it less significant than its predecessors.

Christine Geraghty, commenting on horseplay in RAF mess rooms and POW camps, notes that 'the heroes of the 50s war films become boys again to escape its tensions' (Geraghty, 1984, p. 65). This boyish quality is only occasionally evident in the 1950s films; in *The Password Is Courage* it is all-pervasive. Coward gets himself mixed up with a party of wounded Germans and is decorated with an Iron Cross before his identity is uncovered; he makes fools of the camp commanders by persuading them to believe he knows the secrets of a new British bomb sight; and he causes a buffoonish German to start a conflagration which destroys the whole camp. He has a brief romance with a Polish resistance fighter (Maria Perschy), which gives the film its most serious moments, but as if to bear out Medhurst's earlier claim for the hampering effect of heterosexual relations, Coward chooses to give himself up rather than risk her arrest. The persistently larky tone of the film reasserts itself and he makes his final, successful bid for freedom by commandeering a fire engine with his loyal buddy, Billy Pope (Alfred Lynch).

The Password Is Courage was overshadowed by a much bigger-budget film, *The Great Escape* (John Sturges, 1963), in which Steve McQueen, James Garner, James Coburn and Charles Bronson rub shoulders with British POW camp regulars Richard Attenborough, Gordon Jackson, Donald Pleasence and Nigel Stock.[5] *The Great Escape* is an effective fusion, though no British POW camp film would have attempted to present the old 'slow release down the trousers' trick for getting rid of tunnel soil as a daring innovation. *The Great Escape* was successful in reaching a much wider international audience than the average British POW camp film, but it left little room for further explorations.[6]

The Mackenzie Break twists the conventions by setting its story among German POWs in a Scottish camp. It is directly comparable to Roy Baker's *The One That Got Away*, but whereas the protagonist of Baker's film, Franz von Werra (Hardy Kruger), is very much an individualist, Willi Schleutter (Helmut Griem) is a determined leader intent on imposing Nazi discipline on the camp and organizing a meticulously planned break-out for his U-boat crew. To this end, he contemptuously defies the British camp commander, Major Perry (Ian Hendry), and outwits his guards to have a homosexual Luftwaffe pilot murdered.

Von Werra's progress is wryly observed by his former captors and interrogators but he faces no particular adversary and, like Coward in *The Password Is Courage*, his sheer persistence in pursuing every avenue of escape eventually pays off. Schleutter is more threatening and is not allowed to command our sympathies. He is matched against a maverick army officer, Captain Jack Connor (Brian Keith), drafted into the intelligence section as an alternative to disciplinary action. Connor is a hard-drinking Irish anti-disciplinarian whose hackles are raised by Schleutter's passion for order. In a reminder of the lesson propounded in *The Life and Death of Colonel Blimp*, his unconventional methods are shown to be necessary against an enemy who refuses to play by the rules.

Unexpectedly, however, both Schleutter and Connor overreach themselves. Connor unmasks Schleutter's escape plot but his insistence on allowing it to go ahead in the hope that he can catch the U-boat detailed to pick up the escapees backfires. Schleutter, with exceptional ruthlessness, collapses the attic of one of the huts where the soil from the tunnel has been secreted, burying the Luftwaffe officers housed in it and using the resulting panic as a diversion for the escapees to emerge from their tunnel. The film ends in a stalemate. Schleutter, carried away with trying to shoot down Connor's reconnaissance plane, leaves it too late to board the U-boat before it submerges. The E-boat Connor calls up arrives too late for its depth charges to prevent the escape of the submariners. Connor, on top of a cliff, acknowledges Schleutter in a dinghy below as he takes a swig from his hip flask and sighs, 'Willi, looks like we're both in the shithouse.'

The cynical view that war is a dirty business, where even smart mavericks find it difficult to survive, owed much to the disillusion brought about by American involvement in Vietnam, and it is most

Von Werra (Hardy Kruger, hatless) joins the ranks of German POWs in *The One That Got Away*. Supplied by Flashbacks, © courtesy of Carlton International.

bitterly apparent in films showing small units undertaking dangerous military operations. Robert Aldrich's *The Dirty Dozen* (1967) and *Too Late the Hero* (1969), which have some British input, are essentially American films, but similar tendencies can be seen in *Play Dirty*, *The Long Day's Dying* and *How I Won the War*.

Play Dirty covers the same ground as *Sea of Sand*, but the conflict between officers representing orthodox and unconventional methods is overlain by the machinations of their commanders who unscrupulously use men's lives as pawns in their own power games. Colonel Masters (Nigel Green) runs an unorthodox set-up which operates on his twin principles: that war is a criminal enterprise best carried out by criminals; and that strategies and campaigns planned two thousand years ago by the ancient Egyptians can be re-employed in the current desert war. After a series of failures he is given a last chance and is ordered to destroy one of Rommel's fuel dumps far behind enemy lines. In fact, his commander, Brigadier Blore (Harry

Andrews), plans to use Masters' unit as a decoy and send his own, larger force to claim the glory for what he hopes will be a crushing blow to the German forces. He also insists on one of his own men commanding the Masters unit, though the man he chooses – Captain Douglas (Michael Caine) – is himself something of a maverick. Tension within the unit is maintained by pitting the mildly unortho-dox Douglas against Captain Leech (Nigel Davenport), a murderous, slobbish mercenary, whose contempt for his fellow officer is tempered by the fact that Masters has promised him £2000 for bringing him back alive. Both men prove their worth: Douglas by getting their trucks over seemingly impassable terrain; Leech by allowing Blore's unit – which would have been their own nemesis – to walk into a German ambush. Blowing up the fuel depot proves even more difficult and costly than in *Sea of Sand*. Blore has decided that, with the rapid Allied advance, it is better left intact and he orders Masters to inform the Germans of the whereabouts and intentions of his unit. Douglas and Leech succeed despite the odds, but, their mission over, they are then shot by a trigger-happy British soldier. *Play Dirty*'s bleak vision of war as totally amoral is more interesting than the conven-tional heroism of a film like *Submarine X-1*, which reproduces with less conviction the 1950s conception of an honourable war. But it uses arbitrary death as an easy way of tying up the story and leaves an impression of crudity and insensitivity.

Play Dirty was directed by André de Toth, a Hungarian who had worked with Korda and had forged a successful career in Hollywood; *The Long Day's Dying* was made by Peter Collinson, a prolific young British director who was responsible for films as different as *Up the Junction* (1967) and *The Italian Job* (1969). Whereas *Play Dirty* explores Machiavellian power struggles among an officer class shown as decadent and unscrupulous, *The Long Day's Dying* concen-trates on ordinary soldiers. At the beginning of the decade, *The Long and the Short and the Tall* had been heralded in some quarters as 'the spearhead of the new wave in British cinema', for its boldness in concentrating on a unit of squabbling, foul-mouthed and distinctly unheroic soldiers.[7] It was limited by a profusion of stagy dialogue and a jungle setting which is too obviously part of Boreham Wood. *The Long Day's Dying*, with its constantly moving camera and interior monologue voice-over, is technically more sophisticated and its voice is that of a bright grammar school-educated soldier who – unlike Bogarde's Charlie Coward – clearly holds a different set of values to the officer protagonists of 1950s films.[8] Unfortunately, having shown non-professional soldiers as competent and intelli-gent, and in no need of officer guidance, the film doesn't quite know what to do with them, and, like Douglas and Leech in *Play Dirty*, they are shot down by their own side in the final moments of the film.

How I Won the War works loosely as a parody of *The Way Ahead*, showing a middle-class officer and a fierce but protective sergeant major taking a platoon of conscripts through training to action in North Africa. Instead of engaging in heroic action, they are sent on a mission to establish a cricket pitch behind enemy lines. It is not altogether clear whether this is meant to be endearingly silly or bitingly satirical, and the film only reaches its proper plane of inspired anarchy when the wily shirker played by Jack MacGowran impersonates a general and punches everyone who contradicts him on the nose. Lieutenant Goodbody (Michael Crawford) is a nincompoop, but he is as much a victim as he is a perpetrator of the absurd cruelties of war. His insistence, in the film's epilogue, that he – as the representative of a stupid military juggernaut – won the war certainly challenges the idea of a people's war, but he is too pathetic a figure to give the claim much force.

Epics and Anti-Epics

The early 1950s war films were relatively modest affairs. The POW camp setting of *The Wooden Horse* made few demands on resources and one sees little aerial action in *Angels One Five*. It was not until *The Dam Busters* confirmed the durable popularity of the Second World War as a subject that more extravagant films were proposed. Powell and Pressburger's *The Battle of the River Plate*, David Lean's *The Bridge on the River Kwai* and Leslie Norman's *Dunkirk* were big-budget productions and their commercial success started a trend which lasted for the next two decades.

Faced with the problem of sustaining interest over a long period, these epics interwove various storylines. *The Battle of the River Plate* cuts between the *Graf Spee*, where we see events through the eyes of the captured British merchant seamen, and the Allied battle cruisers attempting to track her down. A third strand is added later with the diplomatic wrangling in Montevideo. *The Bridge on the River Kwai* follows Commander Shears (William Holden) on his escape venture and sets up an alternative site of action to the POW camp; eventually the two strands are brought together with the attack on the bridge. *Dunkirk* intercuts between its two stories – a reluctant corporal (John Mills) shepherding the remnants of his platoon to Dunkirk and the events leading a bellicose reporter (Bernard Lee) and a businessman who is doing well out of the war (Richard Attenborough) to volunteer to take their small boats over to France – until they come together on the beaches. In the 1950s epics, fictional or fictionalized characters participate in real events. Among the later films there is a division between those which meticulously reconstruct major moments of the war, such as *Battle of Britain* and *A Bridge Too Far*, and those which use the war as a setting for high adventure, a process which began with *The Guns of Navarone*.

As in *They Who Dare*, a small commando group lands on a Greek island to carry out a dangerous mission. *The Guns of Navarone* lacks the sour realism of Milestone's film but it is more carefully structured and J. Lee Thompson's direction is inventive enough to maintain interest and suspense over a long period. Carl Foreman's adaptation introduces productive conflicts not provided by Alistair MacLean's novel. Andrea (Anthony Quinn), a Greek resistance fighter, has sworn to kill Mallory (Gregory Peck), the leader of the mission; Mallory leaves the injured Major Franklin (Anthony Quayle) to the mercies of the Gestapo and feeds him with false information in the expectation that he will crack under torture. Mallory's callousness provokes the hostility of Corporal Miller (David Niven), who goads him to kill Anna (Gia Scala), the Greek woman he has a romantic interest in, when she is revealed as a traitor. Maria (Irene Pappas), another Greek partisan, impatient of his sentimental hesitation, shoots Anna herself.[9] Plot complexity, dramatic conflict, exciting action and spectacular locations ensured *The Guns of Navarone*'s international success, but its successors proved less adept at avoiding the pitfalls of epic production.

Operation Crossbow, despite the contribution of Emeric Pressburger (as Richard Imrie), suffers from a ramshackle, shapeless script which makes poor use of its all-star cast. Like *The Battle of the V1*, it begins with the threat posed by the V1 testing programme at Peenemünde on the Baltic coast. Whereas Sewell's film concentrates on resistance activity, *Operation Crossbow* chooses to deal with a female Luftwaffe pilot who volunteers to investigate the V1's steering problems by going up in one herself. She succeeds despite the lack of any mechanism for controlling the speed of the flying bomb or an undercarriage to land it with, but her efforts are soon annulled by an RAF bombing raid which flattens the base. A new set of characters now emerge to carry out the film's main plot – the infiltration of a factory making long-range rockets – and as the film moves away from the wooden Germans and the rhubarbing British chiefs of staff it begins to come alive.

Three scientists – Curtis (George Peppard), Henshaw (Tom

Courtenay) and Bradley (Jeremy Kemp) – are recruited, trained, given false identities, and dropped into Holland, but things rapidly go wrong. Curtis, a womanizing American, is nonplussed to find the divorced wife of the dead man whose identity he has assumed looking for him. He has to tell her at least some of the truth and this is enough for her to jeopardize the mission. When she realizes what she has stepped into, she becomes panicky and frightened. Curtis is an ordinary, decent man and his natural instincts are to calm the fears of this attractive woman (Sophia Loren) and avoid having to kill her. He provides the signature she needed from her husband to allow her to take her children home to Italy and arranges for her to be freed. It seems a plausible enough solution and allows us to believe that the cruel necessities of war can be superseded. Thus, there is a genuine shock when the Dutch hotelier (Lilli Palmer) who is Curtis's contact comes into the room and shoots her. The inexperienced Allied agent might risk sparing a woman who is fearful and probably innocent, but the hotelier, like Léonie in *Orders to Kill* and Maria in *The Guns of Navarone*, has been too long in the field for such sentimentalities.

Unfortunately, this dramatically effective sequence hardly connects with the rest of the film and the other main characters get less chance to display their talents. In a shoddily written subplot, Tom Courtenay's Henshaw is arrested, tortured and shot; and Jeremy Kemp's Bradley, interesting though he is, has no proper dramatic function. The final part of the film, with Curtis and Bradley in the rocket factory, provides an opportunity for pyrotechnic extravagance but it lacks the wit and panache of the equivalent episode of *The Adventures of Tartu*. Wholesale conflagration blows up Curtis and Bradley along with the Germans and their rockets, and the film concludes lamely back at base among the generals and politicians.

The Heroes of Telemark – a fictionalized account of the disruption of German heavy water production at Vemork in Norway – is more competent in its dramatic construction. The SOE agent Knut Haukelid is partially represented by the character played by Richard Harris (Knut Straud), but his SOE connections are lost and he is subordinated to a daredevil Oslo University professor, Rolf Pedersen (Kirk Douglas). Pedersen, the only Norwegian to fully understand the implications of heavy water production in the race to produce an atomic bomb, is an irritating character but he provides a dynamic focus for the narrative. Once the first raid begins, the film becomes impressively taut and assumes a proper epic structure.

The destruction of the Vemork plant was a prime Allied objective and in November 1942 a Combined Operations mission of British engineers made a glider-borne assault. One of the planes was shot down, bringing its glider with it; the other glider crash-landed and the commandos who survived were summarily shot by the Germans. In February the following year, a small Norwegian force led by Haukelid penetrated the factory, blew up the production equipment and destroyed 3000 pounds of heavy water. This raid and a bombing attack by the USAF ended the production of heavy water at Vemork. The remaining stocks were destroyed crossing Lake Tinnsjo en route to Germany.

The film condenses time so that the Norwegian raid on the factory follows immediately on from the crashing of the gliders and the detonation period for blowing up the Lake Tinnsjo ferry is reduced from hours to minutes. More radically, the film transforms Haukelid's remarkable series of coups into a more dramatically satisfying pattern of failure and loss before resounding success is finally achieved. After the disastrous end to the glider-borne assault, the raid on the factory appears to achieve its ends, but such is the wily tenacity of the Nazis that two weeks later production is back to its normal level. A bombing raid, reluctantly sanctioned by Knut and Rolf, kills several civilians and leaves the factory virtually untouched. If substantial stocks of heavy water are transported to Germany, then the production of an atomic bomb can go ahead. Rolf's solution – attacking the convoy while it is confined on the ferry – poses the moral dilemma that the explosion will kill innocent Norwegians and this is compounded when he sees that one of the passengers is a partisan's wife with her baby. Veteran director Anthony Mann died while making the film and there are a number of uncertain moments and loose ends, but its serious subject and impressive visual style give *The Heroes of Telemark* a stature other epics found difficult to emulate.

Operation Crossbow had some basis in fact and represented real characters, such as Duncan Sandys and Lord Cherwell, and *The Heroes of Telemark*, though it has to accommodate an egocentric Hollywood star, adheres closely to real events. *Where Eagles Dare*, like *The Guns of Navarone*, is adapted from an Alistair MacLean adventure story and revels in fictional excess. What appears to be a dangerous but orthodox rescue mission becomes progressively more complicated as treachery is exposed in the highest places and the leader of the mission (Richard Burton) indulges in games of bluff and double bluff which leave his American sidekick (Clint Eastwood) bemused. The suspense and action sequences are effectively maintained and the film meditates productively on British traditions of perfidy and ruthlessness, but it has little to do with the realities of the Second World War.

James Chapman claims that 'the obsession with authenticity in the war film is, in any event, a tedious one which has distracted the attention of film critics from more interesting subjects' (Chapman, 1998a, p. 72). But from *Ships with Wings* and *Mrs Miniver* onwards, the issue of authenticity has remained a vital one and Chapman's comparison between Second World War films and the Western is misleading. A demand for authenticity has never troubled the Western. For the vast majority of its fans, the American West is a mythical place known only through films. Millions of people had direct experience of the Second World War, and if subsequent generations drew on the cinema as their main source of information about the war, it was a knowledge checked against a flood of non-fictional writing and a constant flow of prestigious and influential television documentaries.

While *Where Eagles Dare* borrowed its tone and visual style from the James Bond films, Bond producer Harry Saltzman embarked on a sober and serious reconstruction, *Battle of Britain*. Instead of trying to weave the historic events of 1940 around a personal story, the film offers a series of vignettes: irascible squadron leaders burdened by responsibility, recruits who quickly mature or die, worried older men in positions of power. Despite the star-laden cast, the characters are unmemorable except for Trevor Howard's Keith Park and Laurence Olivier's Hugh Dowding, the two men controlling the battle. Dowding had become almost the forgotten man of the war and the film makes timely acknowledgement of his achievement. But it is typical of its blandness that the argument over strategy which would cost Dowding his job is represented as a conflict between Park and Leigh-Mallory (Dowding's eventual successor), with Dowding adopting a saintly detachment as arbitrator between them.

The aerial combat, which, along with the star cast, pushed the budget up to $12 million, is initially impressive, but without emotional involvement it becomes repetitive, and the film's attempt at impartiality is vitiated by its need for spectacular effects. In total, 1733 German planes were destroyed during the Battle of Britain (compared to RAF losses of 915), but it required more than a short burst of machine gun fire to bring them down. Len Deighton cites the example of Peter Townsend, who fired 220 bullets from his Hurricane's machine guns into a Dornier Do 17 over Lowestoft without destroying it (Deighton, 1977, p. 163). Douglas Bader's biographer points out that the firepower and speed of the monoplane fighters of 1940 did not necessarily make them more deadly than their First World War predecessors:

The greater bullet density of the eight-gun Hurricane and Spitfire over the twin gun Sopwith Camel was offset by the fact that a modern bomber's airframe would deflect or stop a large proportion of the .303-inch-calibre bullets. A 1940 bomber could sustain a large number of hits without lethal damage – and the longer the range, the fewer the bullets that would hit. (Burns, 1998, p. 34)

Such undramatic resilience finds no place in *Battle of Britain*. The epic scope of the film requires it to devote time to Luftwaffe strategy and the fortunes of its aircrew, but it represents them as arrogant fools whose planes explode with monotonous regularity.

Despite their tendencies towards sprawling impersonality, the size and scope of epics often required considerable commitment from their producers. Commitment which resulted in more personal films can be seen in two shoestring productions – *It Happened Here* and *Overlord* – and in Carl Foreman's much bigger-budgeted *The Victors*. Foreman's film, though registered as British and relying on British technicians, is essentially a Euro-American production, but given the important role Foreman played in the British film industry, and the uniqueness of *The Victors*, it is worth considering here. For its first hour, as it follows a platoon of American soldiers through the invasion of Italy, Foreman's film moves in the shadow of Roberto Rossellini's *Paisà* (1946), but as the action moves to France, Belgium and Germany, it comes into its own. The American soldiers played by George Peppard, Eli Wallach and George Hamilton emerge as complex, sympathetic characters and Foreman recreates the world of soldiers on a long-term campaign with unequalled authenticity.

Though it was poorly received at the time, in retrospect many of the film's episodes look definitive: awkward English hospitality is captured more sensitively than in *Yanks*; retribution meted out by partisans more shockingly represented than in *It Happened Here*; battle-hardened cruelty portrayed more impassively than in *The Dirty Dozen*; military execution displayed more sardonically than in *The Affair*. The episodes involving glamorous European stars are solidly written and the performances superb. The brief encounter between Eli Wallach's battle-coarsened sergeant and Jeanne Moreau's sophisticated but shell-shocked French lady captures, with a proper sense of the bizarre, the odd collisions and juxtapositions that war brings about. Moreau's and Wallach's characters span such different worlds that the fact they share a bottle of wine and a bed is extraordinary in itself, and Foreman resists the temptation to push them into a romance. The episodes concerned with more conventional relationships are equally concise and moving. Rosanna Schiaffino, slipping from virtuous wife to cautious infidelity to a sad realization of abandonment; Romy Schneider switching from world-weary innocence to desperate hedonism; Melina Mercouri metamorphosing from barroom slut to criminal godmother, all succeed in stripping away clichés to reveal the wreckage that even a well-intentioned army brings in its wake.

In the penultimate sequence, the handsome, untroubled Chase (Peppard), who has turned his back on promotion and the chance of a lucrative black market career to stay with his mates, is now disabled. On crutches, he makes a long journey to a rural hospital and, after an interlude when an English family rescue him from the rain and ply him with tea, he arrives to be greeted with a 'Stoopid idiot! Get out of here.' Chase, shocked, less by the abuse than by the horribly disfigured appearance of the sergeant who has been his constant companion for the past two years, manages a tearful smile and a cheerful 'Hi Sarge.' It is too poignant a moment on which to end the film and an epilogue follows, set in Berlin after the war.

Trower (George Hamilton), Chase's less smart buddy, is now an officer and has a glamorous German girlfriend, Helga (Elke Sommer). Her sister (Senta Berger), who is involved with a Russian officer, hints that Helga is also sharing her favours with the Russians. The girl he liked in Belgium was seduced by a flashier American and turned into a whore, and Trower is haunted by the fear that the same thing will happen to Helga. Making his way home in the early hours of the morning, he bumps into a drunken Russian officer (Albert Finney) and starts a fight which ends with them stabbing each other to death. Trower's aggression towards the Russian is unreasonable, but it is fuelled by disillusion and the fear of corruption. In Italy, when still a shy and inexperienced private, he is taunted by the sergeant for wanting to meet one of the Russian soldiers who, thousands of miles away, are fighting the same enemy. Now, with the war won and the Russians and Americans together in Berlin, Trower's disappointment and confusion explodes in aggression. The final shot, of the two bodies lying among the ruins of Berlin, might seem an overblown metaphor for the futility of war, but it is also a satisfactory resolution of the film's narrative.

It Happened Here is set in England in 1944. Dunkirk has been followed by a successful invasion, but the Russians are winning the war in the east and American-backed British partisans are gaining ground in the west of England. A district nurse (Pauline Murray) is evacuated to London where she is made to join a fascist organization and sent to a hospital which administers lethal injections to sick labour camp workers. When she objects she is arrested, but is subsequently captured by the partisans and agrees to nurse their wounded. The story plods along uninvolvingly and, with the partisans behaving as badly as the Nazis, there is no catharsis. But the film's evocation of a fascist Britain is fascinating. The newsreels, the propaganda speeches, the anti-Semitic arguments, the policemen loyally enforcing fascist law and order, the German soldiers relaxing in Trafalgar Square conjure up a chilling vision of what it might have been like in Britain if there had been an invasion.

Stuart Cooper and James Quinn's *Overlord* is a gentler, sadder and more diffuse film. A young man (Brian Stirner) from what looks like lower-middle-class suburbia joins up in 1944, gets through army training, although he shows little aptitude for it, makes a friend, begins a romance and is sent to France where he is killed before he can disembark from the landing craft. Whereas in *It Happened Here*, Brownlow and Mollo rely primarily on reconstruction, Chapman and Quinn make extensive use of actuality material which they skilfully interweave with their thin story. It was too gloomily downbeat to have much commercial appeal but its omission from critical consideration is puzzling. The montage of preparations for D-Day accompanied by the hypnotically repetitive song 'We don't know where we're going until we're there', the mechanical monsters clearing the beaches of mines and barbed wire, the tentative love affair consummated in a surreal dream sequence, are remarkable and the film's evocative portrait of a bleak, uncomfortable and unfriendly war is unique.[10]

British Second World War films had been largely financed by American companies in the 1960s, and when backing was withdrawn at the end of the decade, there was no rush to fill the breach. *The Mackenzie Break* was followed only by Norman Cohen's genial comedies *Dad's Army* and *Adolf Hitler – My Part in His Downfall*, Roy Boulting's *Soft Beds, Hard Battles*, Michael Apted's *The Triple Echo*, *Overlord*, and a European co-production, *Hitler – The Last Ten Days*. James Chapman writes that the commercial failure of *A Bridge Too Far* in 1977 'marked the symbolic (as well as the actual) end of the traditional war film' (Chapman, 1998a, p. 74). It would be a fair judgement were it not for the fact that in 1977 there was a remarkable revival of the Second World War film. *A Bridge Too Far*, *Cross of Iron* (Sam Peckinpah) and *The Eagle Has Landed* were followed by a number of other big-budget productions – *Force Ten from Navarone*, *The Passage*, *Escape to Athena*, *Hanover Street*, *Yanks* and *The Sea Wolves*.

A Bridge Too Far is concerned with the Arnhem campaign, which had been more modestly recreated in Brian Desmond Hurst's *Theirs*

Is the Glory. Its Germans are less wooden stereotypes than those of *Battle of Britain* and William Goldman's script creates vivid characters for James Caan, Elliott Gould, Edward Fox and Anthony Hopkins on the Allied side. Although it is sometimes flaccid and diffuse and lacks the immediacy of *Theirs Is the Glory* (where Hurst persuaded British paratroopers to return to Arnhem to recreate the battle), Chapman is right to see it as the last major cinematic monument to the Second World War.[11]

As in 1969, when *Battle of Britain*'s box-office returns were dwarfed by those of Alistair MacLean's *Where Eagles Dare*, *A Bridge Too Far* was much less successful than the adaptation of Jack Higgins' best-selling novel *The Eagle Has Landed*. Though it shares with Lawrence Huntington's *Warn That Man* a plot to kidnap Churchill and with *Went the Day Well?* the idea of German paratroopers in disguise taking over an English village, it carefully repackages the war as an internationally marketable subject. Donald Sutherland makes IRA support for the German cause look fair and reasonable and the division between evil Nazis and good Germans is reopened. Admiral Canaris (Anthony Quayle) might be head of the Abwehr, responsible for all sorts of dastardly deeds of espionage and counter-espionage, and his deputy, Colonel Radl (Robert Duvall), wears an eyepatch and has the stiff military bearing of a Prussian, but they are both honourable men. Colonel Steiner (Michael Caine), the man who leads the German mission, is an unblemished hero. He has received the Iron Cross for bravery and commands the devoted support of his men; he also tries to prevent a Jewish woman from being herded off to an extermination camp. His surprise at the harsh treatment of women and children might seem ingenuous in an officer returning from the notoriously brutal Eastern front, but, as in Peckinpah's *Cross of Iron*, fighting the Russians has a purifying effect which allows German soldiers to be shown in a sympathetic light. In contrast to the arrogant young Luftwaffe officers and U-boat sailors of *The One That Got Away* and *The Mackenzie Break*, Steiner and his men are a noble band of brothers, one of whom sacrifices his own life and jeopardizes the mission to save a little English girl from drowning.

The Eagle Has Landed cannot rewrite history to the extent that Steiner succeeds in kidnapping Churchill, but it breaks so many conventions and taboos that it becomes something more than a simple adventure story. Its big-budget successors had fewer redeeming features. J. Lee Thompson's *The Passage* is turgid and indulgent compared to *The Guns of Navarone*. *Force Ten from Navarone* does make a clear distinction between Yugoslav partisans and Chetniks, but it patronizingly represents the partisans as incapable of blowing up a bridge without help from American rangers and British commandos. *Escape to Athena* makes so little attempt to create a wartime atmosphere that Roger Moore's jokey POW camp commander might be James Bond in disguise and Telly Savalas's Greek resistance leader, Kojak on an undercover operation. *The Sea Wolves*, with its large cast of veterans – David Niven, Gregory Peck, Roger Moore, Trevor Howard, Glyn Houston, Terence Longden and Michael Medwin – seemed to mark a fitting end to the cycle. However, two films released in 1979 – *Hanover Street* and *Yanks* – showed that the Second World War film was still capable of evolution.

War Romance

Hanover Street takes a surprising lurch back to the world of *I Live in Grosvenor Square*. An American airman, David Halloran (Harrison Ford), bumps into an English lady, Margaret Sellinger (Lesley-Anne Down), at a West End bus stop and after initial hostilities they agree to have tea together and fall in love. They enjoy a sexual relationship denied Lady Pat and John Patterson in *I Live in Grosvenor*, but their romance is complicated by the fact that the pleasant, respectable Englishman who also loves Margaret is married to her. With a melodramatic leap which even Herbert Wilcox and Anna Neagle might have balked at, the husband, Paul Sellinger (Christopher Plummer), changes places with an agent he has trained to penetrate Gestapo headquarters in Lyon and is flown out by Halloran. The plane is badly shot up and all the crew killed, apart from Halloran, who jumps out with Sellinger and helps him on his mission. The men have never met before but the taciturn Halloran discovers that the talkative Paul is Margaret's husband and he goes to extraordinary lengths to keep him alive.

There is a pronounced shift in the power balance from the Englishman to the American between *I Live in Grosvenor Square* and *Hanover Street*. Rex Harrison's David Bruce is tetchily put out by Lady Pat's disloyalty but he magnanimously brings the lovers back together and is able to comfort Pat when Patterson is killed. Paul Sellinger keeps his wife but remains innocent of her infidelity and unaware that the man who has saved his life is her lover. Halloran, unlike Patterson, doesn't die and the film ends not on the married couple reunited, but on Margaret thanking Halloran for bringing her husband safely home and saying her last, passionate goodbye.

Hanover Street is interesting in its revival of wartime formulas and motifs (the combination of romance and an undercover operation in occupied France goes back to *Secret Mission*), but it has to cheat continually to bring everything together. The romance between Halloran and Margaret starts and progresses too easily; the mechanism which brings Halloran and Paul together is too contrived (and involves killing off all of Halloran's garrulous and likeable crew); the ease with which they penetrate Gestapo headquarters and make their escape is implausible; and the premise which shows a stronger, more passionate man helping his weaker rival preserve his marriage is not covered with sufficient irony. *Yanks*, released a few months later, is a cleverer and more nuanced film, but it completely eschews war action.

In *Yanks*, Lisa Eichhorn's Jean is characterized by the same determined modesty as Patricia Roc's Celia in *Millions Like Us*. Her relationship with Matt (Richard Gere), an American army cook, is juxtaposed with another, less sentimental romance. The class tension between Charlie and Jennifer is only faintly present in the relationship between Helen (Vanessa Redgrave) and John (William Devane), who classifies himself as a mongrel and looks out of place among Helen's posh friends. But he is a commanding officer with Kennedy-like good looks and he has the assurance to revel in their cultural differences. The easygoing familiarity between this pair allows them both a sexual consummation and a regretful acknowledgement that their relationship is impossible.

The romance between and Jean and Matt is more troubled. They are younger and their emotions are less under control, and though they too establish a friendship which leads inexorably towards a sexual relationship, her engagement to a British soldier, and his scruples about committing himself fully when he is about to be sent into action, prevent sexual consummation. Turbulence, however, also allows obstacles to be overcome, and whereas John goes off to war saddened by the loss of the woman he loves, the broken strands of the relationship between Matt and Jean are magically brought back together.

These sophisticated emotional trajectories give *Yanks* a resonance which inspired a television series (*Wish You Were Here*) and two films, *The Dressmaker* and *The Affair*, which fill out its concerns about relationships between Englishwomen and American servicemen. *The Dressmaker* has a well-worked-out script by John McGrath (from a novel by Beryl Bainbridge) and fine performances by Joan Plowright, Billie Whitelaw and Jane Horrocks. Though it is set during the war and dwells on the sexual impact of the American forces in Britain, it is essentially a melodrama examining the clash between working-class hedonism (Whitelaw) and working-class puritanism (Plowright).

The Dressmaker: Rita (Jane Horrocks) suspicious of the consequences of romance with a good-looking GI (Tim Ransom). Supplied by Flashbacks, © courtesy of Channel 4.

The Affair is more centrally concerned with the war. In *Yanks*, the New Year's Eve dance ends with black GIs being beaten up by their white counterparts after one of them dares put on a display of uninhibited dancing with a white girl. It leads to a crisis between Matt (who refuses to get involved) and Jean (who defiantly asks one of the black GIs to dance). Their divergent view on race illustrates the deep cultural divide between them, but it is a peripheral issue and soon forgotten; in *The Affair*, however, it is the central focus of the film.

Two black GIs, Travis (Courtney Vance) and Charlie (Leland Gantt), become involved with two Englishwomen: Charlie with Esther (Beatie Edney), a servant girl; Travis with Maggie (Kerry Fox), a middle-class lady married to a naval officer. Charlie provokes the ire of Esther's white American ex-boyfriend and he is beaten up; Travis is more circumspect, but is caught having passionate sex with Maggie by her husband, who, having no inkling of their relationship, assumes she is being raped. The film is refreshingly uncoy about sex, but it becomes schematic and one-dimensional in its eagerness to ram home its message about bigotry and injustice. Travis has no flaws. He is patient, considerate and wise. He is kind to children and charms Maggie's unhappy son. He can start temperamental cars and is good at sex. In contrast, Maggie's husband (Ciaran Hinds) is slimy, duplicitous, and has sex with his wife when she obviously doesn't want him to. Travis's terrible fate is so obviously unjust that the film sacrifices emotional complexity for righteous indignation.

The cross-cultural relationships in Mike Radford's *Another Time, Another Place* run deeper. Janie (Phyllis Logan), a married Scots-woman, befriends three Italian POWs consigned to agricultural labour in the cruelly cold northern environment. Luigi (Giovanni Mauriello) is so obviously an opportunistic womanizer that one expects Janie's relationship to be either with the socialist intellectual, Umberto (Gian Luca Favilla), or with the sad, handsome Paolo (Claudio Rosini). But Luigi's insistent enquiries about whether jig-a-jig is possible eventually pay off. Jean's exuberant excitement at the local dance suggests she is not so repressed and demure as she seems. At the Italians' Christmas party, she dances with Luigi before returning to her miserly husband's bed, and the natural rhythm they fall into while dancing presages sex. They are brought together when Janie, touched by his despair of ever returning to the warmth of Naples, embraces him, but what begins as compassion is quickly compounded by desire.

Luigi rather bemusedly reassures Janie that he will love her always and that he would very much like her to come to Naples, but this odd combination of comradeship and sexual passion is less fragile than the romantic love that Halloran and Margaret or Travis and Maggie indulge in. The film ends with Luigi arrested for rape and Janie weeping profusely as she confesses to Jess (Yvonne Gilan), the strong, tempestuous woman who refuses to have anything to do with the Italians, about her relationship with Luigi. But the film is not so gloomily downbeat as it seems. Luigi's singing, Janie's dancing, their urgent, satisfying sex, indicate an emotional resilience which will withstand the mean, petty rules of society. Maggie allows herself to be tricked by her husband into allowing Travis to be found guilty of a rape he did not commit and, to her horror, hanged. Janie is willing to sacrifice her marriage and her reputation to prove that Luigi is innocent of the rape of which he is accused. But once the tears have dried, she will escape from a community where she can find no fulfilment.

Reassessing the War

The war romances tinker with and creatively adapt the myths that surround the war and – as in *The Affair* and *Another Time, Another Place* – shed light on aspects hitherto unrepresented. *Hope and Glory* offers a more thoroughgoing reassessment. War comes to a suburban housing estate in the outer suburbs of London as a time of wonder and adventure. Clive (David Hayman), who fought in the last war, eagerly joins up, though to his rueful amusement he is deemed too old to become an officer and is posted to Cumberland to type for England. His wife, Grace (Sarah Miles), refuses at the last minute to allow her children to be evacuated and braves the bombs that blast out her windows and create a gap in the neat row of Rosewood Avenue. A German pilot bales out among the Brussels sprouts and women eagerly seize his silk parachute. A barrage balloon is launched to deter bombers but breaks loose and has to be shot down by the Home Guard. Nine-year-old Bill (Sebastian Rice Edwards) searches for shrapnel among the ruins and joins a gang which holds the bombed building sites as their territory and exuberantly smashes up the remains of what had been homes.

When the family home is burnt down it is from an ordinary domestic fire and comes as a semi-comical nemesis for Grace's incipient romance with Clive's best friend. Rather than being a tragedy which throws the family into poverty and distress, the fire allows an escape from suburbia to an idyllic setting on the banks of the Thames. Two more bombs follow, but both of them are beneficent. Out on a fruitless fishing trip with his little sister, Bill spies a lone German plane; it drops its bomb load into the Thames and yields a rich harvest of fish. When the holidays end, Bill returns reluctantly to school only to find that it is now a smoking ruin and his joyous days on the river can continue.

Hope and Glory is a film of great charm, warmth and vitality. John Boorman's sunny interpretation of life during the Blitz works by being unabashedly subjective, and avoids or transfigures clichéd representations of the war. Three television films made between 1978 and 1984, *Licking Hitler*, written and directed by David Hare, *The Imitation Game*, written by Ian McEwan and directed by Richard Eyre, and *Rainy Day Women*, written by David Pirie and directed by Ben Bolt, are equally personal, but they incorporate a clear political agenda. All three films depict a dirty war, where the government and its representatives are devious and unscrupulous, distorting truth in the name of national security. Men, far from being heroic, brave and perceptive, are emotionally stunted, cowardly, dishonest and short-sighted. Women, instead of enjoying GI romances or smiling through the Blitz, are abused and exploited by a rigidly patriarchal society.

The three films have several common characteristics. They are written by men who were born in the late 1940s and grew up in the 1950s, a decade saturated in memories of the war. But in place of the nostalgia of *Yanks* and *Hope and Glory*, which draw on the child-hood memories of their writers (Colin Welland and John Boorman, respectively), there is a yearning to uncover secrets about the war, to discover what really happened. All three films reflect contemporary worries about the 'secret state': the operation of intelligence services in ways which seem to undermine democracy. In *Licking Hitler*, the heroine looks back on her wartime experience in a black propaganda unit and links it to 'the 30-year-old deep, corrosive national habit of lying'. In *The Imitation Game*, hypocrisy, injustice and duplicity are condoned in the name of security. In *Rainy Day Women*, a breakdown of law and order in a remote community is cynically manipulated by the authorities.

The other main influence on these films was 1970s feminism. Ian McEwan, discussing the genesis of *The Imitation Game*, recalled that

> The Women's Movement had presented ways of looking at the world, both its present and its past, that were at once profoundly dislocating and infinite in possibility. I wanted to write a novel which would assume as its background a society not primarily as a set of economic classes but as a patriarchy. The English class system, its pervasiveness, its endless subtleties, had once been a rich source for the English novel. The system whose laws, customs, religion and culture consistently sanction the economic ascendancy of one sex over another could be a still richer source; men and women have to do with each other in ways that economic classes do not. (McEwan, 1982, p. 14)

McEwan combined his idea for a novel with research he had done on Alan Turing, the homosexual mathematician who was the key member of the team which cracked German Enigma codes during the war. *The Imitation Game* (the title comes from an article by Turing entitled 'Computing machinery and intelligence') became the story of a bright, discontented woman who joins the ATS and works as a 'special operator' at the Bletchley Park code-breaking centre.

The Imitation Game, like *The Gentle Sex*, shows women joining the ATS, struggling through their basic training, forming close relationships with other women from different backgrounds and learning new skills. In *The Gentle Sex*, a number of crises occur but in the end, all seven women are happily integrated into the Army. By contrast, the heroine of *The Imitation Game* ends the film disgraced and imprisoned. Her downfall is caused by her refusal to act with conventional deference towards men. In *The Gentle Sex* and *Millions Like Us*, there is a certain amount of resentment and suspicion, but the women are allowed to stand up for themselves and prove their equality. The conflict between Jennifer and Charlie is about class rather than gender and there is no hint of discrimination or prejudice against the women workers. Leslie Howard's commentary in *The Gentle Sex* might sound patronizing now, but he is friendly and admiring towards his heroines and the prevailing mood is one of relaxed camaraderie. In *The Imitation Game*, all male–female relationships are troubled by misunderstandings, hostility and prejudice.

In *Licking Hitler*, a young woman from a sheltered upper-class background is brought in to act as interpreter and translator for a black propaganda unit using radio transmissions to spread alarming rumours in Germany. As in *The Imitation Game*, there is a sense of Machiavellian manipulation which troubles the idea of fighting a good war. When Anna (Kate Nelligan) questions the probity of a rumour campaign to convince German soldiers that the blood used in transfusions is non-Aryan and possibly syphilitic, she is told that the German Army went to Russia 'because they were inspired to go by that great genius Joseph Goebbels'. If she feels unable to draft the broadcast, she is told, then she should return to her country estate and leave fighting the war to those with the stomach for it,

> 'because we have as much duty to assist our side as he has his. And if this involves throwing a great trail of aniseed across Europe, if it means covering the whole continent in obloquy and filth, than that is what we shall do.'

As with *The Imitation Game*, male–female relationships are a site of hostility and tension. Anna's sexual relationship with her boss, Archie Maclean (Bill Paterson), a Glaswegian working-class journalist who

Licking Hitler. Karl (Michael Mellinger) broadcasts nasty rumours about the Nazis while the sardonic Will Langley (Hugh Fraser) looks on. Supplied by Flashbacks, © courtesy of BBC Television.

is determined to beat Goebbels at his own game, exposes class differences and conflicts, but the film is also concerned with the way in which men lie to and exploit women and shelter behind an unfair system to avoid the consequences of their actions. Anna struggles to make sense of an education that dissolves her naivety about tea-making and bill-paying but also tries to teach her that sex is brutish and unmingled with tenderness. Archie is psychologically, not physically, damaged, but he is similar to Sammy Rice in *The Small Back Room*: both men are unsmiling and abrasive, have chips on their shoulders and are over-reliant on whisky. In *The Small Back Room*, Sammy is chased through an expressionist nightmare by a giant whisky bottle; in *Licking Hitler*, the progress of Anna and Archie's relationship is indicated by a wardrobe full of Cutty Sark bottles jostling her teddy bear into a corner. But Sammy has a strong, equal, mutually supportive relationship with his fiancée, Susan, which helps the film end on a plausibly optimistic note. Archie is so wrapped up in himself he is unable to acknowledge any need or responsibility for Anna and their relationship is broken off, leaving them both scarred.

Rainy Day Women has a male protagonist, a shell-shocked survivor from the Dunkirk evacuation who is caught in the crossfire between the men and women of the fenland village he is sent to investigate by the Ministry of Information. There is no enemy action. The war against the Germans is significant only in encouraging paranoia and causing smouldering resentments to flare into violence, and men made hysterical by war exert a petty tyranny which results in a group of women being victimized and murdered. Despite the dissimilarities in their stories, there are strong parallels between *Rainy Day Women* and *Went the Day Well?* Both films begin and end with a framing sequence from the present day and look back at a story which represents a violent interlude in a normally quiet and peaceful rural community. Both of them are about things not being what they seem to be. In *Went the Day Well?*, the confusion is straightforward: the troops billeted in the village who are dressed in British Army uniforms are Germans. In *Rainy Day Women*, it is more widespread. The dusty MoI official who sends John Truman (Charles Dance) off on his mission turns out to be an important figure in the intelligence service. Truman, while working for the MoI, is pretending to be an officer on his way to rejoin his regiment. The 'transmitter' which the women are accused of using to send messages to the Germans is an electrolysis machine for removing unwanted hair.

In both films the village community is endangered by a threat from within. In *Went the Day Well?*, it is Oliver Wilsford, the leader of the Home Guard, who is a German agent. In *Rainy Day Women*, it is Alice Durkow (Suzanne Bertish), the widow of a German communist who died in a British internment camp. In 1940 J. B. Priestley had warned that

> any country that allows itself to be dominated by the Nazis will not only have the German Gestapo crawling everywhere, but will also find itself in the power of all its own most unpleasant types – the very people who, for years, have been rotten with unsatisfied vanity, gnawing envy, and haunted by dreams of cruel power. Let the Nazis in, and you will find that the laziest loud-mouth in the workshop has suddenly been given power to kick you up and down the street, and that if you try to make any appeal, you have to do it to the one man in the district whose every word and look you'd always distrusted. (Priestley, 1940, p. 17)

Britain hasn't been invaded in *Rainy Day Women* but the seeds of fascism have already taken root. Alice Durkow's account of her husband's internment deliberately conflates the activities of British policemen with Nazi stormtroopers and the ignorant, prejudiced, paranoid men of the Home Guard act like Nazi thugs.

Alice is innocent of the treachery of which she is suspected, but the real threat she offers is to the power and potency of the village men. In both films, women are called upon to play new and more active roles. In *Went the Day Well?*, the kindly, bumbling postmistress murders the German soldier billeted on her so she can telephone for help, and the clergyman's daughter executes Wilsford, whom she admires and probably hoped to marry. In *Rainy Day Women*, women run the pub and the doctor's practice, and do most of the work on the farm. It is less female independence, though, than male inadequacy which is the problem. John Truman is haunted by nightmares and unable to assert his authority when he needs to. The parson is a sanctimonious fool whose advice the land girls laugh at. The policeman is weak and ineffectual and drinks lemonade instead of beer. The pub landlord, whose sexual problems precipitate the climax, is impotent. *Went the Day Well?* is disturbing in its juxtaposition of pastoral tranquillity and savagery. But the threat to the community is finally overcome. In *Rainy Day Women*, peace is restored, but it is the sullen, shameful silence of a community guilty of an act which can never be spoken of. Similar atrocities in such films as *Witchfinder General* (1968) and *Straw Dogs* (1971) provoke retaliatory vengeance from the hero. But *Rainy Day Women*, like *The Imitation Game* and *Licking Hitler*, refuses us this satisfaction and we are left with wrongs unrighted and evil and injustice triumphant.

The Imitation Game, *Licking Hitler* and *Rainy Day Women* are salutary reminders of the darker side of the war, but their disillusion should not be accepted as definitive truth. Undoubtedly there was betrayal, injustice, abuse and exploitation, but the war effort was not simply a con-trick. People fought against a cruel and oppressive enemy and they gained knowledge and self-respect in that struggle.

In the 1990s, the war attracted only a handful of British films. Michael Caton-Jones' *Memphis Belle*, by casting genuinely young men as the crew of its Flying Fortresses, captures the callowness and inexperience of those who fought and died in the war. It is hampered by a storyline which focuses heavily on a single mission – which we know from the historical record that the Memphis Belle will survive – but it admirably recreates the tensions and fears of a bombing raid. David Leland's *The Land Girls* is equally respectful on the Home Front. The three land girls (Anna Friel, Catherine McCormack and Rachel Weisz) never quite break out of their class stereotypes and the love affair between middle-class Stella (McCormack) and the farmer's son (Steven Mackintosh) is unsatisfactorily resolved. These women face none of the hostility meted out to the land girls of *Rainy Day Women* and none of the hardships faced by men and women alike in *Another Time, Another Place*. The rosy glow of nostalgia only comes into focus when it settles upon the farmer (Tom Georgeson), a true romantic who works himself to death on the land he loves. The meadow where he courted his wife provides the emotional heart of the film. Stella ploughs it up but she understands its significance. She has a feeling for the land which makes her his true successor; but, like Maggie in *The Affair*, she is a broken-backed heroine who allows others to deflect her from her destiny and she slips away into mediocrity.

It is unlikely there will ever again be such a large-scale conflict as the Second World War, and though its echoes are fainter, it still commands interest. Big-budget American films such as *Schindler's List* (1993), *Saving Private Ryan* and *The Thin Red Line* (1998) and popular novels such as Sebastian Faulks' *Charlotte Gray*, Jack Higgins' *Enigma* and Louis de Bernières' *Captain Corelli's Mandolin* suggest that there will continue to be a reworking of ideas and stories about the war as a means of coming to terms with the recent past and of understanding contemporary society.

NOTES

1 Alun Lewis, 'All Day It Has Rained', in Brian Gardner (ed.), *The Terrible Rain: The War Poets 1939–1945* (London: Methuen, 1983), p. 36.
2 Mirisch had been responsible for *The Magnificent Seven* (John Sturges, 1960), *West Side Story* (Robert Wise and Jerome Robbins, 1961), *The Great Escape* (John Sturges, 1963) and the Pink Panther films. Its war films were financed and distributed by United Artists. *Mosquito Squadron* was not technically a Mirisch film, but it employed many of the same personnel and worked within the same ethos.
3 *Mosquito Squadron* incorporates fascinating documentary footage of a Barnes Wallis bouncing bomb designed to bounce on the ground.
4 In *Mosquito Squadron*, Munroe's flight consists of only three planes – acting as pathfinders for a much larger force – but this was probably determined by the film's budget and the numbers of surviving Mosquitoes rather than by the needs of the mission. Similar limitations probably explain the reuse of the sequence of a Mosquito crash landing from *633 Squadron*; it is so dramatic and dangerous it might be actuality footage and certainly bears re-seeing. The raid on the airfield also employs shots used in *633 Squadron*.
5 *The Great Escape* was backed by the Mirisch Corporation but as an American rather than a British film.
6 The continuing resonance of the POW camp myth in Britain was evidenced by the success of the BBC television series *The Colditz Story*

(1972–3), which incarcerated David McCallum and Robert Wagner along with Jack Hedley and Bernard Hepton. The few post-*Great Escape* POW camp films include Bryan Forbes' (American) *King Rat* (1966), Nagisa Oshima's *Merry Christmas, Mr Lawrence*, and Terence Ryan's *The Brylcreem Boys*, which has an interesting premise (German and British prisoners interned in the same camp in Ireland), but is hampered by uncertainty of tone and a weak script.

6 C. A. Lejeune, '*The Long and the Short and the Tall*', *Films and Filming*, March 1961, p. 23. Lejeune herself regards this as an odd way of describing the film but she is glowingly enthusiastic, particularly about Laurence Harvey's performance.

7 The film it most resembles is Alan Clarke's *Contact* (1984), a study of a group of soldiers on an operation in Northern Ireland.

8 For a detailed and sympathetic assessment of *The Guns of Navarone*, see Chibnall (2000).

9 Peter Todd's short film *The Shoreline* (1984) has the same sort of atmosphere.

10 I am writing about British rather than Hollywood films; both *Saving Private Ryan* and Terence Malik's *The Thin Red Line* (which is set in the Pacific) aspire to monumental status.

Filmography

I have included films made during the war where the wartime setting is crucial to the action. Except for *This England*, I have excluded costume films even when parallels are drawn with the contemporary situation. Films made after the war include a selection dealing with the legacy of the war, though I have attempted to confine the sample to those where this is the dominant element of the film. American-backed films registered as British have been included when there is a significant British contribution (as in *The Cockleshell Heroes*) but not (as with *Saturday Island, Heaven Knows, Mr Allison* or *The Dirty Dozen*) where they appear to be primarily American affairs.

For all Ealing films up to the early 1950s, Michael Balcon took the producer credit, the active producer generally being credited as associate producer. For all Gainsborough films between 1939 and 1945, Maurice Ostrer was credited as being 'in charge of production'.

Only long-established production companies are listed; otherwise it is the distribution company which is given.

Abbreviations

ABPC	Associated British Picture Corporation
BL	British Lion
BN	British National
Col	Columbia
CFU	Crown Film Unit
Fox	20th Century-Fox
GFD	General Film Distributors
IFD	Independent Film Distributors
RFD	Rank Film Distributors
UA	United Artists
WB	Warner Bros.

Above Us the Waves. 1955, d. Ralph Thomas, p. William MacQuitty (RFD), sc. Robin Estridge (bk. C.E.T. Warren/James Benson), w. John Mills, John Gregson, Donald Sinden, James Robertson Justice, Michael Medwin, James Kenney. Three British midget submarines attack the German battleship, *Tirpitz*, in a Norwegian fjord. 99 m.

Adolf Hitler – My Part in His Downfall. 1973, d. Norman Cohen, p. Cohen/Gregory Smith (UA), sc. Cohen/Johnny Byrne (bk. Spike Milligan), w. Jim Dale, Arthur Lowe, Bill Maynard, Tony Selby, Geoffrey Hughes, Jim Norton. British conscripts have tragicomic adventures in army training. 102 m.

The Adventures of Tartu. 1943, d. Harold S. Bucquet, p. Irving Asher (MGM), sc. Howard Emmet Rogers/John Lee Mahin/Miles Malleson (st. John C. Higgins), w. Robert Donat, Valerie Hobson, Walter Rilla, Glynis Johns, Phyllis Morris, Martin Miller. A British bomb disposal expert goes undercover in Czechoslovakia to blow up a secret weapons factory. 103 m.

The Affair. 1995, d. Paul Seed, p. David M. Thompson/John Smithson (BBC/HBO-Showcase), sc. Pablo Fenjves/Bryan Goluboff (st. Fenjves/ Walter Bernstein), w. Courtney B. Vance, Kerry Fox, Leland Gantt, Ciaran Hinds, Beatie Edney, Bill Nunn. A married English lady in a rural community has a sexual relationship with a black GI but colludes with her husband in accusing him of rape. 105 m.

Against the Wind. 1948, d. Charles Crichton, ap. Sidney Cole (Ealing), sc. T.E.B. Clarke, w. Simone Signoret, Robert Beatty, Gordon Jackson, Jack Warner, Peter Illing, Paul Dupuis. SOE sends agents into Belgium to carry out resistance. 96 m.

Albert RN. 1953, d. Lewis Gilbert, p. Daniel M. Angel (Eros), sc. Guy Morgan/Vernon Harris (pl. Morgan/Edward Sammis), w. Anthony Steel, Jack Warner, Robert Beatty, William Sylvester, Anton Diffring, Guy Middleton. Naval prisoners of war use a dummy in a bid to escape. 88 m.

Angels One Five. 1952, d. George More O'Ferrall, p. John Gossage/ Derek Twist (ABPC), sc. Twist (st. Pelham Groom), w. Jack Hawkins, Michael Denison, John Gregson, Dulcie Gray, Cyril Raymond, Veronica Hurst. A trainee pilot joins a fighter squadron and is accepted into the group before being killed in action. 98 m.

The Angry Hills. 1959, d. Robert Aldrich, p. Raymond Stross (MGM), sc. A.I. Bezzerides (n. Leon Uris), w. Robert Mitchum, Stanley Baker, Gia Scala, Elizabeth Muller, Leslie Phillips, Marius Goring. A war correspondent is helped by Greek patriots to get a list of resistance contacts to England. 105 m.

Another Time, Another Place. 1958, d. Lewis Allen, p. Allen/Joseph Kaufman, sc. Stanley Mann (n. Lenore Coffee), w. Lana Turner, Barry Sullivan, Glynis Johns, Sean Connery, Sidney James, Terence Longden. An American war correspondent comforts the widow of the British man whom she loved. 95 m.

Another Time, Another Place. 1983, d/sc. Mike Radford (n. Jessie Kesson), p. Simon Perry (Rediffusion/Channel 4), w. Phyllis Logan, Giovanni Mauriello, Gian Luca Favilla, Claudio Rosini, Gregor Fisher, Paul Young. A married Scotswoman has a sexual affair with an Italian prisoner of war working on the land. 102 m.

Appointment in London. 1953, d. Philip Leacock, p. Maxwell Setton/ Aubrey Baring (BL), sc. Robert Westerby/John Wooldridge (st. Wooldridge), w. Dirk Bogarde, Dinah Sheridan, Ian Hunter, William Sylvester, Bryan Forbes, Bill Kerr. A wing commander insists on completing a tour of 90 missions. 96 m.

Appointment with Venus. 1951, d. Ralph Thomas, p. Betty Box (GFD), sc. Nicholas Phipps (st. Jerrard Tickell), w. David Niven, Glynis Johns, George Coulouris, Barry Jones, Kenneth More, Noel Purcell, Bernard Lee. Suzerain's sister and pacifist painter help a major kidnap a prize cow from the German-occupied Channel Islands. 89 m.

Attack on the Iron Coast. 1968, d. Paul Wendkos, p. Irving Tamener/ John C. Champion (Mirisch/UA), sc. Herman Hoffman (st. Champion), w. Lloyd Bridges, Andrew Keir, Sue Lloyd, Mark Eden, Maurice Denham, Glyn Owen. An American officer leads a commando attack on a German submarine base at St Nazaire. 90 m.

Back Room Boy. 1942, d. Herbert Mason, p. Edward Black (Gainsborough), sc. Val Guest/Marriott Edgar/J.O.C. Orton, w. Arthur Askey, Moore Marriott, Graham Moffatt, Googie Withers, Vera Francis, Joyce Howard. A BBC worker takes a job in a remote lighthouse and unmasks German spies. 82 m.

Band Waggon. 1940, d. Marcel Varnel, p. Edward Black (Gainsborough), sc. Marriott Edgar/Val Guest/ J.O.C. Orton/Robert Edmunds, w. Arthur Askey, Richard Murdoch, Moore Marriott, Pat Kirkwood, Jack Hylton, Peter Gawthorne. Unemployed performers take over a television station from spies and transmit a variety show. 85 m.

Battle for Music. 1943, d/p. Donald Taylor (Strand), sc. St John Legh Clowes, w. Hay Petrie, Mavis Claire, Dennis Wyndham, Joss Ambler, Charles Carson, David Keir. An orchestra survives by adapting to the war culture. 89 m.

Battle of Britain 1969, d. Guy Hamilton, p. Harry Saltzman/S. Benjamin Fisz (UA), sc. James Kennaway/Wilfred Greatorex (bk. *The Narrow Margin*, Derek Wood/Derek Dempster), w. Laurence Olivier, Trevor Howard, Christopher Plummer, Michael Caine, Susannah York, Kenneth More. Chronicle of events of the Battle of Britain from various viewpoints. 131 m.

The Battle of the River Plate. 1957, d/p/sc. Michael Powell/Emeric Pressburger (Archers/RFD), w. Peter Finch, Bernard Lee, Anthony Quayle, John Gregson, Ian Hunter, Anthony Bushell. The captain of the *Graf Spee* scuttles his ship rather than be sunk or captured by British battlecruisers. 119 m.

The Battle of the V1. 1958, d. Vernon Sewell, p. George Maynard (Eros), sc. Jack Hanley/Eryk Wlodek (bk. *They Saved London*, Bernard Newman), w. Michael Rennie, Patricia Medina, Milly Vitale, David Knight, Esmond Knight, Christopher Lee. The Polish resistance uncovers the locations of V1 rocket bases and passes the information on to the British. 109 m.

Bees in Paradise. 1944, d. Val Guest, p. Edward Black (Gainsborough), sc. Guest/Marriott Edgar, w. Arthur Askey, Anne Shelton, Peter Graves, Jean Kent, Max Bacon, Antoinette Cellier. Airmen bale out on to an island ruled by women. 75 m.

Before Winter Comes. 1969, d. J. Lee Thompson, p. Robert Emmett Ginna (Col), sc. Andrew Sinclair (st. *The Interpreter*, Frederick L. Keefe), w. David Niven, Topol, Anna Karina, John Hurt, Ori Levy, Anthony Quayle. A Russian deserter makes himself indispensable in a transit camp for displaced persons but is not allowed sanctuary in the West. 107 m.

Bell Bottom George. 1943, d. Marcel Varnel, p. Ben Henry (Col), sc. Peter Fraser/Edward Dryhurst/John L. Arthur (st. Richard Fisher/ Peter Cresswell), w. George Formby, Anne Firth, Reginald Purdell,

Peter Murray Hill, Eliot Makeham, Manning Whiley. A waiter proves his eligibility to join the Navy by exposing a spy ring. 97 m.

The Bells Go Down. 1943, d. Basil Dearden, ap. S.C. Balcon (Ealing), sc. Roger MacDougall/Stephen Black, w. Tommy Trinder, James Mason, Finlay Currie, Mervyn Johns, Philippa Hiatt, Philip Friend. Recruits to AFS fight fires in the London Blitz. 90 m.

The Big Blockade. 1942, d. Charles Frend, ap. Cavalcanti (Ealing), sc. Frend/Angus MacPhail (st. Frank Owen/Michael Foot), w. Leslie Banks, Michael Redgrave, Frank Cellier, Alfred Drayton, John Mills, Robert Morley. An MEW official explains the impact of the British blockade on the German economy. 73 m.

The Black Sheep of Whitehall. 1941, d. Will Hay/Basil Dearden, ap. S.C. Balcon (Ealing), sc. Angus MacPhail/John Dighton, w. Will Hay, John Mills, Basil Sydney, Frank Cellier, Felix Aylmer, Joss Ambler. An incompetent teacher inadvertently foils a plot by fifth columnists. 80 m.

The Black Tent. 1956, d. Brian Desmond Hurst, p. William MacQuitty (RFD), sc. Robin Maugham/Bryan Forbes, w. Anthony Steel, Maria Sandri, Donald Sinden, André Morell, Donald Pleasence, Anthony Bushell. A wounded British officer marries a sheikh's daughter. 93 m.

Bless 'Em All. 1949, d/p. Robert Jordan Hill (Adelphi), sc. Hal Monty/C. Boganny (st. Arthur Dent/Aileen Burke/Leone Stuart), w. Hal Monty, Max Bygraves, Jack Milroy, Les Ritchie, Patricia Linova, Stanley White. Wartime comrades separated after Dunkirk reunite on D-Day. 79 m.

The Bridge on the River Kwai. 1957, d. David Lean, p. Sam Spiegel (Col), sc/n. Pierre Boule, w. Alex Guinness, William Holden, Jack Hawkins, Sessue Hayakawa, James Donald, André Morell. A British commander organizes his men to build a bridge for the Japanese to keep up morale. 161 m.

A Bridge Too Far. 1977, d. Richard Attenborough, p. Joseph E. and Richard P. Levine (UA), sc. William Goldman (n. Cornelius Ryan), w. Sean Connery, Anthony Hopkins, Dirk Bogarde, James Caan, Elliott Gould, Hardy Kruger, Edward Fox. Paratroopers attempt to secure bridges behind enemy lines in Holland. 175 m.

The Briggs Family. 1940, d. Herbert Mason, p. A.M. Salomon (WB), sc. Brock Williams/John Dighton (st. Williams), w. Edward Chapman, Mary Clare, Jane Baxter, Peter Croft, Oliver Wakefield, Glynis Johns. A solicitor becomes a special constable when war breaks out and discovers the truth behind his son's involvement in a jewel theft. 69 m.

The Brylcreem Boys. 1995, d/sc. Terence Ryan, p. Paul Madigan (Sherwood), w. Bill Campbell, William McNamara, Angus Macfadyen, John Gordon Sinclair, Gabriel Byrne, Jean Butler. British and German prisoners are interned together in an Irish POW camp. 106 m.

Bulldog Sees It Through. 1940, d. Harold Huth, p. Walter Mycroft (ABPC), sc. Doreen Montgomery (n. *Scissors Cut Paper*, Gerald Fairlie), w. Jack Buchanan, Greta Gynt, Sebastian Shaw, Googie Withers, Robert Newton, Wylie Watson. A test-pilot exposes enemy agents and foils a plot to blow up parliament. 77 m.

Burma Victory. 1945, d. Roy Boulting, p. David Macdonald (Army Film Unit). Progress of the British Army campaign in Burma. 62 m.

But Not in Vain. 1948, d. Edmond T. Greville, p. Guus E. Ostwalt/ Geoffrey Goodheart (pl. Ben Van Eeslyn), w. Raymond Lovell, Carol Van Derman, Martin Benson, Agnes Bernelle, Julian Dallas, Bruce Lister. Intrigue and betrayal among Dutch resistants. 73 m.

Cage of Gold. 1950, d. Basil Dearden, ap. Michael Relph (Ealing), sc. Jack Whittingham/Paul Stein, w. David Farrar, Jean Simmons, James Donald, Madeleine Lebeau, Herbert Lom, Harcourt Williams. A young woman seduced by an ex-RAF officer is blackmailed after she marries a GP. 83 m.

The Camp on Blood Island. 1958, d. Val Guest, p. Anthony Hinds (Hammer), sc. Guest/Jon Manchip White, w. André Morell, Carl Mohner, Edward Underdown, Walter Fitzgerald, Phil Brown, Barbara Shelley, Michael Goodliffe. Inmates of a Japanese POW camp try to prevent the Japanese finding out that the war has ended to avoid being massacred. 91 m.

Candlelight in Algeria. 1943, d. George King, p. John Stafford (British Aviation), sc. Katherine Stueby, Brock Williams (st. Dorothy Hope), w. James Mason, Carla Lehman, Walter Rilla, Raymond Lovell, Enid Stamp Taylor. A British agent prevents the Nazis from interrupting talks between the Free French and an American general who is planning to invade North Africa. 85 m.

A Canterbury Tale. 1944, d/p/sc. Michael Powell and Emeric Pressburger (Archers/GFD), w. Eric Portman, Sheila Sim, Dennis Price, Sgt. John Sweet, Edward Rigby, Eliot Makeham. A land girl and two sergeants team up to prove the identity of a man who throws glue on women's hair in a small town near Canterbury. 124 m.

The Captive Heart. 1946. d. Basil Dearden, ap. Michael Relph (Ealing), sc. Angus MacPhail/Guy Morgan (st. Patrick Kirwan), w. Michael Redgrave, Basil Radford, Jack Warner, Mervyn Johns, Jimmy Hanley, Gordon Jackson, Rachel Kempson. A Czech captain assumes the identity of a British officer to avoid the Gestapo and is repatriated from a German camp. 98 m.

Carve Her Name with Pride. 1958, d. Lewis Gilbert, p. Daniel M. Angel, sc. Lewis Gilbert/Vernon Harris (st. R.J. Minney), w. Virginia McKenna, Paul Scofield, Jack Warner, Denise Gray, Maurice Roner, Avice Landone. An English girl trained by the SOE goes on two missions into France and is caught and executed by the Nazis. 119 m.

Castle Sinister. 1947, d. Oscar Burn, p. Howard Boler (Equity-British), w. Mara Russell-Tavernan, Alistair Hunter, James Liggatt, Robert Essex, Karl Mier, John Gauntley. In a Scottish castle, an army doctor is unmasked as a Nazi spy. 49 m.

Children of Chance. 1949, d. Luigi Zampa, p. Ludovico Toeplitz/John Sutro (Ortus), sc. Piero Tellini/Michael Medwin, w. Patricia Medina, Manning Whiley, Yvonne Mitchell, Eliot Makeham, Barbara Everest, George Woodbridge. A priest uses a black marketeer's profits to found a home for the illegitimate children of Allied soldiers. 99 m.

Circle of Danger. 1951, d. Jacques Tourneur, p. David E. Rose/Joan Harrison (RKO), sc/n. Philip Macdonald, w. Ray Milland, Patricia Roc, Hugh Sinclair, Marius Goring, Marjorie Fielding, Edward Rigby. An American unravels the truth about his brother's death on a commando raid. 86 m.

Circle of Deception. 1960, d. Jack Lee, p. Tom Morahan (Fox), sc. Nigel Balchin/Robert Musel (n. Alec Waugh), w. Bradford Dillman, Suzy Parker, Harry Andrews, Robert Stephens, Paul Rogers, John Welsh. The SOE sends an agent to France with misinformation to divulge to the Germans. 100 m.

Close Quarters. 1943, d/sc. Jack Lee, p. Ian Dalrymple (CFU). A British submarine sinks a U-boat off Norway and survives a depth charge assault to return to base. 75 m.

The Clouded Yellow. 1950, d. Ralph Thomas, p. Betty Box (RFD), sc/st. Janet Green, w. Trevor Howard, Jean Simmons, Sonia Dresdel, Barry Jones, Kenneth More, Maxwell Reed, André Morell. An ex-SIS agent helps a disturbed girl escape a murder charge. 96 m.

Coastal Command. 1942, d. J.B. Holmes, p. Ian Dalrymple (CFU). An RAF Sunderland flying boat tracks a German surface raider in the

North Atlantic and guides naval fighter planes to attack and sink it. 71 m.

The Cockleshell Heroes. 1955, d. José Ferrer/Alex Bryce, p. Phil C. Samuel (Warwick/Col), sc. Richard Maibaum/Bryan Forbes (st. George Kent), w. José Ferrer, Trevor Howard, Victor Maddern, Anthony Newley, David Lodge, Karel Stepanek. British marines raid Bordeaux docks in canoes and blow ships up with limpet mines. 98 m.

The Colditz Story. 1955, d. Guy Hamilton, p. Ivan Foxwell (BL), sc. P.R. Reid/William Douglas Home/Foxwell/Hamilton (bk. Reid), w. John Mills, Eric Portman, Frederick Valk, Lionel Jeffries, Denis Shaw, Ian Carmichael. Persistent British escapees manage to break out of the German fortress in which they have been confined. 97 m.

Conspiracy of Hearts. 1960, d. Ralph Thomas, p. Betty Box (RFD), sc. Robert Presnell Jr (st. Dale Pitt), w. Lilli Palmer, Sylvia Syms, Yvonne Mitchell, Ronald Lewis, Albert Lieven, Peter Arne. Italian nuns protect Jewish children from the Nazis. 116 m.

Contraband. 1940, d. Michael Powell, p. John Corfield (BN), sc. Powell/Brock Williams (st. Emeric Pressburger), w. Conrad Veidt, Valerie Hobson, Esmond Knight, Raymond Lovell, Hay Petrie, Joss Ambler. A Danish captain rescues British agents from German spies. 92 m.

Convoy. 1940, d. Pen Tennyson, ap. Sergei Nolbandov (Ealing), sc. Tennyson/Patrick Kirwan, w. John Clements, Clive Brook, Judy Campbell, Edward Chapman, Edward Rigby, Michael Wilding. An RN cruiser protects convoys from the depredations of a German battleship. 90 m.

Cottage to Let. 1941, d. Anthony Asquith, p. Edward Black (Gainsborough), sc. Anatole de Grunwald/J.O.C. Orton (pl. Geoffrey Kerr), w. John Mills, Alastair Sim, George Cole, Leslie Banks, Michael Wilding, Carla Lehman, Jeanne de Casalis. An undercover detective catches a gang of spies and fifth columnists. 90 m.

Count Five and Die. 1958, d. Victor Vicas, p. Ernest Gartside (Fox), sc. Jack Seddon/David Pursall, w. Jeffrey Hunter, Nigel Patrick, David Kossoff, Anne-Marie Duringer, Rolf Le Febvre, Larry Burns. Intrigue in the Dutch underground preceding the Allied invasion. 92 m.

Crooks' Tour. 1940, d. John Baxter, p. John Corfield (BN), sc. John Watt/Max Kester, w. Basil Radford, Naunton Wayne, Greta Gynt,

Charles Oliver, Gordon McLeod, Cyril Gardner. English gentlemen abroad get involved in espionage intrigue. 84 m.

The Cruel Sea. 1953, d. Charles Frend, p. Leslie Norman (Ealing), sc. Eric Ambler (n. Nicholas Monsarrat), w. Jack Hawkins, Donald Sinden, Virginia McKenna, Stanley Baker, Denholm Elliott, John Stratton. Five years of grim naval warfare on corvettes guarding convoys. 126 m.

Dad's Army. 1971, d. Norman Cohen, p. John R. Sloan (Col), sc. Jimmy Perry/David Croft, w. Arthur Lowe, John Le Mesurier, Clive Dunn, John Laurie, James Beck, Arnold Rigby. A bank manager organizes the Home Guard in an English seaside town. 95 m.

The Dam Busters. 1955, d. Michael Anderson, p. Robert Clark, W.A. Whittaker (ABPC), sc. R.C. Sherriff (bk. *The Dam Busters*, Paul Brickhill; *Enemy Coast Ahead*, Guy Gibson), w. Michael Redgrave, Richard Todd, Derek Farr, Ursula Jeans, Basil Sydney, Patrick Barr. Planning and execution of bouncing bomb air raids on the Ruhr dams. 125 m.

Danger Within. 1959, d. Don Chaffey, p. Colin Lesslie (BL), sc. Bryan Forbes/Frank Harvey (n. Michael Gilbert), w. Bernard Lee, Richard Todd, Richard Attenborough, William Franklyn, Michael Wilding, Dennis Price, Donald Houston. Allied servicemen in Italian POW camp are plagued by betrayal. 101 m.

Dangerous Moonlight. 1941, d. Brian Desmond Hurst, p. William Sistrom (RKO), sc. Shaun Terence Young/Rodney Ackland/Hurst (st. Young), w. Anton Walbrook, Sally Gray, Derrick de Marney, Cecil Parker, Percy Parsons, Frederick Valk. A Polish flyer raises money for the Polish cause with piano concerts in the USA, but returns to fight in the Battle of Britain. 98 m.

The Day Will Dawn. 1942, d. Harold French, p. Paul Soskin (GFD), sc. Terence Rattigan/Anatole de Grunwald/Patrick Kirwan (st. Frank Owen), w. Hugh Williams, Deborah Kerr, Finlay Currie, Francis L. Sullivan, Griffith Jones, Ralph Richardson, Roland Culver. A racing correspondent undertakes an espionage mission in Norway for naval intelligence. 98 m.

The Deep Blue Sea. 1955, d. Anatole Litvak, p. Anatole Litvak/Alexander Korda (London Films/Fox), sc/pl. Terence Rattigan, w. Vivien Leigh, Kenneth More, Eric Portman, Emlyn Williams, Moira Lister, Dandy Nichols. 99 m. A feckless ex-RAF pilot wrecks the life of a posh lady. 99 m.

Filmography

The Demi-Paradise. 1943, d. Anthony Asquith, p/sc. Anatole de Grunwald (Two Cities), w. Laurence Olivier, Penelope Dudley Ward, Felix Aylmer, Margaret Rutherford, Guy Middleton, Edie Martin. A Russian engineer learns to love the English. 115 m.

Demobbed. 1944, d/p. John E. Blakeley (Mancunian), sc. Roney Parsons/Anthony Toner, w. Norman Evans, Nat Jackley, Dan Young, Betty Jumel, Anne Firth, Tony Dalton. Ex-servicemen take jobs in a factory and expose a crooked manager. 96 m.

Desert Mice. 1959, d. Michael Relph, p. Basil Dearden/Sidney Box (RFD), sc. David Climie, w. Alfred Marks, Sidney James, Dick Bentley, Patricia Bredin, Marius Goring, Dora Bryan. Entertainers root out a German spy in North Africa. 83 m.

Desert Victory. 1943, d. Roy Boulting, p. David Macdonald (Army Film and Photographic Unit/RAF Film Production Unit). Lead-up to and progress of the Battle of El Alamein. 60 m.

The Devil's Jest. 1954, d. Alfred Goulding, p. Paul King (Equity British), sc. Vance Uhden, w. Mara Russell Tavernan, Ivan Craig, Valentine Dyall, Derek Aylwood, Julian Sherrier, Lee Fox. MI5 tracks German spies to a Scottish castle. 61 m. (Remake of *Castle Sinister.*)

The Divided Heart. 1954, d. Charles Crichton, p. Michael Truman (Ealing), sc. Jack Whittingham/Richard Hughes, w. Cornell Borchers, Yvonne Mitchell, Armin Dahlen, Alexander Knox, Michael Ray, Geoffrey Keen. Struggle between Austrian foster-parents and Yugoslav mother over a child adopted during the war. 89 m.

Don't Panic Chaps. 1959, d. George Pollock, p. Ralph Bond/Teddy Baird (ACT/Hammer), sc. Michael Corston/Ronald Holroyd, w. Dennis Price, George Cole, Thorley Walters, Nadia Rejin, Harry Fowler, Nicholas Phipps. Harmony between British and German units in the Adriatic is disrupted by the arrival of a glamorous Italian castaway. 85 m.

Don't Take It to Heart. 1944, d/sc. Jeffrey Dell, p. Sydney Box (Two Cities), w. Richard Greene, Brefni O'Rorke, Edward Rigby, Patricia Medina, Wylie Watson, Alfred Drayton. A ghost's revelations lead an earl and a village poacher to exchange places. 91 m.

Dreaming. 1944, d/p. John Baxter (Ealing), sc. Bud Flanagan/Reginald Purdell, w. Flanagan, Chesney Allen, Hazel Court, Dick Francis, Philip Wade, Robert Adams. A concussed soldier has dreams about escaping hostile natives in Africa, winning a horse race and opening a services canteen. 78 m.

The Dressmaker. 1988, d. Jim O'Brien, p. Ronald Sheldo (British Screen/Film Four), sc. John McGrath (n. Beryl Bainbridge), w. Joan Plowright, Billie Whitelaw, Jane Horrocks, Tim Ransom, Pete Postlethwaite, Pippa Hinchley. A repressed Liverpool girl's love affair with a GI leads to murder. 91 m.

Dunkirk. 1958, d. Leslie Norman, ap. Michael Forlong (Ealing/MGM), sc. W.P. Lipscomb/David Divine (n. *The Big Pickup*, Elleston Trevor; bk. *Dunkirk*, Ewen Butler/J.S. Bradford), w. Richard Attenborough, John Mills, Bernard Lee, Robert Urquhart, Roland Curram, Meredith Edwards. British soldiers cut off from their unit are rescued by civilian and RN sailors from the beaches of Dunkirk. 135 m.

The Eagle Has Landed. 1977, d. John Sturges, p. Jack Wiener/David Niven Jr (ITC), sc. Tom Mankiewicz (n. Jack Higgins), w. Michael Caine, Donald Sutherland, Robert Duvall, Donald Pleasence, Anthony Quayle, Jean Marsh, Jenny Agutter. German commandos attempt to kidnap Churchill. 135 m.

The End of the Affair. 1955, d. Edward Dmytryk, p. David Lewis (Col), sc. Lenore Coffee (n. Graham Greene), w. Deborah Kerr, Van Johnson, Peter Cushing, John Mills, Stephen Murray, Michael Goodliffe. A woman renounces the man she loves because of a vow made to God during a V1 raid. 105 m.

English without Tears. 1944, d. Harold French, p. Anatole de Grunwald/Sydney Box/William Sassoon (Two Cities), sc. Terence Rattigan/de Grunwald, w. Penelope Dudley Ward, Margaret Rutherford, Michael Wilding, Lilli Palmer, Albert Lieven, Claude Dauphin, Roland Culver. A English lady loves her butler but is distracted by flirtatious foreign officers. 89 m.

Escape. 1948, d. Joseph L. Mankiewicz, p. William Perlberg (Fox), sc. Philip Dunne (p. John Galsworthy), w. Rex Harrison, Peggy Cummins, Betty Ann Davis, Norman Wooland, Cyril Cusack. An ex-RAF officer is sent to Dartmoor after killing a man in a fight and escapes. 77 m.

Escape to Athena. 1979, d. George P. Cosmatos, p. Jack Wiener/David Niven Jr (ITC), sc. Edward Anhalt/Richard S. Lochte (st. George P. Cosmatos/Richard S. Lochte), w. Roger Moore, David Niven, Elliott Gould, Claudia Cardinale, Stefanie Powers, Telly Savalas, Richard Roundtree. Allied prisoners of war combine with an Austrian camp commander and a Greek resistance leader to find treasure and destroy a secret Nazi base. 117 m.

Escape to Danger. 1943, d. Lance Comfort/Mutz Greenbaum, p. William Sistrom (RKO), sc. Wolfgang Wilhelm/Jack Whittingham (st. Patrick Kirwan), w. Anne Dvorak, Eric Portman, Karel Stepanek, Brefni O'Rorke, A.E. Matthews, Lily Kann. An English schoolteacher in Denmark uses her contacts in the Gestapo to help resistance fighters and teams up with a British agent. 92 m.

The Evacuees. 1975, d. Alan Parker, p. Mark Shivas (BBC), sc. Jack Rosenthal, w. Garry Carp, Steven Serember, Maureen Lipman, Margery Mason, Ray Mort. Jewish evacuees try to return from the seaside to Manchester. 73 m.

The Eye of the Needle. 1981, d. Richard Marquand, p. Stephen Friedman (UA), sc. Stanley Mann (n. Ken Follett), w. Donald Sutherland, Kate Nelligan, Christopher Cazenove, Ian Bannen, Faith Brook, Barbara Ewing. A Nazi agent is prevented by the neglected wife of a misanthropic cripple from getting secret information back to Germany despite her passionate involvement with him. 113 m

Eyes That Kill. 1947, d/sc. Richard M. Grey (st. Warwick Charlton), p. Harry Goodman (Butchers), w. Robert Berkeley, Sandra Dorne, William Price. An intelligence officer exposes a secret Nazi organization headed by Martin Bormann in Britain. 61 m.

Fiddlers Three. 1944, d. Harry Watt, ap. Robert Hamer (Ealing), sc. Diana Morgan/Angus MacPhail, w. Tommy Trinder, Sonny Hale, Diana Decker, Francis L. Sullivan, Frances Day, Elizabeth Welch, Mary Clare. Two sailors and a Wren are struck by lightning at Stonehenge and sent back in time to Nero's Rome. 88 m.

Fires Were Started. 1943, d/sc. Humphrey Jennings, p. Ian Dalrymple (CFU), w. William Sansom, Philip Dickson, Fred Griffiths, Loris Rey, Johnny Houghton, T.P. Smith, John Barker. Auxiliary firemen fight a dockland blaze during the Blitz. 80 m.

The First of the Few. 1942, d. Leslie Howard, p. George King/Howard/Adrian Brunel/John Stafford (British Aviation), w. Howard, David Niven, Rosamund John, Roland Culver, Derrick de Marney, Anne Firth. A British inventor designs and produces the Spitfire before dying. 117 m.

The Flamingo Affair. 1948, d/p. Horace Shepherd (Grand National), sc. Maurice Moisiewitsch, w. Denis Webb, Colette Melville, Arthur Chesney, Eddie Matthews, Michael Anthony, Geoffrey Wilmer. An ex-commando is ensnared by a femme fatale into black marketeering and robbery. 58 m.

The Flemish Farm. 1943, d. Jeffrey Dell, p. Sydney Box (Two Cities), sc. Dell/Jill Craigie, w. Clifford Evans, Clive Brook, Jane Baxter, Philip Friend, Brefni O'Rorke, Wylie Watson. A Belgian airman returns to occupied Belgium to retrieve his regimental colours. 82 m.

Flying Fortress. 1942, d. Walter Forde, p. A.H. Salomon (WB), sc. Gordon Wellesley/Edward Dryhurst/Brock Williams (st. Williams), w. Richard Greene, Carla Lehman, Donald Stewart, Betty Stockfield, Basil Radford, Edward Rigby. A boastful American flyer learns the virtues of English modesty. 106 m.

For Freedom. 1940, d. Maurice Elvey and Castleton Knight, p. Edward Black (Gainsborough), sc. Miles Malleson/Leslie Arliss/Will Fyffe/Knight, w. Will Fyffe, Anthony Hulme, E.V. Emmett, Guy Middleton, Albert Lieven, Hugh McDermott. A newsreel editor, thwarted in his exposé of Nazi Germany by the Munich agreement, celebrates the sinking of the *Graf Spee*. 87 m.

For Those in Peril. 1944, d. Charles Crichton, ap. S.C. Balcon (Ealing), sc. Harry Watt/J.O.C. Orton/T.E.B. Clarke (st. Richard Hillary), w. David Farrar, Ralph Michael, John Slater, Robert Wyndham, Robert Griffith, John Batten. A reluctant recruit to the Air–Sea Rescue Service learns the value and dangers of their work. 67 m.

Forbidden. 1984, d. Anthony Page, p. Mark Forstater/Hans Brockmann (Enterprise), sc/n. Leonard Gross (*The Last Jews in Berlin*), w. Jacqueline Bisset, Jürgen Prochnow, Irene Worth, Peter Vaughan, Robert Dietl, Avis Bunnage. Aristocrats help Jews in wartime Berlin. 114 m.

Force Ten from Navarone. 1978, d. Guy Hamilton, p. Oliver Unger/John R. Sloan (Col), sc. Carl Foreman/Robin Chapman/George Macdonald Fraser (n. Alistair MacLean), w. Robert Shaw, Harrison Ford, Edward Fox, Franco Nero, Barbara Bach, Alan Badel, Carl Weathers, Richard Kiel. British and American commandos help Yugoslav partisans blow up a bridge. 118 m.

The Foreman Went to France. 1942, d. Charles Frend, ap. Cavalcanti (Ealing), sc. John Dighton/Angus MacPhail/Leslie Arliss/Roger MacDougall/Diana Morgan (st. J.B. Priestley), w. Clifford Evans, Tommy Trinder, Constance Cummings, Gordon Jackson, Robert Morley, John Williams. A foreman goes to France as it collapses before the German advance and brings back essential war machinery. 87 m.

49th Parallel. 1941, d. Michael Powell, p. Powell/John Sutro (Ortus/GFD), sc. Emeric Pressburger, w. Eric Portman, Laurence Olivier,

Anton Walbrook, Glynis Johns, Leslie Howard, Raymond Massie, Niall MacGinnis. A German U-boat crew try to escape from Canada to the neutral USA. 123 m.

Foxhole in Cairo. 1960, d. John Moxey, p. Steven Pallos/Donald Taylor (BL), sc/n. Leonard Mosley (*The Cat and the Mice*), w. James Robertson Justice, Adrian Hoven, Niall MacGinnis, Fenella Fielding, Robert Urquhart, Albert Lieven, Gloria Mestre. Rommel sends a spying mission into Cairo but it is monitored by British Intelligence. 80 m.

Freedom Radio. 1941, d. Anthony Asquith, p. Mario Zampi (Two Cities), sc. Basil Woon/Gordon Wellesley/Louis Golding/Anatole de Grunwald/Jeffrey Dell/Bridget Boland/Roland Pertwee (st. Wolfgang Wilhelm/George Campbell), w. Clive Brook, Diana Wynyard, Raymond Huntley, Derek Farr, Joyce Howard, Morland Graham. A Viennese doctor is revolted by Nazi excesses and starts a radio station to voice opposition. 95 m.

Frieda. 1947, d. Basil Dearden, ap. Michael Relph (Ealing), sc. Ronald Miller/Angus MacPhail (pl. Miller), w. David Farrar, Mai Zetterling, Flora Robson, Glynis Johns, Albert Lieven, Gladys Henson. A British officer returns to an English country town with the German woman who helped him escape. 98 m.

Front Line Kids. 1942, d. Maclean Rogers, p. Hugh Perceval (Butchers), sc. Kathleen Butler/H.F. Maltby/John Byrd, w. Leslie Fuller, Anthony Holles, Marion Garth, John Singer, George Pughe, Ralph Michael. Evacuees return to London and help a hotel porter catch jewel thieves. 80 m.

Garrison Follies. 1940, d. Maclean Rogers, p. Hugh Perceval/Ernest Gartside (Butchers), sc. Rogers/Kathleen Butler/H.F. Maltby, w. Barry Lupino, Nancy O'Neil, H.F. Maltby, John Kevan, Hugh Dempster, Gabrielle Brune. A plumber foils thieving rackets at an RAF base. 64 m.

Gasbags. 1940, d. Marcel Varnel, p. Edward Black (Gainsborough), sc. Val Guest/Marriott Edgar (st. Valentine/Ralph Smart), w. Bud Flanagan, Chesney Allen, Charlie Naughton, Jimmy Gold, Jimmy Nervo, Teddy Knox, Moore Marriott. A barrage balloon crew drift to Germany and return in a secret tunnelling machine. 77 m.

The Gentle Sex. 1943, d. Leslie Howard, p. Derrick de Marney (Two Cities), sc. Moie Charles/Aimee Stuart/Roland Pertwee/Phyllis Rose (st. Charles), w. Rosamund John, Lilli Palmer, Joan Greenwood,

Joyce Howard, Jean Gillie, Joan Gates, Barbara Waring. Seven women join the ATS and become proficient servicewomen. 93 m.

George in Civvy Street. 1946, d. Marcel Varnel, p. Varnel/Ben Henry (Col), sc. Peter Fraser/Ted Kavanagh/Max Kester/Gale Pedrick (st. Howard Irving Young), w. George Formby, Rosalyn Boulter, Ronald Shiner, Philippa Hiatt, Ian Fleming, Wally Patch. An ex-serviceman returns to run a country pub and deal with unfair competitors. 79 m.

Gert and Daisy Clean Up. 1942, d. Maclean Rogers, p. F.W. Baker (Butchers), sc. Kathleen Butler/H.F. Maltby, w. Elsie and Doris Waters, Iris Vandeleur, Joss Ambler, Ralph Michael, Elizabeth Hunt. Cockney sisters expose black market racketeers. 85 m.

Gert and Daisy's Weekend. 1941, d. Maclean Rogers, p. F.W. Baker (Butchers), sc. Rogers/Kathleen Butler/H.F. Maltby, w. Elsie and Doris Waters, Iris Vandeleur, Aubrey Mallalieu, Wally Patch, John Slater. Two working-class women take evacuees to a stately home and help catch country house thieves. 79 m.

Get Cracking. 1943, d. Marcel Varnel, p. Ben Henry (Col), sc. Edward Dryhurst/Michael Vaughan/John Arthur (st. L. DuGarde Peach), w. George Formby, Dinah Sheridan, Edward Rigby, Frank Pettingell, Ronald Shiner, Vera Frances. A mechanic designs a homemade tank and helps his village Home Guard win manoeuvres. 96 m.

The Ghost of St Michaels. 1941, d. Marcel Varnel, ap. Basil Deardon (Ealing), sc. Angus MacPhail, John Dighton, w. Will Hay, Claude Hulbert, Charles Hawtrey, Raymond Huntley, Elliot Mason, Felix Aylmer. A teacher accompanies evacuated schoolboys to a Scottish castle and unmasks fifth columnists. 82 m.

The Ghost Train. 1941, d. Walter Forde, p. Edward Black (Gainsborough), sc. J.O.C. Orton (pl. Arnold Rigby), w. Arthur Askey, Richard Murdoch, Kathleen Harrison, Linden Travers, Raymond Huntley, Peter Murray Hill, Morland Graham. Stranded passengers unmask ghosts as German agents. 85 m.

Gift Horse. 1952, d. Compton Bennett, p. George Pitcher (IFD), sc. William Fairchild/Hugh Hastings/William Rose (st. Ivan Goff/Ben Roberts), w. Trevor Howard, Richard Attenborough, Hugh Williams, Sonny Tufts, James Donald, Joan Rice. A captain with a stained record redeems himself with an old-fashioned destroyer donated by the Americans and uses it to ram the dock gates of St Nazaire. 100 m.

Give Us the Moon. 1944, d/sc. Val Guest (n. *The Elephant Is White*, Caryl Brahms/S.J. Simon), p. Edward Black (Gainsborough), w. Margaret

Lockwood, Vic Oliver, Peter Graves, Jean Simmons, Frank Cellier, Irene Handl. A war hero bored with peacetime life joins a club for those who don't believe in work. 95 m.

Goodnight Mr Tom. 1998, d. Jack Gold, p. Chris Burt (Carlton), sc. Brian Finch (n. Michelle Magorian), w. John Thaw, Nick Robinson, Annabelle Apsion, John Cater, Geoffrey Hutchings, Charles Kay. A grumpy old man takes in an evacuee and rescues him from his psychotic mother. 102 m.

The Goose Steps Out. 1942, d. Will Hay/Basil Dearden, ap. S.C. Balcon (Ealing), sc. Angus MacPhail/John Dighton (st. Bernard Miles/Reginald Groves), w. Hay, Frederick Pettingell, Julien Mitchell, Charles Hawtrey, Anne Firth, Peter Croft. An incompetent schoolteacher impersonates a Nazi spy and steals a secret weapon from Germany. 79 m.

Great Day. 1945, d. Lance Comfort, p. Victor Hanbury (RKO), sc. Wolfgang Wilhelm/John Davenport/Lesley Storm (pl. Storm), w. Eric Portman, Flora Robson, Sheila Sim, Isabel Jeans, Marjorie Rhodes, Walter Fitzgerald, Philip Friend. The Women's Institute organizes a reception for Mrs Roosevelt while a land girl chooses between two men and a WWI captain is caught stealing. 79 m.

The Guns of Navarone. 1961, d. J. Lee Thompson, p. Cecil F. Ford (Col), sc. Carl Foreman (n. Alistair MacLean), w. David Niven, Gregory Peck, Anthony Quinn, Anthony Quayle, Stanley Baker, Irene Pappas, Gia Scala. Commandos and Greek resistants destroy impregnable German guns. 157 m.

The Halfway House. 1944, d. Basil Dearden, a.p. Alberto Cavalcanti (Ealing), sc. Angus MacPhail/Diana Morgan/T.E.B. Clarke/Roland Pertwee (pl. Denis Ogden), w. Françoise Rosay, Tom Walls, Mervyn Johns, Glynis Johns, Alfred Drayton, Esmond Knight. Characters who meet in a ghostly hotel find they have stepped back into the past and are allowed the opportunity to redirect their lives. 95 m.

Hannibal Brooks. 1969, d/p. Michael Winner (UA), sc. Dick Clement/Ian Le Frenais (st. Winner/Tom Wright), w. Oliver Reed, Michael J. Pollard, Wolfgang Priess, John Alderton, James Donald, Peter Karsten. A British POW and an elephant escape from Germany by crossing the Alps. 102 m.

Hanover Street. 1979, d/sc. Peter Hyams, p. Paul N. Lazarus III (Col), w. Harrison Ford, Lesley-Anne Down, Christopher Plummer, Alec McCowen, Patsy Kensit, Max Wall. An American flyer helps his lover's husband to penetrate the Gestapo headquarters in Lyon. 108 m.

Hard Steel. 1942, d. Norman Walker, p. James B. Sloane (GFD), sc. Lydia Hayward (n. *Steel Saraband*, Roger Detaller), w. Wilfrid Lawson, Betty Stockfield, George Carney, John Stuart, Joan Kemp-Walsh, James Harcourt. A tough foreman is promoted to manager and alienates his men by driving them too hard. 86 m.

The Hasty Heart. 1949, d/p. Vincent Sherman (ABPC), sc. Ronald MacDougall (pl. John Patrick), w. Richard Todd, Ronald Reagan, Patricia Neal, Howard Marion Crawford, Ralph Michael, Orlando Martins. A dying soldier overcomes priggish self-pity to form friendships with a nurse and fellow patients. 107 m.

Hell Boats. 1969, d. Paul Wendkos, p. Lewis J. Rachmil (Mirisch/UA), sc. Anthony Spinner/Donald and Derek Ford (st. S.S. Schweitzer), w. James Franciscus, Elizabeth Shepherd, Ronald Allen, Reuven Bar-Yotam, Inigo Jackson, Drewe Henley. An American leads a Royal Naval expedition to destroy a German gun base in Sicily. 95 m.

The Heroes of Telemark. 1965, d. Anthony Mann, p. S. Benjamin Fisz (RFD), sc. Ivan Moffat/Ben Barzman (bk. *Skis against the Atom*, Knut Haukelid; *But for These Men*, John Drummond), w. Kirk Douglas, Richard Harris, Ulla Jacobson, Michael Redgrave, Anton Diffring, Ralph Michael. Norwegian resistants sabotage the Vemork heavy water plant. 131 m.

Hi Gang! 1941, d. Marcel Varnel, p. Edward Black (Gainsborough), sc. Val Guest/Marriott Edgar/Howard Irving Young/J.O.C. Orton, w. Ben Lyon, Bebe Daniels, Vic Oliver, Moore Marriott, Graham Moffatt, Felix Aylmer. Rival American broadcasters adopt an English evacuee. 100 m.

The Hill. 1965, d. Sidney Lumet, p. Kenneth Hyman (MGM), sc. Ray Rigby (pl. Rigby/R.S. Allen), w. Sean Connery, Harry Andrews, Ian Bannen, Alfred Lynch, Ian Hendry, Ossie Davis, Roy Kinnear, Michael Redgrave. Tensions lead to murder at an Army punishment camp in North Africa. 123 m.

Hitler – The Last Ten Days. 1973, d. Ennio de Concini, p. Wolfgang Reinhardt (MGM-EMI), sc. Concini/Reinhardt/Ivan Moffat/Maria Pia Fusco (bk. *The Last Days of the Chancellery*, Gerhardt Boldt), w. Alec Guinness, Doris Kunstmann, Simon Ward, Adolfo Celi, Diane Cilento, Eric Porter. Adolf Hitler and Eva Braun commit suicide in their Berlin bunker. 104 m.

Hitler's SS: Portrait in Evil. 1985, d. Jim Goddard, p. Aida Young (Cannon), sc. Lukas Heller, w. John Shea, Bill Nighy, Lucy Gutteridge, David Warner, Tony Randall, Carroll Baker, José Ferrer. Mixed fortunes of brothers who get involved with the SA and SS. 147 m.

Hope and Glory. 1987, d/p/sc. John Boorman (Col), w. Sarah Miles, Sebastian Rice-Edwards, Ian Bannen, Derrick O'Connor, David Hayman, Sammi Davis, Geraldine Muir, Susan Wooldridge. A boy's experience of the Blitz in the suburban outskirts of London. 112 m.

Hotel Reserve. 1944, d/p. Lance Comfort/Max Greene/Victor Hanbury (RKO), sc. John Davenport (n. *Epitaph for a Spy*, Eric Ambler), w. James Mason, Julien Mitchell, Lucie Mannheim, Raymond Lovell, Herbert Lom. Pre-war intrigue in the South of France. 89 m.

Hotel Sahara. 1951, d. Ken Annakin, p. George H. Brown (GFD), sc. Brown/Patrick Kirwan, w. Peter Ustinov, Yvonne de Carlo, Roland Culver, David Tomlinson, Albert Lieven, Bill Owen. Life in a hotel in a desert area occupied by various Allied and Axis forces. 96 m.

How I Won the War. 1967, d/p. Richard Lester (UA), sc. Charles Wood (n. Patrick Ryan), w. Michael Crawford, John Lennon, Roy Kinnear, Jack MacGowran, Lee Montague, Michael Hordern. A young officer leads a platoon behind enemy lines in North Africa to establish a cricket pitch. 110 m.

I Live in Grosvenor Square. 1945, d/p. Herbert Wilcox (ABPC), sc. Nicholas Phipps/William D. Bayles (st. Maurice Cowen), w. Anna Neagle, Rex Harrison, Dean Jagger, Robert Morley, Nancy Price, Elliot Arluck. An English lady chooses an American air gunner over an English major, but he is killed in action. 115 m.

I See a Dark Stranger. 1946, d. Frank Launder, p. Sidney Gilliat (Individual/GFD), sc. Launder/Gilliat/Wolfgang Wilhelm/Liam Redmond, w. Deborah Kerr, Trevor Howard, Raymond Huntley, Brefni O'Rorke, Liam Redmond, Garry Marsh. An IRA girl is weaned away from the Nazis by a British officer. 111 m.

I Thank You. 1941, d. Marcel Varnel, p. Edward Black (Gainsborough), sc. Marriott Edgar/Val Guest (st. Howard Irving Young), w. Arthur Askey, Richard Murdoch, Moore Marriott, Graham Moffatt, Lily Morris, Kathleen Harrison, Wally Patch. Out-of-work performers persuade a music-hall star to perform to tube shelterers and back their show. 80 m.

I Was Monty's Double. 1958, d. John Guillermin, p. Maxwell Setton (ABPC), sc. Bryan Forbes (bk. M.E. Clifton James), w. Clifton James,

John Mills, Cecil Parker, Bryan Forbes, Sidney James, Leslie Phillips. An actor impersonates General Montgomery to fool the Germans about the invasion plans. 100 m.

Ice Cold in Alex. 1958, d. J. Lee Thompson, p. W.A. Whittaker (ABPC), sc. Christopher Landon/Lee Thompson (n. Landon), w. John Mills, Sylvia Syms, Anthony Quayle, Harry Andrews, Liam Redmond, David Lodge. British soldiers and nurses cross the Libyan desert in an ambulance with a German spy. 129 m.

Ill Met by Moonlight. 1957, d/p/sc. Michael Powell/Emeric Pressburger (Archers/RFD) (bk. Stanley Moss), w. Dirk Bogarde, Marius Goring, Cyril Cusack, David Oxley, Demitri Andreas, Laurence Payne. British agents and Cretan patriots kidnap a German general. 100 m

I'll Walk Beside You. 1943, d. Maclean Rogers, p. F.W. Baker (Butchers), sc. Kathleen Butler (st. Mabel Constanduros), w. Richard Bird, Lesley Brook, Percy Marmont, Beatrice Varley, Irene Handl, George Merritt. An amnesiac sailor's memory is restored by a loving woman who thought he was dead. 88 m.

The Imitation Game. 1980, d/p. Richard Eyre (BBC) sc. Ian McEwan, w. Harriet Walter, Simon Chandler, Nicholas Le Prevost, Brenda Blethyn, Gillian Martell, Bernard Gallagher. An ATS recruit is sent to Bletchley Park, disciplined and accused of treachery. 75 m.

In Which We Serve. 1942, d. David Lean/Noël Coward, p. Anthony Havelock-Allan (Two Cities), sc. Coward, w. Coward, John Mills, Bernard Miles, Celia Johnson, Kay Walsh, Joyce Carey. A captain, a petty officer and an able seaman recollect their war experiences and domestic happiness while clinging to a life-raft. 114 m.

Inspector Hornleigh Goes To It. 1940, d. Walter Forde, p. Edward Black (Gainsborough), sc. Frank Launder/Val Guest/J.O.C. Orton, w. Gordon Harker, Alastair Sim, Raymond Huntley, Phyllis Calvert, Edward Chapman, Percy Walsh. Scotland Yard detectives track down a gang of fifth columnists. 87 m.

The Intruder. 1953, d. Guy Hamilton, p. Ivan Foxwell (BL), sc. Robin Maugham/John Hunter/Anthony Squire (n. *Line on Ginger*, Maugham), w. Jack Hawkins, Michael Medwin, George Cole, Dennis Price, Dora Bryan, Susan Shaw. An ex-tank commander disturbs one of his old soldiers in the act of burglary and seeks to uncover what turned him into a thief. 84 m.

Invasion Quartet. 1961, d. Jay Lewis, p. Ronald Kinnoch (MGM), sc. Jack Trevor Storey/John Briley (st. Norman Collins), w. Bill Travers,

Spike Milligan, Gregoire Aslan, John Le Mesurier, Eric Sykes, Maurice Denham. An ill-assorted team put a German gun that threatens Dover out of action. 87 m.

It Happened Here. 1964, d/p/sc. Kevin Brownlow/Andrew Mollo (UA), w. Pauline Murray, Sebastian Shaw, Nicolette Bernard, Bart Allison, Stella Kimball, Fiona Leland. A district nurse joins a fascist organization after the Nazis invade Britain, but is co-opted by partisans. 99 m.

It's That Man Again! 1942, d. Walter Forde, p. Edward Black (Gainsborough), sc. Ted Kavanagh/Howard Irving Young, w. Tommy Handley, Jean Kent, Jack Train, Sidney Keith, Horace Percival, Dorothy Summers. The mayor of Foaming-at-the-Mouth helps students put on a show. 84 m.

Joey Boy. 1965, d. Frank Launder, p. Launder/Sidney and Leslie Gilliat (BL), sc. Launder/Mike Watts (n. Eddie Chapman), w. Harry H. Corbett, Stanley Baxter, Bill Fraser, Percy Herbert, Lance Percival, Reg Varney. Crooks organize petty scams when they are conscripted into the Army. 91 m.

Johnny Frenchman. 1945, d. Charles Frend, ap. S.C. Balcon (Ealing), sc. T.E.B. Clarke, w. Françoise Rosay, Patricia Roc, Tom Walls, Paul Dupuis, Ralph Michael, Frederick Piper. Rivalry between Cornish and Breton fishermen is superseded by their common opposition to the Nazis. 105 m.

Journey Together. 1945, d/p/sc. John Boulting (RAF Film Unit) (st. Terence Rattigan), w. Richard Attenborough, Edward G. Robinson, Jack Watling, David Tomlinson, George Cole, John Justin. An RAF mechanic fails in his bid to become a pilot but trains as a navigator instead. 95 m.

The Key. 1958, d. Carol Reed, p. Aubrey Baring (Col), sc. Carl Foreman (n. *Stella*, Jan de Hartog), w. Sophia Loren, Trevor Howard, William Holden, Oscar Homolka, Kieron Moore, Bernard Lee, Noel Purcell. Tugboat captains pass on a key to a flat – and a woman – to their successors in the event of their being killed in action. 134 m.

King Arthur Was a Gentleman. 1942, d. Marcel Varnel, p. Edward Black (Gainsborough), sc. Val Guest/Marriott Edgar, w. Arthur Askey, Evelyn Dall, Anne Shelton, Max Bacon, Jack Train, Peter Graves. A small soldier thinks he is invincible because he has King Arthur's sword. 99 m.

Lady from Lisbon. 1942, d. Leslie Hiscott, p. Elizabeth Hiscott (BN), sc. Michael Barringer, w. Francis L. Sullivan, Jane Carr, Martita Hunt, Charles Victor, Anthony Holles, Wilfrid Hyde White. A racketeer agrees to spy for the Nazis in exchange for the Mona Lisa. 75 m.

The Lamp Still Burns. 1943, d. Maurice Elvey, p. Leslie Howard (Two Cities), sc. Elizabeth Baron/Roland Pertwee/Major Neilson (n. *One Pair of Feet*, Monica Dickens), w. Rosamund John, Stewart Granger, Cathleen Nesbitt, Sophie Stuart, Godfrey Tearle, Joyce Grenfell, John Laurie. An architect gives up her profession to train as a wartime nurse. 90 m.

The Land Girls. 1998, d. David Leland, p. Simon Relph (Greenpoint/ Channel 4), sc. Leland/Keith Dewhurst (n. Angela Huth), w. Catherine McCormack, Anna Friel, Rachel Weisz, Steven Mackintosh, Tom Georgeson, Maureen O'Brien. A land girl loves a farmer's son but marries a disabled naval officer. 111 m.

Landfall. 1949, d. Ken Annakin, p. Victor Skutezky (ABPC), sc. Talbot Jennings/Gilbert Gunn/Anne Burnaby (n. Nevil Shute), w. Michael Denison, Patricia Plunkett, Charles Victor, Kathleen Harrison, David Tomlinson, Margaretta Scott. A barmaid proves that the RAF pilot she loves was not responsible for sinking a Royal Navy submarine. 88 m.

Lassiter. 1984, d. Roger Young, p. Albert Ruddy (RFD), sc. David Taylor, w. Tom Selleck, Bob Hoskins, Jane Seymour, Lauren Hutton, Warren Clarke, Joe Regalbuto. A detective blackmails an American into burgling the German embassy. 100 m.

Laugh It Off. 1940, d. John Baxter, p. John Corfield (BN), sc. Bridget Boland/Austin Melford (st. Boland), w. Tommy Trinder, Jean Colin, Anthony Hulme, Marjorie Browne, Edward Lexy, Charles Victor. A variety performer joins the Army and becomes Entertainments Officer. 78 m.

Law and Disorder. 1940, d. David Macdonald, p. K.C. Alexander (RKO), sc. Roger Macdonald, w. Barry K. Barnes, Diana Churchill, Alastair Sim, Edward Chapman, Austin Trevor, Ruby Miller. A lawyer penetrates a fifth columnist gang. 74 m.

The League of Gentlemen. 1960, d. Basil Dearden, p. Michael Relph (Allied Film-Makers/RFD), sc. Bryan Forbes (n. John Boland), w. Jack Hawkins, Nigel Patrick, Roger Livesey, Bryan Forbes, Richard Attenborough, Kieron Moore, Norman Bird. Ex-officers ill-adjusted to peace team up to rob a bank. 113 m.

Let George Do It. 1940, d. Marcel Varnel, ap. Basil Dearden (Ealing), sc. John Dighton/Angus MacPhail/Austin Melford/Dearden, w. George Formby, Phyllis Calvert, Garry Marsh, Coral Browne. A ukulele player uncovers a plot to transmit messages to German U-boats by a treacherous Anglo-German bandleader in Norway. 82 m.

Let the People Sing. 1942, d/p. John Baxter (BN), sc. Baxter/Barbara Emary/Geoffrey Orme (n. J.B. Priestley), w. Alastair Sim, Edward Rigby, Patricia Roc, Fred Emney, Oliver Wakefield, Olive Sloane. A music-hall comedian, a Czech refugee and a magistrate save a concert hall from closure. 105 m.

Letters to an Unknown Lover. 1985, d. Peter Duffell, p. Ian Warren/Jacques Mader/Serge Barry (Channel 4) (st. Pierre Boileau/Thomas Narcejac), w. Cherie Lunghi, Yves Beneyton, Mathilda May, Ralph Bates, Andrea Ferréol. An escaped prisoner of war is hidden by two sisters in France. 101 m.

Licking Hitler. 1978, d/sc. David Hare, p. David Rose (BBC), w. Kate Nelligan, Bill Paterson, Clive Revill, Hugh Fraser, Brenda Fricker, Michael Mellinger, George Herbert. An upper-class girl joins a black propaganda unit. 68 m.

The Life and Death of Colonel Blimp. 1943, d/p/sc. Michael Powell and Emeric Pressburger (Archers/GFD), w. Roger Livesey, Anton Walbrook, Deborah Kerr, James McKechnie, A.E. Matthews, John Laurie. An old soldier relives his life and career and comes to terms with the need for new methods of warfare. 163 m.

Light Up the Sky. 1960, d. Lewis Gilbert, sc. Vernon Harris (pl. *Touch It Light*, Robert Storey), w. Ian Carmichael, Tommy Steel, Benny Hill, Sydney Tafler, Dick Emery, Johnny Briggs. Comic adventures of a searchlight battery crew in 1941. 90 m.

Lili Marlene. 1950, d. Arthur Crabtree, p. William Gell (Monarch), sc. Leslie Wood, w. Lisa Daniely, Hugh McDermott, Richard Murdoch, Leslie Dwyer, John Blythe, Rufus Cruickshank. The Germans force a French girl singer to broadcast in German. 85 m.

The Lion Has Wings. 1939, d. Michael Powell/Adrian Brunel/Brian Desmond Hurst, p. Ian Dalrymple (London Films), w. Ralph Richardson, Merle Oberon, June Duprez, Anthony Bushell, Derrick de Marney. Celebration of RAF and British values. 76 m.

Lisbon Story. 1946, Paul Stein, p. Louis H. Jackson (BN), sc. Jack Whittingham (pl. Harold Purcell/Harry Parr-Davis), w. David Farrar, Patricia Burke, Walter Rilla, Richard Tauber, Laurence O'Madden,

Austin Trevor. An English intelligence officer and a French actress outwit the Nazis to save an atom bomb scientist. 103 m.

The Long and the Short and the Tall. 1961, d. Leslie Norman, p. Michael Balcon (ABPC), sc. Wolf Mankowitz/Willis Hall (pl. Hall), w. Laurence Harvey, Richard Todd, Ronald Fraser, Richard Harris, David McCallum, Kenji Takaki. Internecine conflicts in a British Army patrol group are exacerbated by the capture of a Japanese prisoner. 110 m.

The Long Day's Dying. 1968, d. Peter Collinson, p. Michael Deeley/Harry Fine (Paramount), sc. Charles Wood (n. Alan White), w. David Hemmings, Tom Bell, Tony Jackley, Alan Dobie. Allied paratroopers outwit a German soldier but are gunned down by their own side. 95 m.

The Lost People. 1949, d. Bernard Knowles, p. Gordon Wellesley (Gainsborough), sc/pl. (*Cockpit*) Bridget Boland, w. Mai Zetterling, Richard Attenborough, Siobhan McKenna, Dennis Price, Maxwell Reed, William Hartnell. Displaced persons squabble in a German theatre. 89 m.

Love Story. 1944, d. Leslie Arliss, p. Harold Huth (Gainsborough), sc. Arliss/Doreen Montgomery/Rodney Ackland (n. J.W. Drawbell), w. Margaret Lockwood, Stewart Granger, Patricia Roc, Tom Walls, Reginald Purdell, Moira Lister. A pianist who thinks she has only a short time to live falls in love with a pilot who thinks he is going blind. 108 m.

The Mackenzie Break. 1970, d. Lamont Johnson, p. Jules Levy/Arthur Gardner (UA), sc. William Norton (n. Sidney Shelley), w. Brian Keith, Helmut Griem, Ian Hendry, Jack Watson, Patrick O'Connell, Horst Janson. An intelligence officer investigates a murder in a British POW camp but fails to prevent a breakout by U-boat men. 106 m.

The Malta Story. 1953, d. Brian Desmond Hurst, p. Peter de Sarigny (RFD), sc. William Fairchild/Nigel Balchin (st. Thorold Dickinson/Fairchild/de Sarigny), w. Alec Guinness, Jack Hawkins, Anthony Steel, Flora Robson, Muriel Pavlow, Renee Asherton. Intrigue and romance during the siege of Malta in 1942. 103 m.

The Man from Morocco. 1945, d. Max Greene, p. Warwick Ward (ABPC), sc. Ward/Edward Dryhurst/Margaret Steen (st. Rudolph Cartier), w. Anton Walbrook, Margaretta Scott, Reginald Tate, Mary Morris, Sybilla Binder, Orlando Martins. A Czech radical, interned by the French, escapes to North Africa and aids the resistance. 115 m.

Man on the Run. 1949, d/p/sc. Lawrence Huntington (ABPC), w. Derek Farr, Jean Hopkins, Edward Chapman, Laurence Harvey, John Stuart, Kenneth More. An Army deserter redeems himself by tracking down robbers. 82 m.

The Man Who Never Was. 1956, d. Ronald Neame, p. André Hakim (Fox), sc. Nigel Balchin (bk. Ewen Montagu), w. Clifton Webb, Gloria Grahame, Robert Flemyng, Stephen Boyd, Josephine Griffin, Laurence Naismith. Naval Intelligence attempts to deceive the Germans about the invasion plans for Sicily. 103 m.

A Matter of Life and Death. 1946, d/p/sc. Michael Powell/Emeric Pressburger (Archers/GFD), w. David Niven, Roger Livesey, Kim Hunter, Marius Goring, Raymond Massey, Kathleen Byron. A crashed pilot believes he has cheated death. 104 m.

Medal for the General. 1944, d. Maurice Elvey, p. Louis H. Jackson (BN), sc. Elizabeth Baron (n. James Ronald), w. Godfrey Tearle, Jeanne de Casalis, Morland Graham, Mabel Constanduros, John Laurie, Petula Clark. A Colonel Blimp-like old soldier finds a useful role in war looking after evacuated slum children. 99 m.

Memphis Belle. 1990, d. Michael Caton-Jones, p. David Puttnam/Catherine Wyler (Enigma), sc. Monte Merrick, w. Matthew Modine, Eric Stoltz, Tate Donovan, Billy Zane, David Straithairn, Jane Horrocks. US airmen fly a bombing mission over Bremen to complete their tour of duty. 102 m.

Merry Christmas, Mr Lawrence. 1983, d. Nagisa Oshima, p. Jeremy Thomas (Recorded Picture/Palace), sc. Oshima/Paul Mayersberg (n. *The Seed and the Sower*, Laurens van der Post), w. David Bowie, Tom Conti, Ryuichi Sakamoto, Takeshi Kitano, Jack Thompson, Johnny Okura. A Japanese commander is attracted to a British POW. 123 m.

The Middle Course. 1961, d. Montgomery Tully, p. Brian Taylor (Danziger), sc. Brian Clemens, w. Vincent Ball, Lisa Daniely, Peter Illing, Roland Bartrop, Marne Maitland, Robert Rietty. A crashed flyer helps the French Resistance. 60 m.

Millions Like Us. 1943, d/sc. Frank Launder/Sidney Gilliat, p. Edward Black (Gainsborough), w. Patricia Roc, Gordon Jackson, Eric Portman, Anne Crawford, Moore Marriott, Joy Shelton, Megs Jenkins. Mobile women work in a Castle Bromwich aircraft factory and find romance. 103 m.

Mine Own Executioner, 1947, d. Anthony Kimmins, p. Kimmins/Jack Kitchin (BL), sc/n. Nigel Balchin, w. Burgess Meredith, Dulcie Gray,

Kieron Moore, Christine Norden, John Laurie, Barbara White. A busy psychiatrist, tempted by a femme fatale, fails to prevent a disturbed war hero from killing himself. 104 m.

Miss London Ltd. 1944, d. Val Guest, p. Edward Black (Gainsborough), sc. Guest/Marriott Edgar, w. Arthur Askey, Evelyn Dall, Anne Shelton, Moore Marriott, Graham Moffat, Peter Graves, Richard Hearne. A moribund dating agency is revived by a dynamic American. 99 m.

Mr Emmanuel. 1944, d. Harold French, p. William Sistrom (Two Cities), sc. Gordon Wellesley/Norman Ginsburg (Louis Golding), w. Felix Aylmer, Greta Gynt, Walter Rilla, Ursula Jeans, Peter Mullins, Elspeth March. An elderly Jew's attempt to find a refugee's mother in pre-war Nazi Germany puts him in jeopardy. 97 m.

Mosquito Squadron. 1969, d. Boris Sagal, p. Lewis J. Rachmil (UA), sc. Donald Sanford/Joyce Perry, w. David McCallum, Suzanne Neve, Charles Gray, David Dundas, Dinsdale Landen, Nicky Henson, David Buck. The RAF uses bouncing bombs to attack a rocket base in France. 90 m.

Murphy's War. 1970, d. Peter Yates, p. Michael Deeley/Dmitri de Grunwald (Hemdale), sc. Stirling Silliphant (n. Max Catto), w. Peter O'Toole, Sian Phillips, Philippe Noiret, Horst Janson, Ingo Mogendorf. A merchant skipper attempts to sink a U-boat after his ship is torpedoed. 106 m.

My Ain Folk. 1944, d. Germain Burger, p. F.W. Baker (Butchers), sc. Kathleen Butler, w. Moira Lister, Mabel Constanduros, Norman Prince, Herbert Cameron, Nicolette Roeg, John Turner. A Highland girl goes to work in a factory and organizes a concert. 75 m.

Mystery Submarine. 1963, d. C.M. Pennington-Richards, p. Bertram Ostrer (BL), sc. Jon Manchip White/Hugh Woodhouse/Ostrer (pl. White), w. Edward Judd, James Robertson Justice, Laurence Payne, Joachim Fuchsberger, Albert Lieven, Robert Flemyng. A British crew take over a German U-boat. 92 m.

Neutral Port. 1940, d. Marcel Varnel, p. Edward Black (Gainsborough), sc. J.B. Williams/T.J. Morrison, w. Will Fyffe, Leslie Banks, Yvonne Arnaud, Phyllis Calvert, Hugh McDermott, John Salew. An angry skipper kidnaps a German ship after a U-boat sinks his cargo boat. 92 m.

The Next of Kin. 1942, d. Thorold Dickinson, ap. S.C. Balcon (Ealing), sc. Dickinson/Basil Bartlett/Angus MacPhail/John Dighton, w. Mervyn Johns, Nova Pilbeam, Reginald Tate, Stephen Murray, Geoffrey

Hibbert, Phyllis Stanley, Philip Friend. An Army intelligence officer tries to prevent careless talk revealing the whereabouts of a commando raid. 102 m.

Night Beat. 1948, d/p. Harold Huth (BL), sc. Guy Morgan/T.J. Morrison/Roland Pertwee (st. Morgan), w. Anne Crawford, Ronald Howard, Maxwell Reed, Christine Norden, Hector Ross, Sidney James. Demobilized commandos join the Metropolitan Police. 91 m.

Night Boat to Dublin. 1946, d. Lawrence Huntington, p. Hamilton G. Inglis (ABPC), sc. Huntington/Robert Hall, w. Robert Newton, Raymond Lovell, Muriel Pavlow, Guy Middleton, Herbert Lom, Martin Miller. A British intelligence officer rescues a Swedish atom bomb scientist from Nazi spies. 99 m.

The Night Invader. 1943, d. Herbert Mason, p. Max Milder (WB), sc. Brock Williams/Edward Dryhurst/Roland Pertwee (n. *Rendezvous with Death*, John Bentley), w. David Farrar, Anne Crawford, Carl Jaffe, Sybilla Binder, Marius Goring, George Carney. An RAF intelligence officer is parachuted into Holland to obtain a secret document. 81 m.

The Night of the Generals. 1966, d. Anatole Litvak, p. Sam Spiegel (Col), sc. Joseph Kessel/Paul Dehn (n. Hans Helmut Kirst), w. Peter O'Toole, Omar Sharif, Tom Courtenay, Philippe Noiret, Donald Pleasence, Christopher Plummer. A German intelligence officer tracks down a general who murders prostitutes. 147 m.

Night Train to Munich. 1940, d. Carol Reed, p. Edward Black (Fox), sc. Frank Launder/Sidney Gilliat (st. Gordon Wellesley), w. Margaret Lockwood, Rex Harrison, Paul Henreid, Basil Radford, Naunton Wayne, James Harcourt. A British agent retrieves a Czech scientist from Nazi clutches. 95 m.

The Night We Dropped a Clanger. 1959, d. Darcy Conyers, p. David Henley (RFD), sc. John Chapman, w. Brian Rix, Cecil Parker, Liz Frazer, Leslie Phillips, William Hartnell, Leo Franklyn. A toilet cleaner and a wing commander exchange identities. 86 m.

Nine Men. 1943, d/sc. Harry Watt (st. Gerald Kersh), ap. Charles Crichton (Ealing), w. Jack Lambert, Gordon Jackson, Bill Blewett, Frederick Piper, Eric Micklewood, Grant Sutherland. A British platoon defend a desert tomb against the Italians. 68 m.

No Time to Die. 1958, d. Terence Young, p. Phil C. Samuel (Warwick/Col), sc. Richard Maibaum/Young (st. Merle Miller), w. Victor Mature, Leo Genn, Anthony Newley, Bonar Colleano, David Lodge,

Luciana Paluzzi. Allied soldiers are caught between the Italians and pro-Nazi Arabs. 103 m.

Now It Can Be Told/School for Danger. 1946, d. Teddy Baird (RAF Film Production Unit), w. Harry Rée, Jacqueline Nearne. The SOE trains agents and sends them to run a resistance group in France. 89/69 m.

The Odessa File. 1974, d. Ronald Neame, p. John Woolf/John R. Sloan (Col), sc. Kenneth Ross/George Markstein (n. Frederick Forsyth), w. Jon Voight, Maximilian Schell, Maria Schell, Mary Tamm, Derek Jacobi, Peter Jeffrey. A German journalist uncovers a neo-Nazi organization. 129 m.

Odette. 1950, d/p. Herbert Wilcox, sc. Warren Chetham-Strode (bk. Jerrard Tickell), w. Anna Neagle, Trevor Howard, Marius Goring, Peter Ustinov, Bernard Lee, Maurice Buckmaster. An SOE agent trapped by the Abwehr survives torture and is released from Ravensbrück. 123 m.

Old Bill and Son. 1940, d. Ian Dalrymple, p. Harold Boxall/Josef Somlo (GFD), sc. Bruce Bairnsfather/Dalrymple, w. Morland Graham, John Mills, Rene Ray, Renee Houston, Manning Whiley, Mary Clare. Father, son and adopted daughter all end up serving with the BEF in France. 96 m.

Old Mother Riley Joins Up. 1939, d. Maclean Rogers, p. John Baxter (BN), sc. Kathleen Butler/Maisie Sharman (st. Jack Marks), w. Arthur Lucan, Kitty McShane, Martita Hunt, Bruce Seton, H.F. Maltby, Garry Marsh. An old nurse joins the ATS and unmasks fifth columnists. 75 m.

On the Fiddle. 1961, d. Cyril Frankel, p. S. Benjamin Fisz (Anglo-Amalgamated), sc. Harold Buchman/R.F. Delderfield (n. *Stop at a Winner*, Delderfield), w. Alfred Lynch, Sean Connery, Cecil Parker, Wilfrid Hyde White, Stanley Holloway, Kathleen Harrison. A Cockney and a gypsy get up to tricks in the RAF. 97 m.

One of Our Aircraft Is Missing. 1942, d/p/sc. Michael Powell/Emeric Pressburger (Archers/BN), w. Godfrey Tearle, Hugh Williams, Eric Portman, Bernard Miles, Hugh Burden, Googie Withers, Pamela Brown. The Dutch resistance helps an RAF bomber crew to get back to Britain. 102 m.

The One That Got Away. 1957, d. Roy Baker, p. Julian Wintle (RFD), sc. Howard Clewes (bk. Kendal Burt/James Leasor), w. Hardy Kruger, Michael Goodliffe, Terence Alexander, Colin Gordon, Andrew Faulds,

Alec McCowen. A persistent German POW escapee is sent to Canada and escapes to the neutral USA. 111 m.

Operation Amsterdam. 1959, d. Michael McCarthy, p. Maurice Cowan (RFD), sc. McCarthy/John Eldridge (n. *Adventure in Diamonds*, David E. Walker), w. Peter Finch, Eva Bartok, Tony Britton, Alexander Knox, Malcolm Keen, Melvyn Hayes. Dutch patriots and British agents save industrial diamonds from falling into Nazi hands. 104 m.

Operation Bullshine. 1959, d. Gilbert Gunn, p. Frank Godwin (ABPC), sc. Anne Burnaby/Rupert Lang/Gilbert Gunn (st. Burnaby), w. Donald Sinden, Barbara Murray, Carole Lesley, Ronald Shiner, Dora Bryan, Naunton Wayne. Romantic shenanigans among a mixed-sex anti-aircraft unit. 84 m.

Operation Crossbow. 1965, d. Michael Anderson, p. Carlo Ponti (MGM), sc. Richard Imrie (Emeric Pressburger)/Derry Quinn/Ray Rigby (st. Duilio Coletti/Vittoriano Petrilli), w. George Peppard, Jeremy Kemp, Sophia Loren, Tom Courtenay, Lilli Palmer, Anthony Quayle, Richard Johnson. British scientists infiltrate a V2 rocket base and help the RAF to destroy it. 116 m.

Orders to Kill. 1958, d. Anthony Asquith, p. Anthony Havelock-Allan (BL), sc. Paul Dehn/George St George (st. Donald C. Downes), w. Paul Massie, Irene Worth, Leslie French, John Crawford, Eddie Albert, James Robertson Justice, Lilian Gish. A grounded American airman is trained by the OSS and sent to kill a suspected French collaborator. 111 m.

Our Miss Fred. 1972, d. Bob Kellett, p. Josephine Douglas (MGM-EMI), sc. Hugh Leonard, w. Danny La Rue, Alfred Marks, Lance Percival, Lally Bowers, Walter Gotell, Kristin Hatfield. The comic adventures of a female impersonator in occupied France. 96 m.

The Overlanders. 1946, d/sc. Harry Watt, p. Ralph Smart (Ealing), w. Chips Rafferty, John Nugent Haywood, Daphne Campbell, John Fernside, Jean Blue, Peter Pagan. Australians drive cattle on a thousand-mile trek to save them from the Japanese. 91 m.

Overlord. 1975, d. Stuart Cooper, p. James Quinn (EMI), sc. Cooper/Christopher Hudson, w. Brian Stirner, Davyd Harries, Nicholas Ball, Julie Neesam, Sam Sewell, John Franklyn-Robbins. A young man joins the Army, undergoes training and is killed during the Normandy landings. 83 m.

Pack Up Your Troubles. 1940, d. Oswald Mitchell, p. F.W. Baker (Butchers), sc. Con West (st. Reginald Purdell/Milton Hayward), w.

Purdell, Wylie Watson, Patricia Roc, Wally Patch, Muriel George, Manning Whiley. A garage-owner and a ventriloquist join up and foil the Gestapo. 75 m.

The Passage. 1979, d. J. Lee Thompson, p. John Quested (Hemdale), sc/n. (*The Perilous Passage*) Bruce Nicolaysen, w. Anthony Quinn, James Mason, Malcolm McDowell, Patricia Neal, Kay Lentz, Christopher Lee, Paul Clemens. A Basque shepherd helps a scientist and his family to escape from occupied France across the Pyrenees. 98 m.

The Passing Stranger. 1956, d. John Arnold, p. Anthony Simmons/ Leon Clore/Ian Gibson-Smith (BL), sc. Arnold/Simmons, w. Lee Patterson, Diane Cilento, Duncan Lamont, Liam Redmond, Paul Whitsun-Jones, Alfie Bass. An American deserter hoodwinks a gang of criminals but is betrayed by a jealous rival. 84 m.

The Password Is Courage. 1962, d/sc. Andrew Stone (bk. John Castle), p. Andrew and Virginia Stone (MGM), w. Dirk Bogarde, Maria Perschy, Alfred Lynch, Nigel Stock, Reginald Beckwith, Richard Marner. A British sergeant major makes repeated escape attempts from German POW camps. 116 m.

Pastor Hall. 1940, d. Roy Boulting, p. John Boulting (Charter), sc. Leslie Arliss/Anna Reiner/Haworth Bromley/J. and R. Boulting (pl. Ernst Toller), w. Wilfrid Lawson, Nova Pilbeam, Seymour Hicks, Marius Goring, Percy Walsh, Brian Worth. A German pastor preaches against the Nazis and is shot. 97 m.

Perfect Strangers. 1945, d/p. Alexander Korda (London Films/MGM), sc. Clemence Dane/Anthony Pelissier (pl. Dane), w. Robert Donat, Deborah Kerr, Ann Todd, Glynis Johns, Roland Culver, Elliot Mason. A dowdy married couple are transformed by their war experiences. 102 m.

Piccadilly Incident. 1946, d/p. Herbert Wilcox (ABPC), sc. Nicholas Phipps (st. Florence Tranter), w. Anna Neagle, Michael Wilding, Michael Laurence, Frances Mercer, A.E. Matthews, Brenda Bruce, Edward Rigby. A baronet marries an American after news of his wife's death. But she returns. 102 m.

Pimpernel Smith. 1941, d/p. Leslie Howard (BN), sc. Anatole de Grunwald/Roland Pertwee/Ian Dalrymple (st. A.G. MacDonnell/ Wolfgang Wilhelm), w. Leslie Howard, Mary Morris, Francis L. Sullivan, Hugh McDermott, Raymond Huntley, Manning Whiley. An archaeology professor rescues intellectuals from Nazi concentration camps. 121 m.

Play Dirty. 1968, d. André de Toth, p. Harry Saltzman (UA), sc. Lotte Colin/Melvin Bragg (st. George Martin), w. Michael Caine, Nigel Davenport, Nigel Green, Harry Andrews, Vivian Pickles, Daniel Pilon. An irregular unit sent to blow up a German fuel dump in North Africa is betrayed by their high command. 117 m.

Plenty. 1985, d. Fred Schepisi, p. Edward Pressman/Joseph Papp (Col/EMI/WB), sc/pl. David Hare, w. Meryl Streep, Charles Dance, John Gielgud, Tracey Ullman, Sam Neill, Sting. A woman who worked with the French resistance cannot recapture meaning and purpose in peacetime society. 124 m.

Portrait from Life. 1948, d. Terence Fisher, p. Anthony Darnborough (Gainsborough), sc. Muriel and Sydney Box/Frank Harvey (st. David Evans), w. Mai Zetterling, Robert Beatty, Guy Rolfe, Herbert Lom, Arnold Marle, Sybilla Binder. A British officer traces a girl in a portrait to a German refugee camp and helps restore her memory. 90 m.

Private Angelo. 1949, d/sc. Peter Ustinov/Michael Anderson (n. Eric Linklater), p. Ustinov (Pilgrim), w. Godfrey Tearle, Maria Denis, Peter Ustinov, James Robertson Justice, Robin Bailey, Marjorie Rhodes. A reluctant Italian soldier helps the British against the Germans. 106 m.

Private's Progress. 1956, d. John Boulting, p. Roy Boulting (Charter/BL), sc. John Boulting/Frank Harvey (n. Alan Hackney), w. Ian Carmichael, Dennis Price, Richard Attenborough, Terry-Thomas, Peter Jones, William Hartnell. An Oxbridge student joins the Army and is recruited for crooked enterprises. 102 m.

The Purple Plain. 1954, d. Robert Parrish, p. John Bryan (Two Cities), sc. Eric Ambler (n. H.E. Bates), w. Gregory Peck, Win Min Than, Brenda de Banzie, Bernard Lee, Maurice Denham, Anthony Bushell. A Canadian pilot crashes in Burma and is inspired by the love of a Burmese woman to survive. 100 m.

Rainy Day Women. 1983, d. Ben Bolt (BBC), sc. David Pirie, w. Charles Dance, Lindsay Duncan, Ian Hogg, Cyril Cusack, Suzanne Bertish, Gwyneth Strong. A war-damaged officer investigates rumours in a Fenland village. 75 m.

The Rake's Progress. 1945, d. Sidney Gilliat, p/sc. Gilliat/Frank Launder (Individual/GFD; st. Val Valentine), w. Rex Harrison, Lilli Palmer, Margaret Johnson, Godfrey Tearle, Griffith Jones, Jean Kent. An upper-class wastrel is redeemed by war service. 124 m.

Reach for Glory. 1962, d. Philip Leacock, p. John Kohn/Jud Kinberg (Gala), sc. John Rae/Kohn/Kinberg (n. *The Custard Boys*, Rae), w. Harry Andrews, Kay Walsh, Michael Anderson Jr, Oliver Grimm, Michael Trubshawe, Richard Vernon. Schoolboys persecute an Austrian refugee. 86 m.

Reach for the Sky. 1956, d. Lewis Gilbert, p. Daniel M. Angel (RFD), sc. Lewis Gilbert/Vernon Harris (bk. Paul Brickhill), w. Kenneth More, Muriel Pavlow, Lyndon Brook, Lee Patterson, Dorothy Alison, Sydney Tafler. A pilot loses his legs in a crash but insists on returning to flying duties when war breaks out. 135 m.

The Red Beret. 1953, d. Terence Young, p. Irving Allen/Albert Broccoli/Anthony Bushell (Warwick/Col), sc. Richard Maibaum/Frank Nugent (bk. Hilary St George Sanders), w. Alan Ladd, Leo Genn, Susan Stephen, Harry Andrews, Donald Houston, Anthony Bushell. An American pretends to be a Canadian and joins a British paratroop regiment. 88 m.

Rhythm Serenade. 1943, d. Gordon Wellesley, p. Ben Henry/George Formby (Col), sc. Marjorie Deans/Basil Woon/Margaret Kennedy/Edward Dryhurst (st. Deans), w. Vera Lynn, Peter Murray-Hill, Charles Victor, Julien Mitchell, Jimmy Jewel, Ben Warriss. A young woman forgoes service in the WRNS to set up a crèche for the children of factory workers and help a traumatized commando overcome memory loss. 87 m.

Sabotage at Sea 1942, d. Leslie Hiscott, p. Elizabeth Hiscott (BN), sc. Michael Barringer, w. Jane Carr, David Hutcheson, Margaretta Scott, Wally Patch, Martita Hunt, Ronald Shiner. A captain tries to catch a saboteur on his ship. 76 m.

The Safecracker. 1958, d. Ray Milland, p. David E. Rose/John R. Sloan (MGM), sc. Paul Monash (bk. Rhys Davis/Bruce Thomas), w. Ray Milland, Barry Jones, Cyril Raymond, Melissa Stribling, Jeannette Sterke, Percy Herbert. A burglar is recruited for a mission in Belgium. 96 m.

Sailors Don't Care. 1940, d. Oswald Mitchell, p. F.W. Baker (Butchers), sc. Mitchell/Kenneth Horne, w. Tom Gamble, Edward Rigby, Jean Gillie, Michael Wilding, John Salew, Mavis Villiers. Incompetent and lecherous sailors expose spies and fifth columnists attempting to pass naval secrets to Germany. 79 m.

Sailors Three. 1940, d. Walter Forde, ap. Culley Forde (Ealing), sc. Angus MacPhail/Gordon Wellesley (st. MacPhail/John Dighton/

Austin Melford), w. Tommy Trinder, Claude Hulbert, Michael Wilding, Carla Lehman, James Hayter, Jeanne de Casalis. Hung-over British sailors sabotage a German pocket battleship. 86 m.

Salute John Citizen. 1942, d. Maurice Elvey, p. Wallace Orton (BN), sc. Clemence Dane, Elizabeth Baron (n. *Mr Bunting/Mr Bunting at War*, Robert Greenwood), w. Edward Rigby, Mabel Constanduros, Stanley Holloway, Jimmy Hanley, Dinah Sheridan, George Robey. An ordinary London family carry on through the Blitz. 98 m.

San Demetrio London. 1943, d. Charles Frend, ap. Robert Hamer (Ealing), sc. Hamer/Frend (st. F. Tennyson Jesse), w. Walter Fitzgerald, Mervyn Johns, Ralph Michael, Robert Beatty, Gordon Jackson, Charles Victor. Lifeboat survivors return to a burning tanker and sail her home to Britain. 105 m.

School for Danger, see *Now It Can Be Told*.

School for Secrets. 1946, d/sc. Peter Ustinov, p. Ustinov/George H. Brown (Two Cities), w. Ralph Richardson, Raymond Huntley, Richard Attenborough, Marjorie Rhodes, John Laurie, David Tomlinson. A mixed bag of scientists come together to invent a radar-aided bomb sight. 108 m.

Schweik's New Adventures. 1943, d. Karel Lamac, p. Walter Sors/ Edward G. Whiting (Coronel), sc. Lamac/Con West (st. Jaroslav Hasek), w. Lloyd Bacon, Julien Mitchell, George Carney, Richard Attenborough, Margaret McGrath, Jan Masaryk. A Czech patriot becomes a Gestapo chief's butler and helps the resistance. 84 m.

Sea of Sand. 1958, d. Guy Green, p. Robert Baker/Monty Berman (Tempean/RFD), sc. Robert Westerby (st. Sean Fielding), w. John Gregson, Richard Attenborough, Michael Craig, Vincent Ball, Barry Foster, Ray McAnally, Dermot Walsh. A commando unit cross the desert to blow up a German supply depot. 97 m.

The Sea Shall Not Have Them. 1954, d. Lewis Gilbert, p. Daniel M. Angel (Eros), sc. Gilbert/Vernon Harris (n. John Harris), w. Michael Redgrave, Dirk Bogarde, Anthony Steel, Nigel Patrick, Bonar Colleano, Griffith Jones, Sydney Tafler. An Air–Sea Rescue launch searches the Atlantic for survivors of a crashed plane. 93 m.

Sea Wife. 1957, Bob McNaught, p. André Hakim (Fox), sc. George K. Burke (n. *Seawyf and Biscuit*, J.M. Scott), w. Richard Burton, Joan Collins, Basil Sydney, Cy Grant. Quarrels among the survivors of a ship sunk during the Singapore evacuation lead to tragedy. 82m.

The Sea Wolves. 1980, d. Andrew V. McLaglen, p. Euan Lloyd/Jorge Araneta (Rank), sc. Reginald Rose (n. *Boarding Party*, James Leasor), w. Gregory Peck, Roger Moore, David Niven, Trevor Howard, Barbara Kellerman, Patrick MacNee. Old expatriates sabotage a Nazi installation in India. 122 m.

Secret Mission. 1942, d. Harold French, p. Marcel Hellman (GFD), sc. Anatole de Grunwald/Basil Bartlett (st. Shaun Terence Young), w. Hugh Williams, Carla Lehman, James Mason, Roland Culver, Michael Wilding, Nancy Price. A commando group organizes the destruction of a German submarine base. 94 m.

The Secret of Blood Island. 1964, d. Quentin Lawrence, p. Anthony Nelson Keys, sc. John Gilling, w. Barbara Shelley, Jack Hedley, Patrick Wymark, Charles Tingwell, Bill Owen, Lee Montagu. Prisoners in a Japanese camp sacrifice themselves to help a female agent. 84 m.

Secret Places. 1984, d/sc. Zelda Barron (n. Janice Elliott), p. Ann Skinner/Simon Relph (Rediffusion/Skreba/Virgin), w. Marie-Therese Relin, Tara MacGowran, Claudine Auger, Jenny Agutter, Cassie Stuart, Pippa Hinchley. Experiences of a German refugee at an English boarding-school during the war. 98 m.

Seven Thunders. 1957, d. Hugo Fregonese, p. Daniel M. Angel (RFD), sc. John Baines (n. Rupert Croft-Cooke), w. Stephen Boyd, James Robertson Justice, Tony Wright, Kathleen Harrison, Anna Gaylor, Eugene Deckers. British POWs hiding out in Marseilles are helped by women and outwit a treacherous smuggler. 100 m.

The Ship That Died of Shame. 1955, d. Basil Dearden, p. Michael Relph (Ealing), sc. Dearden/ Relph/John Whiting, w. George Baker, Richard Attenborough, Bill Owen, Virginia McKenna, Bernard Lee, Roland Culver. Ex-naval officers restore their wartime gunboat and use it for smuggling. 95 m.

The Shipbuilders. 1944, d/p. John Baxter (BN), sc. Gordon Wellesley, Reginald Pound, Stephen Potter (n. George Blake), w. Clive Brook, Morland Graham, Nell Ballantyne, Finlay Currie, Geoffrey Hibbert, Moira Lister. The struggle to keep a Clydeside shipyard open is justified by the wartime need for ships. 89 m.

Ships with Wings. 1941, d. Sergei Nolbandov, ap. S.C. Balcon (Ealing), sc. Nolbandov/Patrick Kirwan/Austin Melford/Diana Morgan, w. John Clements, Ann Todd, Leslie Banks, Jane Baxter, Basil Sydney,

Edward Chapman, Hugh Williams. A disgraced flyer redeems himself with a suicide mission. 103 m.

Silent Dust. 1949, d. Lance Comfort, p. N.A. Bronsten (ABPC), sc. Michael Pertwee (pl. *The Paragon*, Roland and Michael Pertwee), w. Stephen Murray, Nigel Patrick, Sally Gray, Beatrice Campbell, Seymour Hicks, Derek Farr. A son returns on the eve of a ceremony to commemorate his death and proves to be a deserter and murderer. 82 m.

The Silent Enemy. 1958, d/sc. William Fairchild (bk. *Commander Crabb*, Marshall Pugh), p. Bertram Ostrer (Romulus), w. Laurence Harvey, John Clements, Michael Craig, Dawn Addams, Sidney James, Alec McCowen. Royal Navy divers protect an invasion fleet from limpet mines by blowing up a secret Italian base. 112 m.

The Silent Invasion. 1962, d. Max Varnel, p. Edward J. and Harry Lee Danziger (Danzigers), sc. Brian Clemens, w. Eric Flynn, Petra Davies, Francis de Wolff, Martin Benson, Jan Conrad, Melvyn Hayes. A girl is torn between a German officer whom she loves and her brother working for the resistance. 70 m.

The Silver Fleet. 1943 d/sc. Vernon Sewell/Gordon Wellesley, p. Michael Powell/Emeric Pressburger/Ralph Richardson (Archers/GFD), w. Ralph Richardson, Googie Withers, Esmond Knight, Beresford Egan, Kathleen Byron, Charles Victor. A Dutch shipbuilder pretends to collaborate with the Nazis in order to sabotage U-boats. 87 m.

Single-Handed/Sailor of the King. 1953, d. Roy Boulting, p. Frank McCarthy (Fox), sc. Valentine Davies (n. *Brown on Resolution*, C.S. Forrester), w. Jeffrey Hunter, Michael Rennie, Wendy Hiller, Bernard Lee, Peter Van Eyck, Victor Maddern. A sailor keeps a German ship confined to harbour with a rifle. 85 m.

Sink the Bismarck! 1960, d. Lewis Gilbert, p. John Brabourne (Fox), sc. Edmund H. North (bk. C.S. Forrester), w. Kenneth More, Dana Wynter, Carl Mohner, Karel Stepanek, Laurence Naismith, Maurice Denham. The Royal Navy hunts down a German battleship. 98 m.

633 Squadron. 1964, d. Walter E. Grauman, p. Cecil F. Ford (Mirisch/UA), sc. James Clavell/Howard Koch (n. Frederick E. Smith), w. Cliff Robertson, George Chakiris, Maria Perschy, Harry Andrews, Donald Houston, Michael Goodliffe. A Mosquito attack on a rocket fuel factory in Norway is made more hazardous by Nazi suppression of local resistance. 94 m.

The Small Back Room. 1949, d/p/sc. Michael Powell/Emeric Pressburger (Archers/BL) (n. Nigel Balchin), w. David Farrar, Kathleen Byron, Jack Hawkins, Cyril Cusack, Anthony Bushell, Leslie Banks. An explosives expert with a tin foot recovers his self-respect by defusing a bomb. 108 m.

The Small Voice. 1948, d. Fergus McDonell, p. Anthony Havelock-Allan (BL), sc. Derek Neame/Julian Orde/George Barraud (n. Robert Westerby), w. Valerie Hobson, James Donald, Howard Keele, David Greene, Michael Balfour, Joan Young. A crippled ex-officer and his wife are held hostage by ex-servicemen turned convicts. 85 m.

So Little Time. 1952, d. Compton Bennett, p. Maxwell Setton/Aubrey Baring (ABPC), sc. John Cresswell, (n. Noelle Henry), w. Marius Goring, Maria Schell, Barbara Mullen, Lucie Mannheim. A Belgian pianist falls in love with a German governor, despite her patriotism. 88 m.

Soft Beds, Hard Battles. 1974, d. Roy Boulting, p. John Boulting (Charter/Fox/Rank), sc. Leo Marks/Roy Boulting (st. Maurice Moisewitch), w. Peter Sellers, Lila Kedrova, Beatrice Romand, Curt Jurgens, Gabriella Licudi, Jenny Hanley. A brothel-owner and her prostitutes help a British agent and the French resistance. 107 m.

Somewhere in Camp. 1942, d/p. John E. Blakeley (Mancunian/Butchers), sc. Anthony Toner/Roney Parsons, w. Frank Randle, Harry Korris, Robbie Vincent, Dan Young, John Singer, Tony Lupino. Army conscripts help a middle-class private win the CO's daughter. 88 m.

Somewhere in Civvies. 1943, d. Maclean Rogers, p. T.A. Welsh (Butchers), sc. Con West, w. Frank Randle, George Doonan, Suzette Tarri, Joss Ambler, H.F. Maltby, Nancy O'Neil. A private leaves the Army on medical grounds but after adventures in Civvy Street is glad to return. 87 m.

Somewhere in England. 1940, d/p. John E. Blakeley (Mancunian/Butchers), sc. Anthony Toner/Roney Parsons, w. Frank Randle, Harry Korris, Robbie Vincent, Dan Young, John Singer, Winkie Turner. Army conscripts help a popular corporal redeem his reputation. 79 m.

Somewhere on Leave. 1942, d/p. John E. Blakeley (Mancunian/Butchers), sc. Anthony Toner/Roney Parsons, w. Frank Randle, Harry Korris, Robbie Vincent, Dan Young, Tony Lupino, Pat McGrath. Army conscripts are invited to spend their leave at a rich private's home. 96 m.

Spare a Copper. 1940, d. John Paddy Carstairs, ap. Basil Dearden (Ealing), sc. Roger MacDougall/Austin Melford/Dearden, w. George Formby, Dorothy Hyson, Bernard Lee, Eliot Makeham, Warburton Gamble, John Warwick. A keen motorcyclist prevents fifth columnists from sabotaging a ship launch. 77 m.

Squadron Leader X. 1942, d. Lance Comfort, p. Victor Hanbury (RKO), sc. Wolfgang Wilhelm/Miles Malleson (st. Emeric Pressburger), w. Eric Portman, Ann Dvorak, Walter Fitzgerald, Barry Jones, Henry Oscar, Beatrice Varley. A German disguised as an RAF pilot is helped by the Belgian resistance. 100 m.

The Square Peg. 1958, d. John Paddy Carstairs, p. Hugh Stewart (RFD), sc. Jack Davies/Henry E. Blyth/Norman Wisdom/Eddie Leslie, w. Norman Wisdom, Edward Chapman, Honor Blackman, Hattie Jacques, Terence Alexander, Campbell Singer. A private in the Pioneer Corps' resemblance to a German general enables him to escape and help resistance fighters. 89 m.

The Steel Bayonet. 1957, d/p. Michael Carreras (Hammer), sc. Howard Clewes, w. Leo Genn, Kieron Moore, Michael Medwin, Robert Brown, Michael Ripper, Percy Herbert. A British Army squad holds an outpost against advancing Germans in Tunisia. 85 m.

Submarine X-1. 1969, d. William Graham, p. Irving Temaner/John C. Champion (Mirisch/UA), sc. Donald Sanford/Guy Elmes (st. Champion/Edmund North), w. James Caan, Norman Bowler, David Sumner, Brian Grellis, Paul Young, Rupert Davies. Royal Navy midget submarines attack the German battleship *Lindendorf* in a Norwegian fjord. 90 m.

Target for Tonight. 1941, d. Harry Watt, p. Ian Dalrymple (CFU), sc. Watt/Budge Cooper. RAF Wellington bombers raid Germany. 48 m.

Tarnished Heroes. 1961, d. Ernest Morris, p. Edward J. and Harry Lee Danziger (Danzigers), sc. Brian Clemens, w. Dermot Walsh, Anton Rodgers, Patrick McAlinney, Richard Carpenter, Maurice Kaufmann, Max Butterfield. Court-martialled soldiers blow up a bridge behind German lines. 75 m.

Tawny Pipit. 1944, d. Bernard Miles/Charles Saunders, p. Sydney Box (Two Cities), w. Rosamund John, Niall MacGinnis, Bernard Miles, Brefni O'Rorke, Jean Gillie, Wylie Watson. A recuperating airman and a nurse recruit a retired colonel, evacuees and a village community to protect rare nesting birds. 85 m.

A Terrible Beauty. 1960, d. Tay Garnett, p. Raymond Stross (UA), sc. Richard Wright Campbell (n. Arthur Roth), w. Robert Mitchum, Anne Heywood, Dan O'Herlihy, Cyril Cusack, Richard Harris, Niall MacGinnis. Split loyalties within the IRA over collaboration with the Nazis. 89 m.

Theirs Is the Glory. 1946, d. Brian Desmond Hurst, p. Castleton Knight (Castleton Knight Productions), sc. Louis Golding. Re-creation of the campaign by British paratroopers to secure bridges behind enemy lines in Holland using soldiers of the First British Airborne Division. 82 m.

They Flew Alone. 1942, d/p. Herbert Wilcox (RKO), sc. Miles Malleson (st. Viscount Castlerosse), w. Anna Neagle, Robert Newton, Edward Chapman, Nora Swinburne, Brefni O'Rorke, Martita Hunt. A head-strong girl becomes a record-breaking aviator and dies while working as a wartime ferry pilot. 103 m.

They Made Me a Fugitive. 1947, d. Cavalcanti, p. N.A. Bronsten (WB), sc. Noel Langley (n. *A Convict Has Escaped*, Jackson Budd), w. Trevor Howard, Griffith Jones, Sally Gray, Rene Ray, Mary Merrall, Charles Farrell. A wartime pilot turns to crime for excitement and is framed by a gang boss out to steal his girl. 103 m.

They Met in the Dark. 1943, d. Karel Lamac, p. Marcel Hellman (Excelsior for Independent Producers), sc. Anatole de Grunwald/ Miles Malleson/Basil Bartlett/Victor Maclure/James Seymour (n. *The Vanishing Corpse*, Anthony Gilbert), w. James Mason, Tom Walls, Joyce Howard, Phyllis Stanley, Karel Stepanek, Edward Rigby, David Farrar. A naval commander and a young woman unmask theatrical agents as fifth columnists. 104 m.

They Were Not Divided. 1950, d/sc. Terence Young, p. Herbert Smith (Two Cities), w. Edward Underdown, Ralph Clanton, Helen Cherry, Stella Andrews, Michael Trubshawe, Michael Brennan. An American and an Englishman become officers in the Welsh Guards, fight in France and Belgium and are killed in the Ardennes. 102 m.

They Who Dare. 1953, d. Lewis Milestone, p. Maxwell Setton/Aubrey Baring (BL), sc. Robert Westerby, w. Dirk Bogarde, Denholm Elliott, Akim Tamiroff, Eric Pohlmann, Sam Kydd, Gerard Oury. SAS officers lead marines and commandos on a mission to destroy enemy airfields on Rhodes. 107 m.

This England. 1941, d. David Macdonald, p. John Corfield (BN), sc. Emlyn Williams (st. A.R. Rawlinson/Bridget Boland), w. John

Clements, Constance Cummings, Emlyn Williams, Frank Pettingell, Ronald Ward, Charles Victor. A yeoman farmer and a labourer explain the history of an English village to an American journalist. 84 m.

This Happy Breed. 1944, d. David Lean, p. Anthony Havelock-Allan (Cineguild/Two Cities), sc. Lean/Ronald Neame/Havelock-Allan (pl. Noël Coward), w. Robert Newton, Celia Johnson, John Mills, Stanley Holloway, Kay Walsh, Amy Veness, Alison Leggatt. Trials and tribulations of a London family between the wars. 114 m.

This Was Paris. 1942, d. John Harlow, p. Max Milder (WB) sc. Brock William/Edward Dryhurst (st. Gordon Wellesley/Basil Woon), w. Ann Dvorak, Ben Lyon, Robert Morley, Griffith Jones, Mary Maguire, Harold Huth. A British agent unmasks Nazi plotters as Paris falls. 88 m.

Those Kids from Town. 1942, d. Lance Comfort, p. Richard Vernon (BN), sc/n. Adrian Arlington (*These Our Strangers*), w. Jeanne de Casalis, Percy Marmont, Shirley Lenner, D.J. Williams, Harry Fowler, George Cole. Cockney evacuees are billeted with an earl in his stately home. 82 m.

Those People Next Door. 1953, d. John Harlow, p. Tom Blakeley (Eros), sc/pl. (*Wearing the Pants*) Zelda Davees, w. Jack Warner, Patricia Cutts, Charles Victor, Marjorie Rhodes, Peter Forbes-Robertson, Garry Marsh, Gladys Henson. Romance between a working-class girl and an aristocratic RAF officer causes class problems for their families. 77 m.

Thunder Rock. 1941, d. Roy Boulting, p. John Boulting (Charter), sc. Wolfgang Wilhelm/Jeffrey Dell/Bernard Miles/Anna Reiner (pl. Robert Ardney), w. Michael Redgrave, Finlay Currie, James Mason, Lilli Palmer. A misanthropic lighthouse keeper determines to end his isolation after a therapeutic encounter with ghosts. 112 m.

Tiger in the Smoke. 1956, d. Roy Baker, p. Leslie Parkyn (RFD), sc. Anthony Pelissier (n. Margery Allingham), w. Muriel Pavlow, Donald Sinden, Tony Wright, Bernard Miles, Laurence Naismith, Alec Clunes, Beatrice Varley, Charles Victor. Ex-soldiers seek out treasure hidden during the war. 94 m.

Tomorrow We Live. 1943, d. George King, p. King/John Stafford (British Aviation), sc. Anatole de Grunwald/Katherine Strueby (st. Dorothy Hope), w. John Clements, Greta Gynt, Yvonne Arnaud, Godfrey Tearle, Hugh Sinclair, Judy Kelly. A French resistance group blows up an ammunition train but is broken up by the Gestapo. 85 m.

Tower of Terror. 1941, d. Lawrence Huntington, p. John Argyle (ABPC), sc. John Reinhart/Argyle (st. Reinhart), w. Wilfrid Lawson, Movita, Michael Rennie. A British agent saves a refugee from the Nazis and a mad lighthouse keeper. 78 m.

A Town Like Alice. 1956, d. Jack Lee, p. Joseph Janni (RFD), sc. W.P. Lipscomb/Richard Mason (n. Nevil Shute), w. Virginia McKenna, Peter Finch, Marie Lohr, Renee Houston, Eileen Moore, Jean Anderson, Kenji Takaki. Women trapped by the Japanese invasion of Malaya are forced to walk to POW camps, which refuse to accept them. 117 m.

The Traitor. 1957, d/sc. Michael McCarthy, p. E.J. Fancey (New Realm), w. Donald Wolfit, Anton Diffring, John Van Eyssen, Rupert Davies, Carl Jaffe, Christopher Lee, Karel Stepanek. A wartime resistance leader brings together colleagues for a reunion to unmask the traitor who betrayed them to the Gestapo. 88 m.

Traitor Spy. 1939, d. Walter Summers, p. John Argyle (Pathé), sc. Summers/Argyle/R.G. Bettinson/Jan Van Lusil (n. T.C.H. Jacobs), w. Bruce Cabot, Marta Labarr, Tamara Desni, Romilly Lunge, Percy Walsh, Edward Lexy. A spy with secret documents is chased by German agents and British intelligence. 75 m.

Triple Cross. 1967, d. Terence Young, p. Jacques-Paul Bertrand (WB), sc. René Hardy/William Marchant (bk. *The Eddie Chapman Story*, Frank Owen), w. Christopher Plummer, Yul Brynner, Romy Schneider, Gert Frobe, Trevor Howard, Claudine Auger. A safebreaker is imprisoned in Jersey and becomes a double agent when the Nazis invade. 126 m.

The Triple Echo. 1972, d. Michael Apted, p. Graham Cottle (Hemdale), sc. Robin Chapman (n. H.E. Bates), w. Glenda Jackson, Oliver Reed, Brian Deacon, Anthony May, Gavin Richards, Jenny Lee Wright. A deserter disguises himself as a woman and works on a farm. 94 m.

The True Glory. 1945, d. Carol Reed/Garson Kanin, p. MoI/Office of War Information, sc. Eric Maschwitz/Arthur Macrae/Jenny Nicholson/Gerald Kersh/Guy Trosper/Harry Brown/Peter Ustinov/Saul Levitt/Paddy Chayefsky. The last year of the war pieced together from newsreel footage. 87 m.

Tunisian Victory. 1944, d. Frank Capra/Hugh Stewart (British and American Service Film Units). Advance of the British Army through North Africa. 76 m.

The Two-Headed Spy. 1958, d. André de Toth, p. Hal E. Chester/Bill Kirby (Col), sc. James O'Donnell (st. J. Alvin Kugelmass), w. Jack Hawkins, Alexander Knox, Felix Aylmer, Gia Scala, Eric Schumann, Kenneth Griffith. A British officer penetrates the German high command and remains undetected. 93 m.

Two Thousand Women. 1944, d. Frank Launder, p. Edward Black (Gainsborough), sc. Launder/Michael Pertwee (st. Launder/Sidney Gilliat), w. Phyllis Calvert, Patricia Roc, Jean Kent, Flora Robson, Renee Houston, James McKechnie. British women interned in France help an RAF bomber crew to escape. 97 m.

Uncensored. 1942, d. Anthony Asquith, p. Edward Black (Gainsborough), sc. Wolfgang Wilhelm/Terence Rattigan/Rodney Acland (n. Oscar Millard), w. Eric Portman, Peter Glenville, Phyllis Calvert, Raymond Lovell, Frederick Culley, Irene Handl. A music-hall performer helps the publisher of a Belgian resistance newspaper. 108 m.

Under Your Hat. 1940, d. Maurice Elvey, p. Jack Hulbert (Grand National), sc. Rodney Acland/Anthony Kimmins (pl. Hulbert/Geoffrey Kerr), w. Jack Hulbert, Cicely Courtneidge, Austin Trevor, Leonora Corbett, Austin Trevor, Cecil Parker, Glynis Johns. A show-biz couple outwit German spies in the South of France. 79 m.

Undercover. 1943, d. Sergei Nolbandov, ap. S.C. Balcon (Ealing), sc. John Dighton/Monja Danischewsky/Milosh Sokulich/Nolbandov (st. George Slocombe), w. John Clements, Mary Morris, Stephen Murray, Tom Walls, Godfrey Tearle, Michael Wilding. Two Yugoslav brothers adopt different strategies but work together to oppose the Nazis. 80 m.

Underground. 1970, d. Arthur H. Nadel, p. Jules Levy/Arthur Gardner/Arnold Laven (UA), sc. Ron Bishop/Andy Lewis (st. Marc L. Roberts), w. Robert Goulet, Daniele Gaubert, Lawrence Dobkin, Carl Duering, Joachim Hansen, Roger Delgardo. An unbalanced US major and a French resistance group kidnap a Nazi general. 100 m.

Unpublished Story. 1942. d. Harold French, p. Anthony Havelock-Allan (Two Cities), sc. Anatole de Grunwald/Patrick Kirwan/Lesley Storm (st. Havelock-Allan/Alan McKinnon), w. Richard Greene, Valerie Hobson, Brefni O'Rorke, Basil Radford, Roland Culver, Miles Malleson. A journalist exposes a peace organization as a Nazi front. 92 m.

The Valiant. 1962, d. Roy Baker, p. Jon Penington (UA), sc. Willis Hall/Keith Waterhouse (pl. *L'Equipage au Complet*, Robert Mallet), w. John Mills, Ettore Manni, Roberto Risso, Robert Shaw, Liam Redmond, Laurence Naismith. A British battleship is mined by Italian frogmen in Alexandria harbour. 90 m.

Very Important Person. 1961, d. Ken Annakin, p. Julian Wintle/Leslie Parkyn (Independent Artists/RFD), sc. Jack Davies/Henry Blyth (st. Davies), w. James Robertson Justice, Leslie Phillips, Stanley Baxter, Eric Sykes, Richard Wattis, Godfrey Winn. British officers organize the escape of a scientist from a POW camp. 98 m.

The Victors. 1963, d/p/sc. Carl Foreman (Col) (n. *The Human Kind*, Alexander Baron), w. George Peppard, George Hamilton, Eli Wallach, Melina Mercouri, Romy Schneider, Jeanne Moreau. Episodes in the lives of an American Army platoon as it fights its way through Italy, France, Belgium and Germany. 175 m.

Violent Moment. 1959, d. Sidney Hayers, p. Bernard Coote (Independent Artists), sc. Peter Barnes, w. Lyndon Brook, Jane Hylton, Rupert Davies, Moira Redmond, Bruce Seton, Martin Miller. A deserter kills his wife and becomes a successful businessman, but the past catches up with him. 61 m.

The War Lover. 1962, d. Philip Leacock, p. Arthur Hornblow Jr (Col), sc. Howard Koch (n. John Hersey), w. Steve McQueen, Robert Wagner, Shirley Ann Field, Michael Crawford, Gary Cockrell, Bernard Braden. A womanizing USAF pilot tries to seduce his co-pilot's lover and reveals his fallibility during a bombing mission against Leipzig. 105 m.

Warn That Man. 1943, d. Lawrence Huntington, p. Warwick Ward (ABPC), sc. Vernon Sylvaine/Huntington (pl. Sylvaine), w. Gordon Harker, Philip Friend, Jean Kent, Raymond Lovell, Finlay Currie. Sailors on leave and a showgirl foil a plot to kidnap Churchill. 82 m.

Waterloo Road. 1945, d/sc. Sidney Gilliat (st. Val Valentine), p. Edward Black (Gainsborough), w. John Mills, Joy Shelton, Stewart Granger, Alastair Sim, Jean Kent, Beatrice Varley. A soldier goes AWOL to check on his wife's fidelity. 76 m.

The Way Ahead. 1944, d. Carol Reed, p. John Sutro/Norman Walker (Two Cities), sc. Eric Ambler/Peter Ustinov, w. David Niven, William Hartnell, James Donald, Jimmy Hanley, Stanley Holloway, Raymond Huntley, John Laurie, Leslie Dwyer. Army conscripts are moulded into an effective fighting force. 115 m.

The Way to the Stars. 1945, d. Anthony Asquith, p. Anatole de Grunwald (Two Cities), sc. Terence Rattigan/de Grunwald (st. Rattigan/Richard Sherman), w. Michael Redgrave, John Mills, Rosamund John, Douglass Montgomery, Renee Asherson, Stanley Holloway. A hotelier forms a close friendship with an American airman after her RAF husband is killed. 109 m.

We Dive at Dawn. 1943, d. Anthony Asquith, p. Edward Black (Gainsborough), sc. J.B. Williams/Val Valentine/Frank Launder, w. John Mills, Eric Portman, Reginald Purdell, Niall MacGinnis, Joan Hopkins, Josephine Wilson. A submarine crew is recalled from leave to hunt down a German battleship. 98 m.

Welcome Mr Washington. 1944, d. Leslie Hiscott, p. Elizabeth Hiscott (BN), sc. Jack Whittingham (st. Noel Streatfeild), w. Barbara Mullen, Donald Stewart, Peggy Cummins, Graham Moffatt, Martita Hunt, Leslie Bradley. An American army unit makes friends and enemies among the English villagers they are billeted on. 90 m.

We'll Meet Again. 1942, d. Phil Brandon, p. Ben Henry/George Formby (Col), sc. James Seymour/Howard Thomas (st. Derek Sheils), w. Vera Lynn, Patricia Roc, Geraldo, Ronald Ward, Donald Gray, Frederick Leister. A singer loses her soldier sweetheart to a glamour girl. 84 m.

We'll Smile Again. 1942, d/p. John Baxter (BN), sc. Baxter/Austin Melford/Barbara Emary/Bud Flanagan, w. Bud Flanagan, Chesney Allen, Phyllis Stanley, Charles Austin, Horace Kenney, Wally Patch. A down-and-out roots out spies in a film studio. 93 m.

Went the Day Well? 1943, d. Cavalcanti, ap. S.C. Balcon (Ealing), sc. Angus MacPhail/John Dighton/Diana Morgan (st. *The Lieutenant Died Last*, Graham Greene), w. Leslie Banks, Edward Rigby, Valerie Taylor, Basil Sydney, David Farrar, Harry Fowler. A troop of German paratroopers takes over an English village. 92 m.

Western Approaches. 1945, d/sc. Pat Jackson, p. Ian Dalrymple (CFU), w. Bob Banner, Captain Pycraft, Alf Rawson, John Walden, Fred Armistead, C.P.O. Hills, Lt. Meeke. A U-boat uses a lifeboat as a decoy to attack a merchant ship. 87 m.

Where Eagles Dare. 1968, d. Brian G. Hutton, p. Elliott Kastner (MGM), sc/n. Alistair MacLean, w. Richard Burton, Clint Eastwood, Mary Ure, Patrick Wymark, Michael Hordern, Anton Diffring. A mission to rescue an American general is used to unmask spies in MI6. 155 m.

The Wind Cannot Read. 1958, d. Ralph Thomas, p. Betty Box (RFD), sc/n. Richard Mason, w. Dirk Bogarde, Yoko Tani, Anthony Bushell,

John Fraser, Ronald Lewis, Michael Medwin. A British officer marries a Japanese woman in India and escapes from Burma to nurse her. 115 m.

The Woman with No Name. 1950, d. Ladislas Vajda/George More O'Ferrall, p. John Stafford, sc. Vajda/Guy Morgan (n. *Happy Now I Go*, Theresa Charles), w. Phyllis Calvert, Richard Burton, Edward Underdown, Helen Cherry, James Hayter, Betty Ann Davies. A woman with amnesia is reunited with her crippled husband despite the machinations of his jealous sister. 83 m.

Women Aren't Angels. 1942, d. Lawrence Huntington, p. Warwick Ward (ABPC), sc. Huntington/Bernard Mainwaring/Vernon Sylvaine (pl. Sylvaine), w. Robertson Hare, Alfred Drayton, Polly Ward, Joyce Heron, Ethel Coleridge, Mary Hinton. Music publishers wearing their wives' ATS uniforms break up a fifth column gang. 85 m.

The Wooden Horse. 1950, d. Jack Lee, p. Ian Dalrymple (Wessex/BL), sc/bk. Eric Williams, w. Leo Genn, David Tomlinson, Anthony Steel, Michael Goodliffe, Anthony Dawson, Bryan Forbes. POWs tunnel out of a German camp. 101 m.

The World Owes Me a Living. 1945, d. Vernon Sewell, p. Louis H. Jackson (BN), sc. Sewell/Erwin Reiner (n. John Llewellyn Rhys), w. David Farrar, Judy Campbell, Sonia Dresdel, Jack Livesey, John Laurie, Anthony Hawtrey. Disillusioned WWI flyers find they are needed again as WWII looms. 91 m.

Worm's Eye View. 1951, d. Jack Raymond, p. Henry Halstead (ABFD), sc. R.F. Delderfield/Jack Marks (pl. Delderfield), w. Ronald Shiner, Garry Marsh, Diana Dors, John Blythe, Bruce Seton, Digby Wolfe. Comic adventures of airmen billeted on a seaside landlady. 77 m.

Yanks. 1979, d. John Schlesinger, p. Joseph Janni/Lester Persky (UA), sc. Colin Welland/Walter Bernstein (st. Welland), w. Richard Gere, Vanessa Redgrave, Lisa Eichhorn, William Devane, Chick Vennera, Rachel Roberts. Romance between an American army cook and a postmistress's daughter, and an American major and a naval officer's wife in the months leading up to D-Day. 141 m.

The Years Between. 1946, d. Compton Bennett, p. Sydney Box (RFD), sc. Muriel and Sydney Box (pl. Daphne du Maurier), w. Michael Redgrave, Valerie Hobson, Flora Robson, Felix Aylmer, Dulcie Gray, Edward Rigby. A wife fills her husband's parliamentary seat after he is reported dead, but he returns. 100 m.

Yellow Canary. 1943, d/p. Herbert Wilcox, sc. Miles Malleson/DeWitt Bodeen (st. Pamela Bower), w. Anna Neagle, Richard Greene, Albert Lieven, Lucie Mannheim, Margaret Rutherford, Nova Pilbeam. A pro-Nazi society lady deported to Canada is a British agent sent to expose a German spy ring. 98 m.

Yesterday's Enemy. 1959, d. Val Guest, p. Michael Carreras (Hammer), sc/pl. Peter Newman, w. Stanley Baker, Guy Rolfe, Leo McKern, Gordon Jackson, David Oxley, Richard Pasco. A British officer in Burma shoots civilians to obtain information and is later shot by the Japanese when he refuses to divulge what he knows. 95 m.

Where possible, I have taken credits directly from the films. For those films I have been unable to view, I have relied upon the *Monthly Film Bulletin*, Gifford (1986), Quinlan (1984) and the *Time Out Film Guide*.

Bibliography

Addison, Paul (1977) *The Road to 1945*. London: Quartet Books.

Addison, Paul (1985) *Now the War Is Over*. London: Jonathan Cape.

Aitken, Ian (1990) *Film and Reform: John Grierson and the Documentary Film Movement*. London: Routledge.

Aitken, Ian (2000) *Cavalcanti: Strange Realisms*. Trowbridge: Flicks Books.

Aldgate, Anthony and Jeffrey Richards (1986) *Best of British: Cinema and Society 1930–1970*. Oxford: Blackwell.

Aldgate, Anthony and Jeffrey Richards (1994) *Britain Can Take It: The British Cinema in the Second World War*. Oxford: Blackwell.

Anderson, Lindsay (1954) 'Only connect: some aspects of the work of Humphrey Jennings', *Sight and Sound*, vol. 23, no. 4 (April–June).

Armes, Roy (1978) *A Critical History of British Cinema*. London: Secker and Warburg.

Aspinall, Sue (1983), 'Women, realism and reality in British films, 1943–53', in James Curran and Vincent Porter (eds), *British Cinema History*. London: Weidenfeld and Nicolson.

Aspinall, Sue and Robert Murphy (eds) (1983) *Gainsborough Melodrama*. London: BFI Publishing.

Asquith, Anthony (1945) 'Realler than the real thing', *Cine-Technician*, vol. 11, no. 53 (March–April).

Badder, David (1978) 'Powell and Pressburger: the war years', *Sight and Sound*, vol. 48, no. 1 (Winter).

Balcon, Michael (1944) *Realism or Tinsel*. London: Workers' Film Association.

Balcon, Michael (1946) 'The British film during the war', *The Penguin Film Review*, no. 1. Harmondsworth: Penguin.

Balcon, Michael (1969) *A Lifetime in Films*. London: Hutchinson.

Barnett, Correlli (1986) *The Audit of War*. London: Macmillan.

Barr, Charles (1974) 'Projecting Britain and the British character', *Screen*, vol. 15, no. 1.

Barr, Charles (1977) *Ealing Studios*. London: Cameron and Tayleur/David and Charles.

Barr, Charles (1984) 'A conundrum for England', *Monthly Film Bulletin*, vol. 51, no. 607 (August).

Barr, Charles (ed.) (1986) *All Our Yesterdays*. London: BFI Publishing.

Barr, Charles (1987) 'Hope and glory', *Monthly Film Bulletin*, vol. 54, no. 644.

Barr, Charles (1989) 'War record'. *Sight and Sound*, vol. 58, no. 4 (Autumn).

Bernstein, Sidney (1945) *The Film and International Relations*. London: Workers' Film Association.

Betts, Ernest (1973) *The Film Business*. London: Allen and Unwin.

Bogarde, Dirk (1978) *Snakes and Ladders*. London: Chatto and Windus.

Braine, John (1978) *J. B. Priestley*. London: Weidenfeld and Nicolson.

Brown, Geoff (1977a) 'Ealing your Ealing', *Sight and Sound*, vol. 46, no. 3 (Summer).

Brown, Geoff (1977b) *Walter Forde*. London: BFI Publishing.

Brown, Geoff (1977c) *Launder and Gilliat*. London: BFI Publishing.

Brown, Geoff (1978) 'Which way to the way ahead?', *Sight and Sound*, vol. 47, no. 4 (Autumn).

Brown, Geoff (1997) 'Paradise found and lost: the course of British realism', in Robert Murphy (ed.), *The British Cinema Book*. London: BFI Publishing.

Brown, John (1984) 'Home fires burning', *Sight and Sound*, vol. 53, no. 3 Summer.

Brownlow, Kevin (1968) *How It Happened Here*. London: Secker and Warburg/BFI Publishing.

Brunel, Adrian (1949) *Nice Work*. London: Forbes Robertson.

Brunsdon, Charlotte and Rachel Moseley (1997) ' "She's a foreigner who's become a British subject", *Frieda*', in Alan Burton, Tim O'Sullivan and Paul Wells (eds), *Liberal Directions: Basil Dearden and Postwar British Film Culture*. Trowbridge: Flicks Books.

Buckman, Keith (1997) 'The Royal Air Force Film Production Unit, 1941–45', *Historical Journal of Film, Radio and Television*, vol. 17, no. 2.

Burns, Michael G. (1998) *Bader: The Man and His Men*. London: Cassell.

Burton, Alan (1997) 'Love in a cold climate: critics, filmmakers and the British cinema of quality – the case of *The Captive Heart*, in Alan Burton, Tim O'Sullivan and Paul Wells (eds), *Liberal Directions: Basil Dearden and Postwar British Film Culture*. Trowbridge: Flicks Books.

Butler, Ivan (1974) *The War Film*. London: Tantivy Press.

Calder, Angus (1971) *The People's War*. London: Granada.

Calder, Angus (1991) *The Myth of the Blitz*. London: Jonathan Cape.

Cardiff, Jack (1996) *Magic Hour*. London: Faber and Faber.

Chapman, James (1995) '*The Life and Death of Colonel Blimp* (1943) reconsidered', *Historical Journal of Film, Radio and Television*, vol. 15, no. 1.

Chapman, James (1996) ' "The Yanks are shown to such advantage": Anglo-American rivalry in the production of *The True Glory* (1945)', *Historical Journal of Film, Radio and Television*, vol. 16, no. 4.

Chapman, James (1998a) 'Our finest hour revisited: the Second World War in British feature films since 1945', *Journal of Popular British Cinema*, no. 1.

Chapman, James (1998b) *The British at War: Cinema, State and Propaganda 1939–1945*. London: I. B. Tauris.

Chibnall, Steve (2000) *J. Lee Thompson*. Manchester: Manchester University Press.

Christie, Ian (ed.) (1978) *Powell, Pressburger and Others*. London: BFI Publishing.

Christie, Ian (1994) *Arrows of Desire*. London: Faber and Faber.

Clark, Kenneth (1977) *The Other Half: A Self Portrait*. London: John Murray.

Clay, Andrew (1999) 'Men, women and money: masculinity in crisis in the British professional crime film 1946–1965', in Steve Chibnall and Robert Murphy (eds), *British Crime Cinema*. London: Routledge.

Cook, Jim (1986) '*The Ship That Died of Shame*', in Charles Barr (ed.), *All Our Yesterdays*. London: BFI Publishing.

Cook, Judith (1997) *Priestley*. London: Bloomsbury.

Cook, Pam (1996a) 'Neither here nor there: national identity in Gainsborough costume drama', in Andrew Higson (ed.), *Dissolving Views*. London: Cassell.

Cook, Pam (1996b) *Fashioning the Nation: Costume and Identity in British Cinema*. London: BFI Publishing.

Coote, Jack H. (1993) *The Illustrated History of Colour Photography*. Surbiton: Fountain Press.

Costello, John (1986) *Love, Sex and War*. London: Pan.

Coultass, Clive (1984) 'British feature films and the Second World War', *Journal of Contemporary History*, vol. 19.

Coultass, Clive (1988) 'British cinema and the reality of war', in Philip Taylor (ed.), *Britain and the Cinema in the Second World War*. London: Macmillan.

Coultass, Clive (1989) *Images for Battle: British Film and the Second World War 1939–1945*. London and Toronto: Associated University Presses.

Cruickshank, Charles (1986) *SOE in Scandinavia*. Oxford: Oxford University Press.

Cultural History Group (1976) 'Out of the people: the politics of containment 1935–45', *Working Papers in Cultural Studies*, no. 9.

Dalrymple, Ian (1982) 'The Crown Film Unit, 1940–43', in Nicholas Pronay and D. W. Spring (eds), *Propaganda, Politics and Film, 1918–45*. London: Macmillan.

Dalton, Hugh (1957) *The Fateful Years: Memoirs 1931–1945*. London: Frederick Muller.

Danischewsky, Monja (1966) *White Russian, Red Face*. London: Victor Gollancz.

Darlow, Michael and Gillian Hodson (1979) *Terence Rattigan*. London, Melbourne and New York: Quartet Books.

Davidson, Bruce (1980) *Special Operations in Europe*. London: Victor Gollancz.

Dean, Basil (1973) *Mind's Eye*. London: Hutchinson.

Deighton, Len (1977) *Fighter: The True Story of the Battle of Britain*. London: Jonathan Cape.

Deighton, Len (1993) *Blood, Tears and Folly*. London: Jonathan Cape.

Dickinson, Margaret and Sarah Street (1985) *Cinema and State*. London: BFI Publishing.

Dickinson, Thorold (1951) 'The work of Sir Michael Balcon at Ealing Studios', in Roger Mansell (ed.), *The Year's Work in Film (1950)*. London: Longmans Green.

Doherty, Thomas (1993) *Projections of War: Hollywood, American Culture and World War II*. New York: Columbia University Press.

Drazin, Charles (1998) *The Finest Years: British Cinema of the 1940s*. London: André Deutsch.

Durgnat, Raymond (1970) *A Mirror for England*. London: Faber and Faber.

Ellis, John (1975) 'Made in Ealing', *Screen*, vol. 16, no. 1.

Ellis, John (1996) 'The quality film adventure: British critics and the cinema 1942–1948', in Andrew Higson (ed.), *Dissolving Views*. London: Cassell.

Farson, Negley (1941) *Bomber's Moon*. London: Victor Gollancz.

Faulks, Sebastian (1998) *Charlotte Gray*. London: BCA.

Firth, Vincent (1977) '50 years of war films', *Film Review*, vol. 27, no. 10 (October).

Foot, M. R. D. (1966) *SOE in France*. London: HMSO.

Forman, Helen (1982) 'The non-theatrical distribution of film by the Ministry of Information', in Nicholas Pronay and D. W. Spring (eds), *Propaganda, Politics and Film, 1918–45*. London: Macmillan.

Geraghty, Christine (1984) 'Masculinity', in Geoff Hurd (ed.), *National Fictions: World War Two in British Films and Television*. London: BFI Publishing.

Geraghty, Christine (1996) 'Disguises and betrayals: negotiating nationality in three wartime films', in Christine Gledhill and Gillian Swanson (eds), *Nationalising Femininity: Culture, Sexuality and British Cinema in the Second World War*. Manchester: Manchester University Press.

Gibson, Guy (1995) *Enemy Coast Ahead*. Wrexham: Bridge Books.

Gifford, Denis (1986) *The British Film Catalogue 1895–1985*. London: David and Charles.

Gillman, Peter and Leni Gillman (1980) *Collar the Lot: How Britain Interned and Expelled Its Wartime Refugees*. London: Quartet.

Gledhill, Christine (1996) '"An abundance of understatement": documentary, melodrama and romance', in Christine Gledhill and Gillian Swanson (eds), *Nationalising Femininity: Culture, Sexuality and British Cinema in the Second World War*. Manchester: Manchester University Press.

Gledhill, Christine and Gillian Swanson (eds) (1996) *Nationalising Femininity: Culture, Sexuality and British Cinema in the Second World War*. Manchester: Manchester University Press.

Gough-Yates, Kevin (1997) 'Exiles and British cinema', in Robert Murphy (ed.), *The British Cinema Book*. London: BFI Publishing.

Gray, Hugh (ed.) (1974) *What Is Cinema?: Essays by André Bazin*, vols 1 and 2. Berkeley, Los Angeles and London: University of California Press.

Hall, Stuart (1972) 'The social eye of *Picture Post*', *Working Papers in Cultural Studies*, No. 2.

Hardy, Forsyth (ed.) (1979) *Grierson on Documentary*. London: Faber and Faber.

Harper, Sue (1994) *Picturing the Past*. London: BFI Publishing.

Harper, Sue (1996) 'The years of total war: propaganda and entertainment', in Christine Gledhill and Gillian Swanson (eds), *Nationalising Femininity: Culture, Sexuality and British Cinema in the Second World War*. Manchester: Manchester University Press.

Harper, Sue (1997) 'Nothing to beat the Hay diet', in Pam Cook (ed.), *Gainsborough Pictures*. London: Cassell.

Harrisson, Tom (1976) *Living through the Blitz*. London: Collins.

Hawkins, Jack (1973) *Anything for a Quiet Life*. London: Elm Tree Books/ Hamish Hamilton.

Higson, Andrew (1984) 'Five films', in Geoff Hurd (ed.), *National Fictions: World War Two in British Films and Television*. London: BFI Publishing.

Higson, Andrew (1986) 'Britain's outstanding contribution to the film: the documentary–realist tradition', in Charles Barr (ed.) *All Our Yesterdays*. London: BFI Publishing.

Higson, Andrew (1995) *Waving the Flag: Constructing a National Cinema in Britain*. Oxford: Clarendon Press.

Hinsley, F. H. and C. A. G. Simkins (1990) *British Intelligence in the Second World War*: Volume 4, *Security and Counter Intelligence*. London: HMSO.

Hollins, T. J. (1981) 'The Conservative Party and film propaganda between the wars', *English Historical Review*, vol. 96, no. 379 (April).

Hopkins, Harry (1963) *The New Look*. London: Secker and Warburg.

Houston, Penelope (1992) *Went the Day Well?* London: BFI Publishing.

Howard, Anthony (1986) 'We are the masters now', in Philip French and Michael Sissons (eds), *The Age of Austerity*. Oxford: Oxford University Press.

Hurd, Geoff (ed.) (1984) *National Fictions: World War Two in British Films and Television*. London: BFI Publishing.

Jackson, Pat (1999) *A Retake Please: Night Mail to Western Approaches*. Liverpool: Liverpool University Press.

James, Robert Rhodes (ed.) (1969) *Memoirs of a Conservative: J. C. C. Davidson's Memoirs and Papers 1910–37*. London: Weidenfeld and Nicolson.

Jarvie, Ian (1988) 'The Burma Campaign on film: *Objective Burma* (1945), *The Stilwell Road* (1945) and *Burma Victory* (1945)', *Historical Journal of Film, Radio and Television*, vol. 8, no. 1.

Jeavons, Clyde (1974) *A Pictorial History of the War Film*. London: Hamlyn.

Jennings, Mary-Lou (ed.) (1982) *Humphrey Jennings: Film-Maker, Painter, Poet*. London: BFI Publishing.

Jones, Liane (1990) *A Quiet Courage*. London: Corgi.

Jordan, Marion (1980/81) 'Yanks', *Movie*, no. 27/28.

Kennedy, A. L. (1997) *The Life and Death of Colonel Blimp*. London: BFI Publishing.

Kirkham, Pat and David Thomas (eds) (1995) *War Culture: Social Change and Changing Experience in World War Two Britain*. London: Lawrence and Wishart.

Kuhn, Annette (1981) '*Desert Victory* and the People's War', *Screen*, vol. 22, no. 2.

Landy, Marcia (1991) *British Genres: Cinema and Society, 1930–1960*. Princeton: Princeton University Press.

Landy, Marcia (1997) 'Melodrama and femininity in World War Two British cinema', in Robert Murphy (ed.), *The British Cinema Book*. London: BFI Publishing.

Lant, Antonia (1991) *Blackout*. Princeton: Princeton University Press.

Last, Nella (1981) *Nella Last's War*. London: Sphere.

Leites, Nathan and Martha Wolfenstein (1950) *Movies: A Psychological Study*. Glencoe, Illinois: Free Press.

Lewis, Peter (1986) *A People's War*. London: Thames Methuen.

Litewski, Chaim and Vincent Porter (1981) *'The Way Ahead*: case history of a propaganda film', *Sight and Sound*, vol. 50, no. 2 (Spring).

Longmate, Norman (1971) *How We Lived Then*. London: Hutchinson.

Longmate, Norman (1975) *The GIs: The Americans in Britain 1942–1945*. London: Hutchinson.

Lovell, Alan and Jim Hillier (1972) *Studies in Documentary*. London: Secker and Warburg.

Lovell, Terry (1984) *'Frieda'*, in Geoff Hurd (ed.), *National Fictions: World War Two in British Films and Television*. London: BFI Publishing.

Lusted, David (1984) *'Builders* and *The Demi-Paradise'*, in Geoff Hurd (ed.), *National Fictions: World War Two in British Films and Television*. London: BFI Publishing.

Macdonald, Kevin (1994) *Emeric Pressburger: The Life and Death of a Screenwriter*. London: Faber and Faber.

McEwan, Ian (1982) *The Imitation Game: Three Plays for Television*. London: Picador.

McFarlane, Brian (1992) *Sixty Voices*. London: BFI Publishing.

McFarlane, Brian (1997) *An Autobiography of British Cinema*. London: Methuen.

McFarlane, Brian (1998) 'Losing the peace: some British films of postwar adjustment', in Tony Barta (ed.), *Screening the Past: Film and the Representation of History*. Westport, CT: Praeger.

McFarlane, Brian (2000) *Lance Comfort*. Manchester: Manchester University Press.

Macksey, Kenneth (1975) *The Partisans of Europe in World War II*. London: Hart-Davis, MacGibbon.

McLaine, Ian (1979) *Ministry of Morale*. London: Allen and Unwin.

Maclean, Fitzroy (1949) *Eastern Approaches*. London: Jonathan Cape.

Macnab, Geoffrey (1993) *J. Arthur Rank and the British Film Industry*. London: Routledge.

Manvell, Roger (1943) 'They laugh at realism', *Documentary News Letter*, vol. 4, no. 3 (March).

Manvell, Roger (1944) *Film*. Harmondsworth: Penguin.

Manvell, Roger (1947) 'The British feature film from 1940 to 1945', in Michael Balcon, Ernest Lindgren, Forsyth Hardy and Roger Manvell (eds), *Twenty Years of British Films*. London: Falcon Press.

Manvell, Roger (1953) 'Britain's self-portraiture in feature films', *Geographical Magazine*, August.

Manvell, Roger (1974) *Films and the Second World War*. London: J. M. Dent.

Marks, Leo (1998) *Between Silk and Cyanide: The Story of SOE's Code War*. London: HarperCollins.

Marshall, Robert (1988) *All the King's Men: The Truth behind SOE's Greatest Wartime Disaster*. London: Collins.

Mass Observation (1943) *War Factory*. London: Victor Gollancz.

Mass Observation (1944) *The Journey Home*. London: John Murray.

Medhurst, Andy (1984) '1950s war films', in Geoff Hurd (ed.), *National*

Fictions: World War Two in British Films and Television. London: BFI Publishing.

Millar, Daniel (1969) *'Fires Were Started'*, *Sight and Sound*, vol. 38, no. 2 (Spring).

Mills, John (1980) *Up in the Clouds Gentlemen Please*. London: Weidenfeld and Nicolson.

Minney, R. J. (1973) *Puffin Asquith*. London: Leslie Frewin.

Minns, Raynes (1980) *Bombers and Mash*. London: Virago.

Moorehead, Caroline (1984) *Sidney Bernstein*. London: Jonathan Cape.

Morgan, Guy (1948) *Red Roses Every Night*. London: Quality Press.

Morley, Sheridan (1969) *A Talent to Amuse: A Biography of Noël Coward*. London: Heinemann.

Morley, Sheridan (1984) *Tales from the Hollywood Raj*. New York: Viking.

Murphy, Robert (1989) *Realism and Tinsel: Cinema and Society, 1939–49*. London: Routledge.

Murphy, Robert (1997) *'Cage of Gold'*, in Alan Burton, Tim O'Sullivan and Paul Wells (eds), *Liberal Directions: Basil Dearden and Postwar British Film Culture*. Trowbridge: Flicks Books.

Murphy, Robert (1997) 'The heart of Britain', in Robert Murphy (ed.), *The British Cinema Book*. London: BFI Publishing.

Narracott, A. H. (ed.) (1947) *In Praise of the Few: A Battle of Britain Anthology*. London: Frederick Muller.

Nuttall, Jeff (1978) *King Twist: A Portrait of Frank Randle*. London: Routledge and Kegan Paul.

Oakley, Charles (1964) *Where We Came In*. London: Allen and Unwin.

Orwell, George (1968) 'The lion and the unicorn', in vol. 2, and 'The English people', in vol. 3, of his *Collected Essays*. Harmondsworth: Penguin.

O'Sullivan, Tim (1997) 'Not quite fit for heroes: cautionary tales of men at work – *The Ship That Died of Shame* and *The League of Gentlemen*', in Alan Burton, Tim O'Sullivan and Paul Wells (eds), *Liberal Directions: Basil Dearden and Postwar British Film Culture*. Trowbridge: Flicks Books.

Palmer, Scott (1981) *A Who's Who of British Film Actors*. Metuchen, NJ, and London: Scarecrow Press.

Paris, Michael (2000) 'Filming the People's War: *Dawn Guard, Desert Victory Tunisian Victory*, and *Burma Victory*', in Alan Burton, Tim O'Sullivan and Paul Wells (eds), *The Boulting Brothers*. Trowbridge: Flicks Books.

Perkins, Tessa (1984) 'Struggles over the meaning of *The Imitation Game*', in Geoff Hurd (ed.), *National Fictions: World War Two in British Films and Television*. London: BFI Publishing.

Perry, George (1981) *Forever Ealing*. London: Pavilion/Michael Joseph.

Perry, George (1985) *The Great British Picture Show*. London: Pavilion.

Pimlott, Ben (1985) *Hugh Dalton*. London: Jonathan Cape.

Political and Economic Planning (1952) *The British Film Industry*. London: PEP.

Ponting, Clive (1990) *1940 – Myth and Reality*. London: Sphere.

Poole, Julian (1987) 'British cinema attendance in wartime: audience preference at the Majestic, Macclesfield, 1939–46', *Historical Journal of Film, Radio and Television*, vol. 7, no. 1.

Powell, Dilys (1947) *Films since 1939*. London: Longmans Green.

Powell, Michael (1986) *A Life in Movies*. London: Heinemann.

Powell, Michael (1995) *Million Dollar Movie*. New York: Random House.

Powell, Michael and Emeric Pressburger (1994) *The Life and Death of Colonel Blimp*, edited and introduced by Ian Christie. London: Faber and Faber.

Priestley, J. B. (1940) *Postscripts*. London: Heinemann.

Priestley, J. B. (1941) *Out of the People*. London: Collins/Heinemann.

Priestley, J. B. (1979) *English Journey*. Harmondsworth: Penguin.

Pronay, Nicholas (1982) 'The news media at war', in Nicholas Pronay and D.W. Spring (eds), *Propaganda, Politics and Film, 1918–45*. London: Macmillan.

Pronay, Nicholas (1983) 'The land of promise: the projection of peace aims in Britain', in K. R. M. Short (ed.) *Film and Radio Propaganda in World War II*. London: Croom Helm.

Pronay, Nicholas (1988) 'The British post-bellum cinema: a survey of the films relating to World War II made in Britain between 1945 and 1960', *Historical Journal of Film, Radio and Television*, vol. 8, no. 1.

Pronay, Nicholas and Jeremy Croft (1983) 'British film censorship and propaganda policy during the Second World War', in James Curran and Vincent Porter (eds), *British Cinema History*. London: Weidenfeld and Nicolson.

Pronay, Nicholas and Francis Thorpe (1980) *British Official Films in the Second World War*. London: Clio.

Pulleine, Tim (1997) 'A song and dance at the local: thoughts on Ealing', in Robert Murphy (ed.), *The British Cinema Book*. London: BFI Publishing.

Pulleine, Tim (1999) 'Spin a dark web', in Steve Chibnall and Robert Murphy (eds), *British Crime Cinema*. London: Routledge.

Quinlan, David (1984) *British Sound Films: The Studio Years 1920–1959*. London: Batsford.

Ramsden, John (1998) 'Refocusing "The People's War": British war films of the 1950s', *Journal of Contemporary History*, vol. 33, no. 1.

Rattigan, Neil (1994a) '*The Demi-Paradise* and images of class in British wartime films', in Winston Wheeler Dixon (ed.), *British Cinema Revisited*. New York: State University of New York Press.

Rattigan, Neil (1994b) 'The last gasp of the middle class: British war films of the 1950s', in Winston Wheeler Dixon (ed.), *British Cinema Revisited*. New York: State University of New York Press.

Richards, Jeffrey (1986) *Thorold Dickinson*. London: Croom Helm.

Richards, Jeffrey (1987) 'Wartime British cinema audiences and the class system: the case of *Ships with Wings* (1941)', *Historical Journal of Film, Radio and Television*, vol. 7, no. 2.

Richards, Jeffrey (1997) 'Basil Dearden at Ealing', in Alan Burton, Tim O'Sullivan and Paul Wells (eds), *Liberal Directions: Basil Dearden and Postwar British Film Culture*. Trowbridge: Flicks Books.

Richards, Jeffrey and Dorothy Sheridan (1987) *Mass Observation at the Movies*. London: Routledge.

Robertson, James (1982) 'British film censorship goes to war', *Historical Journal of Film, Radio and Television*, vol. 2, no. 1.

Robertson, James (1985) *The British Board of Film Censors*. London: Croom Helm.

Robertson, James (1989) *The Hidden Cinema*. London: Routledge.

Robson, E. W. and M. M. (1943) *The Shame and Disgrace of Colonel Blimp*. London: Sidneyan Society.

Samuels, Charles Thomas (1978) 'Interview with Carol Reed', in Brenda Davies (ed.), *Carol Reed*. London: BFI Publishing.

Short, K. R. M. (1997a) 'RAF Bomber Command's *Target for Tonight* (1941)', *Historical Journal of Film, Radio and Television*, vol. 17, no. 2.

Short, K. R. M. (1997b) *Screening the Propaganda of British Air Power*. Trowbridge: Flicks Books.

Simpson, Philip (1984) '*Yanks* and popular memory', in Geoff Hurd (ed.), *National Fictions: World War Two in British Films and Television*. London: BFI Publishing.

Smith, Harold L. (1986) 'The effect of the war on the status of women', in Harold L. Smith (ed.), *War and Social Change*. Manchester: Manchester University Press.

Smith, Michael (1998) *Station X: The Codebreakers of Bletchley Park*. London: Macmillan.

Spicer, Andrew (1997) 'Male stars, masculinity and British cinema 1945–1960', in Robert Murphy (ed.), *The British Cinema Book*. London: BFI Publishing.

Spicer, Andrew (1999) 'The emergence of the British tough guy: Stanley Baker, masculinity and the crime thriller', in Steve Chibnall and Robert Murphy (eds), *British Crime Cinema*. London: Routledge.

Spicer, Andrew (2001) *Typical Men: The Representation of Masculinity in Popular British Cinema*. London: I.B. Tauris.

Stafford, David (1983) *Britain and European Resistance 1940–1945*. London: Macmillan.

Stead, Peter (1988) 'The people as stars: feature films as national expression', in Philip Taylor (ed.), *Britain and the Cinema in the Second World War*. London: Macmillan.

Stead, Peter (1989) *Film and the Working Class*. London: Routledge.

Stent, Ronald (1980) *A Bespattered Page: The Internment of 'His Majesty's Most Loyal Enemy Aliens'*. London: André Deutsch.

Stevenson, John (1986) 'Planner's moon? The Second World War and the planning movement', in Harold L. Smith (ed.), *War and Social Change*. Manchester: Manchester University Press.

Summerfield, Penny (1984) *Women Workers in the Second World War: Production and Patriarchy in Conflict*. London: Croom Helm.

Summerfield, Penny (1986) 'The levelling of class', in Harold L. Smith (ed.), *War and Social Change*. Manchester: Manchester University Press.

Sussex, Elizabeth (1975a) *The Rise and Fall of British Documentary*. Berkeley and London: University of California Press.

Sussex, Elizabeth (1975b) 'Cavalcanti in England', *Sight and Sound*, vol. 44, no. 4 (Autumn).

Swann, Paul (1989) *The British Documentary Film Movement*. Cambridge: Cambridge University Press.

Bibliography

Taylor, A. J. P. (1983) *English History 1914–1945*. Harmondsworth: Penguin.

Taylor, Philip (ed.) (1988) *Britain and the Cinema in the Second World War*. London: Macmillan.

Thumin, Janet (1996) 'The female audience: mobile women and married ladies', in Christine Gledhill and Gillian Swanson (eds), *Nationalising Femininity: Culture, Sexuality and British Cinema in the Second World War*. Manchester: Manchester University Press.

Vaughan, Dai (1983) *Portrait of an Invisible Man*. London: BFI Publishing.

Wapshott, Nicholas (1990) *The Man Between: A Biography of Carol Reed*. London: Chatto and Windus.

Watt, Harry (1974) *Don't Look at the Camera*. London: Paul Elek.

Williams, Raymond (1977) 'A lecture on realism', *Screen*, vol. 18, no. 1.

Winston, Brian (1999) *Fires Were Started*. London: BFI Publishing.

Wood, Alan (1952) *Mr Rank*. London: Hodder and Stoughton.

Wood, Linda (1987) *The Commercial Imperative in the British Film Industry: Maurice Elvey, a Case Study*. London: BFI Publishing.

Worpole, Ken (1983) *Dockers and Detectives*. London: Verso.

Wright, Patrick (1985) *On Living in an Old Country*. London: Verso.

Index of Film Titles

Page numbers in **bold** indicate illustrations.

Index of Film Titles

Index of Names

Page numbers in **bold** indicate illustrations.